# Twenty-First Century Macroeconomics

## Responding to the Climate Challenge

---

*Edited by*

Jonathan M. Harris and Neva R. Goodwin

*The Global Development and Environment Institute, Tufts University, USA*

**Edward Elgar**
Cheltenham, UK • Northampton, MA, USA

Published by
Edward Elgar Publishing Limited
The Lypiatts
15 Lansdown Road
Cheltenham
Glos GL50 2JA
UK

Edward Elgar Publishing, Inc.
William Pratt House
9 Dewey Court
Northampton
Massachusetts 01060
USA

A catalogue record for this book
is available from the British Library

Library of Congress Control Number: 2008942910

ISBN 978 1 84720 848 4

Printed and bound in Great Britain by the MPG Books Group

# Contents

## PART III POLICY OPTIONS FOR RESPONDING TO CLIMATE CHANGE

# Figures

# Tables

# Contributors

**Frank Ackerman** is a Senior Economist at the Stockholm Environment Institute US Center (SEI-US), and Senior Research Fellow at the Global Development and Environment Institute, Tufts University, Medford, Massachusetts.

**Tom Athanasiou** is Director of EcoEquity, an activist think tank focused on the development of equitable approaches to emergency climate stabilization.

**Paul Baer** is the Research Director for EcoEquity.

**James K. Boyce** is Professor of Economics and Director of the program on development, peacebuilding, and the environment at the Political Economy Research Institute, University of Massachusetts at Amherst.

**Lloyd J. Dumas** is Professor of Economics and Public Policy, University of Texas at Dallas. He chaired the national Working Group on Climate Change of the Civil Society Institute.

**Christian Egenhofer** is Senior Fellow, Centre for European Policy Studies; Jean-Monnet Lecturer, Centre for Energy, Petroleum and Law and Policy, University of Dundee, Scotland/UK; and Lecturer, MBA Programme, Solvay Business School, Brussels.

**Duncan Foley** is Leo Model Professor of Economics, New School for Social Research, New York, New York.

**Neva R. Goodwin** is Co-Director of the Global Development and Environment Institute, Tufts University, Medford, Massachusetts.

**Jonathan M. Harris** is Director of the Theory and Education Program at the Global Development and Environment Institute, Tufts University, Medford, Massachusetts.

**Sivan Kartha** is Senior Scientist at the Stockholm Environment Institute's US Center (SEI-US) and Director of SEI's Climate and Energy Program.

**Andrzej Kassenberg** is President of the Institute for Sustainable Development in Warsaw, Poland

**Mohan Munasinghe** is Chairman of the Munasinghe Institute for Development (MIND), Colombo, Sri Lanka; Vice Chair, UN Intergovernmental Panel on Climate Change (IPCC); and Visiting Professor, Institute of Advanced Studies, United Nations University.

**Matthew Riddle** is a PhD candidate in Economics at the University of Massachusetts.

**Brian Roach** is Research Associate at the Global Development and Environment Institute, Tufts University, Medford, Massachusetts.

**Adam Seitchik** is Executive Vice President and Chief Investment Officer, Trillium Asset Management Corporation.

**Lance Taylor** is Arnhold Professor of International Cooperation and Development at the New School University, New York, New York.

# Acknowledgments

This volume represents the collective achievement of many colleagues. The ideas presented here were originally discussed at a conference sponsored by the Tufts University Global Development and Environment Institute in November 2006, held at the Pocantico Conference Center of the Rockefeller Brothers Fund. The conference brought together scholars from different countries including China, the Czech Republic, Ecuador, Malaysia, Mexico, Poland, Sri Lanka, Thailand, and the US, to focus on the challenge of responding to climate change, in the context of broader issues of macroeconomic growth and sustainable development.

In addition to conference participants whose work is presented in this collection, we are indebted to Peter Dorman, Kelly Sims Gallagher, Eban Goodstein, Richard Howarth, Sitanon Jesdapipat, Nadia Johanisova, Alejandro Nadal, Julie Nelson, Conn Nugent, David Seckler, Jomo Kwame Sundaram, Betsy Taylor, Pam Velez, and Shiqui Zhang for their contributions to the continuing conversation among scholars that is helping to show the way forward on climate change. Authors who were not at the original conference but later contributed to the book include Lloyd Dumas, Paul Baer, Tom Athanasiou, Sivan Kartha, Matt Riddle, and Christian Egenhofer. The papers presented in this volume, of course, represent the views of their authors, not necessarily those of other conference participants or of the Rockefeller Brothers Fund.

Colleagues at the Tufts University Global Development and Environment Institute and the Stockholm Environment Institute's US Center, located at Tufts University, have contributed valuable ideas and comments during the period that the book was in preparation. Particular thanks are due to Suzanne Bremer, who served as conference coordinator, and to Julia DiGiammarino, Patrick Roath, Curt Campbell, and Allison Schuster, who worked tirelessly and with conscientious attention to detail on the preparation of the manuscript. Administrative support for the conference and manuscript preparation process was provided by Joshua Berkowitz and Mukhtar Amin.

We are grateful for financial support provided by the Rockefeller Brothers Fund for the conference and book, as well as to the staff of the Pocantico Conference Center.

# Introduction: Reforming Macroeconomics for a Century of Climate Change

**Jonathan M. Harris and Neva R. Goodwin**

Climate change has moved to the center of the political and economic agenda. The period during which the validity of climate science could be debated, or the importance of the issue questioned, has ended. The work of the Intergovernmental Panel on Climate Change, which published its Fourth Assessment Report in 2007, has left no doubt about the urgency of the issue. Now that the message from the scientific side is clear, the economics of the issue have become a major focus of discussion. What are the likely economic effects of climate change? What are the costs of substantial action to avert climate change? This debate has broad implications for public policy. But it also raises fundamental questions about economic analysis itself, and moves issues of environmental policy from the microeconomic to the macroeconomic level.

To address these issues, the Tufts University Global Development and Environment Institute (http://ase.tufts.edu/gdae) convened a conference of scholars from the global North and South in November 2006 to address the issues of economic growth and sustainability, with a special focus on climate change. That conference, and subsequent discussions, led to the preparation of this volume, which brings together a wide range of contributions on the economic theory and policy issues surrounding climate change.

## FUNDAMENTAL SCIENTIFIC AND ECONOMIC ISSUES

The first part of the book discusses the scope of the challenges raised by climate change. Lloyd Dumas reviews the science and economics concerning the impacts of global warming. Impacts on health, agriculture, extreme weather events, water resources, and sea levels, together with other ecological impacts, are projected to have extensive economic costs, mounting into hundreds of billions annually. The difficulty of valuing ecosystem losses, the profound uncertainty surrounding the course of climate change, and the

the profound uncertainty surrounding the course of climate change, and the possibility of abrupt or catastrophic change, make it likely that economic valuations of potential losses are understated. The inertial nature of global climate systems means that impacts of current carbon-generating activities will continue for centuries. Dumas argues that while this poses a huge challenge for a global system of economic development that depends so heavily on carbon fuels, it also creates huge opportunities for economic transformation, and that economic analysis can help to identify cost-minimizing, return-maximizing response strategies.

One of the most influential, and controversial, analyzes of the economics of climate change is the 2006 *Stern Review* commissioned by the government of the UK. Frank Ackerman evaluates the debate over the *Stern Review*, which has highlighted key issues of economic valuation of social and environmental costs. These include valuation of the future through use of a discount rate. Discounting makes good sense for many economic issues such as valuing bonds and mortgages, but has drawn criticism when used to evaluate more sweeping issues of present versus future well-being. The use of a standard discount rate, favored by most mainstream economists, places a very low value on damages occurring much more than 20 years in the future, leading critics to question whether it is appropriate for estimating climate change damages that will tend to mount over decades and even centuries. Stern deals with the issue by using a low, non-standard discount rate that places much greater weight on future damages. Ackerman explores both the technical and the ethical implications of this controversy, concluding that 'Stern's general arguments for a low discount rate are persuasive'. But he also questions the validity of attempting to get a 'bottom-line' estimate of costs when great uncertainty and potentially catastrophic damages are involved. He advocates instead a two-stage process of a (primarily scientific) determination of a maximum acceptable level of atmospheric $CO_2$ concentration, followed by a (primarily economic) analysis of the least-cost method of achieving this target. This sounds like simple common sense, but it upends much of the standard economic paradigm for valuation that many economists have adopted as the primary criterion for determining climate policy. It also provides strong support for Stern's recommendations for aggressive action to combat global warming.

## CLIMATE CHANGE AND GLOBAL DEVELOPMENT

The climate issue does not stand alone, but must be viewed in the context of broader issues of equitable and sustainable development. Neva Goodwin addresses this question, presenting a critique of the limitations of standard of both adaptation and mitigation that will require modifications in economic systems to improve resilience and equity. This is particularly important in the poorest nations, which will suffer some of the worst effects of climate change while possessing the least ability to respond to it. Some of the needed modifications, such as changes in price incentives, are within the scope of market-oriented theory, but others involve a broader view of such issues as citizen rights, basic needs and income equity, non-profit and household activities, and management of the global commons. There are many other good reasons to challenge the relatively narrow scope of standard economic theory, but its constricting view of the possibilities for responses to climate change adds urgency to these critiques.

A broader view of the global climate crisis focuses attention on existing global inequities, and in particular on the tension between the need for reductions in carbon emissions and the need of much of the developing world for expanded energy use. Paul Baer, Tom Athanasiou, and Sivan Kartha define this tension sharply, showing both the urgency of the need for drastic emissions cuts, and the strong constraints on the 'development space' left for poorer nations even if richer nations were to follow a path of rapid emissions reduction. They propose a system of 'Greenhouse Development Rights', giving priority to energy needs for development, and assigning responsibility for emissions reductions based on a combination of economic capacity and cumulative emissions since 1990. Thus some nations such as the United States would be required both to reduce their current emissions and to contribute to needed reductions elsewhere in the world; nations such as India and China would have some responsibility for reductions below a 'business as usual path', but would receive international funding for a transition to low-carbon development paths; and low-income nations would have little or no responsibility for reductions, but could also receive international support for low-carbon development. This result could be achieved through a global 'cap and allocate' system assigning emissions rights to countries based on a combination of economic capacity and cumulative past emissions. The measures proposed by Baer, Athanasiou, and Kartha set a high bar for global responses to the climate challenge, but the authors make a persuasive case that the alternative is bitter deadlock between global North and South on the issue, and an increased chance of climate catastrophe.

## MACROECONOMIC THEORY AND CLIMATE CHANGE

What does economic theory have to tell us about the sweeping economic adjustments required to respond to climate change? Duncan Foley offers a surprising answer: standard economic theory indicates that an aggressive policy to reduce global warming will impose no substantial costs on the current generation. The reason for this is that measures to avert warming are primarily a matter of investment, not of consumption. In common-sense terms, we can invest in coal plants or wind power, and we can build structures and machinery that are energy-efficient or energy-inefficient. We are making the investment anyway, and the object of the investment is to create productive capital stock for the future. What is at issue, Foley suggests, is the balance between *conventional capital stock* (usually carbon-intensive) and *climatological capital stock* (reduced carbon accumulations due to investment in mitigation). If averting global climate change required large *additional* investments, in excess of current investment levels, then this would indeed require a reduction in current consumption. But to the extent that what is needed is a *shift* in investment from carbon-intensive to non-carbon energy sources (including energy efficiency), that shift can be achieved through altered price incentives. This internalization of climate externalities should make both current and future generations better off, when the effects of climate on human well-being are taken into account.

Lance Taylor offers a more sobering perspective on the scope of the task involved in reducing carbon energy use. He reviews historical evidence to show that economic growth has been accompanied by steadily increasing energy/labor ratios – that is, increasing use of energy per worker. To reverse the accompanying pattern of ever-increasing carbon emissions, energy use per capita must fall at 1 percent per year or more – something that has rarely been observed except in countries in economic stagnation or decline. Another way of putting this is that energy productivity growth rates must rise at a rate far exceeding the rates currently experienced in either developed or developing countries. This may not be impossible, but it will mandate a dramatically different pattern of economic development from that of the past. Social, institutional, and technological factors must combine to produce forms of development that steadily reduce energy use per worker even as they maintain or improve well-being. The record of economic growth to date, together with the lack of serious policy efforts to redirect growth patterns, is not conducive to optimism about our future ability to achieve this demanding goal.

The concept of reorienting macroeconomic development to include the environment is not new, although climate change represents perhaps the most demanding problem in this area. Mohan Munasinghe, Vice Chair of the UN Intergovernmental Panel on Climate Change (IPCC), reviews the record of theory and practice in sustainable macroeconomic development. He points out that, unlike some pollutants, carbon emissions so far exhibit no 'turning point' with relation to economic growth, but tend to increase steadily in correlation with GDP per capita. This reinforces the need for 'comprehensive environmental policies to counteract any adverse impacts of growth oriented macroeconomic policies'. 'Win-win' policies that can benefit both economy and environment can include markets for emissions permits, the removal of policy distortions such as subsidies for energy use, market reforms to improve energy efficiency and reduce waste, and proper pricing of natural resources. Munasinghe also emphasizes the danger of 'structural adjustment' reforms that slash social and environmental spending. A possible remedy for this would be international funding for low-carbon development strategies, as suggested by Baer et al. (this volume). On the theory side, Munasinghe reviews efforts to integrate environmental concerns into formal macroeconomic analysis such as the IS-LM framework. This involves supplementing the standard conditions for macroeconomic equilibrium in goods and financial markets with an equilibrium condition representing a stable stock of environmental assets. On a global scale, this stock of environmental assets would clearly include atmospheric carbon levels. This suggests that economic growth policies should be specifically evaluated with regard to their impact on atmospheric carbon accumulation.

Does integrating environmental factors into macroeconomic and growth theory imply merely an adjustment of existing theory or an essentially new direction? Jonathan Harris argues for a return to the Keynesian roots of macro theory, but with a broader view of environmental and social goals, and different definitions of key concepts in macroeconomic measurement. By specifying sustainable forms of consumption, as well as defining specific categories of investment in energy-efficiency and in human and natural capital, traditional Keynesian concepts of demand management can be reoriented to the world of the 21st century, in which environmental constraints, in particular carbon limits, threaten to derail growth. Fiscal and monetary policy can be 'greened', and combined with new instruments such as cap-and-trade policies to promote income equity and increased employment while reducing 'throughput' of energy and materials.

## FORMULATING POLICY RESPONSES

A detailed analysis of policies to reduce carbon emissions while maintaining equity and employment is provided by Boyce and Riddle. Their focus is on the United States, but the policies they advocate could be applied in other countries, or globally (as proposed by Baer et al. in this volume). Boyce and Riddle address one of the basic problems with 'green' taxes or carbon cap-and-trade policies: the increased energy prices that result will have a regressive impact, since energy represents a higher proportion of domestic budgets for lower-income households. Their solution is to link cap-and-trade to a guaranteed rebate of permit auction revenues. This 'cap-and-dividend' policy is based on the concept of an atmospheric commons, in which each person holds an equal right. The distributional impacts of such a policy are progressive rather than regressive, with the progressive effect depending on the complete auction of permits. To the extent that carbon permits are distributed to existing firms for free, a cap-and-trade policy moves back towards regressivity, with complete give-away benefiting primarily high-income energy stockholders at the expense of low- and middle-income consumers.

More socially beneficial uses of revenue, such as investment in public goods or aid to promote decarbonized economic development in lower-income countries, are also possible, but Boyce and Riddle argue against devoting more than a small share of revenues to these uses, in order to preserve the basic principle of cap-and-rebate: an inherent right to an equitable share of the revenues from an environmental commons. This raises the issue of national equity versus global equity. Different balances could be struck between the Boyce/Riddle proposal at a national level and the type of global cap-and-trade system advocated by Baer et al., or the 'Earth Atmospheric Trust' proposed by Barnes et al. (2008). Both, however, offer economic mechanisms for redirecting economic growth to low-carbon paths while promoting intranational and international equity.[1]

One of the key issues in promoting the transition to a low-carbon economy is technological progress in non-carbon energy source and energy efficiency. Brian Roach discusses the critical role of public R&D funding in this area. Even with market incentives for clean energy technology, based on carbon taxes or cap-and-trade policies, Roach argues that private R&D will still be underfunded. Basic research in particular requires public investment. Such investment could be financed by taxes, but could also be voluntarily funded through private savings under a government-sponsored plan that provided tax advantages and significant potential for financial returns. The funds would be used for joint public-private investments that would generate financial returns, with a minimum return guaranteed by the government. This would provide a direct mechanism for individuals to participate directly in a redirection of investment towards clean energy alternatives, as well as promoting increased savings.

## LESSONS FROM PRACTICAL EXPERIENCE

While little has been done in the United States under the Bush Administration to address global climate change, the European Union has made a serious effort to incorporate carbon reduction into macroeconomic policy through an

EU-wide carbon trading scheme. Christian Egenhofer of the Center for European Policy Studies analyzes the successes and failures of the scheme through 2007, with a focus on efforts to strengthen the scheme during its second phase in 2008-2012. Despite 'teething problems',the EU Emissions Trading Scheme represents by far the largest working carbon cap-and-trade system in the world, and Egenhofer suggests that it may eventually form the basis for a global carbon market, both through linkage with other national trading systems and as a blueprint for design of other international agreements.

A practical example of the difficulties in departing from a carbon-centered path for economic development is offered in Andrzej Kassenberg's review of the Polish experience since the fall of Communism. On paper, Poland has adopted principles of sustainable development and goals for reduced carbon emissions. But there has been considerable resistance to implementing environmental tax policies or effective measures to promote low-carbon development. Carbon emissions did fall significantly during the decade of the 1990s, but this was primarily a function of the collapse of Communist-era industries. Current projections are for a sharp rise in emissions through 2020, associated with a rapid increase in automobile transport and weak progress in energy efficiency. Government policies are heavily oriented towards traditional, energy-intensive growth models, and EU assistance for developing alternative paths has so far been ineffective and contradictory, with most funds going to support traditional carbon-based development. Kassenberg, the President of the Institute for Sustainable Development in Warsaw, offers a menu of alternative development options, but fears that Poland will continue to emulate the Western model of expanding energy production rather than improving energy efficiency.

The contribution by Adam Seitchik adds an optimistic note to conclude this volume. Seitchik, Chief Investment Officer for Trillium Asset Management Corporation, provides an overview of the rapidly expanding market for clean technology and climate solutions. Both on the negative side – assessment of climate risk – and the positive side – the potential for profit in carbon-reducing technologies – investors are becoming widely aware of the importance of climate change. Venture capital opportunities in clean technology and 'green' real estate are in the tens of billions of dollars. The Investor Network on Climate Risk, representing over $3 trillion in assets (and still rapidly growing), including state treasurers, public pension funds, and labor pension funds, supports policies for mandatory climate disclosure and government action to provide a level playing field for low-carbon development. This activity is taking place with essentially no leadership at the Federal level; a true national commitment to climate action would greatly reinforce the already vigorous moves in the private sector to redirect investment towards climate solutions.

## LOOKING TO THE FUTURE

The field of macroeconomics developed in the twentieth century in response to massive economic problems of unemployment and depression. The theory and institutions that evolved from the initial impetus for new thinking in the 1930s shaped the post-World War II world, and have continued to guide economic development to the present day. Now it is time for another renaissance in macroeconomic thought.

The new challenge – to achieve drastic reduction of global carbon emission while preserving and advancing economic well-being – requires a fundamental change in how we define the economic goals of growth and well-being, and which economic goals take priority. As the contributions to this volume make clear, there is a rich variety of economic thinking, drawn both from mainstream and ecological perspectives, that can be brought to bear on the problem. Too often, economists have played the role of defending the status quo, unwilling to depart far from traditional assumptions about macroeconomic growth goals. The growing urgency of achieving a reversal in patterns of carbon emissions will force the discipline to accept new theory and new policies. Once this crucial shift in thinking has begun, economics can once again help to lead the way towards solutions that promote both human development and wise stewardship of planetary resources.

The selections in this book represent some of the best thinking available right now to move forward the iterative process of proposing *what can and should be done*, while also revising theoretic understandings of the realities within which action is required. As exemplified in the discussion in note 1, below, this process is – fortunately – moving extremely rapidly. We hope that this book, with its wide variety of innovative perspectives, will be useful in representing the leading edge of movements in action and theory, while also helping to support this forward motion.

## NOTE

1. The Boyce and Riddle proposal should be viewed as part of a highly creative ongoing research and policy discussion. An earlier presentation of the cap-and-dividend concept appeared in Barnes' 'Sky Trust' proposal (Barnes, 2006), while the 2008 'Earth Atmospheric Trust' (Barnes et al., 2008) represents the most recent phase. Much can be learned from comparing the differences, similarities, and (in some areas) gradual convergence of this approach with another, which is being developed at the Stockholm

Environment Institute's US Center at Tufts University, and which is represented in this volume by Baer, Athanasiou, and Kartha.

Cap-and-dividend proposals are seriously limited so long as the project is addressed solely to the United States. That is, the funds to be collected, as described in Boyce/Riddle, are intended to internalize the global cost of US $CO_2$ emissions, which represent about 25 percent of the global damage to the atmosphere. The atmosphere is understood to be a common resource, belonging to all of humanity. However, a US based cap-and-dividend policy distributes the funds, per capita, only among US citizens – who represent only 5 percent of the human 'owners' of the atmospheric commons.

Practical politics may make it impossible to redistribute the funds received by sales of $CO_2$ emission permits in the United States in a fully equitable way – either in a global per capita distribution in which everyone in the world receives the same amount (as suggested in Barnes at al., 2008), or in the more progressive distribution suggested by Baer, Athanasiou, and Kartha. Much of the essential redistribution for equitable development will need to come through the 'trade' aspect of cap and trade, in which poorer countries can receive payments for the environmental services for which they are stewards. Nevertheless, a comparison of the two papers in this volume that are specifically directed to economic policies for mitigation of $CO_2$ emissions – Boyce and Riddle, and Baer, Athanasiou, and Kartha – demonstrate that excellent thinking is being applied to the knotty issue of how to respond to the climate challenge in a way that is truly equitable. It is especially encouraging that this thinking is evolving very rapidly – proceeding, indeed, about as rapidly as the growth in scientific understanding of the seriousness of the challenge.

# REFERENCES

Barnes, Peter (2006), *Capitalism 3.0: A Guide to Reclaiming the Commons*, San Francisco: Berrett-Koehler Publishers.

Barnes, Peter et al. (2008), 'Creating an Earth Atmospheric Trust', *Science* **319**, 724, February 8.

# PART I

# The Scope of the Challenge

# 1. Understanding the Challenge of Global Warming

**Lloyd J. Dumas**[1]

## GLOBAL WARMING AND CLIMATE CHANGE

Though the terms 'global warming' and 'climate change' are often used interchangeably, they are not actually the same thing. Global warming refers to the rise in average global temperature. Climate change refers to changes in long-term average weather patterns, including changes in either the regional or global patterns of temperature, humidity, precipitation, wind, and so on. The two are connected because global warming provides more energy to the processes that drive the wind patterns and ocean currents, key forces that determine the long-term average weather.

Higher ocean temperatures, for example, are more conducive to hurricane formation than lower temperatures. Warmer temperatures tend to fuel the winds and increase the rains (and therefore the flooding) associated with these storms. More generally, atmospheric temperature differences (which are influenced by the amount of heat rising from the surface of the land or water, as well as by solar radiation) create pressure differences that affect wind patterns, and wind patterns are very important in determining where rain falls and where it does not.[2]

Since it is notoriously difficult to predict the weather in many parts of the world even a week in advance, it is reasonable to ask how it is possible to make meaningful predictions about climate change over a span of decades. The answer is that climate is a kind of 'average weather', and it is generally much easier to predict averages than the individual numbers from which averages are derived. Insurance companies, for example, have little trouble developing actuarial tables that can dependably predict the average number of 80-year-olds who will die within the next twelve months. But it is an entirely different and much more difficult problem to predict which 80-year-olds will die on which day of the coming year. Similarly, although they are short-term and closer to the present, weather forecasts are more difficult because they try to predict specific magnitude and timing of temperature, humidity, rainfall, wind direction and strength, etc. Even though climate forecasts are made over much longer periods of time, they are only trying to predict general average temperatures, humidity, rainfall and the like. That is not all that easy to do, but it is easier than forecasting the details of weather.

## Climate Change

When longer-term and broader trends cause a shift in the average weather the climate changes. Places that were usually cool become warmer, places that were usually dry get more rain, the intensity and track of storms change, and so on. The atmospheric, terrestrial and oceanic systems that drive weather – and therefore climate over the long term – are complex in themselves, and their many-sided interactions with each other only add to this complexity. A level-headed, objective assessment would recognize that we now understand these systems far better than we did 100 (or even 50) years ago, but there is still much that we do not completely understand and are unlikely to understand for many years to come. There is thus an unavoidable degree of uncertainty attached to any detailed prediction we try to make about patterns or even trends in climate change.

From a policy point of view, it would be better if we could have complete confidence in our predictions as to what will happen and why. But while it would be ideal, we rarely have that degree of certainty in any policy arena. There is still much debate, for example, about how children learn and what teaching techniques and institutional settings work best to educate them. Yet we know we cannot afford to throw up our hands and wait for complete understanding before we try to improve the quality of their education. We cannot predict with any real degree of certainty when and where the next major terrorist attack will occur, but we all know that we cannot wait until we understand terrorism well enough to make such predictions before we take action.

Perhaps it is because the issue of global warming and the climate change it produces is surrounded by the aura of science that we even think we can nail down all the details and settle this debate before we have to decide what action to take, if any. We have every reason to have confidence in the ability of science to extend the boundaries of our knowledge, but the reality is that it rarely gives us complete answers with perfect accuracy. While scientific research answers some of our questions, it almost invariably raises new ones. And the processes of serious science take time. So we must always ask, can we afford to wait until every detail is settled and everyone is convinced before we take action? Or is a preponderance of evidence good enough?

There is, in fact, a broad scientific consensus on human-induced climate change. The Intergovernmental Panel on Climate Change (IPCC), created by the World Meteorological Association and the UN Environmental Program in 1988, for example, has written, 'Human activities... are modifying the concentration of atmospheric constituents... that absorb or scatter radiant energy. ...most of the observed warming over the last 50 years is likely to have been due to the increase in greenhouse gas concentrations' (McCarthy et al., 2001, p. 21). The IPCC's summary of basic climate science released almost two decades later reinforces that message, concluding with 90 percent confidence that humans have been the major cause of global warming since 1950 (Kanter and Revkin, 2007; IPCC, 2007). The National Academy of Sciences (2001, p.1) clearly agrees, 'Greenhouse gases are accumulating in the Earth's atmosphere as a result of human activities, causing surface air temperatures and subsurface ocean temperatures to rise'. The National Academy's report then went on to declare, 'The IPCC's conclusion that most of the observed warming of the last 50 years is likely to have been due to the increase in greenhouse gas concentrations accurately reflects the current thinking of the scientific community on this issue' (ibid, p. 3).

This conclusion is further strengthened by an analysis of 928 abstracts in relevant refereed scientific journals with the key words 'climate change' reported in an essay in *Science* magazine. The survey revealed that 75 percent of the papers either implicitly or explicitly accepted the consensus view that climate change is at least partly human-induced, and the remaining 25 percent took no position at all on the issue. Not a single paper disagreed (Oresekes, 2004, p. 1686). The real scientific debate is over how much and how fast global warming will increase as a result of human activity, not whether human activity contributes to global warming.

## Greenhouse Gases (GHGs) and Global Warming

Radiant energy in the form of sunlight easily passes through the glass of a conventional greenhouse. When it hits the floor, the plants, the soil, etc. inside the greenhouse, part of it is reflected as light, which passes easily back through the glass. But part of the sunlight's energy is also absorbed and re-emitted as heat. While the glass ceiling and walls of the greenhouse are transparent to light, they are not nearly as 'transparent' to heat. Much of the heat therefore remains trapped, raising the temperature inside the greenhouse. It is the same process by which the inside of a car heats up when it is parked outside on a sunny summer day

When 'greenhouse gases' (GHGs) accumulate in the atmosphere, they have an effect similar to the glass of the greenhouse, allowing light to pass easily through but trapping heat. The heat that they trap is partly heat that has been produced by the sunlight's warming of the earth's surface, and partly heat that has been generated by other activities within the biological and physical environment of the earth – including heat produced by cars burning gasoline, power plants burning coal, and many other human activities.

There is nothing unnatural about the greenhouse effect of the Earth's atmosphere. In fact, it is vital. If it did not occur, the average temperature of the earth would be –18°C (0°F), rather than the current average temperature of +15°C (+59°F), and life as we know it could not exist on this planet (Environment Canada, 2005, p. 1). The problem is that when too much greenhouse gas accumulates in the atmosphere, there is too much trapping of heat. This causes global warming, which in turn changes the climate.

As it turns out, most greenhouse gases are produced even in the absence of human intervention. The main naturally occurring GHGs are:

- water vapor, the result of the evaporation phase of the hydrological (water) cycle that is vital to life on this planet
- carbon dioxide ($CO_2$), the waste product of plant and animal respiration, and a crucial input to photosynthesis, the foundation of the food chain
- methane ($CH_4$), emitted as the result of the decomposition of dead organisms and organic waste
- nitrous oxide ($N_2O$), emitted from the microbial breakdown of animal and human waste

Other GHGs include perfluorocarbons (PFCs), hydrofluorocarbons (HFCs), chlorofluorocarbons (CFCs) and sulphur hexafluoride ($SF_6$), all of which are the results of various industrial processes.[3]

The naturally occurring GHGs are also produced as the result of human activity: carbon dioxide is a major byproduct of the combustion of fossil fuels (oil, coal and natural gas); methane is emitted in the production and transport of fossil fuels, as well as by agricultural processes; and nitrous oxide is produced by both agricultural and industrial activities.

Before the Industrial Revolution, there was a relative balance between the huge amount of carbon dioxide and other GHGs emitted from natural sources and the amounts absorbed by natural 'sinks' – parts of the ecosystem whose processes prevent the release of the gas or remove it from the atmosphere. Since that time, human activity has put something on the order of twice as much $CO_2$ into the atmosphere annually (chiefly by burning wood and fossil fuels) as remaining natural sinks have been easily able to remove. By some estimates, atmospheric levels of $CO_2$ are now the highest they have been in 420,000 years (Wang and Oppenheimer, 2005).

Forests and other land- and sea-based photosynthetic plant ecosystems are very large and important carbon sinks. That is one of the reasons why global deforestation and pollution of the oceans is a matter of real significance for the problem of global warming. There is, in fact, a large carbon sink within the contiguous US that is very much affected, among other things, by processes of land use (such as land clearing and logging) and fire management. Projecting the future of the US carbon sink, a study published by the National Academy of Sciences concluded that 'without dramatic increases in the area of forests, without substantial positive changes in land-use practices, [etc.]... the US carbon sink will decrease substantially over the 21st century. ... Total US fossil fuel emissions would need to be reduced by an additional 7-30 percent to compensate for the declining sink'. The study went further, arguing that if fire suppression efforts were a complete failure, the land-based ecosystems of the US would turn into a source of carbon to the atmosphere, rather than a sink, during the whole 21st century because of 'extensive burning from large-scale fires' (Hurtt et al., 2002).[4]

## WHY IS GLOBAL WARMING A PROBLEM?

Current average global temperatures are now about 0.8°C (1.4°F) above what they were in pre-industrial times. The 2001 IPCC projections of the rise in average temperature likely by the end of this century (2100) range from 1.4°C (2.5°F) to 5.8°C (10.4°F) (Kintisch, 2005, p. 496). These projections were reaffirmed in the IPCC 2007 report, but with a slightly higher upper range for temperatures (IPCC, 2007, p. 45). If this meant that every place on earth would be a few degrees warmer every day than it is now, this change in climate (especially at the low end of these estimates) would not make such a big difference. The problem is that this small average global increase does not represent a slight uniform change everywhere, but much greater changes in individual temperatures and their variation from place to place and over time. For example, a year that was only a few degrees warmer than usual might be a year with many more extremely hot summer days, along with some winter days than were much colder than normal. Especially when we are averaging temperatures across the whole Earth, averages can hide a substantial amount of variability from place to place and time to time.

Because of this, even small average changes in climate can have dramatic effects on the physical environment (such as wind patterns, rainfall, storms) that in turn have powerful impacts on the biological environment. The change in global average temperature between the peak of the last ice age 25,000 years ago and today was only of the order of 5°C (9°F) (Environment Canada, 2005, p. 2). That is within the upper limit of IPCC's 2001 projection of increase in the global average temperature by 2100.

The ecology of the planet consists of a complex web of interdependent physical and biological systems. It is a matter of fact – not opinion – that our lives literally depend directly and indirectly on these systems. When climate changes, the balance of these systems is disrupted. Although it is difficult to predict all of the detailed implications of this disruption, it cannot help but have powerful effects on us.

By the year 2050, according to the Worldwatch Institute (2001, 2002), the total worldwide economic costs of global climate change are expected to be $300 billion per year [5] But using models developed by both the Goddard Institute for Space Studies and the Princeton Geophysical Fluid Dynamics Laboratory, James Titus of the US Environmental Protection Agency estimated that the costs of a doubling of carbon dioxide levels to the United States alone would be from $37 billion to $351 billion per year by 2060, depending on the model used and the scenario followed (Titus, 1992, pp. 1 and 16). This illustrates two important points: first, that the climate change produced by global warming is likely to impose very substantial economic costs on the US and the wider world; and second, that there is considerable uncertainty as to exactly how large those costs will be. There is, however, much more agreement on the pathways through which costs, economic and otherwise, will be transmitted. We look at the more important of these pathways in turn.

## Health Impacts

Global warming and the climate change it produces can directly affect human health by increasing the rate of heat- and cold-related illnesses and death, and increasing the frequency and/or intensity of violent storms and other extreme weather events (such as floods and drought). It can also affect human health indirectly, through its impact on food supply and patterns of disease. In the US and beyond, all of these effects are likely to fall more heavily on the poor, who live in more difficult conditions and have less of a buffer against adversity (as we have seen with great clarity in the aftermath of Hurricane Katrina). But it would be foolish to see the potential health impacts of the climate change produced by global warming only as a problem of poverty.

The World Health Organization has argued that among the first impacts on human health produced by global warming will be changes in the geographical range and seasonality of certain infectious diseases. This includes both illnesses borne by vectors (organisms that carry disease-causing microorganisms from one host to another) such as malaria and dengue fever, and food-borne illnesses such as salmonellosis, both of which tend to be more common in the warmer seasons (World Health Organization, 2005). Although the effect on the populations of countries with less well-developed systems of public health is likely to be greater, these problems will certainly not bypass the US, with potentially large effects on public health costs.

The principal vector-borne diseases that currently threaten people living in the US are transmitted by mosquitoes (for example, West Nile virus), ticks (for example, Lyme disease) and fleas (for example, plague). Studies have shown that climate is important in the life cycle, survival and behavior of these hosts, and that is vital to the development and transmission of the disease-causing microorganisms they carry. Global warming is expected to increase the likelihood that infectious diseases that are currently more common in lower latitudes, as well as diseases that are primarily transmitted by insects such as mosquitoes, will increasingly be experienced in more northern locations of the hemisphere (US Environmental Protection Agency, 2005). Together with temperature changes, changes in rainfall amounts may contribute to increases in insect and even rodent populations that will in turn enhance the prevalence and spread of water and food-borne diseases (Hopfl-Harris, 2005, p. 3).

Even if we do all the right things to protect the US population, the reality is that there is so much movement of people and goods in this globalizing world that disease can spread almost before we know what has happened. The SARS virus, for example, contracted in China in 2003 became, with alarming speed, a threat to the health of people living in Europe and North America. According to the World Health Organization, more than 30 new diseases have emerged since the mid-1970s, along with new drug-resistant forms of old diseases such as tuberculosis we once thought we had completely under control (Epstein, 1997, p. 3).

On the other hand, it is also possible that some of the changes in climate will actually help to suppress some forms of disease or the vectors that transmit them, at least in some parts of the country. The US should be able to avert the worst health consequences of global warming with sufficient investment in public health, but while a precise estimate of cost is difficult, it will not be cheap.

Finally, some of the greenhouse gases that contribute to global warming are also air pollutants that have negative effects on health. Nitrogen oxides, for example, are not only heat-trapping gases, they are key ingredients of smog and atmospheric ozone near enough to the ground to be breathed. They damage lung tissue, increase sensitivity to other irritants, and reduce lung function (especially troubling for asthmatics), causing chest pain, congestion and coughing.[6]

## Impacts on Agriculture

Variations in temperature, especially unseasonable variations – for example, unusually cold days during critical parts of the normally warm growing season – can substantially reduce crop yields. Plants are affected by higher concentrations of $CO_2$ in the atmosphere as well, though in this case the effect seems to be positive: their growth is stimulated by it. In the absence of irrigation systems, crops are also especially sensitive to precipitation. Because warm air can carry more water, the IPCC's 1996 report projected that the global warming that would be expected from a doubling of $CO_2$ would increase precipitation by 10–15 percent on average (IPCC, 1996). Since global warming shifts wind and rainfall patterns, it is not difficult to predict that it will also change where (and when) the precipitation falls – a critical matter for agriculture.

Working with the UN's Food and Agricultural Organization (FAO), the International Institute of Applied Systems Analysis (IIASA) concluded '[O]n average, industrialized countries stand to make substantial gains in production potential, while developing countries are expected to lose. In the developing world, climate change would lead to an increase in lands that are arid and lands experiencing moisture stress... [leading to] an 11 percent decrease in cultivable rain-fed land, with consequent decline in cereal production' (United Nations Food and Agricultural Organization, 2005, p. 2). These results were not uniform throughout the developing world. For example, although India was projected to experience an 18 percent decline in rain-fed cereal output, China was projected to gain 15 percent. In Africa, a continent that has had more than its share of food security problems, some 29 countries would lose about 35 million tons of cereal production (ibid.).

Aside from humanitarian concerns, there are at least three reasons to be concerned about the impacts on US agriculture. The first is that these projections do not take into account the potential spread of animal and plant diseases and pests, which is likely to be provoked by global warming for the same reasons given in the discussion of human health. Temperature increases can speed up the growth rates of insects and plant pests, decreasing their mortality in winter at the same time they are affecting crops in ways that make these crops more vulnerable to pests (ibid. pp. 4–6). We need to be concerned about the effect of the spread of animal diseases on agriculture as well. Losses to agriculture resulting from foot and mouth disease, mad cow disease, swine flu and, more recently, bird flu have been in the billions of dollars – and they were most certainly not confined to the less developed countries. Some diseases of farm animals have also shown a disturbing tendency to jump species and infect people. Mad cow disease has been implicated in producing Creutzfeldt-Jakob disease in humans, and the virus that causes virulent bird flu has also infected people.

The second reason is that while general climate change projections are reasonably sound, it is extremely difficult to predict the details of exactly where and when the extra rain that is projected to help US crops grow will actually fall within the country. If the forecasts are a bit off and the change results in a lot more rain along the Boston–Washington corridor and a lot less in Kansas and Nebraska, the same total US rainfall will have very different implications for American agriculture. Finally, some of the most important 'ambitious adaptations' in agriculture that are needed to adjust to global warming could be quite expensive. Changing planting time and harvest time to adjust to a longer growing season will not cost much, but the investment in research required to understand all the downsides of global warming for agriculture and develop technologies (for instance, new pest control techniques) to deal with them may not come cheap. And some of the equipment and supplies needed to make the necessary changes in agricultural practices may be expensive. In the end, these adjustments may prove to be more or less costly. Still, this adds yet another element of uncertainty to thinking realistically about climate change.

**Impacts on Severe Weather**

According to a UN Environmental Program (UNEP) report published in 2002, 'Worldwide economic losses due to natural disasters appear to be doubling every ten years, and have reached almost $1 trillion over the past 15 years.... Each year now brings four times as many weather related disasters as 40 years ago.... If current trends persist, the annual loss amount will, within the next decade, come close to $150 billion' (Innovest Strategic Value Advisors, 2002, p. 6).

There is no doubt that human-induced global warming affects weather patterns, and little doubt that it plays some role in the patterns and severity of drought and floods, since it clearly does affect rainfall. But there is still an unsettled and ongoing scientific debate as to just what affect it has in generating the most severe and violent storms, hurricanes and tornadoes.

In August 2005, Kerry Emanuel, a noted atmospheric physicist from MIT, published the results of a study he had done in *Nature*. Emanuel found that the power output of storms in the Atlantic and western North Pacific cycled up and down over the decades since 1930, but shot upward 30 years ago. Although he cannot be sure, he now believes global warming may very well be the reason why (Monastersky, 2005). The following month, meteorologist Peter Webster of Georgia Institute of Technology and his colleagues reported the results of their study of satellite records of tropical storms around the world from 1970 to 2004. They found no long-term trend in the number of storms, but a dramatic increase of nearly 80 percent in the number of category four and five hurricanes (Webster et al., 2005). In this same 35-year period, global warming had raised sea surface temperatures worldwide 0.5°C (0.9°F) (Kerr, 2005, p. 1844). Of course, correlation is not the same as causation. The fact that sea surface temperatures rose due to global warming at the same time that storm intensities increased certainly does not prove that global warming has caused hurricanes to become more powerful. But this pattern is consistent with that predicted by recent climate model simulations (and with the pattern Emanuel observed). So it is quite possible that global warming may be the culprit.

In the 25 years between 1980 and 2004, there were 62 weather-related disasters in the US that did at least $1 billion worth of damage. These events included hurricanes and tropical storms, tornadoes, snow and ice storms, wildfires, floods, and droughts. Hurricanes were the most frequent of these extreme weather events, accounting for about 30 percent of the disasters. But the most damaging of these events by far was not a hurricane; it was not even a storm. It was the killer drought and heat wave that gripped the central and eastern US in the summer of 1988, doing nearly $62 billion worth of damage and taking the lives of 5,000–10,000 people. Hurricane Andrew (1992) did the second most damage, almost $36 billion, and took 61 lives. The third most damaging event was the Midwest flooding due to persistent heavy rains in the summer of 1993 – close to $27 billion of damage and 48 deaths. (Some 17 percent of all the urban land in the US lies within the 100-year flood plain) (Reid et al., 2005, p. 192). The total money-valued loss from these 62 major disasters was more than $390 billion (US Department of Commerce, 2005).[7]

The Association of British Insurers (ABI) concluded recently that global warming was probably helping to intensify the extreme weather patterns that in the past few years have produced heavy insured losses. In June 2005, ABI issued a report on the financial risks associated with climate change. Based on IPCC's scenarios, the report indicated that by 2080, insured losses from hurricanes in the US could increase by as much as 75 percent ($62 billion) over present losses. Under the high emissions scenario ($CO_2$ levels double), insurers' capital requirements could increase by more than 90 percent. If emissions were controlled enough to match the low emissions scenario, increased losses from US hurricanes would be 80 percent lower than under the high emissions scenario, saving $35–$50 billion per year – the equivalent of avoiding one to one-and-a-half Hurricane Andrews per season (Association of British Insurers, 2005, pp. 8, 23 and 28).

**Impacts on Water Resources and Sea-Level Rise**

Global warming affects many aspects of the global water cycle: cloud characteristics, rainfall, soil moisture, patterns of snowfall and snowmelt, the rate at which water evaporates from the Earth's surface, and the rate at which it is released to the atmosphere by plants (transpiration). The higher $CO_2$ levels that contribute to warming also increase transpiration rates, because they increase plant growth. About a third of the 25 billion metric tons of carbon dioxide released into the air by burning fossil fuels each year is absorbed by the ocean, according to a report by Britain's leading scientific organization (the Royal Society). It is turning ocean water more acidic, damaging plankton, and disrupting the food chain (Chang, 2005).[8]

Many of the expected changes in the water cycle will affect US water resources directly by altering total availability, and more importantly, by changing the quantity and quality of water available to different regions of the country. In general, the northern US is likely to have more precipitation and runoff, while the southern US is expected to have less. Changes in seasonal patterns within regions are also likely. For example, areas where snow falls, such as the Rockies and the Sierra Nevada, are expected to have greater runoff in winter and early spring, and less in late spring and summer. Changes in the amount and timing of runoff affect not only water supply, but also river navigation, hydropower and aquatic ecosystems. The semi-arid and arid western parts of the US might see greater drying of soils during the growing season and perhaps more variability in water supply. But there is also a risk that other changes due to global warming, such as the expected rise in sea level, will indirectly affect regional water supply by increasing the intrusion of saltwater into freshwater aquifers along the coasts, in places like Cape Cod, Long Island, central coastal California, Hawaii, and Florida (Claussen, 2001, pp. 66–67).

It has been estimated that additional costs imposed by global warming on the water industry alone could reach $47 billion per year by 2050 (Coalition for Environmentally Responsible Economics, 2001, p. 10). But there is considerable uncertainty in such estimates, because the details are hard to predict and the details make a very big difference to projections of economic costs. For example, using the least-cost management scenario, the Canadian climate change model projects much higher annual costs of meeting water demands in the contiguous United States – $105 billion. On the other hand, the so-called Hadley2 model projects that climate change will actually cause these costs to be $5 billion lower than they would be without climate change (Claussen, 2001, p. 75).

It is by now well accepted that higher global temperatures will cause increased melting of glaciers that will lead to a rise in sea level.[9] This is already happening. In Antarctica, the Larsen A ice shelf collapsed in 1995; in 1998, the Wilkinson ice shelf also disintegrated. In a period of about a month in early 2002, the Larsen B ice shelf lost more than 25 percent of its total mass, launching thousands of icebergs into the Weddell Sea (Rohter, 2005). But global warming is also causing additional snowfall in the East Antarctic icecap, an area in which it was previously too cold to snow. The snow is causing the ice sheet to grow about enough to offset the roughly 45 billion tons of water flowing into the ocean each year as a result of the melting Greenland icecap (Hotz, 2005).

When the ice in land-based glaciers (or their melt water) flows into the sea, it increases the volume of water. Unless this flow is offset by another process (such as increased evaporation) that is removing as much or more water, the sea level naturally rises. A study sponsored by the EPA suggests that there is a 50 percent chance that global warming will cause as much as a 20-inch rise in the sea level at Miami Beach, a 25-inch rise in Charleston, South Carolina, and a 55-inch rise for Grand Isle, Louisiana (about 50 miles south of New Orleans) (Pacific Institute for Studies in Development, 2005).

According to the EPA, global warming could cause sea level to rise by 0.5 meters (20 inches) to 2 meters (6.5 feet) by 2100. A 1-meter rise could drown 25–80 percent of the US coastal wetlands and inundate 5,000–10,000 square miles of dry land if shores were not protected. The capital costs of protecting developed areas at risk against such inundation and erosion by building bulkheads and levees, pumping sand and raising barrier islands could be $73–$111 billion by the year 2100 (US Environmental Protection Agency, 2005).

## Ecological Impacts

It is difficult to separate out the ecological effects of the increase in $CO_2$ and other greenhouse gases from those of other sources of human-induced ecological change, since the ecology is, almost by definition, a complex intensely interconnected system. Still, it is clear that global warming works with these other sources of change to alter the environment. For example, heavy commercial fishing is no doubt the most important factor in driving some aquatic species to the edge of extinction. But a recent study of Europe's heavily fished North Sea concluded that the warming of its waters over the past 25 years has driven indigenous fish populations northward and to greater depths. As a result, the North Sea's ecosystem is changing in ways whose effects on commercial fishing are difficult to predict (Inman, 2005, p. 937).

The effect of rapid climate change on biodiversity is a major concern, although various plant and animal species have shown a greater ability to adapt to past climate changes than was at first thought likely. Ice core records extracted from Greenland and Antarctica in the 1990s showed considerable variability in climate over the past 200,000 years. 'Yet biodiversity has survived these past rapid changes largely intact. There is no reliable record of mass extinctions in the Pleistocene' (Lovejoy and Lee, 2005, p. 388).[10] Range shifts (movement to habitats in new places), rather than genetic changes, seem to have been the main mechanism for surviving dramatic changes in climate over very long periods of time. But the migration of plant and animal species to new areas is now hampered by human activities that have destroyed or fragmented new habitats and/or blocked the routes that might have made these habitats more accessible in the very distant past. The fragmentation or outright destruction of habitats has also reduced the number of individuals, making the species less viable. Because it is difficult to isolate the effects of climate change on biodiversity, its effects are therefore best understood in combination with those of other human-induced stresses, such as habitat destruction and environmental pollution.

Biodiversity as such is not the only relevant ecological issue. According to UNEP, not only could about 3°C–4°C (5.4°F–7.2°F) worth of global warming eliminate 85 percent of all remaining wetlands, it could cause the permafrost in arctic habitats to thaw, releasing vast stores of additional GHGs trapped in the soil. Through this positive feedback effect, global warming could make itself worse (UN Environmental Program, 2005). Researchers studying western Siberia have found that an area of permafrost the size of France and Germany combined has already begun to melt – for the first time in 11,000 years. The entire sub-Arctic region of western Siberia is one gigantic peat bog, and as it thaws it could release billions of metric tons of methane into the atmosphere. Methane, produced as a result of the decomposition of organisms and organic waste, is a much more potent GHG than carbon dioxide. It would most likely take many decades for the Siberian permafrost to thaw, and therefore for all that methane to be released. But climate scientist Stephen Sitch and his colleagues have calculated that even if it took 100 years, it would still add 700 million metric tons of carbon to the atmosphere per year. That's about as much carbon as is released each year from all the world's wetlands and agriculture. By itself, this could increase global warming by 10–25 percent (Sample, 2005).

Siberia is not alone in this. According to a 2004 report prepared for the Pew Center on Global Climate Change, 'The Alaskan tundra has already experienced much stronger warming trends than the rest of the United States. At some point, as deeper layers remain above freezing, the rate of decomposition of dead matter will exceed the rate of plant growth, and the tundra will turn from a net sink to a net source of $CO_2$. … [D]uring 1983–1987 and 1990, the tundra across the North Slope of Alaska was acting as a source of $CO_2$ to the atmosphere, instead of the sink it had been' (Parmesan and Galbraith, 2004, p. 33).

## WHY IT IS IMPORTANT TO ACT SOONER RATHER THAN LATER

The problem posed by global warming is particularly challenging because it combines a serious degree of uncertainty with the need to intervene in a system that is inertial and yet capable of abrupt change, in a situation where the stakes are very high. In order to understand how to make sensible, practical and effective policy under these difficult conditions, it is first worth considering the nature and implications of each of these characteristics of the global warming problem in turn.

### Uncertainty

It is certain that global warming is occurring, and it is clear that human activity is one of the causes. But there is great uncertainty as to exactly how much human activity is contributing to each of the drivers of global climate change, how much each of the drivers is individually contributing to the overall problem, and precisely how these drivers are interacting with each other. The strongest evidence for this is that there is such a wide range of estimate for the projected value of almost every physical and economic dimension of the impact of global climate change among the many studies that have been done.

For example, consider the most basic physical estimate, the rise in global temperatures expected by the end of this century (2100). The upper limit of the 2001 IPCC projections (5.8°C) is more than four times as large as the lower limit (1.4°C). On the economic side, the upper estimate of the costs that would be imposed on the US by 2060 as a result of doubling carbon dioxide levels given in the study by James Titus of the EPA cited earlier ($351 billion) is more than nine times the size of the lower end estimate ($37 billion). Such wide ranges of estimate are in part due to different model structures and assumptions, as well as varying scenarios that include differences in the human response to the problem, a notoriously difficult factor to predict. But, apart from the human factor, there would not be such a wide variation in these structures, assumptions and scenarios if we knew better how all the factors that affect climate actually work and interact.

It is worth pointing out that the situation we face here is one of true uncertainty, not just risk. We are dealing with 'risk' when we cannot predict what will happen, but we know all the possible outcomes, along with how likely each of these outcomes is to actually happen. For example, when we roll a pair of dice, we know all the numbers that could possibly come up, and if the dice have not been loaded, we can easily calculate the chance of each of these numbers occurring. 'Uncertainty' means we are missing some of this information – either we do not know all of the outcomes that are possible, or we do not know how likely some of the possible outcomes are, or both.

An honest, objective assessment of the present state of knowledge about climate change is that while we do know quite a lot, we cannot be sure that we are aware of everything that could possibly happen, given the complexity of the planet's meteorological system and ecology. We cannot even be certain of our ability to calculate the chances of the outcomes we do know about. When it comes down to it, much that we would like to know to understand the details of the climate change problem more precisely is still beyond the boundary of what we now do know. As Leonard Smith of the London School of Economics put it, 'At best, our models hold only in certain circumstances.... All results at the boundaries of our understanding must be treated as fundamentally uncertain' (Smith, 2002, p. 2487).

The natural impulse in such a situation is to do more research to try to clear up enough of the uncertainty so that we can work out the best approach to solving the problem. That is a healthy impulse; it has been the impulse behind much of our intellectual progress, especially in science and engineering. I think any sensible person would agree that doing more research on climate change is a good idea. But the problem is, since climate change is happening here and now, the longer we wait to act, the more painful and extreme the action needed to solve the problem may turn out to be. As a result, there is likely to be a great advantage to acting sooner rather than later.

## The Possibility of Abrupt Change

We know from our experience with complex, interacting systems (including ecological systems) that for a while, slow, bit-by-bit changes may produce only slow, predictable, incremental changes in system behavior, if any. But when a threshold or 'tipping point' is reached and then crossed, they can suddenly undergo major changes in behavior that may be very difficult or impossible to predict or to undo.

For example, when increased sensitivity caused by highly interactive computerized program trading helped push the stock market across a critical threshold in 1987, the value of stocks on the New York exchange dropped precipitously. For that matter, an even more spectacular example occurred when low margin requirements and that era's version of 'irrational exuberance' combined to push the stock market of the 1920s over the edge, leading to the crash of 1929 that ushered in the Great Depression.

Until the levees built around New Orleans were pounded by storm forces that exceeded the strength of their weakest points, or were faced with water levels higher than the levees themselves, they could protect the city. But when Hurricane Katrina and (a few weeks later) Hurricane Rita took the levees over those critical thresholds, the city was quickly flooded. Something similar had happened years earlier in Grand Forks, North Dakota. Grand Forks had been successfully protected against flood since the 19th century, despite frequent threats from river surges up to a stage of 49 feet. But in 1997, the river crested just 10 percent higher than before (54 feet), and the result was catastrophic damage (National Research Council, 2002, pp. 121–122).

We know that such thresholds exist within the environment and that crossing them can trigger major ecological damage, but we often do not know where these 'ecotriggers' are, or how they work. This is especially true with respect to climate change. According to the National Research Council of the US, 'the quintessential abrupt climate change was… about 11,500 years ago, when… climate shifted dramatically in many regions by about one-third to one-half the difference between ice age and modern conditions, with much of the change occurring over a few years' (ibid., p. 14).

The recent discovery that a million square miles of permafrost in western Siberia is now melting (mentioned earlier in the section on ecological impacts) raises the possibility that billions of metric tons of methane, a potent greenhouse gas, will be released to the atmosphere. Sergei Kirpotin, one of the two discoverers of this phenomenon, said that the thaw, which had probably begun only a few years ago, was an 'ecological landslide that is probably irreversible and is undoubtedly connected to climatic warming'. Reacting to Kirpotin's discovery, British climate researcher David Viner said, 'When you start messing around with these natural systems, you can end up in situations where it's unstoppable. There are no brakes you can apply' (Sample, 2005).

Summarizing the results of its analysis of abrupt climate change, the National Research Council pointed out, 'Abrupt climate changes were especially common when the climate system was being forced to change most rapidly. Thus, greenhouse warming and other human alterations of the earth system may increase the possibility of large, abrupt, and unwelcome regional or global climatic events. The abrupt changes of the past are not fully explained yet, and climate models typically underestimate the size, speed, and extent of those changes. Hence, *future abrupt changes cannot be predicted with confidence, and climate surprises are to be expected.*'[11]

**Inertia**

It is not unusual for time lags to be built into the structure of large, complex, interactive systems. These delays tend to make the system sluggish in responding to changes in the external forces that drive it. As a result, after a change is made, it can take some time for the system to respond at all, and considerably longer for the change to work its way completely through the system.

There are many examples of systems with this kind of inertia. In the demographic system, for example, a precipitous drop in the birth rate in the US would take about five years to have any effect on grade school enrollment, and about 13 years more to have any major effect on the number of new entrants to the labor force. Further along in the life cycle, it is predictably taking about 65 years for the population bulge created by the post-war baby boom to work its way through to retirement, with all that implies for social security and other pension systems.

The Earth's ecology is also a large, complex interactive system with considerable inertia. It took more than a decade after the peak use of the pesticide DDT for peak levels of DDT to be detected in fish. The Montreal Protocol on Substances that Deplete the Ozone Layer was created in 1987, and ultimately signed by more than 180 nations. Eighteen years later, it was finally noted that the amount of ozone-depleting chlorofluorocarbons (CFCs) in the lower atmosphere had started to decline. It is expected to take decades before the ozone layer in the upper atmosphere is restored to pre-1970 levels (Leahy, 2005).

The climate system too is inertial. Many greenhouse gases (GHGs) are long-lived in the atmosphere, and they are continuing to accumulate because of current GHG emission levels. Even if the amount of GHGs in the atmosphere were stabilized today, average global temperature would continue to rise. So would sea level, because the oceans take a long time to heat up. According to T.M.L. Wigley of the National Center for Atmospheric Research, 'Ocean thermal inertia causes climate change to lag.... Because of this lag..., and because of the changes in atmospheric composition [and changes in the buildup of heat]... that have already occurred, the climate system will continue to change for many decades (centuries for sea level) even in the absence of future changes in atmospheric composition' (Wigley, 2005, p. 1766).

According to Gerald A. Meehl (also of the National Center for Atmospheric Research) and his colleagues, 'even if the concentrations of greenhouse gases in the atmosphere had been stabilized in the year 2000, we are already committed to further global warming of about another half degree and an additional 320 percent sea level rise caused by thermal expansion by the end of the 21st century… At any given point in time, even if concentrations are stabilized, there is a commitment to future climate changes that will be greater than those we have already observed' (Meehl et al., 2005, p. 1769).

Inertial systems put a premium on starting now rather than later to make a change when a change is needed. Anticipation becomes crucial. Just as someone at the helm of an oil supertanker must begin to turn the ship much earlier than someone at the helm of a small speedboat, there is so much inertia in the climate system that we must start 'turning the ship' now, if we are to successfully turn toward a more viable course. There is no need to panic, but we cannot afford to wait until global temperatures and sea level have risen to dangerous levels before we begin to take some corrective action.

## High Stakes

According to British Petroleum (BP), world energy consumption rose 4.3 percent in 2004, the biggest percentage rise in 20 years and the largest absolute increase ever. The company's annual statistical review also indicated that the increased burning of fossil fuels the following year resulted in the biggest absolute increase ever in carbon emissions, boosting the atmosphere's burden of greenhouse gases. The fast-growing Asian economies were responsible for an important part of the rise in GHGs: energy consumption in China increased by 15.1 percent; in India, the increase was 7.2 percent (Catan, 2005).

As long as the developing economies continue to grow – and that has long been not only their dream, but also ours – we are likely to see more of the same. Yet neither their continued growth nor ours can be sustained without finding a way to disconnect economic progress from the voracious consumption of nonrenewable, environmentally damaging energy resources. Otherwise, we will find ourselves in increasing competition for a dwindling stock of nonrenewable resources, a competition that has already caused a more than its share of conflict costly in both money and blood. And we will find ourselves burdened by higher and higher cost as a result of the environmental and climatic forces we are unleashing. Nothing less than the quality of our common – and individual – economic futures is at stake.

As we have seen, the direct economic costs of the climate change induced by global warming are high, estimated to reach as much as $351 billion per year in the US alone by 2060. They have the potential to become much higher. Whether or not the United States takes strong action to deal with the problem, many other nations are in the process of doing so. As a result, global markets for technologies and devices designed to reduce greenhouse emissions are large today and will grow over time. UNEP projects that sales in the market for renewable energy will reach $234 billion to $625 billion worldwide within a few years (2010), and as high as $1.9 trillion by 2020.

Because business people cannot pay attention to everything at once, even profitable opportunities will sometimes slip by them when their attention is focused elsewhere. US companies may be disadvantaged in the competition for these profitable markets if strong leadership is not taken to push them to pay attention to climate change. If it is not, we will eventually wind up buying the equipment and technology needed to address global warming from other nations, rather than selling it to them.

The stakes are high, both in terms of the costs likely to be imposed on us by the climate change that results from global warming, and the economic opportunities now being created by global action to mitigate the problem.

## KEY CHARACTERISTICS OF SENSIBLE STRATEGIES TO MITIGATE CLIMATE WARMING

Global warming presents us with a high stakes problem characterized by great uncertainty, system inertia and the likelihood that crossing thresholds we cannot even foresee may cause sudden escalation that is very difficult to predict or control. What is the most sensible strategy to follow in this kind of challenging situation?

We could wait until the scientific community is able to gain enough knowledge to understand all the details of the problem, so that we can be sure we know what the best solution is. But while climate change research should be encouraged, it is likely to be a long time before we understand the situation even close to that well. In the meantime, business-as-usual could easily carry us across one of those unseen escalation thresholds – or even just build up enough momentum that by the time we know what the best approach would have been, the inertia of the climate system will have rendered it unworkable.

Alternatively, we could wait until the worst that is going to happen actually does start happening before taking action, and then try to deal with the problems after the fact, say a few decades from now. But if anything near the worst-case scenario does happen, dealing with the problem after the fact could absorb so much of the nation's available resources that we won't be able to do anything else.

On the other hand, if we act strongly enough now to even significantly reduce the scope of the problem, we can preserve the nation's ability to take care of the population's educational and health care needs, to provide a strong national defense – and to maintain the flexibility that will allow us to successfully deal with and overcome other unforeseen (and perhaps unforeseeable) problems. Just as the events of September 11th, 2001 (and more recently, Hurricane Katrina) suddenly called upon the nation to take strong and expensive action we did not expect to have to take, there is no way to be sure future events will not once again hand us an expensive 'bad surprise'. Preserving our fiscal flexibility is critical to keeping the nation and its people secure.

Although on the surface it seems like a more conservative strategy to wait to see how bad the problem really is before taking action, when it comes to global warming, it is actually a far safer, more conservative strategy to take reasonable but bold action sooner rather than later.

We know that many meaningful actions we can take to deal with global warming involve bearing significant costs now. Since strong action taken in the presence of considerable uncertainty could turn out to be more than was strictly necessary to deal with the problem, it makes sense to look for ways of minimizing the cost of taking effective action. Even better, if we can find effective programs that actually have the promise of generating future returns, we can turn the costs we have to bear now into an investment, rather than an expenditure.

**Cost Minimizing**

The first step toward minimizing the cost of mitigating global warming is to take advantage of whatever effective costless or even 'negative cost' (money saving) options are available. It is not difficult to believe that consumers or government agencies might be overlooking such possibilities, but it is harder to understand how they could also be overlooked by the private sector. After all, we normally think of private sector firms as being focused on minimizing costs as a means to maximizing profits (that is certainly the way it is in standard economic theory). It is surprising that firms could actually be ignoring significant money saving opportunities. But let us remember that attention is a limited resource: the managements of real world firms cannot pay attention to everything at once. If their attention is focused elsewhere, it is easy for costless or even money saving options for reducing global warming to slip by them.

As an example, energy has been so cheap for so long in the United States that we have not worried very much about how to conserve it. When energy prices skyrocketed in the mid-1970s, it suddenly seemed to make sense to pay more attention to how much energy we were consuming. Once our attention was focused on the issue, we began to see changes we could make some of which would have saved us a significant amount of money even before energy prices took off. In a book I wrote on energy conservation nearly 30 years ago, I cited the example of an office building designed for Toledo Edison. The architects discovered that by using specially coated double-glazed windows to save energy, they could reduce the size of the building's heating, ventilating and air conditioning (HVAC) system. The space needed for the air ducts could then be reduced, shrinking the size of the building without reducing the amount of useable interior space. It turned out that the money saved by using a smaller HVAC system and making the building smaller was greater than the extra cost of the more expensive energy-conserving windows. In other words, in addition to saving tens of thousands of dollars a year in energy costs, the newly designed building actually cost less to build! It would therefore have made sense to build it that way even before energy became so expensive. But neither the architects nor their clients thought of that until much higher energy prices focused their attention on trying to save energy (Dumas, 1976, pp. 47 and 103–105).

As Lawrence Goulder of Stanford University points out, 'Several studies indicate that, in many circumstances, firms fail to minimize their private costs by overlooking pre-existing zero or negative cost opportunities for emissions reductions.... A public policy intervention can stimulate 'discovery' of costless emissions reduction opportunities that, in a sense, were already there for the taking' (Goulder, 2004).[12] Though it is unlikely to be enough, we should always go after such 'low-hanging fruit' first.

As we introduce policies that are more costly, it is important to work out ways of implementing them that are as cost effective as possible. The key to doing that is to create incentives that are sensitive to differences in both the technical difficulty and the financial cost of implementing climate change mitigation policies to those targeted by the policies. This is one of the great advantages of a properly designed 'cap and trade' approach (discussed in the chapters by Egenhofer and Boyce in this volume).

## Return Maximizing

Since we can be reasonably sure that there will be a large and growing market worldwide for technologies and equipment useful in addressing the problem of global warming, one obvious approach to turning mitigation from an expense into an opportunity to earn a healthy return is to encourage research and development (R&D) aimed at finding those technologies and developing that equipment.

There are basically four types of technologies that should prove to be profitable, if they can be made cost-effective: 1) those that reduce emissions of greenhouse gases; 2) those that conserve energy; 3) those that are useful in artificially sequestering (storing) greenhouse gases; and 4) those that increase the efficiency of alternative, ecologically benign energy sources. Their development involves varying degrees of risk. There may be little need to encourage low-risk projects, since the risks involved are within boundaries that the private sector normally finds acceptable. But some of the projects involving the largest outlays and the highest risks may actually have the greatest social value, as well as the greatest profit potential, should they succeed. Because of the scale required and the risk involved, they might well not be undertaken by the private sector in the absence of additional incentives or support (see the chapter by Roach in this volume).

Another important way to achieve a greater return from resources spent on mitigating global warming is to look for strategies that work to solve more than one problem at the same time. That way, if it turns out that we have unintentionally done more than was actually necessary to deal with the problem (because we had to act despite considerable uncertainty), the approach we have taken will still be beneficial, rather than excessively costly. For example, a focus on improving energy efficiency would not only reduce greenhouse gas emissions, but would reduce other forms of environmental pollution too. By stretching out the life of existing secure nonrenewable energy sources, it would also buy time for doing the longer term R&D needed to improve more environmentally benign energy sources, and at the same time lower the nation's dependence on energy from troubled (or troublesome) foreign suppliers. Mitigating global warming this way thus brings three additional payoffs: less money spent on energy, additional pollution reduction, and increased national security.

## Robustness and Adaptability

If we could be sure how the processes driving global warming would play out in the real world, it would make sense to look for the single best way of dealing with the problem. But since the characteristics of the problem require us to act while there is still a lot of uncertainty, it makes more sense to look for an approach or approaches that are 'robust' – that is, they work reasonably well under a wide range of plausible scenarios. The problem is that the 'best' policy is often best only under a relatively narrow set of circumstances. Since we have no way of knowing which of the scenarios we think are plausible will actually happen, we can hedge our bets in this high stakes game by going for solutions that are robust, rather than betting our future on trying to find the one strategy that will turn out to have been best when the fog of uncertainty finally clears.[13]

The advantages of robustness are complemented by those of adaptability. Both the problems we face and the strategies we choose are processes rather than events. They will take some time to work themselves out. As time passes there will be less uncertainty, particularly if we continue to do more research. We will learn more about what has actually happened, what is likely to happen next, and how well our approaches to mitigating or at least coping with climate change are working. This puts a premium on choosing approaches now that are flexible enough to allow us to adapt as we see later that a change of plan would be a good idea.

**A Cautionary Note**

If we are too narrowly focused in our search for approaches that are effective in dealing with global warming, we are liable to fall into a trap. We may take actions that help solve that serious problem, but actually make other serious problems we face worse. This has happened all too frequently in the past.

For example, the Montreal Protocol on Substances that Deplete the Ozone Layer included an agreed phase-out of a number of stratospheric ozone depleting chemicals, among them hydrochlorofluorocarbons (HCFCs). This stimulated the development of other fluorocarbons that were much less of a threat to the ozone layer to replace those being phased-out. Among these were hydrofluorocarbons (HFCs). As it turns out, although HFCs have far less potential for depleting ozone, they are greenhouse gases with a much higher potential for making global warming worse (see the list of GHGs given earlier) (Checklick, 2004a).

Such is the case with nuclear power. Although no one could reasonably put nuclear power forth as a *cheap* solution to the problem of climate change, many reasonable people have begun to put it forth as an effective solution. There are at least three reasons to be cautious about this approach.

First, while it is true that nuclear power plants generate electricity without emitting greenhouse gases, it is not true that the nuclear fuel cycle is free of such emissions. Depending on how the process is carried out, substantial amounts of chlorofluorocarbons (CFCs), for example, may be emitted during uranium enrichment (Checklick, 2004b). A 1997 assessment of life cycle GHG emissions per kilowatt-hour (GHG/kw-hr) for a number of methods of generating electricity done by the Öko Institute in Germany estimated that nuclear power generated about 6 percent more GHG/kw-hr than hydroelectric power and 75 percent more GHG/kw-hr than wind power (although it was much lower in carbon emissions than fossil fuel plants).[14] Second, we are still far from having a technically efficient, cost-effective solution to storing and protecting the nuclear waste we have already generated (and are continuing to generate). It does not make sense to do anything to make that problem worse. Finally, encouraging large-scale growth of the nuclear power industry here will inevitably encourage its expansion abroad, with all the negative implications that has for nuclear proliferation and hence national security.

**A Note on Equity**

It seems clear that the overall social benefits – and often enough, even the overall private benefits (such as job creation and profit generation) – of many available global warming mitigation policies far exceed their total cost. In our enthusiasm for this situation, it is easy to overlook the important question of equity: Do those particular individuals who bear the costs of the policies also receive enough of the benefits to make these policies beneficial to them? After all, it might well be that the society as a whole gains, but the some people bear much more cost and get much less benefit than others. This is not simply a theoretical possibility; it is often enough what happens.

Fairness matters, for both moral and political reasons. Yet in the 'real world', it is rare for any particular policy to provide the same net benefit to everyone. One way around this dilemma is to design and implement a group of policies that have different net benefits to different groups of individuals. Even if all the policies within the package address the same underlying problem (in this case, global warming), by including policies that come at the problem from different angles, the package as a whole can be made more equitable than any single policy within the package. There is certainly enough flexibility within the group of effective global warming/climate change mitigation policies discussed in the chapters of this report to put together a variety of relatively equitable policy packages. Still another classic approach is to provide mechanisms by which those who get a disproportionate share of the gains must compensate those who bear a disproportionate share of the costs (see the chapter by Boyce in this volume).

As a practical matter, reasonable attention to equity is not all that difficult to achieve. It does not require everyone to gain equally, merely that when the dust settles, on the whole, those who bear greater costs in proportion to their income or wealth also receive greater proportionate benefits.

## CONCLUSIONS AND IMPLICATIONS

Human-induced global warming and the climate change it produces are not phantoms or misinterpretations. They are real. They threaten us with disease, more powerful storms, droughts and floods. They threaten our ecology, our coastal population, our water supplies and the food supply of many of the world's most vulnerable people.

At the same time, the commitment of many local, state and national governments – and a growing number of private sector firms – to finding cost-effective approaches to mitigation has created great opportunity. On the one hand, there is the potential for earning substantial profits and creating large numbers of productive jobs by joining the effort. On the other, there is the very real prospect of undoing some of the damage that the image and reputation of the US has suffered in recent years by asserting our willingness to take effective action in finding and implementing solutions to this matter of vital importance to all the world's people, rich and poor.

Global warming presents us with a high stakes problem that is still surrounded by considerable uncertainty. Yet we cannot wait to take bold and decisive action, due to the significant time-lags in climate system adaptation processes, and the ever-present chance that it will cross an unseen threshold that will suddenly accelerate the problem beyond our control. Such a problem is best solved by implementing policies that are robust (effective under a wide range of plausible scenarios) and adaptable (flexible enough to be modified 'on the fly' as progress is made and some of the uncertainty clears), while minimizing costs and maximizing returns (by creating profit-making opportunities or helping to solve more than one problem at the same time).

We can find ways to mitigate, if not reverse, human-induced global warming and we can do so without seriously threatening either the present standard of living of those who live in the developed countries or the future prospects of those who live in the developing world. Finding these ways will require mobilizing and coordinating the best efforts of government, the private sector, and the public at large, while playing to the strengths of each.

One useful role of government is to get the attention of business aimed in the right direction by, for example, setting energy and environmental performance requirements for energy-using systems (such as cars), and leaving it up to the creativity of private business to work out the details. Another useful role for government is to serve as a proto-market for new technologies and devices, helping American business get a running start at servicing important but financially risky new markets whose products are valuable to society, as well as potentially profitable. The Internet and satellite communications are just two of many examples of markets where the US government played a key role in giving American business a head start.

There is no single change in our behavior or our policies that is likely to solve the problem of global warming, but there are many changes that together add up to a solution. Although it would be simpler, and it might seem more desirable, to try to find one approach that addresses the problem, we are actually better off looking for a variety of paths to the solution. This makes it easier to achieve equity. It also allows us to spread our risks. Diversification is nearly always a risk management strategy worth considering, especially when there is a lot at stake.

There is reason to be optimistic. We certainly cannot afford to be complacent, but there is no need to panic. We still have the time to take a measured approach, to roll up our sleeves and build the political will to take sensible, pragmatic actions that will make global warming a problem of the past, rather than a threat to our future.

## NOTES

1. Professor of Economics and Public Policy, University of Texas at Dallas. This chapter was written with the research assistance of Irene Ngugi, Kruti Dholakia, and Nazia Arbab, and has appeared as part of the series 'Growing the Economy through Global Warming Solutions' sponsored by the Civil Society Institute http://www.civilsocietyinstitute.org/. The author would also like to express his appreciation to Teresa D. Nelson for her valuable substantive contributions to this work, and to the Civil Society Institute for providing funding and inspiration.
2. The temperature-related processes that drive winds and create storms are considerably more complicated than these simple statements indicate. For example, a natural regional cycle of climate known as the North Atlantic Oscillation that influences ocean temperatures seems to be a major determinant of long-term hurricane frequency. In the part of the cycle where ocean temperatures are higher, hurricanes tend to be more frequent and more severe there. But the warm phases of the short-term El Niño Southern Oscillation in the tropical Pacific (known as El Niño events) have the opposite effect, tending to reduce the frequency and severity of hurricanes in the Atlantic.
3. All of these gases, except for water vapor, were included in the Kyoto treaty.
4. Assuming stable atmospheric concentrations of $CO_2$ and constant climate to focus attention on land-use and fire-management changes, the researchers used computer models to project the future of the US carbon sink. (The carbon sink was estimated to have accumulated between 0.37 and 0.71 billion metric tons of carbon per year during the 1980s).
5. See Abramovitz (2001) (citing the Munich Reinsurance Company and the UN Environmental Program), p.38, and Worldwatch Institute (2002), p.41.
6. Nitrogen oxides include: nitrous oxide ($N_2O$), a colorless gas used as anesthetic; nitric oxide (NO), a clear poisonous gas; and nitrogen dioxide ($NO_2$), a poisonous brown gas found in automobile exhaust fumes. In the lower atmosphere, sunlight breaks molecules of nitrogen dioxide (from automobile exhaust and industrial pollution) into nitric oxide gas and single atoms of oxygen that combine with free oxygen in the air to create ozone. Volatile organic compounds (also from automobile exhaust and industrial pollution) convert nitric oxide back into nitrogen dioxide, which sunlight then breaks apart again, generating still more ozone. For a clear and simple explanation of both stratospheric (upper atmosphere) and tropospheric (lower atmosphere) ozone formation, see National Center for Atmospheric Research and University Corporation for Atmospheric Research, Current Research Spotlight, 'How It Forms' (http://eo.ucar.edu/spotlight/ozone/page3.html, 21 July 2005).
7. The $390 billion figure is adjusted for inflation.
8. Ocean water today is somewhat alkaline, with a $pH \approx 8.1$. It is expected to become more acidic (although still alkaline), with a $pH \approx 7.7$ by 2100. A $pH = 7$ is neutral, $< 7$ is acid and $> 7$ is alkaline. The pH scale is logarithmic (base 10), so each 1 unit change represents a change of a factor of 10.
9. This process is already well under way. For example, in August 2005, I visited the Athabasca Glacier, flowing out of the Columbia Icefield in Canada's Alberta Province (the only icefield on Earth that feeds glacial waters into three different oceans). In the past century and a half, the glacier has lost more than 30 percent of its volume of ice. 'The rate of glacial retreat in the early 1990's has accelerated to a rate that that is four times greater than the recession… of the 1960's…. If global warming continues, the glacier front will recede at this rapid rate' (Kucera, 1999, p. 62).
10. The Pleistocene began nearly 2 million years ago and encompassed a number of ice ages.
11. Emphasis added.

12. Goulder explicitly cites studies by Laitner et al. (2000) and DeCanio (1998).
13. For an interesting discussion of 'robustness' as a criterion for choosing options under deep uncertainty and its connection to computer simulation, see Popper et al. (2005).
14. As cited in Nuclear Information and Resource Service and World Information Service on Energy (2005) 'Nuclear Power: No Solution to Climate Change', *Nuclear Monitor* (621–622), February 2005)

# REFERENCES


Abramovitz, Janet N. (2001), 'Unnatural Disasters', Worldwatch Paper No. 158, Washington, DC: Worldwatch Institute.

Association of British Insurers (2005), 'Financial Risks of Climate Change: Summary Report',http://www.abi.org.uk/Display/File/Child/552/Financial_Risks_of_Climate_Change.pdf.

Catan, Thomas (2005), 'Record Volume Rise in World Energy Consumption', *Financial Times*, 15 June 2005.

Chang, Kenneth (2005), 'British Scientists Say Carbon Dioxide is Turning Oceans Acidic', *New York Times*, 1 July 2005.

Checklick, Nancy E. (2004a), Email correspondence, 3 June 2004, Lead Environmental Analyst, US Department of Energy.

Checklick, Nancy E. (2004b), Email correspondence, 5 June 2004, Lead Environmental Analyst, US Department of Energy.

Claussen, Eileen (2001), *Climate Change: Science, Strategies and Solutions*, Arlington, VA: The Pew Center on Global Climate Change.

Coalition for Environmentally Responsible Economics (2001), 'Value at Risk: Climate Change and the Future of Governance'.

DeCanio, S., (1998) 'The Efficiency Paradox: Bureaucratic and Organizational Barriers to Profitable Energy-Saving Investments', *Energy Policy*, **26** (5): 441–454.

Dumas, Lloyd J. (1976), *The Conservation Response: Strategies for the Design and Operation of Energy-Using Systems*, Lexington, MA: Lexington Books.

Environment Canada (2005), 'The Science of Climate Change', http://www.ec.gc.ca/climate/overview_science-e.html.

Epstein, Paul R. (1997), 'Climate, Ecology and Human Health', *Consequences*, **3** (2): 3.

Goulder, Lawrence H. (2004), 'Induced Technological Change and Climate Policy', Pew Center on Global Climate Change.

Hopfl-Harris, Karen (2005), 'Impacts of Climate Change in the United States: The Potential Impacts of Global Warming on Public Health', http://www.climatehotmap.org/impacts/humanhealth.html.

Hotz, Robert Lee (2005), 'As Climate Shifts, Antarctic Ice Sheet is Growing', *Los Angeles Times*, 20 May 2005.

Hurtt, G.C., et al. (2002), 'Projecting the Future of the U.S. Carbon Sink', *Proceedings of the National Academy of Sciences*, 5 February 2002, p. 1393.

Inman, Mason (2005), 'Fish Moved by Warm Waters', *Science*, **308**: 937.

Innovest Strategic Value Advisors (2002), 'Climate Change and the Financial Services Industry: Module 1 – Threats and Opportunities', prepared for the UN Environmental Program Finance Initiatives Climate Change Working Group (July 2002), p. 6.

Intergovernmental Panel on Climate Change (1996), *Climate Change 1995: Impacts, Adaptations and Mitigation of Climate Change: Scientific-Technical Analysis*, Cambridge, UK: Cambridge University Press.

Intergovernmental Panel on Climate Change (2007), *Climate Change 2007 Synthesis Report*, http://www.ipcc.ch/ipccreports/ar4-syr.htm.

Kanter, James and Andrew Revkin (2007), 'Scientists Detail Climate Changes, Poles to Tropics', *New York Times*, 7 April 2007.

Kerr, Richard A. (2005), 'Is Katrina a Harbinger of Still More Powerful Hurricanes?', *Science*, **309** (5742): 1807.

Kintisch, Eli (2005), 'Climate Change: Panel Urges Unified Action, Sets 2° Target', *Science*, **307** (5709): 496.

Kucera, Richard E. (1999), *Exploring the Columbia Icefield*, Calgary, Canada: High Country Colour.

Laitner, J.A., et al. (2000), 'Incorporating Behavioral, Social, and Organizational Phenomena in the Assessment of Climate Change Mitigation Options', in E. Jochem et al (eds), *Society, Behavior and Climate Change Mitigation*, Dordrecht, Netherlands: Kluwer Academic Publishers.

Leahy, Stephen (2005), 'Ozone Heal Thyself, US Declares', IPS (Brooklin, Canada), as published in *Other News*, 25 June 2005.

Lovejoy, Thomas E., and Hannah Lee (2005), 'Global Greenhouse Gas Levels and the Future of Biodiversity', in Thomas E. Lovejoy and Lee Hannah (eds), *Climate Change and Biodiversity*, New Haven, CT: Yale University Press, p. 388.

McCarthy, J.J. et al. (eds) (2001), *Climate Change 2001: Impacts, Adaptation and Vulnerability*, Cambridge, UK: Cambridge University Press.

Meehl, Gerald A. et al. (2005), 'How Much More Global Warming and Sea Level Rise?', *Science*, **307** (5716): 1769.

Monastersky, Richard (2005), 'Stronger Hurricanes? Researchers Debate Whether Global Warming Will Make Storms More Destructive', *New York Times*, 8 September 2005.

National Academy of Sciences (2001), *Climate Change Science: An Analysis of Some Key Questions*, Washington, DC: National Academy Press.

National Research Council (2002), *Abrupt Climate Change: Inevitable Surprises*, Washington, DC: National Academy Press.

Nuclear Information and Resource Service and World Information Service on Energy (2005), 'Nuclear Power: No Solution to Climate Change', *Nuclear Monitor* (621 and 622).

Oreskes, Naomi (2004), 'The Scientific Consensus on Climate Change', *Science*, **306** (5702): 1686.

Pacific Institute for Studies in Development, Environment and Security (2005), 'US National Assessment of the Potential Consequence of Climate Variability and Change', http://pacinst.org/reports/national_assessment/natl_assessment_water.pdf.

Parmesan, Camille and Hector Galbraith (2004), 'Observed Impacts of Global Climate Change in the US', prepared for the Pew Center on Global Climate Change.

Popper, Stephen W., Lempert, Robert J., and Steve C. Bankes (2005), 'Shaping the Future', *Scientific American*, April 2005.

Reid, Walter V. et al. (2005), *Millennium Ecosystem Assessment Synthesis Report*, Washington, DC: World Resources Institute.

Rohter, Larry (2005), 'Antarctica, Warming, Looks Ever More Vulnerable', *New York Times*, 25 January 2005.

Sample, Ian (2005), 'Warming Hits Tipping Point', *Guardian*, 11 August 2005.

Smith, Leonard A. (2002), 'What Might We Learn from Climate Forecasts?', *Proceedings of the National Academy of Sciences*, **99** (3): 2487.

Titus, James G. (1992), 'The Costs of Climate Change to the United States', in S.K. Majumdar, et al. (eds), *Global Climate Change: Implications, Challenges and Mitigation Measures*, Philadelphia, PA: Pennsylvania Academy of Sciences.

United Nations Environmental Program (2005), 'Biodiversity and Climate Change: Sensitive Ecosystems', http://www.unep-wcmc.org/climate/impacts.htm.

United Nations Food and Agricultural Organization (2005), 'Background Document: Special Event on Impact of Climate Change, Pests and Diseases on Food Security and Poverty Reduction', 31st Session of the Committee on World Food Security, 23–26 May 2005.

US Department of Commerce (2005), 'Billion Dollar Climate and Weather Disasters, 1980-2004', http://www.gesource.ac.uk/hazards/billion.html.

US Environmental Protection Agency (2005), 'The Potential Impacts of Global Climate Change on the United States', http://yosemite.epa.gov/OAR/globalwarming.nsf/UniqueKLeyLookup/JSAW5HJQQB/$File/rte_sealevel rise.pdf.

US Environmental Protection Agency (2005), 'Global Warming – Impacts: Health', http://yosemite.epa.gov/OAR/globalwarming.nsf/content/ImpactsHealth.html.

Wang, James and Michael Oppenheimer (2005), *The Latest Myths and Facts on Global Warming*, New York: Environmental Defense Fund.

Webster, Peter J., et al. (2005), 'Changes in Tropical Cyclone Number, Duration, and Intensity in a Warming Environment', *Science*, **309** (5742): 1844.

Wigley. T.M.L. (2005), 'The Climate Change Commitment', *Science*, **307** (5716): 1766.

World Health Organization (2005), 'Climate Change and Human Health: Risks and Responses', http://www.who.int/globalchange/climate/summary/en/.

Worldwatch Institute (2002), *State of the World 2002*, New York and London: W.W. Norton.

# 2. The New Climate Economics: The Stern Review versus its Critics

**Frank Ackerman**[1]

The economic analysis of climate change has been characterized by many controversies, and these have become more heated in the wake of the 2006 Stern Review. Some of the issues raised relate to economic techniques and data, but others deal more fundamentally with the nature of economic analysis and its ability to inform policy decisions. This chapter reviews some of the major areas of debate in climate economics, and evaluates the contribution of the Stern Review as well as the points raised by its critics. While the discussion of some areas can become quite technical, it is important for the public process of policy debate to demystify the economics and present the issues in a way that reveals the value judgments involved in cost–benefit analysis.

The basic questions include:

- The relationship between present and future. Standard economic analysis uses a discount rate to translate future costs and benefits into present value terms. The choice of discount rate is crucial. For long-term effects, a high discount rate will reduce the formal present value of future costs dramatically even though those costs, will, of course, be felt unabated by people in the future. Those, including Stern, who choose a low discount rate, in effect give greater weight to future impacts, but this has drawn criticism from economists who argue for the use of a more familiar, higher rate.
- How to deal with risk and uncertainty. Since many of the consequences of climate change cannot be predicted precisely, including potentially catastrophic effects, it is necessary to have some way either of quantifying risk or of developing other principles for responding to uncertain but potentially serious impacts.
- How (and whether) to calculate costs and benefits in monetary terms. In part, this is a discussion about techniques for translating non-monetary

impacts, such as loss of life, into monetary values. But a broader issue is whether this kind of monetization can or should be done at all. The full extent of human and ecological damages that could result from higher-range climate change possibilities may defy expression as dollar values. An alternative approach, suggested here, is to define what levels of climate change impact should be considered unacceptable, and then work to develop a least-cost strategy for preventing these outcomes.

## THE STERN REVIEW

In 2005, British Chancellor (now Prime Minister) Gordon Brown asked Sir Nicholas Stern to conduct a major review of the economics of climate change as a guide to developing government policy. Stern is a well-respected, established economist: he has been the chief economist at the World Bank, the second permanent secretary of HM Treasury, and the head of the (UK) Government Economic Service. It is not a background that suggested he would make radical new departures in his latest report.

However, the Stern Review,[2] released in late 2006, expressed alarm at the impending climate damages that will result from business as usual, and presented novel economic arguments endorsing prompt and vigorous action. Other economists were quick to respond, in many cases quite critically. How could Stern have strayed so far from the majority of economic analyses, which tend to recommend much smaller and slower responses? Stern was accused of numerous violations of standard economic methodology, which supposedly led to his ‘errors’.

While the Stern Review is a ponderous and imperfect document, it rests on much sounder ground than the economists who have attacked it. The Stern Review illustrates important ways in which economic analysis can be made to reflect the urgency of the climate problem. And it raises crucial questions about the economic aspects of climate change even though it ultimately fails to find successful solutions to some of the important problems.

‘The scientific evidence is now overwhelming: climate change presents very serious global risks, and it demands an urgent global response… The benefits of strong, early action considerably outweigh the costs’ (Stern, long executive summary, 2006, pp. 1–2). This central conclusion from the Stern Review will not come as a surprise to scientists who study climate change. Nor will it startle those who are troubled by the early signs of global warming, including the intensification of extreme and variable weather conditions. But in the world of academic economics, it is unusual enough to require detailed justification.

Stern found that under business as usual (that is assuming no new policies to reduce carbon emissions), the concentration of greenhouse gases in the atmosphere could reach double the pre-industrial level as early as 2035. This would essentially commit the world to more than 2°C of warming. By the end of the century, business as usual would lead to more than a 50 percent chance of exceeding 5°C of warming, implying disastrous changes in natural ecosystems and human living conditions around the world. (All temperatures cited here are in degrees Celsius, which can be converted to Fahrenheit by multiplying by 1.8; for example, 5°C equals 9°F.)

Stern describes the impacts of unchecked warming in both qualitative and quantitative terms; the qualitative images are perhaps more sweeping and powerful. For example, human actions create 'risks of major disruption to economic and social activity, on a scale similar to those associated with the great wars and the economic depression of the first half of the 20th century' (Stern, short executive summary, 2006, p. 1). American readers should remember that this was written in a country where World Wars I and II loomed considerably larger than in the US.[3] An average global warming of 5° would cause 'a radical change in the physical geography of the world [that] must lead to major changes in the human geography – where people live and how they live their lives' (Stern, short executive summary, 2006, p. 1). The qualitative descriptions of climate impacts are discussed in the final section, below. Most of the economic debate, however, concerns Stern's quantitative estimates.

The economic model used in the Stern Review finds that the damages from business as usual would be expected to reduce GDP by 5 percent based on market impacts alone, or 11 percent including a rough estimate for the value of health and environmental effects that do not have market prices ('externalities', in the jargon of economics). If the sensitivity of climate to $CO_2$ levels turns out to be higher than the baseline estimates, these losses could rise to 7 percent and more than 14 percent, respectively. A disaggregated description of impacts by sector and region is generally in agreement with these numbers, according to the Review. Stern speculates that an adjustment for equity weighting, reflecting the fact that the impacts will fall most heavily on poor countries, could lead to losses valued at 20 percent of global GDP. These figures are substantially greater than the comparable estimates from most economists.

These damages can be largely avoided, at much lower cost, through emissions reduction (or 'mitigation', in the jargon of climate change). Stabilization at 500–550 parts per million (ppm) of $CO_2$-equivalent[4] in the atmosphere would avoid most, though not all, of the 'business as usual' damages. Both direct estimates of mitigation costs and a review of results from many different models suggest that stabilization at this level would cost about 1 percent of GDP. Stabilization below 450 ppm, according to Stern, is no longer feasible in view of the large amount of carbon already in the atmosphere; he suggests the relevant range of targets is now 450–550 ppm of $CO_2$-equivalent.[5]

Later chapters of the Review make many interesting and insightful comments about national policy options and the role of international agreements. However, the principal controversies have concerned the economic analysis described above, with its conclusion that for an immediate and vigorous mitigation effort, the benefits (avoided damages) far exceed the costs.

## CRITICISMS OF THE STERN REVIEW

The extensive criticisms of the Stern Review's economics raise three principal points:

- the discount rate is said to be too low;
- the treatment of risk and uncertainty is inappropriate; and
- the calculation and comparison of costs and benefits is done incorrectly.

### 1. Is the Stern Discount Rate Too Low?

One of the most important factors in the economic analysis of climate change is the choice of a discount rate. Stern's preferred discount rate, 1.4 percent (explained below), is much lower than the rates used in traditional climate economic models. For William Nordhaus, 'the *Review*'s radical view of policy stems from an extreme assumption about discounting … this magnifies impacts in the distant future and rationalizes deep cuts in emissions, and indeed in all consumption, today' (Nordhaus, 2007b, p. 689). As Nordhaus suggests, a lower discount rate makes the far future look more important today, and supports greater future-oriented investment.

In selecting the appropriate discount rate for long-term public policy decisions, economic theory often distinguishes between two components. The *rate of pure time preference* is the discount rate that would apply if all present and future generations had equal resources and opportunities. In addition, there is a *wealth-based component* of the discount rate, reflecting the assumption that if future generations will be richer than we are, then there is less need for us to invest today in order to help them protect themselves. In the notation of the Stern Review, the discount rate, $r$, is the sum of these two parts:

$$r = \delta + \eta g \quad (2.1)$$

Here δ (delta) is the rate of pure time preference, and $g$ is the growth rate of per capita consumption. If per capita consumption is constant, implying that $g = 0$, then the discount rate $r = \delta$. The second parameter, η (eta), determines how strongly economic growth affects the discount rate. A larger value of η implies a larger discount rate, and hence less need to provide for future generations today (as long as per capita consumption is growing).

Nordhaus' critique centers on Stern's value for δ, the discount rate that would apply if all generations were equally well off. Stern reviews and endorses the philosophical arguments for viewing all generations as people of equal worth, deserving equal rights and living conditions (Stern, 2006, chapter 2 and appendix). These arguments are often taken to imply that pure time preference should be zero. However, many economists believe that people reveal their time preferences through choices about savings and other actions affecting the future – and deduce from this that the rate of pure time preference must be greater than zero. (If every generation was equally important to people today, wouldn't we all be saving a lot more for the future?) In addition, pure time preference precisely equal to zero causes technical problems in some economic theories.[6]

Stern just barely avoids setting pure time preference equal to zero. While generally accepting the philosophical arguments for treating all generations equally, he also observes that there is a small, but non-zero, probability that future generations will not exist – for example, if a natural or man-made disaster destroys most or all of the human race. The probability of destruction of humanity is, arbitrarily, assumed to be 0.1 percent per year; pure time preference is therefore set equal to 0.1 percent. That is, Stern suggests that we are only 99.9 percent sure that humanity will still be here next year, so we should consider the well-being of people next year to be, on average, 99.9 percent as important as people today.

To calculate the discount rate using equation (2.1), Stern estimates that the growth of per capita income will average 1.3 percent per year, and sets $\eta = 1$. Thus his discount rate is

$$r = \delta + \eta g = 0.1\% + (1 * 1.3\%) = 1.4\% \quad (2.2)$$

In contrast, the UK Treasury's Green Book (UK Treasury, 2007), providing the government's current guidance for policy appraisal, discusses catastrophic risk and other grounds for pure time preference, recommending $\delta = 1.5$ percent. (While employing the same logical framework, it uses different notation and terminology, and offers only limited explanation of its estimates.[7]) Like Stern, the Green Book assumes $\eta = 1$; it estimates the long-term growth rate of per capita income, $g$, at 2 percent, implying

$$r = \delta + \eta g = 1.5\% + (1 * 2.0\%) = 3.5\% \tag{2.3}$$

The Green Book also calls for a gradual decline in discount rates over the very long run, dropping in several stages to 2.5 percent after 75 years and 1.0 percent after 300 years. However, such a decline may be less significant than it looks; the first few decades of discounting at higher rates are the most important in terms of evaluation of future costs and benefits.[8]

Nordhaus believes that the discount rate should match observed interest rates, or rates of return on capital. In a theoretical world of perfect markets and perfect rationality, the discount rate would be equal to the interest rate, since both would express the trade-off between current and future incomes. Nordhaus estimates that the relevant interest rate is about 5 percent above inflation. (This discussion uses 'real', or inflation-adjusted, quantities throughout.) To achieve this goal he argues that pure time preference, $\delta$ should, at least initially, be as high as 1.5 percent.[9]

To confirm the significance of this technical debate, Nordhaus runs his own DICE model with Stern's 1.4 percent discount rate, and again with Nordhaus' preferred, much higher rate. The results can be compared by looking at the 'social cost of carbon', or 'optimal carbon tax', a measure of the incremental benefits of reducing carbon emissions. The social cost of carbon starts out at $35 per ton of carbon (in 2015, at 2005 prices) with the Nordhaus discount rate, vs. $360 when Nordhaus uses the Stern discount rate. The latter number essentially matches the Stern Review's own estimate of $350 per ton (again, in 2015 at 2005 prices).

Partha Dasgupta presents a complementary critique of Stern, addressing a different aspect of the discount rate (Dasgupta, 2006). Focusing on the ethical implications of discounting, he interprets $\delta$ as the measure of the trade-off between present and future, independent of wealth differences, and $\eta$ as the measure of the trade-off between rich and poor, independent of time differences. In this framework,

- $\eta = 0$ implies that *every dollar is of equal value* regardless of who receives it;
- $\eta = 1$ implies that *every 1 percent increase in a person's income is of equal value* regardless of the wealth of the person who receives it; and
- $\eta > 1$ implies that *a 1 percent increase in income is of greater value* to a poorer person.

Dasgupta endorses Stern's argument that $\delta$ is close to zero, but maintains that equity requires much more concern for the poor, reflected in a larger $\eta$; Dasgupta suggests a range of two to four. If per capita incomes are expected to continue growing in spite of climate change, as most economists (including Stern) assume, then using a larger $\eta$ in equation (2.1) leads to a higher discount rate, and indirectly to less investment in the future. The logic of this conclusion is that, if this generation has lower incomes than all the ones that will follow, equity requires taking from the rich (that is, the future) and giving to the poor (that is, the present). However, if economic growth stops and future incomes decline, due to climate change or other problems, Dasgupta's argument reverses itself: in that case, the present generation should do much more for its poorer descendants. Dasgupta has raised this possibility in other writings on the subject.

Of course, not everyone is equally wealthy within any generation; Dasgupta's strong views on equity would also call for substantial redistribution within the present generation. Indeed, he hints that Stern's $\eta$=1 reflects an insufficient concern for the problems of poverty today – as well as an excessive concern for the well-being of more affluent generations to come. Dasgupta also objects that Stern's low discount rate and heightened concern for future generations should imply an implausibly high savings rate, far higher than observed rates of saving. If you cared that much about the future in general, and if you made all your economic decisions on a consistent, theoretically sound basis, you would be saving a huge proportion of your income for your descendants. In a short, technical response specifically to this point, Brad DeLong argues that the implausible savings rate results from the additional assumption that there is no technological progress; in a world with technical change, Stern's discount rate implies entirely believable savings rates.[10]

In a review of the Stern Review, Martin Weitzman (2007) suggests that differing discount rates can account for the entire disagreement between Stern and his critics. Weitzman proposes, in terms of equation (2.1), his guess at the consensus estimates among economists studying climate change: $\delta$ = 2%, $\eta$ = 2, $g$ = 2%. The result is a discount rate of $r$ = 2% + 2 * 2% = 6%. For events 100 years from now, the present value of future damages is 100 times greater at Stern's 1.4 percent discount rate than at Weitzman's 'consensus' 6 percent discount rate. This gap is sufficient to make Stern's proposal for spending 1 percent of GDP on mitigation obviously attractive at Stern's discount rate, and, equally obviously, unattractive at the 'consensus' rate.

The notion that discount rates should in theory match current interest rates is a surprisingly complex question, requiring a prior determination of which interest rate to use. Weitzman himself, drawing on his work on the economics of uncertainty, favors a discount rate that declines sharply over time, approaching the Stern level as time goes on. While criticizing several aspects of Stern's presentation of the issue, Weitzman ultimately concludes that 'Stern may be right for the wrong reasons', as explained below in the discussion of risk and uncertainty.

Stern's initial response to criticisms on the discount rate[11] reiterates the ethical arguments for pure time preference ($\delta$) being close to zero. At $\delta = 1.5$ percent, he suggests, you are telling your grandchildren that their lives and incomes are only half as important as your own, simply because they live 50 years after you. Stern is more willing to consider changes in $\eta$, though not to the extent that Dasgupta proposes. (If Dasgupta's proposed values for $\eta$ were appropriate, Stern observes, very radical redistribution within the present generation, from rich to poor, should be high on the political agenda.) The appendix to the Review's postscript shows that with $\eta$ as high as 1.5, the key conclusion of the review clearly survives, although the numbers are changed: the costs of mitigation remain smaller than the damages from business as usual

## 2. How Do Risk and Uncertainty Affect Climate Economics?

The second major innovation in the Stern analysis is the treatment of risk and uncertainty connected to climate change.[12] Although the broad outlines and major findings of climate science are increasingly definite, many crucial details remain uncertain, and may not be known until it is too late to do anything about the problem. Both the expected severity of climate impacts and the probability of an abrupt catastrophe are strongly connected to temperature increases, which in turn are strongly connected to atmospheric concentrations of greenhouse gases. However, the precise strength and timing of these relationships remain uncertain. Some of the uncertainty can be addressed by further research, but some may reflect the inherent unpredictability of nonlinear systems such as the earth's atmosphere – the problem that motivates the fields of chaos theory and complexity theory.

Stern introduces issues of uncertainty into the economic calculations in three ways.[13] The first involves the sensitivity of climate to greenhouse gas concentrations. The baseline scenario follows the Intergovernmental Panel on Climate Change (IPCC)'s Third Assessment Report (2001) in assuming that a doubling of pre-industrial $CO_2$ concentrations would lead to warming of $1.5^{\circ}$–$4.5^{\circ}$. Some newer research suggests that climate feedback mechanisms may increase sensitivity beyond that level. Accordingly, Stern's high climate sensitivity scenario assumes that the same doubling of atmospheric $CO_2$ would lead to $2.4^{\circ}$–$5.4^{\circ}$.

Second, the PAGE model, used in the Stern Review, includes an estimate for the risk of an abrupt climate catastrophe. The model assumes that once a threshold temperature is reached (the threshold itself is uncertain, but averages 5° above pre-industrial temperatures) the probability of catastrophe increases by 10 percent for every additional °C of warming; the catastrophe has a value of 5–20 percent of output (Stern, 2006, p. 153). As Stern notes, this is similar to the treatment of catastrophe in Nordhaus' DICE model. Most other economic models, however, do not include estimates for catastrophic events.

Finally, PAGE is designed to reflect risks throughout its calculations, through a statistical technique known as Monte Carlo analysis. For 31 key parameters, PAGE assumes that there is a range of possible values. For each of these parameters, the model randomly selects a value from the range of possibilities, each time it is run. The model is run repeatedly – 1000 times, in this case – and the weighted average of the results is used as the model's estimate.[14]

For example, one of the most important parameters governs the relationship between temperature and economic damages. A simple way for an aggregate economic model to estimate climate damages is to use the equation

$$D = kT^{\gamma} \tag{2.4}$$

Here $D$ is damage (either as a monetary amount, or as a fraction of output), $T$ is temperature above pre-industrial levels, or above a base year such as 1990, and $\gamma$ (gamma) is the exponent on temperature. There is no experiment that determines the correct value of $\gamma$; it is an assumed, not an observed, value. Yet, as we will see, assumptions about $\gamma$ are of critical importance. (More broadly, the form of equation (2.4) itself is an important simplifying assumption, but is not subject to empirical testing except in retrospect, when it will be much too late.)

A common assumption, used in DICE and elsewhere, is that equation (2.4) is valid, and that $\gamma = 2$, which is to say that damages are proportional to the square of the temperature increase. PAGE makes a similar assumption, but with more uncertainty about the exponent: it allows $\gamma$ to be anywhere from one to three, with 1.3 as the most common value, and an average of 1.8. Thus most PAGE runs have a lower value of $\gamma$ than DICE, but some PAGE runs have larger values of $\gamma$ – and hence much larger damages at high temperatures.

Each of these three methods of modeling uncertainty has an important influence on the results. Sensitivity analyses by the Stern team show that the estimated cost of 'business as usual' climate damages would be increased by

3.6 percentage points (that is, 3.6 percent of global consumption) by the high climate sensitivity assumptions. Similarly, removal of the calculation of catastrophic risks would reduce estimated damages by 2.9 percentage points. Elimination of the Monte Carlo analysis, doing one run of PAGE using the most common value for each parameter (such as 1.3 for $\gamma$), would reduce damage estimates by 7.6 percentage points (Dietz et al., 2007, p. 144). In short, Stern's treatment of uncertainty is comparable in importance to the discount rate in determining the outcome of the model.

Despite its quantitative importance and its methodological innovation, the Stern treatment of uncertainty has received relatively little attention from economists. In some cases, aspects of the Review that reflect its treatment of uncertainty are mistakenly attributed to other factors: Nordhaus comments on the escalation from damages averaging 5 percent of output, up to a 14 percent reduction in consumption 'now and forever', but then asserts that it is due to inappropriate discounting (Nordhaus, 2007b, p. 696).[15] Gary Yohe, on the other hand, correctly describes some aspects of Stern's approach to uncertainty as a source of the high estimates of damages; he does not directly express agreement or disagreement (Yohe, 2006, pp. 65–72). David Maddison mentions the Stern analysis of uncertainty approvingly, as correcting a deficiency in most studies; he does comment that the economic valuation of catastrophe, and the range of possible values for the uncertain parameters, are themselves quite uncertain, and beyond the scope of the published economics literature. He concludes that despite these limitations, constructing a model with multiple methods for incorporating uncertainty 'is a perfectly legitimate endeavor not least because so little is currently known about the nature of such damages' (Maddison, nd, p. 3).

In a brief comment specifically on Stern's treatment of catastrophic damages, Paul Baer (2006) argues that much greater catastrophic impacts should have been included, starting at lower temperatures. Stern's target for climate stabilization, according to Baer, would entail significant risks of the complete melting of the Greenland ice sheet, an important, much-discussed example of a climate catastrophe. Based on the non-zero risk of catastrophic damages at lower temperatures, Baer speculates that the optimal target for $CO_2$ reduction and temperature stabilization should be lower than Stern's levels.

Weitzman argues at length that uncertainty is the key to the climate problem. He describes Stern as being 'right for the wrong reason', because Stern places too much emphasis on a debatable cost–benefit analysis, but too little on the need for social insurance against low-probability, catastrophic events. Weitzman applies a framework developed in the analysis of financial markets, where standard theories fail to explain puzzling patterns of behavior. Those standard theories assume investors can learn, through repeated experience, the probability distribution of the full range of possible market outcomes. But when (as usual) market structures are changing over time, there is never enough experience that is relevant to the current structure. In particular, it is intrinsically impossible to learn much from experience about the probability and magnitude of the extreme tails of a changing distribution, such as the worst-case outcomes that could lead to very large losses. Investors appear to worry a great deal about those unpredictable worst-case outcomes, a fact that explains a number of otherwise puzzling financial market results.

The analogy to climate change, according to Weitzman, is that we should worry less about calibrating the most likely outcomes, and more about insurance against worst-case catastrophes. Thus the IPCC's Fourth Assessment Report (2007) offers six 'equally sound' scenarios, with a mean temperature increase over the next century of 2.8°, well within the range of the ongoing debate over the impacts of predictable and expected damages. (Stern follows one of the IPCC scenarios, namely A2, in projecting somewhat greater damages from a century of business as usual.) Much more important than the mean prediction is the fact that, according to Weitzman, the same IPCC report can be read as implying a 2 percent probability of a temperature increase greater than 6°: a point at which we 'are located in the terra incognita of what any honest economic modeler would have to admit is a planet Earth reconfigured as science fiction… [where] mass species extinctions, radical alterations of natural environments, and other extreme outdoor consequences will have been triggered by a geologically-instantaneous temperature change that is significantly larger than what separates us now from past ice ages' (Weitzman, 2007, p. 18).

When it comes to policy implications, Weitzman offers only scattered comments, which he refers to at one point as 'highly-speculative examples'. (ibid., p.24). But his theory suggests a profound reframing of the issue. When homeowners buy fire insurance, or when healthy young adults buy life insurance, they are spending money to insure against accidents that are much less likely than 2 percent. If those expenditures are worthwhile, then perhaps we should be talking about the cost, and value, of insurance against the 2 percent chance of a 6° warming, which would truly be a climate catastrophe.

In view of the limited economic commentary on Stern's treatment of risk and uncertainty, there is little in the way of a response. One major response from the Stern team explains their approach to risk and uncertainty, and rebuts a technical claim that they have double-counted the risk of catastrophe in their use of estimates from Nordhaus' earlier work (Dietz et al., 2007).

## 3. How Should Climate Damages and Mitigation Costs be Estimated and Compared?

In addition to criticisms of the discount rate and the treatment of uncertainty, economists have also criticized Stern's estimates of the expected damages from climate change, the costs of mitigating those damages, and the comparison of damages and mitigation costs. The comments in this area are more detailed and less philosophical than the debates over discounting and uncertainty.

When it comes to estimating climate damages, Richard Tol and Gary Yohe believe that Stern has exaggerated throughout: 'The *Stern Review* consistently selects the most pessimistic study in the literature for water, agriculture, health, and insurance' (Tol and Yohe, 2006, p. 236). On the question of refugees who may be displaced by climate change, they maintain that Stern has relied on the work of 'a known alarmist'. (Ironically, their other criticisms of Stern's damage estimates include Stern's excessive reliance on work by Nordhaus, and use of the wrong numbers from previous work co-authored by Tol himself (ibid., pp. 236–237).)

Robert Mendelsohn adds the claim that Stern has overstated the effects, or the certainty, of extreme weather events, and has downplayed the likely extent of adaptation to a changing climate. In general, Mendelsohn believes the damages from the early stages of warming to be quite small: 'there are hardly any damages associated with a 2°C increase in temperature' (Mendelsohn, 2007, p. 46). The ever-imaginative Bjorn Lomborg reveals that Stern's damage estimates are inflated because 'he assumes that we will continue to pump out carbon far into the 22nd century – a rather unlikely scenario given the falling cost of alternative fuels' (Lomborg, 2006).[16] Lomborg also echoes many of the other criticisms discussed here, and asserts that Stern must be wrong because Nordhaus is known to be right.

A massive, two-part response by a group of British academics, including some well-known climate skeptics, critiques both the science and the economics of the Stern Review. In the economic critique, Ian Byatt et al. emphasize the uncertainty of events more than 100 years in the future, and the importance of Stern's low discount rate in highlighting those far-future impacts (Byatt et al., 2006, pp. 199–229). They object that the Stern damage estimates are dominated by the effects of extreme weather, social and political instability, and 'knock-on effects'.[17] All of these, they feel, are less certain and more conjectural than the better researched, and much smaller, estimates of predictable climate damages that are recognized by 'everybody else'.

Many economists also believe that Stern has underestimated the costs of mitigation. Tol thinks that Stern relies too heavily on one group of models, while other models would estimate higher costs of emission abatement (Tol, 2006, pp. 233–250). Tol and Yohe present technical criticism of Stern's background paper on abatement costs. Mendelsohn observes that carbon recapture (one of Stern's solutions) is not yet a proven technology; in addition, Mendelsohn views renewable energy as expensive and problematical, and thinks Stern is too optimistic about future technological change reducing abatement costs.

Byatt et al. believe that costs of alternative energy sources are normally underestimated in advance, as shown by the history of nuclear power. They object that Stern relies too heavily on too few sources (although noting that those include meta-analyses of many different studies). They also complain that Stern includes estimates of cost reduction via active revenue recycling (using carbon tax revenues to reduce other taxes), induced technological change, and reductions in other pollutants that result from the decreases in fossil fuel combustion (in climate jargon, the 'co-benefits' of carbon reduction).

In addition, there are criticisms of the manner in which the Stern Review compares costs and benefits. Tol and Yohe, among others, point out that Stern's mitigation expenditures of 1 percent of GDP, holding atmospheric greenhouse gas concentrations to 550 ppm $CO_2$-equivalent, will not avoid all climate damages and therefore should be compared to the damages it will avoid, not to total damages. Tol and Yohe also express surprise that although Stern's marginal damage cost estimate is three times the previous estimate from HM Treasury, Stern's target for stabilizing greenhouse gas emissions is unchanged from the earlier Treasury study. If damages are so much higher, why isn't the stabilization target lower?

On the other hand, Mendelsohn thinks that Stern should have explored the costs and benefits of higher stabilization targets, such as 650 or 750 ppm; with Mendelsohn's low estimates of damages, these targets might be the optimal ones to aim for. Byatt et al. worry about the inefficiency that would result if climate-related investments were evaluated using Stern's low discount rate, while ordinary investments were evaluated using higher discount rates. (This inefficiency would mean that 'too much' was being invested in climate protection, relative to other industries.) Lomborg repeats his longstanding claim that public funds would be better spent addressing other priorities rather than climate change.

According to the initial responses on the Stern Review website, the damage estimate of 5 percent of GDP is based on the science in the IPCC's Third Assessment Report (2001), and does not include externality values for unpriced damages to human health and the environment. It is higher than other estimates due to the lower discount rate applied to future damages, the expanded treatment of uncertainty, and the enormous impact of the risk of

5°C or more warming within the 200-year time frame of the study. Many other studies focus on the important, but much smaller, damages expected from 2°C to 3°C of warming. The Stern scenario with higher climate sensitivity, which puts business as usual damages at 7 percent of GDP, attempts to incorporate newer developments in science since the 2001 IPCC report (see discussion of uncertainty, above). Stern emphasizes that the externality valuations, boosting damages to 11 percent of GDP, or 14 percent with higher climate sensitivity, are uncertain and should be treated with caution, as should the guess at an equity adjustment, raising the total as high as 20 percent of GDP. The postscript to the Stern Review offers an expanded set of sensitivity analyses in its appendix, identifying several key factors that influence the damage estimates.

The mitigation cost estimate of 1 percent of GDP, according to the Stern website responses, is supported both by aggregate modeling exercises, and by more detailed, disaggregated studies of costs of carbon-reducing technologies. As a relatively constant cost throughout this century, it does not depend on the choice of discount rates. It does not include estimates of the value of the co-benefits of $CO_2$ reduction. It assumes a flexible market economy and sensible policies; in contrast, studies that assume economic rigidity and inappropriate policies naturally produce higher cost estimates. Stabilization at 450–550 ppm $CO_2$-equivalent, Stern's target range, would eliminate more than 90 percent of the damages from business as usual; those damages are heavily influenced by the risks at high concentrations and temperatures. Stern rejects Lomborg's imagined tradeoff between climate mitigation and other spending priorities, and reminds Lomborg that if we delay, climate mitigation will become much more expensive, if not impossible.

## TOWARD AN EVALUATION OF THE DEBATE

The debate over the Stern Review has captured the attention of a wide range of economists, most of them critical of Stern's conclusions. How should we evaluate this debate? This section briefly reviews the three areas of criticism discussed above; the next section raises a fourth major point that has received too little attention to date.

On discounting, the choices of both $\delta$ and $\eta$ affect the discount rate. The choice of pure time preference ($\delta$) is an ethical question, involving the value placed on the intrinsic well-being of future generations, independent of income. Stern favors a much lower value than most (not all) other economists, but the choice is not a matter of technical analysis. Rather, as the Review puts it, 'if you care little about future generations you will care little about climate change. As we have argued that is not a position which has much foundation in ethics… [It is a position] which many would find unacceptable' (Stern, 2006, Appendix to Chapter 2, p. 48). To quantify an ethical perspective that respects and validates the future, it is essential to set pure time preference close to zero.

Regarding the choice of the second parameter, η, involving the value placed on changes in wealth, the arguments are less clear. Sensitivity analyses show that the exact Stern Review value of η is not crucial to the general conclusions, that is, that the benefits of active, immediate mitigation far outweigh the costs. The argument that discount rates should match current interest rates is surely a mistake, since interest rates reflect the short-run private decisions of those who can afford to participate in financial markets today, not public decisions about intergenerational ethics.

In short, whenever there are data sufficiently precise to justify discounting (a topic discussed below), Stern's general arguments for a low discount rate are persuasive. As Weitzman and others have noted, this alone is sufficient to flip the outcome of cost–benefit analysis: the high discount rates favored by many economists justify doing very little for now; Stern's low discount rate, applied to the same data, endorses dong much more, much sooner.

This is not to say that Stern's specific discount rate is precisely correct; it is hard to be confident of Stern's 0.1 percent annual risk of global catastrophe, an admittedly arbitrary estimate. The 1.3 percent average growth rate of per capita consumption is plausible but far from proven to be correct. A balanced conclusion might be that Stern demonstrates that 1.4 percent is among the plausible discount rates and that such low rates have profoundly different implications from rates like 5–6 percent, used in many other analyses.

On the treatment of uncertainty, Stern is certainly right that this is a critical, under-analyzed feature of the problem. The relative paucity of comments suggests the difficulty of following the details of the Stern analysis of uncertainty. Again, it is more appropriate to interpret the Stern results as showing that thoughtful guesses about uncertainty can have a big effect on the bottom line, rather than attempting to defend the details of the results. As Maddison suggests, the damage estimates involved here are out beyond the frontiers of the economics literature.

Baer argues in a specific case, and Weitzman demonstrates in theoretical terms, that uncertainties and catastrophic risks may be more serious and decisive than Stern recognizes. Valuations for a climate catastrophe, apparently built on Nordhaus estimates from some years ago (which in turn were originally based on an early poll of climate experts' best guesses, plus ad hoc adjustments over the years), seem particularly deficient in empirical support. The PAGE model's Monte Carlo analysis, with 31 parameters allowed to vary, provides an insightful, graphic illustration of the effects of uncertainty in many corners of the analysis; but is it believable that the modelers know the probability distribution for all 31 parameters with any certainty?

Some of the uncertain parameters in PAGE have an enormous effect on the results. Recall that in equation (2.4), relating damages to temperature, the (unobservable) exponent $\gamma$ is often set to 2 in other models, but varies between 1 and 3 in PAGE. There seems to be widespread belief that damages will increase more than proportionally to temperature, implying $\gamma > 1$. But how do we know whether $\gamma$ is 1.3 or 2 or 3, or something in between? In the latest version of DICE, Nordhaus offers monetary estimates of damages at 2.5° and at 6° of warming which are almost perfectly consistent with $\gamma = 2$, but these two data points are each based on pyramids of indirect and incompletely documented hypotheses (Nordhaus, 2007a, pp. 35–39). If one accepts Weitzman's reasonable characterization of the world at 6° of warming as 'science fiction', then Nordhaus' data is not, and could not be, persuasive evidence as to whether damages will increase proportionally to the square of temperature (that is, whether $\gamma = 2$).

Sensitivity analyses by the Stern team show that using a fixed value $\gamma = 3$, rather than allowing $\gamma$ to vary between one and three, would make the estimated climate damages skyrocket, increasing by 23.3 percentage points (Dietz et al., 2007, p. 144). That is, virtually an additional quarter of worldwide consumption is lost to climate damages, if the (unobservable) exponent in equation (2.4) turns out to be three. A sensitivity analysis of this magnitude seems to support Weitzman's suggestion that the worst-case damages of greatest concern are inherently incalculable. The pursuit of greater precision in other parts of the modeling effort cannot eliminate the staggering uncertainty caused by not knowing the exact shape of the damage function.

In the third area of the discussion, the (non-catastrophic) impact estimates and mitigation costs, it is hard to see any points where the critics have damaged the Stern argument. The massively documented Review, its supporting papers, and the detailed responses to the initial criticisms, all illustrate the thoroughness of research that went into the Review.

Yet there is one major outstanding puzzle about the cost–benefit comparison, involving the narrow range of plausible targets. Stabilization at less than 450 ppm of $CO_2$-equivalent is no longer possible at affordable cost, according to Stern, while anything above 550 ppm is too dangerous to consider. Moreover, the costs of reaching 550 ppm are much smaller than the enormous costs of targets just below that level. This pattern is hard to understand; Baer, as well as Tol and Yohe, object that Stern's account of damages should lead to a lower stabilization target.

An abstract argument can be constructed for Stern's narrow window, in terms of the shapes of the damage curve and/or the mitigation cost curve; perhaps it should have been more explicit in the Review. The Review compares costs and benefits in Chapter 13. In that chapter, the sole graphic representation of the comparison (Stern's Figure 13.3, reproduced below as Figure 2.1) is cluttered, and visually suggests that the relevant portions of both curves are fairly flat, and the window of plausible stabilization targets is quite wide.

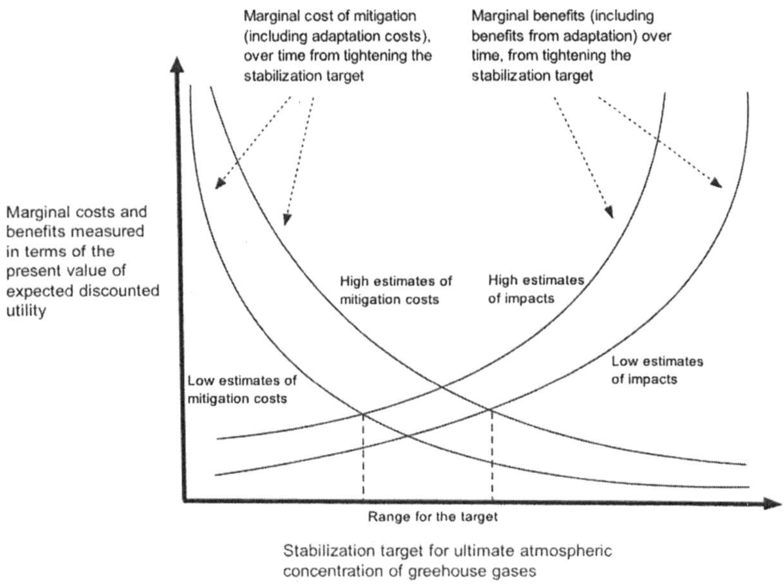


*Source*: The Stern Review

*Figure 2.1 Stern's graphical presentation of how to select a stabilization level*

The flavor of the Review's argument would be better captured by an alternative version, such as the one shown in Figure 2.2. In the alternative graph, a narrow window of plausible stabilization targets emerges naturally, due to the limited space between the steep portions of the (dashed) cost curve and the (solid) damage curve.[18] The arrows show what will happen if emission reduction is delayed: as atmospheric concentrations of greenhouse gases rise, the cost of achieving any fixed stabilization target will rise as well.

This visualization of the cost–benefit problem suggests a possible answer to the question posed by Baer, and by Tol and Yohe: even a big change in estimated damages (that is, the position of the damage curve) might have little effect on the stabilization target, due to both the steep slopes and the movement of the curves. In recent years, costs of mitigation have risen due to relative inaction, shifting the cost curve to the right as shown by the arrows. At the same time, climate research has identified increasingly serious damages at any fixed stabilization level, shifting the damage curve to the left. The result of these two opposite movements could easily be no change in the stabilization target, or a small net change in either direction.

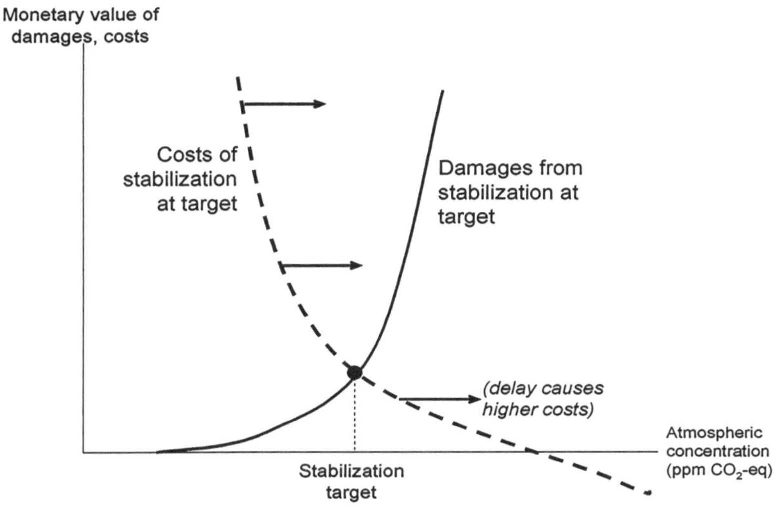


*Figure 2.2 Alternative representation of stabilization level*

This graphic visualization of the Stern analysis is not an alternative to the issues discussed earlier; rather, it depends on, and, somewhat cryptically, summarizes those issues. The position and shape of the damage curve depends on the discount rate and the treatment of uncertainty, and on damage estimates for specific climate impacts such as sea level rise. The position and shape of the cost curve depends on estimates and assumptions about costs of energy-saving and emission-reducing technologies; questions of discounting and uncertainty also play a role here, although to a much lesser extent than on the damage side.

It would be a difficult task to translate the numerous facets of the Stern analysis into a rigorous diagram along these lines. The conclusions reached in Chapter 13 of the Review, about the relatively narrow window of plausible stabilization targets, imply that the diagram, if constructed, would be shaped somewhat like the alternative sketch above. On the other hand, the (appropriate) emphasis on uncertainty in many parts of the Review implies that the location of the 'optimal' stabilization target, where the two curves cross, is itself uncertain. Definitive information on the shape and position of the curves, particularly the damage curve, will not be available until it is much too late to take the needed actions.

If there is a remaining problem here, it is the latent conflict between the treatment of uncertainty versus the apparent precision of the range of stabilization targets, 450–550 ppm $CO_2$-equivalent. Among the economists discussed above, Baer poses the question most sharply, suggesting that the Stern Review itself implies a significant risk of complete melting of the Greenland ice sheet, and consequent enormous sea level rise, even if the Review's stabilization target is reached.

What would a central focus on uncertainty suggest about the Stern Review stabilization targets? One might begin by asking, not what is the most likely value of the damages if the targets are achieved, but rather what is the worst case that is credible under those targets? If there were a precisely defined probability distribution of outcomes expected at 550 ppm, or 450 ppm, the question could be translated into: what does, say, the 98th percentile outcome look like?[19] What is the worst result that has at least a 2 percent chance of occurring, if the Stern Review stabilization targets are met? Once the question is posed this way, it is easy to understand Baer's suspicion that the Stern targets are too high. For confidence at, say, a 98 percent or 95 percent level that climate catastrophe will be avoided, a lower – that is, more ambitious – carbon stabilization target may be needed.

Such a conclusion casts doubt on the entire analytical framework of comparison of costs and benefits, and begs for a different approach to decision-making – which is the topic of the next section.

## PRICING LIVES AND WAYS OF LIFE

Finally, a fourth area of concern about the Stern Review is only hinted at in the economic commentaries to date. Do the monetary damage estimates, expressed as losses of a fraction of per capita consumption 'now and forever', actually convey the seriousness of the problem? As Maddison observes, Stern's estimate of a 1.3 percent long-term annual growth in real per capita consumption implies that in 2200 the world will be 12.3 times as rich as today.[20] Even a 35 percent reduction in consumption, a figure mentioned in the Stern Review for an extreme worst-case scenario, would leave the world of 2200 'only' eight times as rich as today. This hardly sounds like a measure of worrisome harms.

Consider the estimate of 20 percent loss of consumption, offered by the Review as the likely value for the high climate sensitivity scenario with catastrophic risk, non-market damages, and an equity adjustment thrown in.

Over the 200-year span of the Stern analysis, in the context of a steadily growing economy, a 20 percent loss is essentially an insignificant perturbation. After a period of rapid growth, the Japanese economy experienced a decade of stagnation in the 1990s; in recent years, it has begun to grow again. Suppose that Japan lost 2 percent of economic growth per year for ten years,[21] then resumed its long-term trend rate of growth for the next few centuries. Under that assumption, the macroeconomic problems of the 1990s would have caused Japan to lose 20 percent of the consumption that would otherwise have been available, 'now and forever'. In a faster-growing country, such as China, which has reached 10 percent annual growth rates, a 20 percent permanent loss of consumption could result from a mere two-year pause, followed by resumption of long-term rapid growth.

Neither Japan's lost decade of growth in the 1990s, nor an imaginary two-year hiatus in China's faster growth, represents a qualitative disaster for the societies involved. No great loss of life, or of a way of life, is involved. To return to the Stern Review's evocative metaphor, the impacts of World War II on Japan and China were of an entirely different nature and magnitude. There were, of course, vast, economically important wartime losses of property and income. But it is difficult to imagine any single monetary estimate that conveys the qualitative impact of a major war. If the expected impact of climate change resembles the effects of the great wars of the early twentieth century, then it does not look much like a 20 percent loss of consumption in a steadily growing economy, even if that loss is experienced now and forever.

A more up-to-date example illustrates the same point, and provides a model for understanding the role of economic and non-economic aspects of climate damages. In 2005, the impact of Hurricane Katrina on New Orleans and surrounding areas is estimated to have caused as much as $135 billion in property damage; the state of Louisiana as a whole may have lost 15 percent of its income in the months following the hurricane.[22] On the one hand, these numbers are quite large; on the other hand, they are not even candidates for being the most memorable or disturbing evidence of the damage caused by the hurricane. Rather, the impact of the hurricane is measured in the loss of more than 1,000 (perhaps as many as 1,800) lives, the flooding and destruction of countless households and entire neighborhoods, the displacement and impoverishment of several hundred thousand people, and the destruction, perhaps permanent, in part, of a city that has made unique contributions to American music and culture.

The most important impacts of Katrina do not have price tags attached. Some of the lasting impacts could have been ameliorated by a more generous and competent governmental response. This might be viewed as a separate problem; however, climate impacts will at times occur in situations where the resources, generosity, and competence of public authorities cannot be relied on. In other words, the unexpectedly feeble public sector response to Katrina underscores the importance of questions of resilience and capacity to respond to climate change.

What, then, is the importance of the estimates of property damage and income loss from Katrina? It is significant that the losses were many times the cost of building adequate storm defenses in advance, an issue that was frequently raised in the years before 2005. Thus building higher and more reliable levees would have easily passed a cost–benefit test, even without any attempt at valuing externalities; avoided property damage alone would have sufficed to tip the scales in favor of protecting the city. Available, proven methods, long implemented in the Netherlands and elsewhere, would have easily prevented the flooding and destruction of New Orleans.

But this cost–benefit calculation should be done humbly: it is useful, but it is far from the whole story. It may be as far into the story as the monetary damages can take us. Monetary losses do not measure the full human and ecological impact of Katrina, and cannot meaningfully be extended to put a price tag on the whole of the tragedy. Vast sums of wealth and income were needlessly lost and so were lives, and ways of life. The most important damages are, in a word, priceless.[23] In addition, the ruined houses and urban infrastructure (many of which have not been rebuilt because of a lack of financial and social resilience) were quite expensive.

The same interplay of economic and non-economic damages applies to the projections of climate change impacts, in the Stern Review and elsewhere. The significance of the economic damages is that, even in their narrowest interpretation, they tip the balance of a cost–benefit calculation, demonstrating that it is well worth it to invest now in an active program of mitigation and adaptation. For this purpose, the narrowest interpretation of damages is more persuasive, staying closer to estimates of actual losses of market income.

As to the ambition of monetizing the entire range of impacts, and telling the entire story in a single number: give it up. The profundity of human and ecological loss implied in the portraits of climate change, especially at higher temperatures, is only cheapened and diminished by pretending that all of it has a price. At the depths of greatest tragedy, as at the heights of proudest collective response, we leave the market far behind. The reason to avoid another world war is not primarily because repairing bombed-out buildings is so costly. The urgency of preparing wisely in advance for two, three, many Hurricane Katrinas is not strengthened by a hypothetical monetary valuation of the lives lost to the storm in 2005. Our moral obligation to protect the lives and livelihoods of future generations is not adequately conveyed by a numerical discount rate – even a low one.

## A BETTER APPROACH TO ANALYSIS AND POLICY

In the absence of complete monetization of climate impacts, how should policy be determined? In this framework, it is no longer possible to carry out the cost–benefit calculation, comparing mitigation and damage costs, as in the Stern Review's Figure 13.3 or the alternative figure presented above. Indeed, that calculation is doubly impossible, both because of the uncertainty about the extent of damages at any particular atmospheric concentration of $CO_2$, and because of the lack of meaningful monetary values for many of the damages.

Instead, the immensely valuable compendium of information assembled by the Stern Review can be interrogated from a different perspective. A linked pair of questions must be answered:

- First, what is the maximum atmospheric concentration of $CO_2$ at which unacceptable climate outcomes can be ruled out with a high degree of confidence?
- Second, what is the least-cost strategy for stabilizing at that concentration?

The first question is the essence of a precautionary approach to policy, in a context of complex and uncertain scientific information. It involves several difficult, but not impossible judgments: about the (probabilistic) link between $CO_2$ levels and climate outcomes; about which climate outcomes are unacceptable; and about how high a degree of confidence is required that we can avoid those outcomes.

The second question involves cost-effectiveness analysis: given a fixed target, what is the cheapest way to get there? This is far from being easy to answer, for a problem as complex as reducing carbon emissions. Yet it is much more tractable than cost–benefit analysis, since it includes only costs, not benefits (or avoided damages) of mitigation. While challenges and uncertainties will arise in calculating costs, the most difficult problems discussed above are all on the benefit (avoided damage) side of the analysis. Costs are generally well-defined in monetary terms, and subject to engineering and economic research that reduces the remaining uncertainties. Costs occur sooner, on average, than benefits, for this and for many public policy problems. Thus the dilemmas of discounting are much less important for cost-effectiveness calculations.

Such an approach would not be governed by estimates of the social cost of carbon, although it could be made compatible with those figures. The urgency and the required extent of mitigation would be derived from the atmospheric concentration target, which is itself derived from an analysis of the first point at which unacceptable consequences could occur. Once the carbon stabilization target is determined, it is in principle possible to find the least-cost path for reaching the target. The most expensive measure required, in the least-cost path to the target, determines the social cost of carbon. Everything possible that can be done to reduce emissions at a lower cost, per ton of carbon, must be included in the plan.[24]

In conclusion, the Stern Review takes us a long way toward understanding the economics of climate change, posing many big questions and answering some of them quite well. The arguments against conventional, high discount rates, and the massive review of sectoral estimates of damages and mitigation costs, will be hard to improve on, except in issues of detail. The central issue of uncertainty is raised forcefully, though resolved less adequately. The Review offers interesting illustrative calculations of how important uncertainty might be, though it effectively ends up demonstrating how hard it is to put meaningful numbers on the inherently unknown dimensions of the problem.

Finally, the Review episodically suggests an understanding of the priceless, nonmonetary dimensions of loss, which are more serious and profoundly damaging than the – ultimately modest – reductions in long-term growth found by its models. The cost–benefit calculation on the one hand, and the deeper description of damages on the other hand, are important, and importantly separate, dimensions of the discussion. This distinction is unfortunately obscured by the intense debates about exactly how large the monetary damages might be. A better approach would involve deliberation over an acceptable target, followed by calculation of the cost-effective means of achieving the target.

The Stern Review is far from being the last word on every aspect of the economics of climate change – but it is much less wrong than the analyses that preceded it. It has decisively laid to rest the notion that standard economic methods somehow counsel timidity in the face of global crisis.

## NOTES

1. Global Development and Environment Institute, Tufts University, Medford MA 02155, USA. This chapter is based on an analysis of the Stern Review written for Friends of the Earth. Thanks to Simon Bullock and Elizabeth Stanton for helpful comments on an earlier draft.
2. The Stern Review is available online, with background and other related documents, at http://www.hmtreasury.gov.uk/independent_reviews/stern_review_economics_climate_change/sternreview_index.cfm.
3. Unlike the US, the UK experienced heavy bombing during World War II. UK deaths, as a percent of the population, were three times the US level in World War II, and 20 times the US level in World War I. (Wikipedia entries on 'World War I casualties', and 'World War II casualties'.)

4. These Stern calculations of $CO_2$-equivalent emissions include about 50 ppm contribution from non-$CO_2$ greenhouse gases; thus this range is comparable to 450–500 ppm of $CO_2$ alone.
5. This is comparable to 400–500 ppm of $CO_2$ alone (see note 4). The rationale for this target range is spelled out in Chapter 13 of the Review, and discussed below.
6. With zero pure time preference, models of economic growth behave illogically when extended to an infinite time horizon. It is not clear whether this is a fatal flaw in an analysis limited to a few centuries.
7. The calculation of discount rate is explained in Annex 6 of the Green Book, at http://greenbook.treasury.gov.uk/annex06.htm. In the Green Book, the symbol $\delta$ and the term 'pure time preference' both exclude catastrophic risk, while in the Stern Review and this book, the same symbol and term include catastrophic risk. The Green Book's $\rho$ corresponds to Stern's $\delta$; likewise, the Green Book's $\mu$ corresponds to Stern's $\eta$.
8. This point is explained in greater detail in Ackerman and Finlayson (2006).
9. Nordhaus uses different notation, and refers to the rate of pure time preference as the 'social discount rate'. (This report uses the Stern notation and terminology throughout.) In subsequent work Nordhaus (2008) has decreased $\delta$ and increased $\eta$, suggesting that these offsetting adjustments are needed to keep the discount rate consistent with interest rates.
10. Brad DeLong, 'Partha Dasgupta Makes a Mistake in His Critique of the Stern Review', a blog entry for November 30, 2006, http://delong.typepad.com/sdj/2006/11/index.html. Discussion between Dasgupta and DeLong continues on December 7, at http://delong.typepad.com/sdj/2006/12/brad_delongs_se.html.
11. See the Stern Review's postscript, appendix to the postscript, and other recent writings on the Stern Review website.
12. Formally, risk is often taken to mean events where different outcomes have known probabilities, in contrast to uncertainty, where the probabilities are unknown. However, this distinction is often blurred in informal discussion, such as the text of this section.
13. See the summary in one of the Stern team's responses to critics in Dietz et al. (2007).
14. The results are weighted by 'utility', or consumer satisfaction, which Stern assumes is equal to the logarithm of consumption. (This is a common, but far from universal, assumption in economic analyses.) Compared to an unweighted average, this procedure gives greater weight to model runs where climate damages are greater and incomes are lower.
15. In fact, 5 percent is the Stern damage estimate with baseline climate sensitivity, and without non-market impacts, while 14 percent is the high climate sensitivity estimate, with non-market impacts included. Both use the same method of discounting.
16. Unlike other authors discussed here, Lomborg is not an economist; he is a political scientist who frequently raises economic critiques of climate mitigation and other environmental policies.
17. Note for American readers: 'knock-on effects' means indirect, usually undesirable, side effects. The term originated in rugby, where it refers to accidentally knocking the ball forward while trying to pick it up.
18. Damages are zero at the pre-industrial concentration of greenhouse gases, 280 ppm, while costs are negative at high concentrations due to the existence of substantial no-cost and negative-cost energy-saving opportunities. The horizontal axis is not drawn to scale here – nor in the Review's Figure 13.3.
19. The quantitative meaning of 'worst case' is itself a debatable policy decision. Here the 98th percentile, or worst 2 percent outcome, is arbitrarily chosen for comparability with the discussion of Weitzman's comments.
20. This appears to be a calculation of 194 years of compound growth at 1.3 percent, that is, from 2006 to 2200.
21. In fact, the slowdown was even greater than this: Japan's real GDP growth averaged 3.9 percent per year from 1980 to 1990, then fell to 1.5 percent from 1990 to 2000. Calculated from Statistics Bureau, Ministry of Internal Affairs and Communication, *Historical Statistics of Japan*, available at http://www.stat.go.jp/data/chouki/zuhyou/03-21.xls. More recently, Japan's growth rate has risen, although not back to the 1980s level.
22. See Ackerman and Stanton (2006), pp. 3-4.

23. The logical paradoxes and political mischief associated with assigning prices to such damages are explored in Ackerman and Heinzerling (2004).
24. If not, then stabilization costs could be reduced by substituting a lower-cost measure for the most expensive measure in the plan.

# REFERENCES


Ackerman, Frank and Ian Finlayson (2006), 'The Economics of Inaction on Climate Change: A Sensitivity Analysis', *Climate Policy*, **6** (5): 509–526.

Ackerman, Frank and Lisa Heinzerling (2004), *Priceless: On Knowing the Price of Everything and the Value of Nothing*, New York: The New Press.

Ackerman, Frank and Elizabeth Stanton (2006), 'Climate Change: The Costs of Inaction', http://www.ase.tufts.edu/gdae/policy_research/CostsofInaction.html.

Baer, Paul (2006), 'The Worth of an Ice-Sheet: A Critique of the Treatment of Catastrophic Impacts in the Stern Review', 23 December, http://www.postnormaltimes.net/blog/ archives/2006/12/the_worth_of_an_1.html.

Byatt, Ian, Ian Castles, Indur M. Goklany, David Henderson, Nigel Lawson, Ross McKitrick, Julian Morris, Alan Peacock, Colin Robinson and Robert Skidelsky (2006), 'The Stern Review: A Dual Critique – Part II: Economic Aspects', *World Economics*, **7** (4): 199–229.

Dasgupta, Partha (2006), 'Comments on the Stern Review's Economics of Climate Change', revised 12 December, http://www.econ.cam.ac.uk/faculty/dasgupta/STERN.pdf.

Dietz, Simon, Chris Hope, Nicholas Stern and Dimitri Zenghelis (2007), 'Reflections on the Stern Review (1): A Robust Case for Strong Action to Reduce the Risks of Climate Change', *World Economics*, **8** (1): 121–168.

Lomborg, Bjorn (2006), 'Stern Review: The Dodgy Numbers Behind the Latest Warming Scare', *Wall Street Journal*, 2 November.

Maddison, David (nd), 'Further Comments on the Stern Review', p. 3, http://www.economics.bham.ac.uk/maddison/Stern%20Comments.pdf.

Mendelsohn, Robert O. (2007), 'A Critique of the Stern Report', *Regulation*, **24** (4): 42–46.

Nordhaus, William (2007a), 'Accompanying Notes and Documentation on Development of DICE-2007 Model', 12 April, http://www.econ.yale.edu/~nordhaus/DICEGAMS/AccomNotes_041207.pdf.

Nordhaus, William (2007b), 'The *Stern Review* on the Economics of Climate Change', *Journal of Economic Literature,* **45** (3): 686–702.

Nordhaus, William (2008), *A Question of Balance: Economic Modeling of Global Warming,* New Haven and London: Yale University Press.

Stern, Nicholas (2006), *The Stern Review: The Economics of Climate Change*, London: HM Treasury. http://www.hm-treasury.gov.uk/independent_reviews/stern_review_economics_climate_change/stern_review_report.cfm.

Tol, Richard S.J. (2006), 'The Stern Review of the Economics of Climate Change: A Comment', http://www-iam.nies.go.jp/aim/stern/Tol_sternreview.pdf.

Tol, Richard S.J. and Gary W. Yohe (2006), 'A Review of the *Stern Review*', *World Economics*, **7** (4), 233–250.

UK Treasury (2007), *Green Book*, http://greenbook.treasury.gov.uk/

Weitzman, Martin (2007), 'The Stern Review of the Economics of Climate Change', *Journal of Economic Literature*, **45** (3): 703–724.

Yohe, Gary (2006), 'Some Thoughts on the Damage Estimates Presented in the Stern Review – An Editorial', *Integrated Assessment Journal*, **6** (3): 65–72.

# 3. Economics and Climate Change: Resilience, Equity, and Sustainability

**Neva R. Goodwin**

Climate change is a force that will dramatically affect economic realities – at worst in the form of emergency adaptation, and at best in the form of intelligently planned mitigation activities. In the face of this crisis, in a world where material progress has benefited a large proportion of humanity and left another large portion behind, it is essential to work towards four goals:

1. *Well-being and equity in the present*: Maintain or increase human well-being in the present, especially among those who lack the essentials for a healthy life
2. *Productive capital for the future*: Maintain and, where necessary, rehabilitate, the productive resources required to preserve or increase human well-being in the future
3. *Mitigation of climate change*: Reduce to an acceptable level, as quickly as possible, the environmental harms that result from economic activity
4. *Adaptation to climate change*: Cope with unavoidable harms to the natural and social environments

Standard economic theory, as it is now taught and applied, is not well suited to address these goals. To the extent that standard theory admits to having goals or values, it aims to maximize utility. However, because utility cannot be directly observed, measured, or compared across individuals, this goal has very often been reduced to that of maximizing consumption – with the obvious, though not absolutely necessary corollary of maximizing production. This impetus is in conflict with the goal of mitigating climate change and other environmental harms. It also ignores the equity goal – well-known to the early utilitarians, and to John Rawls, among others – of devoting greatest efforts to helping the people with the greatest needs.

In fact, the standard economic theory of the second half of the twentieth century puts up at least as many impediments as it offers assistance to meeting the challenges of the twenty-first century. A quick run-down of the impediments in the standard theory includes:

1. *Inappropriate goals*: standard economic theory prizes wealth creation above all, and most often defines this goal in terms of steadily growing GDP – instead of focusing on what economies should really produce, which is human well-being, in the present and the future.
2. *A de-contextualized view of the economy*: economic systems are viewed as operating in a vacuum, without regard for the critical ways in which the economy affects, and is affected by, the ecological and social contexts.
3. *A truncated list of essential economic activities and concerns*: the standard list of economic activities is 'production, exchange, and consumption'. As feminists, environmentalists and contextual economists[1] point out, this omits critical aspects of resource maintenance (including environmental sustainability and caring activities).
4. *Difficulty in dealing with the future*: the standard use of discounting often drives conclusions that make future concerns seem insignificant.
5. *Bias toward monetary values*: application of cost/benefit analysis often leads to an effort to apply monetary values to human values, such as dignity, health, or fairness. This can be seriously misleading. Moreover, the focus on what can be submitted to the measure of money leads to an overemphasis on formal markets, and insufficient attention to critical unpaid economic activities.
6. *Bias toward the status quo*: a number of conceptual tools and concepts used in economic analysis accept the existing distribution of resources as 'given' – not really up for discussion. These include the concepts of Pareto optimality, aspects of the Coase theorem, and a focus on aggregate growth indices at the expense of disaggregated inequality indicators.
7. *Bias against the public sector*: economists, business people and politicians have joined in a chorus of disparagement against government, buttressed by an increasingly blind, but fervent, belief, that markets can solve all problems. While markets can be a part of the solution to many human needs, they rarely can be the whole of the solution; markets need boundaries, rules, and safeguards against their internal tendency toward concentration of power and their lack of internal motivation to work for the wider good. In many situations insufficiently regulated markets are, in fact, the problem.

These are some of the reasons why new – and some revived old – thinking in economics is required, if the human race is to mitigate the danger of climate change and adapt to the climate-related catastrophes that will occur within this generation and all the generations we can now foresee. A successful effort to meet these challenges will bring together streams of thought that have sometimes, in the past, seemed to be in conflict. People have often felt that they had to choose whether to emphasize social justice, individual well-being, or environmental sustainability – and, in embracing one value, have felt that they might have to accept sacrifices in one or both of the others. Resolution of this apparent conflict is essential, but standard economics is poorly equipped for the task. Responding to global inequity as well as global climate change requires coordinated public policy for the fundamental redirection of economic systems. The status-quo bias inherent in standard economics is no help, and is, indeed a significant barrier, to accomplishing this task.

## ADAPTATION TO CLIMATE CHANGE

In the context of climate change, the issue of adaptation has received less attention than that of mitigation. In part this is because the more mitigation is done right away, the less adaptation will be required. Substantial climate change, however, is already inevitable, bringing changes to which humans will have to adapt – and for which most are very ill prepared. A focus on adaptation makes it especially important to address simultaneously the four goals of well-being, maintaining productive capital, mitigation, and adaptation,.

Discussions of adaptation have increasingly emphasized two essential social characteristics: social cohesion and resilience.

*Social cohesion*, sometimes examined as an aspect of social capital, implies, among other things, that people identify with larger social goals than their own immediate interest; it is undermined by wide inequalities. Unfortunately, at this time, income and wealth inequality in the United States are at or close to their high-water marks for the last hundred years; inequality is also high, by recent standards, in many other parts of the world.

*Resilience* is a concept that combines economic, environmental, and social aspects. The field of resilience studies is a relatively new one which has its roots in ecology, especially in studies of how natural systems react to strong, usually human-induced perturbations. The application of these concepts to the social sciences is even more recent.[2] One definition of resilience is 'the capacity of a system to absorb disturbance and reorganize while undergoing change so as to still retain essentially the same function, structure, identity, and feedbacks' (Folke et al., 2005, p. 443). Using this definition, of course, social cohesion is an essential aspect of overall resilience. Given that resilience is a capacity that is needed not only in whole systems, but also in individuals, and in the connections among people, and between people and institutions, I would like to propose that, if socio-economic systems were organized *to support resilient individuals in resilient networks in resilient societies*, efforts to this end would entail progress towards the other four goals.

The following discussion is offered as a first step toward filling out the concepts just mentioned, specifically with an eye to the kind of economic organization required in a century where capacities for adaptation will be extraordinarily important.

*Individual resilience* is supported by physical and mental health (both are essential for coping under great stress); general knowledge about how things work – such as simple mechanical skills, the basics of nutrition and health, more specialized technical knowledge, or social skills in persuading people to work together; and creativity, or the ability to apply existing knowledge in unfamiliar situations.

A good education is important for developing these qualities; an education that is best supplied by a collaboration between schools and families. Schools and families need to work together to support physical and mental health, for example by discouraging bullying and other kinds of abuse, by discussing ethics and values openly, and by encouraging collaborative behavior and sufficient physical exercise. Families can further support a practical and liberal education by limiting the amount of time spent in passive or overly stimulating entertainment such as TV shows and computer games.

However, for families to play such roles in their children's lives requires that there be adults who are available – that is, not at work – during a reasonable portion of the time the children are home. This opens up much broader issues about the organization of work, the structure of pay, and the inducements in the culture to increase earnings by working long hours. Both education and work organization issues are crucial aspects of social and economic policy, often neglected in market-oriented economics.

'*Resilient networks*' refer to relations among individuals, as well as connections between individuals and a variety of institutions and other social structures. Social networks connect individuals to one another, so that they are prepared to cope collaboratively, rather than competing for resources. They also connect individuals to the larger social systems, so that the people know where to turn for help, and the systems trust that the individuals will not misuse the help they receive.

The concept of *resilient societies* refers to the characteristics of the institutions in the society, which are essential aspects of social cohesion. If it is important for individuals to possess the characteristics that make them trustworthy, it is equally important for institutions also to be trustworthy. Social systems, above the community level, must exist to supply materials –

food, shelter, medicines, to start with – to the most affected individuals. Larger social systems are also necessary in cases of conflict or disaster to help rebuild physical and economic structures.

Resilience may be seen as having two aspects: one is anticipation and preparation for abrupt, catastrophic change; the other is the ability to respond in ways that create a viable future. Some large organizations can be effective at anticipation and preparedness. As an example, although there was almost no warning for the Asian tsunami, at the peak of the global response to this disaster the World Food Programme coordinated the delivery of food aid to two and a quarter million people in six countries (Indonesia, Sri Lanka, Somalia, Myanmar, Maldives and Thailand). This UN agency uses a variety of methods to anticipate and prepare for disasters; for example, crop assessments that can help predict harvests, satellite weather technology, and tracking political situations that might affect the hunger of a population. The Programme has relationships with a huge network of global, regional and local aid agencies that can channel donations of food or money rapidly and, on the whole, efficiently.

The local, regional and national response to Hurricane Katrina is in stark contrast, both in terms of anticipation and preparedness, and in terms of the ability to respond. Many systemic failures in anticipation occurred in state and local governments; an example is the destruction of swamps and wetlands that would, if left intact, have greatly dampened the force of the wind and water. These were followed by even more dramatic failures in response mechanisms after the disaster.

A major impediment to successful adaptation immediately after the 2005 hurricanes hit, especially in New Orleans, was the lack of trust between the larger social systems and the affected individuals. For example, individuals who banded together for mutual support were often viewed as mobs of looters and forced, sometimes at gunpoint, to disperse.

Another corrosive factor for the resilience of individuals in New Orleans was inequality. Given the affluence in the rest of the US, the relative poverty of New Orleans residents was debilitating. Richer communities dominate the political structure and demand its resources for their own needs; the resilience of the poor is undercut by a lack of political support. In the case of Katrina, this was compounded by a national administration particularly insensitive to the needs of poorer citizens. Paradoxically, people are less disempowered by poverty when it is not experienced as being far outside of the norm. This fact is cited to explain why many of the communities hit by the Asian tsunami responded more effectively than did the city of New Orleans in 2005.

# IMPLICATIONS FOR ECONOMIC SYSTEMS

What do these considerations mean for economic systems? There are some characteristics that are needed in any economy if it is to address the threat of climate change. Both adaptation and mitigation require that the economy is managed with a long time horizon, and that powerful economic actors act in ways that are good for people and their environments over the long term. These characteristics will be especially essential as we face a likely time of increased energy prices, whether due to political disruptions of supply, oil-field depletion with rising costs of extraction, or national and international regulation of carbon emissions.

The replacement of fossil fuels with sustainable alternatives may ultimately relax the requirement to reduce the total global consumption of energy, and of materials with energy-intensive requirements. However it is a reasonable guess to anticipate at least a 50-year transition period while those alternatives are developed, mass-produced, and their costs lowered. For this transition to take place in a way that increases, rather than reduces, resilience and social cohesion, economies – and economic theory – require not only a fundamental shift towards a well-being orientation; they also need to contain more effective mechanisms for promoting resilience and equality. Such mechanisms must include excellent education for all children – not just for the children of the wealthy. Also essential are systems of health care and nutrition that allow all people to develop their physical and mental capacities. Other needs that should be considered among the basic rights of all people are access to clean drinking water, and sufficient sources of inanimate energy to allow them to participate in global communications and education systems.

The last of these desiderata – sufficient energy for everyone – may seem to contradict the necessity to reduce global energy consumption, at least over the next half-century. It is, of course, the rich whose energy consumption must decline drastically until sustainable replacements can be found and made available. In 1998 the wealthiest 20 percent of the world's population consumed about 68 percent of the world's commercial energy, while the lowest quintile consumed less than 2 percent of these resources (Podobnik, 2002). These percentages have been shifting somewhat, as less developed countries have increased their energy consumption – too often adopting, as the only affordable or available energy sources, technologies that are especially high in greenhouse gas emissions.

In the critical times immediately ahead it will be essential for the rich nations to provide both money and technology to allow the poorest peoples to increase their energy consumption, and to do so in the most efficient, least polluting manner. The wealthy, industrialized countries have contributed over 90 percent of the $CO_2$ now in the atmosphere, but it is the poor countries who will suffer most from the consequences of climate change. Currently developing nations have contributed the least to the existing atmospheric stock of greenhouse gases, but are now confronted with 'full skies', and urgent pleas, or demands, that they not add any more atmospheric pollution. An especially compelling argument, along with a program for implementing a better sharing of pollution space, is presented in the Greenhouse Development Rights framework set forth in Chapter 4 of this volume.

## Consumption and Equity

Equity is not only a moral issue; in light of what will be required to support resilient individuals in resilient networks in resilient societies, it is a very practical one. Getting from our present world to a less unequal one is an enormously complex matter, with cultural change at the center. Writers such as Robert Frank and Robert Lane (Frank, 1999 and 2007; Lane, 2005, pp. 46-52) have emphasized that the reduction of inequality strongly implies the need to depress conspicuous consumption, and to encourage societies to define success in terms other than material possessions. These suggestions, however, run directly contrary to the way economies are understood today.

In approaching the analysis of consumption, economics can be usefully influenced by the findings of another relatively new science, hedonic psychology. Some of the findings of hedonic psychology are reassuringly obvious. They conclude that, until basic needs for survival and minimal comfort are satisfied, additional wealth, which allows for the fulfillment of these needs, strongly increases people's sense of well-being.[3] After that threshold additional wealth has diminishing marginal returns – John Stuart Mill knew this, and some of the rest of us have held on to this obvious corollary of utility theory, even while it was forgotten in the mainstream of the economics discipline. In the United States and Japan, for example, while per capita income has increased many-fold since the 1950s, it appears that the level of happiness throughout these societies has not increased at all during this period (see, e.g., Inglehart, 1982. p. 465; Lane, 2000, pp. 60-62).

In rich countries, more no longer necessarily equates with better. Increasing materialism and worse eating habits are resulting in growing mental and physical health disorders. There is a growing understanding that a switch of emphasis, away from status and status goods, could produce a happier, healthier society. Luxuries not only have a lower 'happiness pay-back' per dollar spent, they also generate dissatisfactions which may partially or wholly counterbalance the pleasure they give (see e.g. Goodwin, Ackerman, and Kiron,, 1997).

As we learn more about human happiness and well-being, we cannot ignore the fact that wealth very much beyond basic needs which belongs to, and is spent on behalf of, individuals operates within a zero-sum game wherein success creates envy, and overall well-being is not increased. By contrast, wealth that belongs to, and is spent on behalf of, a whole society can be used to promote public goods such as environmental protection and restoration, to protect the well-being of future generations.

These observations are certainly not new – but they may get new traction at a time when two realities converge. One is that, for environmental reasons, global aggregate production – or at least the kind of energy and resource-intensive consumption that characterizes modern industrialized countries – probably needs to decrease, until we can convert our systems to lower carbon methods of production. The other is that the prospect of climate chaos makes it essential to organize societies to be ready to adapt.

## Meta-externalities

In addition to a much greater emphasis on equity, economic theory that is appropriate to the needs of the 21st century will need to be more concerned with the meta-externalities of the economic system. Meta-externalities are unwanted side-effects of the whole economic system on its physical and social contexts – effects in which the economic culture fouls its own nest, if the 'nest' is understood broadly as all the social and physical contexts for economic activity. The replacement of thrift with conspicuous consumption, and of concern for integrity with concern for winning, are examples, in the cultural context, of meta-externalities that emanate from the economic system we now have. Climate change is perhaps the largest meta-externality ever imposed by human economic systems on the natural world. Positive meta-externalities include the common assets on which society at large depends. A sustainable system works to ensure, for example, an ethically and intellectually educated populace and a supportive physical environment.

A host of meta-externalities arise from the fact that market economies are oriented toward the goals of maximizing profits, production and consumption – not toward increasing well-being. The social sciences have been making considerable progress on understanding what does contribute to well-being. To the extent that these findings become part of common knowledge, this could provide a counter-weight to the social meta-externality of market economies, wherein consumers (including the very youngest children) are persuaded to want many purchases that will not increase (and may reduce) their well-being (Kasser, 2005; Nairn et al., 2007). In other words, many people in rich countries, and some elites in poor countries, could actually be better off with less stuff. Reduced material throughput in the global economy would help with climate change mitigation; at the same time, resilience and social cohesion would be increased by policies that depress conspicuous consumption and encourage societies to define success in terms other than material possessions.

The response in standard theory to this kind of critique of excessive consumption is to assert that that the system of market prices should indicate what should be produced less, and what more, to achieve a 'social optimum' – and if it does not, the first line of defense is to internalize the externalities. Well-designed regulations can find ways to provide the market with more complete feedback to force economic actors to pay for the social and ecological costs of their actions (so long as the regulations stay in place and are obeyed). However such feedback can probably never be perfect; it certainly cannot be perfected in time to be the only force inducing adequate climate mitigation. Most importantly, the incentives to internalize externalities must come from outside the market system. Cost-internalization is not in the interest of the individual market actors who, if they can shift to others the true costs of production, marketing or other activities, will gain a market advantage or larger profits. It is even harder for any system to block its own meta-externalities.

The considerations outlined above make it clear that the alternative economic theory that is needed is not just a theory of markets. Markets are not the whole economy; and markets alone create externalities and meta-externalities that they can not control from the inside. And they do not promote the resilience and social cohesion that will be more and more essential, at every level, during the remainder of this century. So what else is there for an economist to think about besides markets?

## Alternatives to Markets

One additional economic sphere is what contextual economists – and, increasingly, others – call the 'core sphere': the economic activity that goes on in homes and communities.[4] This is the focus of a good deal of work in feminist and social economics. Second, the 'public purpose sphere' includes governments as well as institutions that are both non-governmental and not-for-profit. Well-known examples of social-goods-providing NGOs include not-for-profit hospitals and universities, environmental advocacy groups, and foundations. The for-profit business sphere is currently creating meta-externalities of culture and politics that place great burdens on the core sphere, and that tie the hands of governments. This does not necessarily imply that the for-profit sphere is 'bad' and the others 'good' – rather that institutional changes must be made to bring the purposes and functions of the three spheres into better harmony.

If we want to look for still other approaches to serving the common good, there are spaces where the different spheres overlap, as well as, perhaps, spaces outside of them. One such is a property-based approach to the commons. A creative exponent, Peter Barnes, says that commons

> refers to all the gifts we inherit or create together. ... A gift is something we receive, as opposed to something we earn. A shared gift is one we receive as members of a community, as opposed to individually. Examples of such gifts include air, water, ecosystems, languages, music, holidays, money, law, mathematics, parks, the Internet, and much more. (Barnes, 2006, pp. 4–5)

When the atmosphere, the oceans, the Internet, etc., are defined as commonwealth they can be held in trusts, like the land trusts and forest trusts that are coming to be fairly well known, or the petroleum resources of Alaska, which are managed for the enrichment of the citizens of that state (but not, unfortunately, for the wellbeing of citizens of the future, or of the rest of the planet).

Another alternative is rights-based. It focuses, in the United States, on the rights that have been acquired by corporations, and uses citizen-driven democratic action to subordinate corporate decision making to local, community control. For example, the Community Environmental Legal Defense Fund, based in Pennsylvania, assists communities to draft and adopt ordinances which put into the hands of local people the power to prevent corporations from locating environmentally and economically unsustainable activities in resistant communities. These ordinances cover such topics as sludge dumping, corporate water withdrawal, destructive mining, and corporate farming. By now more than a hundred communities in Pennsylvania – 10 percent of the state's municipalities – have adopted such ordinances (see http://www.celdf.org/).

These two approaches have in common a perception that corporations do *not* always serve the public good. They are backed up by research and writing on the history of corporations, describing how, in the 19th century, corporate charters in the US specified the social function to be performed by the corporations to which they were given, and often expired when a particular function was achieved, or at the end of a specified time. The concept that the legal purpose of corporations is to enrich their shareholders has grown gradually, just since the late 19th century; the idea that this is their only legitimate purpose goes back less than half a century.

A slim counterweight to the growth of corporate power has been the movement, starting in the 1970s, to attempt to balance the rights of other 'stakeholders' against the rights of shareholders. This movement has been strongly reinforced by the growing urgency of environmental considerations, and has resulted in an upsurge of 'socially responsible investing' that can claim a number of notable achievements, such as the way Nike has implemented some measures to improve the working conditions of its suppliers, or the 2007 agreement between the purchasers of TXU and Environmental Defense Fund, scrapping plans for building a number of coal-burning power plants in favor of alternatives such as wind energy.[5]

## A SUMMARY OF SOLUTIONS

The essential question facing humankind is: how can we define and shape a healthy path of economic development for the 21st century? An obvious first answer is that any healthy kind of development must be 'sustainable'. Definitions of sustainable development require, among other things, that economic activities are undertaken in ways that maintain or increase the essential capital stocks that are necessary for production. A sustainable socioeconomic system creates a flow of desirable goods and services by using its renewable capital stocks without depleting them. Although some portion of some (especially nonrenewable) capital stocks may be used up in the process of production, the overall quantity and quality of the resource base for sustaining life and well-being must be preserved.

The resource base that is critical for sustainable development includes the well-known natural capital resources of soil, plants, fish, water, ores, etc., as well as the manufactured capital elements of the built environment that allow people to work with efficient (that is, labor-, energy- and materials- saving) machines, in healthy environments, aided by effective communications and transportation infrastructure. There is increasing recognition, as well, of the importance of human and social capital. Human capital refers to the productive capacities of individuals: inherited, acquired through education and training, and maintained by supporting physical and mental health. Social capital includes such cultural attributes as trust, socially held knowledge, mutual understanding, and constructive shared norms and values. It is critically important to sustain and build human and social capital in a context where continued economic development faces such huge challenges as those now confronting humanity.

The following list outlines some of the major requirements for achieving a healthy path of economic development for the 21st century. Not every element on this list is directly or obviously related to the pressing task of ceasing to destabilize the Earth's climate. However, the definition of sustainability given above takes into account the preservation not only of natural resource stocks – including a stable and hospitable climate – but also the human (social and individual) resources that are essential to manage the large tasks ahead of us. For example, item A.3 has to do with human health. Mental health depends to a significant extent on physical health; both must be supported in populations that will need intelligence, knowledge, will, and social cohesiveness to address the mitigation and adaptation challenges ahead. As other examples, C.2 and C.4 are about nurturing the social capital that will encourage people to make decisions in a broad social context, not just on the basis of individual or short-term advantage.

In the list below all the activities listed under A are essential for mitigation, and will also lay the groundwork for adaptation. They all offer opportunities for profitable investment and for job creation. The activities listed under B are also highly relevant to both mitigation and adaptation. They do not directly offer opportunities for investment, but alter or create the institutional and regulatory environment within which businesses will operate. Investors would therefore be well advised to anticipate the changes in relative prices that are likely in a sustainable economic development regime. The political/institutional changes under C, and the cultural changes suggested in D, take a still broader view of the transition to sustainability. They are especially geared toward the creation of the social resilience required for adaptation.

### A. Massive Shifts in Investment Priorities[6] will be Needed to:

1. Develop renewable energy sources including wind and solar energy, and efficient energy carriers such as hydrogen.
2. Develop sustainable technologies for the activities involved in production, transportation, domestic life, entertainment, etc. These should include cradle-to-grave technologies and systems (putting materials into a system of 'circumput' instead of throughput).[7]
3. Replace and (where possible) withdraw toxic substances that have, over the last century, been introduced widely throughout the world's ecosystems and the bodies of living beings, including humans
4. Develop methods of restoring productivity to land and water areas that have suffered degradation.
5. Rebuild cities to include public transportation, low energy use buildings, and excellent public amenities, with the triple goals of improved livability, cost control, and reduced environmental impact

### B. It will be Necessary to Reduce Ecosystem or Resource-degrading Economic Activities through Modified Price Structures:

1. Prices are incentives, motivating purchasers to use more or less of things when their prices fall or rise. The injunction to 'internalize externalities' means to include in the costs of all raw and produced goods the costs that are born by society and the environment in the extraction, production or use of the goods. For example, if all the

now-externalized costs of burning petroleum were internalized in the price, a gallon of gas would cost some large multiple of the present price, representing its contribution to the human and financial adaptation costs that will fall on present and future people affected by climate change.[8]

2. A variety of market (price based) and other incentives will be required, to influence the decisions of producers and consumers away from ecosystem or resource-degrading economic activities. For example, a combination of regulations and prices can motivate electricity companies to sell negawatts rather than megawatts, or make it profitable for consumers to conserve energy in other ways (see Laitner, 2007).
3. Research and planning are needed to anticipate where, in different economies, the requirement to reduce climate-altering activities suggests a shift toward relatively more human inputs, and less material and energy inputs, in the production of marketed or non-marketed goods. Efforts should be made to substitute technology and 'information intensive' human inputs[9] for energy and materials; ideally such a substitution can continue the process of 'ephemeralization' wherein given goals can be achieved with decreasing material quantities.

**C. Political/Institutional Changes will be Needed to:**

1. Increase the power of entities representing the social interest vs. those (such as corporations, in the existing system) that pursue a narrow or short-term interest.
2. Create a substantial floor under the political, economic, and decision-making power of individuals and communities, for example, through legal instruments such as trusts, charters, and ordinances.
3. In order to increase system resilience, intensify efforts to move toward more equal power and access to resource, within nations and among them.
4. Create appropriate means of managing assets which are defined as 'common wealth'.

**D. Necessary Cultural Changes will Likely Include:**

1. Recognition of and adaptation to changing demographics. The rich countries, which must take leadership in significant aspects of the development of new, sustainable patterns of economic activity, will simultaneously need to cope with new demographic/economic issues:

a growing proportion of elderly people, with their particular medical and social needs, along with a shrinking proportion of people in the formal workforce. Existing norms project relatively fewer job-seekers in aging populations. Will there also be fewer jobs? What does this mean for the standard of living of those who are, and those who are not, working at formal jobs? How can societies respect and make use of the potential contributions of the elderly?

2. Changing attitudes toward work and leisure, along with possibly changed definitions of 'work' or 'a job', will likely result from the demographic changes, and may also be necessary concomitants to an economy with reduced throughput. Decreased labor income relative to the value of energy and materials may revise the balance between marketed and non-marketed goods consumed by households. (This carries the danger of counteracting the progress made in gender equality, since in many societies women have traditionally been the major providers of non-marketed goods and services.)
3. Revised understanding of what contributes to well-being. The culture of consumerism includes beliefs that 'more is better', 'happiness can be bought', etc. There is much evidence that these beliefs are false, but they are actively fostered by the many businesses that perceive a consumerist culture as in their interest. This requirement is closely related to a need for revised definitions of individual and business success; hence, revised individual and corporate goals.

## CONCLUSION

The critical role for economic theory is no longer to explain how the existing system works, but to explore ways that it can be changed to become more adaptive and resilient, and more directly designed to support human well-being, in the present and the future. Simultaneous changes are needed in the actual economy – how it functions, by what rules, how it can be made responsive to contextual constraints – and in economic theory. The two largest changes required in economic theory and policies are a shift in emphasis and a shift in goals.

Regarding emphasis – the economy is not just about business. And the economy does not stand alone. What is required is a contextual theory that, first, describes and understands the economy as containing at least three spheres – the core sphere, of families and communities; the public purpose sphere, of business and non-profits, and the business sphere. Second, the economy must always be understood as embedded within the social and environmental contexts on which the economy is dependent, and which it can strongly affect, for better or worse.

Regarding goals – it is important to make the distinction between final and intermediate goals. Of all the goals mentioned in this chapter, the only one that, outside of economics, would be almost universally accepted as a final goal – an end that is worth achieving in itself – is that of maintaining and enhancing human well-being, in the present and the future.

Increasing production and consumption are intermediate goals; they are means to the ends of human welfare. They are important if, and only if, they work to enhance well-being. Indeed, at least two-fifths of the world's people suffer from nutritional, health and educational deficits that severely depress their well-being and that could be overcome with some of the things that money can buy. With respect to these individuals, increased production and consumption are obviously very important intermediate goals. However, under present conditions these are not the people who will receive most of the benefits of increased efficiency and productivity.

This is a reason to accept, as another critically important intermediate goal – some people would regard it as a final goal – the reduction of inequality. The focus here should be on concentrations of power and assets in corporations, which have infinite lives and insufficient accountability. Hedonic psychology, as well the requirements for social cohesion, strongly support the idea that the human race would, on the whole, be happier and more resilient if power and possessions were more evenly distributed. But the corporate culture, and the rules that allow it to dominate our social and political space, are working in the opposite direction.

Other critical intermediate goals are climate mitigation and adaptation. A focus on the final goal of human well-being in the present and the future makes it imperative to reduce threats from extreme weather events, rising sea-levels, and other climate related dangers to people, land, homes, and other structures; and, where these threats turn into realities, to be prepared to survive, to rebuild our lives, and to help others do the same.

To change the direction of our economy towards these goals – well-being for all, realistic coping with climate change, and a more equal allocation of the world's wealth and power – will require different rules and policies for the behavior of corporations, and for a variety of government activities, from their treatment of corporations to their provisions for health and education. For governments to alter their goals and behaviors, it will be necessary for citizens to understand, and want, and work for, such alteration. Economic theory, and the teaching about economics that reaches young people in high school and college, has some part to play in bringing about the cultural changes that will help people to see what is in their interest, and to express values, other than simple materialism, that are at present given short shrift.

# NOTES

1. For a detailed explanation of what is meant by contextual economics, see http://ase.tufts.edu/gdae/advancing_theory/theory_overview.html.
2. For current thinking on the topic some useful references are *Global Environmental Change*, **16** (3) – a Special Issue titled 'Resilience, Vulnerability, and Adaptation - A Cross-cutting Theme of the Human Dimensions of the Global Environmental Change Program'. See also Resilience Alliance: http://www.resalliance.org/1.php; also Walker and Salt (2006),.
3. See Kahneman et al. (1999), for the seminal work on this field; also see Diener and Diener 1995), Diener and Oishi (2000); Diener et al (1995) and Veenhoven (1993).
4. For a definition and discussion of the 'core sphere', see Goodwin et al. (2008), Chapter 1.
5. For insight into the movement for corporate responsibility see, for example, POCLAD – Program on Corporations, Law and Democracy: http://www.poclad.org/; also Ceres, http://www.ceres.org/NetCommunity/page.aspx?pid=705; and Investor Responsibility Research Network, http://bapd.org/ginler-1.html.
6. Returns to investment of financial capital have been rising over the last quarter century, in the US and Europe, as compared to payments to labor. There are equity reasons for reversing this trend, but this may contradict the need to encourage investment in new technologies. It is not clear how this contradiction should play out.
7. See Goodwin (1991).
8. In fact it is virtually impossible to identify what all of these costs will be, to people born and unborn, and beyond impossible to represent in dollar figures the 'true' cost of this disruption. Estimates of the 'full cost' of a gallon of gas vary widely, depending on how much the estimator discounts future costs, as well as on other variables.
9. See Goodwin (1991).

# REFERENCES


Barnes, Peter (2006), *Capitalism 3.0: A Guide to Reclaiming the Commons*, San Francisco, CA: Barrett-Koehler Publishers, Inc.

Diener, Ed and Marissa Diener (1995), 'Cross-Cultural Correlates of Life Satisfaction and Self-Esteem', *Journal of Personality and Social Psychology*, **68**: 653–663.

Diener, Ed, Marissa Diener and Carol Diener (1995), 'Factors Predicting the Subjective Well-being of Nations', *Journal of Personality and Social Psychology*, **69**: 851–864.

Diener, Ed and Shigehiro Oishi (2000), 'Money and Happiness: Income and Subjective Well-being Across Nations', in Diener and E.M. Suh (eds), *Subjective Well-being Across Cultures*, Cambridge, MA: MIT Press.

Folke, Carl, Thomas Hahn, Per Olsson and Jon Norberg (2005), 'Adaptive Governance of Social-Ecological Systems', *Annual Review of Environmental Resources*, **30**: 441– 473

Frank, Robert H. (1999), *Luxury Fever: Money and Happiness in an Era of Excess*, Princeton, NJ: Princeton University Press.

Frank, Robert H. (2007), *Falling Behind: How Rising Inequality Harms the Middle Class*, Berkeley, CA: University of California Press.

Goodwin, Neva (1991), 'Lessons for the World from US Agriculture: Unbundling Technology', *World Development*, **19** (1): 85–102.

Goodwin, Neva, Frank Ackerman and David Kiron (eds.) (1997), *The Consumer Society*, Washington, DC: Island Press.

Goodwin, Neva, Julie A. Nelson, Frank Ackerman and Thomas Weisskopf (2008), *Microeconomics in Context*, 2nd edition, Armonk, NY: M.E. Sharpe.

Inglehart, Ronald (1982), 'Changing Values in Japan and the West', *Comparative Political Studies,* **14**: 447–479.

Kahneman, Daniel, Ed Diener and Norbert Schwarz (eds.) (1999), *Well-being: The Foundations of Hedonic Psychology*, New York: Russell Sage Foundation.

Kasser, Tim (2005), 'Frugality, Generosity, and Materialism in Children and Adolescents' in K.A. Moore and L.H. Lippman (eds.), *What do Children Need to Flourish?: Conceptualizing and Measuring Indicators of Positive Development*, New York: Springer Science, pp. 357 – 373.

Laitner, John A. (2007), *Growing the Economy through Global Warming Solutions*, Newton, MA: Civil Society Institute, http://www.civilsocietyinstitute.org/.

Lane, Robert E. (2000), *The Loss of Happiness in Market Democracies*, New Haven, CT: Yale University Press.

Lane, Robert E. (2005), *After the End of History: The Curious Fate of American Materialism*, Ann Arbor, MI: University of Michigan Press.

Nairn, A., J. Ormrod, and P. Pottomley (2007), *Watching, Wanting, and Well-Being: Exploring the Links: A Study of 9–13-year-olds in England and Wales,* London, UK: National Consumer Council.

Veenhoven, Ruut (1993), *Happiness in Nations: Subjective Appreciation of Life in 56 Nations 1946–1992*, Rotterdam: Erasmus University, RISBO Press.

Walker, Brian and David Salt (2006), *Resilience Thinking; Sustaining Ecosystems and People in a Changing World*, Washington, DC: Island Press.

# 4. The Right to Development in a Climate-Constrained World

**Paul Baer, Tom Athanasiou and Sivan Kartha**[1]

---

## THE GREENHOUSE DEVELOPMENT RIGHTS FRAMEWORK

The climate crisis is upon us. Indeed, it is long past time for an emergency mobilization designed to stabilize the global climate and minimize the now inevitable damages. Most of us know this, yet despite our knowledge, the pace of our response has been profoundly inadequate. Nor is this slow pace entirely attributable to the intransigence of the Bush Administration and its allies. There are deeper problems as well, and it is time now for them to take center stage. This chapter begins with some clear assertions about the climate challenge, and the global climate policy impasse that must be broken if we are to face it successfully. We believe that all of these assertions are true. If so, they are also quite inconvenient.

First, the science now tells us that we are pushing beyond 'dangerous anthropogenic interference with the climate system', and are on the verge of committing to catastrophic interference. Yet even the more aggressive of today's 'realist' scenarios (which seek to stabilize atmospheric greenhouse-gas concentrations at about 450 ppm $CO_2$-equivalent) accept a strong likelihood that we will soon lock in the melting of the Greenland ice sheet, and with it a seven meter rise in the sea level.[2] In fact, if we want a good chance of preventing this melting, and a *decent likelihood* of staying below the widely endorsed 2°C threshold (and this would hardly mean that we were 'safe'), global emissions must peak very soon, and concentrations must be brought back to 400 ppm $CO_2$-equivalent or below. The best remaining path to such a goal requires that emissions peak within ten years – the sooner the better – and then decline precipitously.[3] As implausible as this may seem, it is the trajectory that the climate science is forcing us to accept, if we actually want a reasonable likelihood of keeping below 2°C. To achieve such a trajectory, however, we'll have to be far more aggressive than even the most ambitious of the current EU and US proposals.[4]

Second, we confront the climate crisis, and the consequent need for an emergency mobilization, in a profoundly divided world characterized by both staggering levels of poverty and enormous (and growing) wealth. This is a world in which the usual path from poverty to prosperity is via a development process that entails dramatic increases in the per capita use of fossil fuel energy. And this path, alas, must be closed. Indeed, any future in which it is taken by even a significant fraction of the world's poor is a future in which dramatically rising carbon emissions make a mockery of emergency rhetoric. Yet, if an emergency program is to have any hope of being embraced, it must not threaten to lock in today's vast disparities of wealth and income. Rather, it must show that it can drive down emissions, globally, even while ambitious development goals are met and surpassed.[5] To this end, it must slash the emissions of the already wealthy and, at the same time, prevent the unbounded emissions growth of those rising out of poverty. And, it must do so without stifling their development aspirations.

This is a tall order, and it leads us, inevitably, to the intersection of the climate crisis and the development crisis, and to the core of the climate challenge: The world's wealthy minority has left precious little space for the poor majority. So little space that, even if industrialized country emissions were suddenly and magically halted, the dramatic emissions reduction demanded by the climate crisis would still require the developing countries to decarbonize their economies rapidly, and to do so while they were still combating endemic poverty. This conclusion – a direct consequence of the implacable mathematics of our vanishing emissions budget – is not only the core of the physical challenge, but also the crux of the international political impasse that has overtaken the negotiations.

As long as there is no acceptable burden-sharing proposal on the table, one that ensures that an emergency program can be executed without stifling development in the South, developing country negotiators can be forgiven if they conclude that their countries have more to lose than to gain from earnest engagement. This is especially true because an emergency program would be costly. We might be smart, and lucky, and rapid mitigation might actually be cheap. It might even provide so much economic stimulus that overall costs would be negative.[6] But such outcomes are not particularly likely. Given this, and given the social, sectoral and political dynamics that would attend any true emergency mitigation program, its costs may in the end be quite large. And to them must be added the costs of adaptation, as essential as mitigation in any emergency program and quite possibly even more costly.

Conventional wisdom tells us that the world's wealthier citizens cannot be expected to pay more than a trivial amount for climate change, and even less if the payments go to people and projects in 'other countries'. In fact, given today's extremely limited 'willingness to pay', the costs of a true emergency program may be politically unsupportable even if the overall costs of mitigation turn out to be quite low, and even without considering the costs of adaptation. Thus, southern negotiators may be forgiven if they fear that a stringent global climate agreement would saddle them with unacceptable costs and permanently constrain their development. Recent history, after all, is one in which high-sounding schemes, celebrated in the halls of global power, seldom resolve, in the villages and megacities, into just and adequate results. Before finally throwing their support behind an emergency program, southern negotiators will need to see a proposal that, above all else, explicitly safeguards the right to development.

The Greenhouse Development Rights (GDR) Framework proposed here is designed to do just that. It embodies the right to development as a 'development threshold' below which low-income individuals are not expected to share the burden of mitigating the climate problem. The 'development threshold' that we suggest reflects a level of welfare beyond basic needs, but well short of today's levels of 'affluent' consumption. People below it have little responsibility for the climate problem and relatively little capacity to invest in solving it. Indeed, they have development as their proper priority, and should not be saddled with the costs of keeping society as a whole within the starkly limited global carbon budget.

People above the development threshold, who have arguably realized their right to development, face the corresponding responsibility to preserve that right for others. It is they who must share the burden – in accordance with the UNFCCC's broad principle of 'common but differentiated responsibility and respective capabilities' – of funding the emergency program.[7] It is they who must bear the costs of not only curbing the emissions associated with their own consumption, but also of ensuring that, as those below the threshold rise towards and then above it, they are able to do so along sustainable, low-emission paths.

In the discussion below, we show calculations illustrating the implications of a consistent responsibility- and capacity-based approach that's designed to safeguard the right to development. In particular, we calculate a national Responsibility and Capacity Indicator (RCI) that takes explicit account of the highly unequal distribution of income and emissions within countries. We then use this RCI to quantify national mitigation and adaptation obligations corresponding to an emergency program. And we demonstrate that even if its costs were fairly large, the world's wealthier citizens could easily bear an emergency global climate stabilization program; it would not impoverish them. In fact they could do so with relatively modest reductions in their luxury consumption.

## THE URGENCY

It is not our task to justify the 2°C threshold. There's little doubt that even before the temperature increase reaches that level, our ability to meet critical objectives – food and water security in poor countries, for example, or the preservation of ecological diversity – will be severely challenged. And while adaptation can help, and indeed will be an absolute necessity if we are to avoid the worst effects of even the most immediate impacts, it is not sufficient. Indeed, the IPCC's recent Fourth Assessment Report of Working Group II makes clear that increasingly severe consequences are largely inevitable, given the warming that is already 'in the pipeline'.

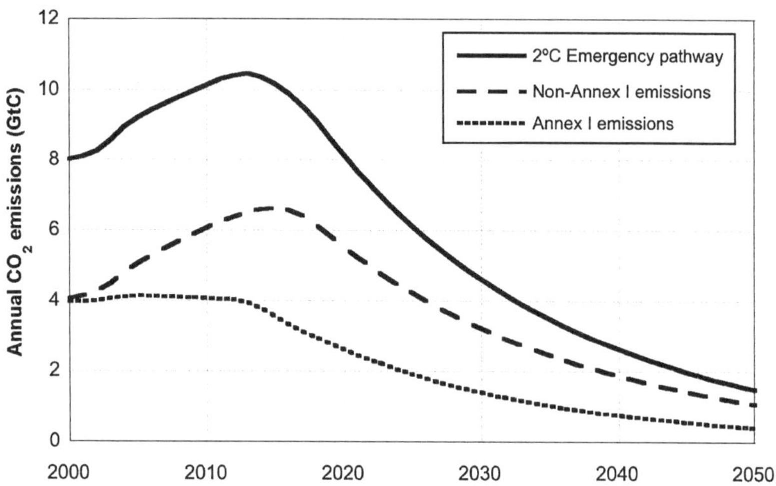


*Note:* This 'thought experiment' shows the global emissions trajectory that entails a 15–30 percent risk of exceeding 2°C (solid line, top). The Annex 1 trajectory assumes an aggressive reduction of 90 percent below 1990 levels by 2050 (dotted line, bottom), with the remaining carbon budget available to non-Annex 1 countries (dashed line, middle).

*Figure 4.1 Global emissions budget for 2°C emergency pathway*

Figure 4.1 puts the climate problem in context. It conveys a simple 'thought experiment' consisting of a bit of science, bit of conjecture, and a bit of arithmetic. The solid line is the science; it shows a global emission trajectory which declines rapidly and deeply enough to preserve a reasonable likelihood of keeping global temperature rise within the widely endorsed 2°C threshold for maximum tolerable warming. It is labeled 'Emergency pathway' because it requires extremely rigorous mitigation indeed, sufficient to force global emissions to peak before 2015 and to fall by at least 80 percent below 1990 levels by 2050.[8] Still, even this ambitious trajectory might not be enough. It subjects the earth to a worrisome 15–30 percent risk[9] of exceeding the 2°C threshold, which, in the language of the IPCC[10], means it is 'likely', but not 'very likely', to keep warming below 2°C[11]. Moreover, recent science suggests that stabilizing the climate and avoiding catastrophic climate disruption may require an even more stringent course, one sufficient to return emissions ultimately to zero and to stabilize atmospheric $CO_2$ concentrations no higher than 350 ppm.[12]

The dotted line ('Annex 1') in Figure 4.1 reflects a simple conjecture. It shows the emission trajectory that would result if all Annex 1 countries quickly adopted an ambitious program that forced their emissions to drop to 90 percent below 1990 levels by 2050, by falling nearly 6 percent annually from 2015 onward. It would require intense and concerted effort, and is just barely within the bounds of what can be considered politically plausible today. Indeed, it exceeds the objectives of the even the strictest of the bills now in play in the US Congress (the House of Representative's Safe Climate Act and the Senate's Global Warming Pollution Reduction Act) and the various aspirational targets put forward by EU members states. As such, this line does not represent the maximum rate of emissions reductions that may be technically feasible; it is merely a reflection of what level of Annex I reductions can be considered politically plausible today, though just barely.

The dashed line ('Non-Annex 1') in Figure 4.1 is the arithmetic. It shows, simply by subtraction, what is left of the global budget (solid line) after Annex 1 has consumed its indicated proportion (dotted line). It is, in other words, the remaining space within which non-Annex I countries would be constrained to develop, and it is quite bracing. It peaks well before 2020, and is soon racing downward at nearly 6 percent annually. It is this Non-Annex 1 line that captures the truly daunting nature of the climate challenge. It is an ambitious trajectory in any event, but especially so in light of the fact that developing countries need to continue to expand energy services in order to meet basic development goals.[13] In the less than fifteen years between now and 2020, incomes in developing countries are likely to grow substantially; but even assuming optimistic growth rates, incomes will still be only one third of current developed country levels on average. In other words, the developing world will still be struggling to eradicate endemic poverty, even while its emissions will need to be rapidly declining.

This brings into stark focus the true nature of the climate challenge, and the source of the current negotiating predicament. The climate crisis calls for a regime that can rapidly curb emissions globally, without impeding the prospects for developing countries to grow economically, to expand access to energy services, and to earnestly combat poverty. In other words, what is needed is a climate regime that, by its very design, preserves a right to development. Unless a climate regime preserves a right to development, it can not engender the necessary scale of developing country engagement, and is therefore not politically or practically feasible.

## HUMAN DEVELOPMENT AND CLIMATE PROTECTION

It is understandable, therefore, why even as a sense of impending climate catastrophe grows, many of the world's people are necessarily preoccupied with the other, even more pressing crisis: that of poverty. Much can and has been said about this crisis – scandalously high infant mortality rates, horrific though easily preventable disease as a miserable fact of life and death, physical insecurity, denial of opportunity and the right to a productive, fulfilling and dignified life; all in a world of extreme affluence and growing middle-class wealth. We shall not attempt to repeat it all here.

But there are things that must be said about poverty – and therefore inequality and wealth – and the climate crisis. First, there is no road to development, however conceived, that does not greatly improve access to energy services. Yet, as economies are now structured, as development is now envisioned, and as long as we rely on today's energy technologies, this will imply increases in $CO_2$ emissions that are entirely incompatible with a precautionary climate policy. And thus our dilemma: there is simply not enough 'environmental space' for the still-poor to develop in the same way – or in anything like the same way – as that which was taken by the already-rich.

It is no mystery where this environmental space has gone. The 15 percent of the world's population that lives today in the roughly 40 high-income countries uses about half the world's energy, produces about half the world's $CO_2$, and consumes about half the world's goods and services. Further, the world's wealthy, as they developed into this current resource-intensive state, consumed so great a fraction of the carbon budget that, today, we are faced with the task of allocating an entirely inadequate remainder.

And herein lies the crux of the climate-development dilemma: Under a global emergency pathway, carbon constraints would be so tight that, in the absence of explicit efforts to enable low-emissions development, the poor would be badly squeezed. In effect, they would lose their right to development. More precisely, the emergency pathway would be seen as requiring development to be deferred, so that that limited resources could be invested instead in mitigation, and in consequence it would be resisted. Nor would this resistance be mere intransigence or brinksmanship. It would, in many cases, be a rational accounting of necessity.

## The Right to Development

The agenda for an emergency climate stabilization program must expand beyond climate stabilization. A global climate regime with any promise of success must also *embrace the right to sustainable human development, and it must do so explicitly.* This right must be declared and protected, despite even the dire pressures of the climate crisis. Any emergency program that does not do so will flounder and fail. There are so many intrinsic connections between the climate and human development challenges that, as a practical matter, the climate problem can only be successfully engaged if the poor majority is visibly progressing toward genuine human development.

These connections, though manifold and complex, can be briefly outlined with respect to both mitigation and adaptation. In the former case, an emergency program would require dramatic technological transformation, amounting to a wholesale reinvention of the global energy infrastructure on the basis of low-emission technologies. In the South, this reinvention would require large-scale investment in training and education, as well as creating the institutional capacity to adopt, develop, and implement revolutionary solutions, all while simultaneously meeting the growing needs of expanding populations and economies. An emergency program would also require far-reaching changes in agricultural and land-use practices, which currently account for as much as one-third of southern greenhouse-gas emissions. These changes are possible, but only if there's a real commitment to grassroots empowerment in poor communities that are now dependent on land-clearing for subsistence farming, fuel wood harvesting, grazing, and timber extraction.[14]

As far as adaptation is concerned, the importance of human development is even clearer. Adaptation to climate change clearly requires a level of 'resilience' that is far beyond the grasp of the billions of people that are still mired in poverty (see Chapter 3 in this volume for more on the resilience issue). Adaptation calls for investments that create options and reserves. It requires improved access to finance and technology, but just as importantly it demands social capital and enfranchisement. In other words, it takes more than narrow, climate-focused measures to build 'adaptive capacity'. For example, while it might help to provide an agricultural household a more drought-resistant variety of a staple crop, it will not alone enable them to weather the next drought. Such a family will have far better odds if there is a literate family member, if they can access investment capital through local financial institutions, if they enjoy relatively intact social networks, if they can hold policymakers accountable. As Amartya Sen famously said, famines don't happen in democracies.

Though these arguments echo a deep sense of ethical propriety, the Greenhouse Development Rights approach is not fundamentally an appeal to morality. Its justification is a realist one. The GDRs framework, or something like it, will be necessary if we are to break the global impasse and rise to the demands of the climate crisis. The North can not stabilize the climate without the full commitment of the South, and the South can not make that commitment if doing so would threaten to undermine its development. In practice, this means that a global alliance to stabilize the climate can only arise, and survive, on terms that honor the poor world's right to development. The wealthy countries must not only cut their own emissions, deeply and soon, but also do whatever is necessary to help the poor leapfrog into a low-emissions, high-adaptation future.

## A Development Threshold

Greenhouse Development Rights suggests a framework for such an alliance, by way of this simple but critical bit of clarification: In our environmentally-constrained world, the right to development is not a right to economic growth as such, but rather the right to a modest but dignified level of well-being. We define this level by way of a *development threshold.* Below this threshold, individuals must be allowed to prioritize development. This means that they should not have to help bear the burdens of dealing with the changing climate, on either the mitigation or the adaptation sides. Those above the threshold, on the other hand, must help to shoulder these burdens, regardless of whether they happen to live in the North or in the South.

The level at which such a development threshold would best be set is a matter for debate, but the relevant principles are clear, as is the goal. The development threshold should differentiate the global poor, who have pressing and legitimate unmet needs, from the 'global middle class', which has reached a level of consumption that yields an appreciable contribution to the climate problem, and has also acquired enough capacity to help bear the costs of managing that problem, whatever they ultimately turn out to be.

Defining the development threshold in a concrete and quantitative sense is, not surprisingly, tricky. The most straightforward option is to define it in terms of income level, though this option suffers a number of obvious problems. Income, after all, is a simplistic and one-dimensional indicator that quite imprecisely reflects sustainable human development. It prioritizes a certain mode of development – economic growth – while obscuring the importance of human rights, political enfranchisement, liberty, social capital, health, environmental and physical security, all of which are essential to a decent standard of human well-being. Nevertheless, we will stick for now with this purely economic indicator, for three principal reasons. First, income is highly correlated with important indicators of well-being, particularly at the income levels that span the low and middle income countries, where there is an indisputable linkage between income and basic indicators such as infant mortality, life expectancy, malnourishment, and educational attainment. Second, income does indeed reflect the capacity to pay for mitigation and adaptation, especially once a country is wealthy enough for basic needs to be met. Third, income is a helpful proxy for consumption, and hence for responsibility.

How then, should we set the development threshold? We will assume that a 'dignified level of human development free from the privations of poverty' implies a line higher than a 'poverty line', perhaps 125 percent of a poverty-line income. This particular level is, of course, somewhat arbitrary, but its appropriateness is supported by the many other contexts in which such a level is taken to define the upper boundary of 'exempt' or 'lifeline' income. These include starting points for income tax calculations, eligibility thresholds for social services, and criteria for defining 'economically vulnerable' or 'near-poor' populations.

So, what is a sensible 'global poverty line'? Not the typical figures of $1 per person per day or $2 per person per day.[15] Such low figures obscure the real meaning of poverty, and the real nature of the poverty crisis. The $1/day line, more precisely, is a '*destitution line*', and the $2/day line an '*extreme poverty line*'. People at incomes much higher than $2/day can still face pervasive exposure to the plagues of poverty: malnutrition, high infant mortality, low educational attainment, high relative food expenditures. A defensible global poverty line must reflect the income level at which these plagues begin to disappear, or at least become exceptions to the rule. This can be examined empirically, and the evidence suggests that the global poverty line can reasonably be approximated by $16/day, or, equivalently, $6,000/year.[16]

Taking $6,000/year as the global poverty line, we then have an indicative development threshold of $7,500/year (125 percent of this global poverty line). This is well above the global median income (of about $3,500 in 2005), and below the global mean income (of about $8,500). It might reasonably be called a 'global middle class' income level (not to be confused with the significantly higher rich-world middle-class standard), and indeed it corresponds fairly well with the income level at which the bottom boundary of the lower middle class in China and India. In terms of the relevant climate policy trade-off – at what point should poorer people help bear the burden, so that wealthier people would bear less? – it draws the line at a defensible level.

This development threshold represents an individual income level, not a national average. Countries with per capita incomes below $7,500/year always have subpopulations with higher incomes, and smaller subpopulations with far higher incomes, while higher-income countries have subpopulations below the poverty level. The more unequal a country, the more this is the case. Thus, we stress that it should be poor individuals, not poor nations, who are excused from bearing climate-related obligations. Individuals with incomes above the development threshold – even if they live in countries with average incomes below the threshold – should be accountable for their fair share of the global climate burden. Similarly, national obligations should be reckoned in accordance with the obligations of their individual inhabitants. This, in a world of nations, is the only reasonable approach to the problem.

This proposition – that the consuming class in developing countries has no greater claim on the remaining environmental space than do its peers in wealthy countries – will of course be controversial. Taken seriously, it necessarily challenges the conventional wisdom that there is a unified 'South' whose peoples have overwhelmingly common interests. Nevertheless, the realities here can no longer be denied, as was illustrated in 'Worlds collide in India over global warming', an article that appeared in the *Financial Times* during 2007's G8+5 meeting (Johnson, 2007). Its central point – indeed its central warning – was that Mukesh Ambani, the world's 14th richest man, is now busily building himself a 60-story glass palace in Mumbai. The key statistic is that this 'home', which sports a helipad, a pool, parking for 168 luxury cars and quarters for an army of staff, is estimated to cost half a billion US dollars. The key quote: 'Such self-indulgence should be a reminder that the G8 is dealing with not one India when it comes to climate change, but two: first-world India and third-world India'.

To be sure, Bill Gates[17] is three times richer than Mukesh Ambani. But the point is still clear. The developing world, despite its millions of desperately poor people, contains a substantial and growing class of people who enjoy northern-style consumption – some of it quite absurd in its conspicuousness. Just as obviously, this wealthy class has both a non-negligible degree of responsibility for the climate problem and the capacity to help solve it. More particularly, intranational inequality must be taken into account explicitly if we want to calculate, and compare, the capacities of wealthy countries such as the United States with those of emerging but still developing countries such as China and India.

Not that all cases are as clear cut. The 'global middle class' holds a more ambiguous position than either Mukesh Ambani or Bill Gates, and the precise location of the development threshold may be quite fairly debated. But the main point is obvious. Recognizing inequality within countries is as unavoidable as recognizing inequality between countries.

# BURDEN SHARING IN THE GREENHOUSE

Fundamentally, the GDRs framework is a rich/poor burden sharing arrangement designed to support an emergency program while protecting the right to development. It does so by allocating the costs of that program among those above the development threshold – irrespective of whether they live in wealthy or developing countries – while allowing those below that threshold to attend to their development priorities.

The keys here are the two notions that lie at the core of most burden-sharing discussions: capacity and responsibility. The idea that burden sharing should be based on a systematic treatment of responsibility and capacity is not new, and is reflected in most if not all contemporary proposals. These tend to be 'multi-stage' proposals that, at a minimum, exempt poor countries from any quantified (or, more importantly, cost-bearing) obligations, and at a maximum divide countries into classes defined by measures of income and emissions.[18] Not only are these moves intuitively sensible, but they're consistent with the principle of 'common but differentiated responsibilities and respective capabilities' enshrined in the UNFCCC itself.

## Defining Capacity

Capacity reflects wealth. For our purposes, it reflects the portion of national wealth that can reasonably be tapped to respond to the climate crisis. But all wealth is not equal. Its definition must be reconciled with the right to development, which is to say that capacity must be calculated, and the climate burden shared, in a manner that takes proper account of intranational inequality.

To see this, assume that the emergency program is to be funded through a global tax on each country's capacity. Now consider an overly-simplified example in which a country's capacity is defined as its total income (GDP). Thus, a country's share of the global mitigation and adaptation burdens would be exactly equal to its share of total global income. Thus if the total 'global bill' for the emergency program is 1 percent of the total global income (the GWP), this bill would be covered if each country paid 1 percent of its national income.

But this sort of 'flat tax', when used within countries to raise domestic revenue, is almost uniformly rejected as unfair. The poor are generally seen as deserving lower tax rates because, the poorer you are, the more of your income you spend on 'necessities', and the richer you are, the more of your income you spend on 'luxuries'. So if an extra dollar in taxes has to be taken from someone, it is fairer to take it from someone who will then have to reduce their luxury consumption than from someone who would have to reduce their consumption of necessities. For this reason, tax systems are generally progressive. They typically exempt from taxation income below some specified minimum threshold. In addition, the tax rate on income above this threshold typically increases as income rises, increasing the progressivity of the overall system. But the exemption alone is enough to ensure that the distribution of the tax burden is at least somewhat progressive.

One simple way to approximate the same progressive effect in a global burden sharing system is to define national capacity as the amount by which a country's average per capita income exceeds some minimal level, and by setting this level at the development threshold, as defined above, it would explicitly reflect a right to development by ensuring that the portion of a country's GDP that fell below the development threshold would be exempt from being 'taxed' to pay for the global emergency program.

The logic here is akin to that of the southern negotiators who have, in the past, successfully argued that developing countries should be granted an exemption from any obligation to pay for climate mitigation. This argument, however, is fast losing its moral force, and for the entirely justifiably reason that it ignores the 'North within the South' – the rising consuming class in the developing world that has more in common with its brethren in the North than with the poor majorities within its own countries. In other words, by focusing on average per capita income, this traditional argument obscures income disparities within countries, which are fully as significant as income disparities between countries.

Our approach is to define capacity in a manner that accounts for income disparities within countries. To define it, that is, as individual income in excess of the development threshold, summed across all the individuals in a country, from the poorest peasant to the wealthiest tycoon. Ultimately, since this is all toward the end of a global climate agreement between nations, capacity will be defined – and the climate burden allocated – on a national basis. But the point here is that, unless capacity is calculated in a manner that accounts for intranational inequality, it will not meaningfully reflect the development status – the wealth and poverty – of nations.

## Defining Responsibility

Responsibility, of course, is the central concept behind the 'polluter pays principle'. And, like capacity, it has a strong common-sense resonance. The notion of national 'responsibility for greenhouse gas pollution' is intuitively – and correctly – understood in terms of the greenhouse gases that nations have emitted. As such, the baseline definition of responsibility must be in terms of cumulative emissions, though there are obviously complications in defining and measuring it unambiguously.

From what point should historical emissions count toward a nation's responsibility? The potential risks of global warming were first identified by Svente Arrhenius in 1896, were included in some university curricula in the 1940s, and were recognized in studies by the Johnson Administration in the US in the 1960s. It is commonplace to suggest that 'responsibility' for greenhouse pollution should start in 1990, when the first report of the IPCC made the risks widely and publicly evident, but as even this capsule history makes plain, some people, including advisers to the president of the United States, have known about the risks for a much longer time.

This issue of knowledge raises the question of intention. Initially, our nations had a *default* policy of inaction, one that arose from simple ignorance and was entirely excusable. Over time, however, this ignorance was attenuated. Dangers were mooted, but in general they were brushed aside and we shifted to a policy of active inaction, of denial disguised as 'risk management'. This policy was, of course, based on short-term and sectoral interests, and on the desire to continue emitting, profiting, and consuming as usual – until at some point it became demonstrably clear that drastic emissions cuts were inevitable. And once that shift had occurred, we were no longer innocent, but were rather making the sometimes explicit, sometime implicit, decision to accept the consequences of delayed action. We would continue to enjoy our easy ways, or – as might be argued by a neoclassical economist – we would delay the reckoning until we were more technologically advanced, and richer, and the costs of action would be lower and more bearable.

More issues arise when we try to choose an appropriate metric of responsibility. Bear in mind that we are actually concerned with two different impacts of greenhouse gas pollution – first, the exhaustion of the available 'sinks', which has radically reduced the future opportunities of others to use those sinks, and second, the harm caused by greenhouse gas pollution. We must in both cases deal with complex links between emissions and impacts, and of course multiple gases. Even if we were concerned only with $CO_2$ emissions, we could choose to measure them, alternatively, as cumulative emissions over time, as the fraction of historical emissions that remain in the atmosphere, as the fraction of realized temperature change attributable to those emissions, or as the long-term contribution to expected temperature change. There are many issues here, and some are controversial (the inclusion of $CO_2$ emissions from deforestation first among them[19]), and no doubt countries will tend to favor definitions that favor their particular interests.

The critical question, though, from a 'right to development' perspective, is: are all emissions created equal? Should we count 'survival' and 'luxury' emissions in the same way?[20] Should $CO_2$ emissions from cooking and heating or methane emissions from subsistence rice agriculture be treated the same way as $CO_2$ from jet travel or CFCs from air conditioners? We argue that they should not be, that these different types of emissions are of fundamentally different natures, and that survival emissions do not imply responsibility, whereas luxury emissions do. Recognition of this difference is critical to any burden-sharing framework designed to protect the right to development.

**Allocating Obligations**

Obligations, for their part, must be defined in a manner that combines capacity and responsibility. However this is done, the underlying principle is clear. No national obligations should arise from the economic activities of individuals at low levels of development, as reckoned in terms of either wealth or emissions. Only when people cross the development threshold and enter the consuming class should their activities affect the obligations of the nation in which they live.

As it happens, most of the consuming class lives in the industrialized countries. Given our assumption that a true emergency program may have relatively high costs, the GDRs framework thus allocates obligations to industrialized countries that significantly exceed any levels that might currently be considered 'realistic'. But it also assigns obligations to developing countries, and, even though it specifies these obligations entirely by reference to the responsibility and capacity of their wealthier citizens, this assignment clearly violates a second principle of today's climate realism, that countries cannot be asked to incur any mitigation costs as long as they are 'developing.' So we hope that we have at least shown ourselves willing to be unrealistic on both sides of the great divide.[21]

## QUANTIFYING THE GDR FRAMEWORK

At the core of the GDRs framework is the right to development, from which we seek to derive a consistent burden-sharing system that combines a measure of responsibility (historic contributions to greenhouse gas pollution) with a measure of capacity (broadly, the ability to pay for mitigation and adaptation). Crucially, these are defined in a manner that is sensitive to inequality within countries, which is to say that we treat nations as collections of economically unequal individuals. By so doing, we calculate national shares of the global mitigation and adaptation burden in a manner that, we believe, is truly consistent with the UNFCCC's broad principle of 'common but differentiated responsibilities and respective capabilities'.

**Calculating Capacity**

We define capacity as the aggregate individual income in excess of the development threshold, summed across all the individuals in a country. Figure 4.2 illustrates this calculation for three countries: India, China, and the United States.

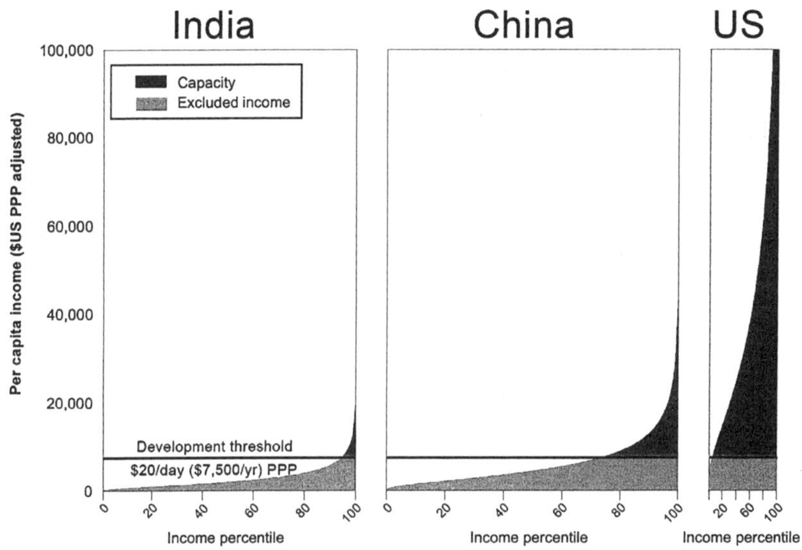


*Note:* Capacity is shown as the dark portion on each graph, using a $7,500 per capita per year (PPP-adjusted) development threshold.

*Figure 4.2 Income and capacity chart for India, China and the US*

Figure 4.2 shows the income distribution for each country, estimated on the basis of national per capita income and Gini coefficient (a measure of national income inequality). These charts array each person along the x-axis from poorest (on the left) to wealthiest (on the right), and plot their (PPP adjusted) income. The development threshold at $7,500 is shown, cutting through each country's income distribution curve and thus dividing total national income into a fraction (light portion) below the development threshold, and a fraction (dark portion) that the wealthier portion of the population earns in excess of the development threshold. This darker area thus graphically presents an quantification of each country's capacity that is approximate, but still a defensible estimate of the national income that could legitimately be 'taxed' to help shoulder the climate burden.

Consider India, shown in the left panel. By our estimate, nearly 6 percent of the Indian population earn incomes above the $7,500 development threshold. These are the members of that burgeoning 'Indian middle class' that has so captured the attention of the media. In terms of sheer numbers, they comprise a large and growing consuming class, one that is roughly the size of the population of the consuming class in, say, the United Kingdom or France. But this is where the similarity ends. For these Indian consumers have a much lower aggregate income, and the amount of India's income in excess of the $7,500 development threshold is less than one-sixth as large. Plainly, in India as in other low-income countries, total national capacity – the ability to pay for development, adaptation, or mitigation, or for that matter luxury consumption – is dwarfed by the national 'development need' – the income shortfall that would have to be filled to raise the entire population to the development threshold. Yet, just as plainly, India and other poor countries contain large (in absolute terms) middle classes and even a subclass of truly rich people (though these latter are so few as to be effectively invisible in these low-resolution charts).[22]

The center panel of the chart shows China. It has much more capacity than India, both in absolute terms and relative to its development need, but note as well that more than 70 percent of the Chinese population is still below the $7,500 threshold. Clearly, China, taken as a whole, is not a wealthy country, though at the same time its absolute capacity is rather high, and the claim that shortages of investment capital (rather than consumption choices or institutional priorities) are limiting efforts at human development (and thus that few resources are available for climate mitigation) is not very credible.

Finally, on the right, we see the US. Here, graphically, is an image of wealth. The 'development need' of the small number of people with incomes under the threshold is entirely dwarfed by the 'capacity' of the rest. This is not to say that this need is in any way irrelevant, or tangential to our concerns. Indeed, the continued existence of injustice and vulnerability within the wealthy world (think of New Orleans) is a critical political challenge to any international burden-sharing regime, in the sense that rich-world obligations must not be met at the expense of the rich-world poor. In any case, the financial capacity of Americans with incomes above the development threshold (the only income that counts towards the calculation of capacity) is extremely large, both absolutely and in relation to the national development need. A good fraction of the US population has incomes so high that they are literally 'off the charts'.

These charts largely speak for themselves, but one point, at least, should be explicit. Even though GDR framework attributes capacity to both poor and wealthy countries, its implications are quite different in these two cases. Poor countries, as befits their small capacity, have small obligations, which can be discharged entirely through domestic action. Wealthy countries will not generally have such an option, for as we will show, their obligations tend to be too great to be discharged with domestic action alone.

*Table 4.1 Characteristics of low-income, middle-income and high-income countries*

| | Low income | Middle income | High income | World |
|---|---|---|---|---|
| Income (projected 2010) ($ trillion PPP) | 6 | 25 | 38 | 69 |
| Share of global Income (percent) | 8 | 36 | 55 | 100 |
| Share of population 2005 (percent) | 38 | 47 | 15 | 100 |
| Per capita income (projected 2010) ($ thousands PPP ) | 2.2 | 7.9 | 36.9 | 10.1 |
| Capacity ($ trillion PPP) | 0.4 | 9.4 | 30.5 | 40 |
| Share of global capacity (percent) | 1.0 | 23.4 | 76 | 100 |
| Percentage of population over $7500 dev't threshold | 3.8 | 34 | 97 | 32 |

*Note:* 'Capacity' is defined by a $7,500 development threshold.

Using the method described above, Table 4.1 shows the capacity for low-, middle- and high-income countries (as per the World Bank's categories[23]), along with the share of global income, the share of global population, and the fraction of the population over the $7,500 development threshold in each group. Much can be read from this table, but note in particular that less than 4 percent of the people in poor countries and 34 percent of the people in middle-income countries have incomes over the development threshold, and that the 'capacity' of these countries (which together contain 85 percent of the global population) is only 25 percent of the global total.

## Calculating Responsibility

As noted above, there is no uniquely 'correct' or uncontroversial definition of responsibility. We suggest, however, that cumulative per capita $CO_2$

emissions from fossil fuel consumption since 1990 is a reasonable one, largely because emissions made prior to this date were usually (though not always) made in ignorance rather than by deliberate policy. One can certainly argue that an earlier start year would be appropriate, and, all else equal, an earlier start would decrease the relative responsibility of the developing countries relative to industrialized countries, which began their intensive use of fossil fuels long in the past.

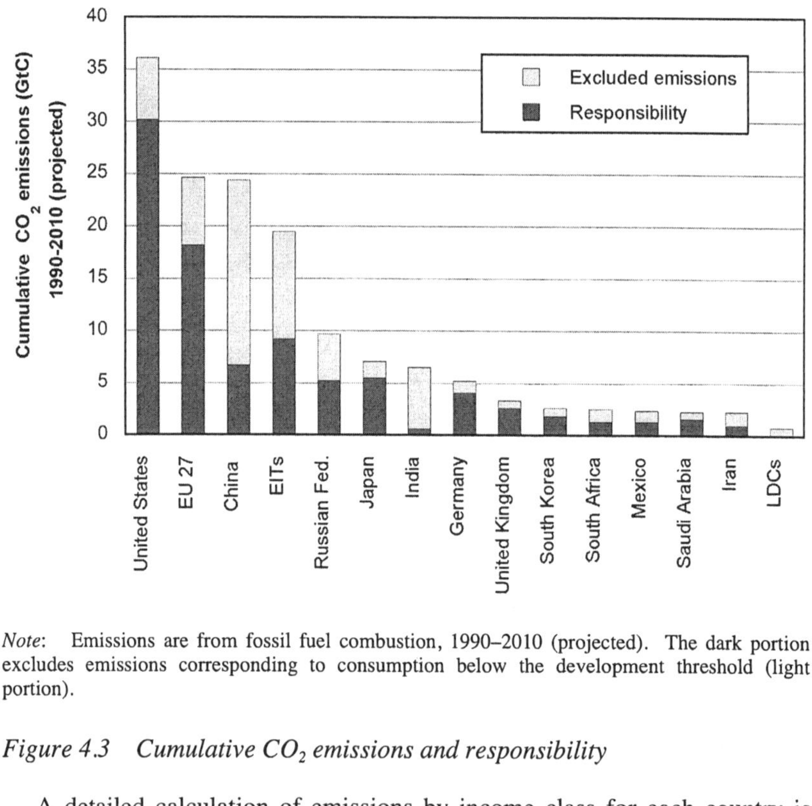


*Note*: Emissions are from fossil fuel combustion, 1990–2010 (projected). The dark portion excludes emissions corresponding to consumption below the development threshold (light portion).

*Figure 4.3 Cumulative $CO_2$ emissions and responsibility*

A detailed calculation of emissions by income class for each country is beyond the scope of our analysis, although it is possible and such analyses have indeed been done for some countries (see, for example, Metcalf (2007) for the US, Brenner et al. (2007) for China, and Ananthapadmanabhan et al. (2007) for India). For the purposes of our indicative calculation, we make the simplifying assumption that (within any given country) emissions are proportional to consumption, which is in turn proportional to income. (See appendix for data sources and calculations.) Given this, we can straightforwardly generate national responsibility graphs exactly analogous to the Figure 4.2 graphs of national capacity. To show more countries, however, we present in Figure 4.3 a condensed graph that shows a number of nations and regions, with the total height of each bar reflecting the cumulative emissions since 1990 (projected out to 2010). The light portion shows the emissions corresponding to consumption below the development threshold, and the dark portion the aggregate responsibility. (These are analogous to the light and dark portions of the graphs in Figure 4.2, except that they are not presented as full distributions across national populations.)

By this metric, responsibility is, not surprisingly, higher in wealthy countries, and effectively zero in the poorest countries (including but not limited to the UN 'Least Developed Countries'). The US, for instance, has not only very high total cumulative emissions but high responsibility as well, because a relatively small portion of its emissions are excluded as 'subsistence' emissions. This is also true for the EU15 and for other industrialized countries. China, on the other hand, and India as well, have significant emissions, but a relatively small fraction count towards their respective responsibility. Note for example that India and Germany have about the same level of emissions, though Germany's responsibility is of course much higher. Note also that the EITs (like Russia) have little responsibility relative to their total emissions, which nicely illustrates that only a framework that takes explicit account of both responsibility and capacity can appropriately account for the fact that these countries, despite being in Annex 1 and despite having high per capita emissions, are in fact poorer than many non-Annex 1 countries.

This raises the question of how capacity and responsibility should be combined into a single obligation indicator capable of meaningfully driving the allocation of the global burden. We now turn to that question.

## The Responsibility and Capacity Indicator

The purpose of this quantitative exercise is to define and calculate a single indicator that properly combines responsibility and capacity and, in so doing, allows us to assign shares of the global mitigation and adaptation burdens to individual countries. Further, this responsibility and capacity indicator (RCI) must – following our claim that the right to development adheres to individuals and not nations – reflect the distribution of income and emissions within countries. When used to calculate national obligations, it should specifically exclude the responsibilities and capacities of individuals below the development threshold.

Again, there cannot be any uniquely correct way to do this, but there are more or less reasonable possibilities.[24] Plainly, the RCI must be defined so that, among countries with the same capacities but different responsibilities, the country with greater responsibility has the greater obligation. Just as plainly, among countries with the same responsibility but different capacities, the one with the greater capacity must have the greater obligation.

There are many formulas which have this property. We use one which multiplies responsibility and capacity, in a way that allows different weights to be given to each:

$$\text{RCI} = R^a \bullet C^b$$

We specify that the exponents $a$ and $b$ sum to one, so that, as the paired weights go from $a = 1$ and $b = 0$ at one extreme to $a = 0$ and $b = 1$ at the other, the RCI goes from being exactly equal to responsibility ($R$) to being exactly equal to capacity ($C$). For our reference calculations, we set $a = 0.4$ and $b = 0.6$, which is to say that we give capacity somewhat higher weight than responsibility. This is just one of many possible choices, but we make this choice as an (admittedly ad hoc) compensation for the fact that an RCI of the above form does not actually make for a very 'progressive' tax. (In fact, relative to income, the RCI actually declines after a certain point.)

We can now estimate the joint responsibility/capacity indicator for any segment of the population. By integrating, we can then estimate the country's total RCI, and compare it with the global total to calculate each country's share. The results of this calculation for selected countries and groups of countries are shown in Table 4.2.

As Table 4.2 makes evident, by excluding the income of poor people (wherever they live), our measure of capacity for a rich country will be larger in percentage terms than its share of global income, and for a poor country will be lower. Similarly, though less transparently, a wealthy country's responsibility will be larger than its share of cumulative emissions, because less of its historical emissions will be excluded.

One notable feature of our results is that the US has the largest share of global capacity, the largest share of global responsibility, and the largest share of combined RCI. By any reasonable standard of 'common but differentiated responsibilities,' the United States would have to pay the largest share of the *global* climate 'bill'. In general, wealthy country 'bills' properly include much of the burden of accelerated decarbonization globally, and of the robust adaptation program that will be needed if we are to maintain a workable measure of international solidarity and cooperation – in addition to aggressive domestic reductions. But, thus far, the US and EU climate communities have generally failed to even raise these issues, let alone campaign on them. Obviously, this is a very serious problem.

*Table 4.2 Global percentage shares of population, income, capacity, cumulative emissions, responsibility, and RCI for selected countries and groups of countries*

| | Percentage share of Global Total | | | | | |
|---|---|---|---|---|---|---|
| | Population | Income | Capacity | Cumulative Emissions (1990–2010) | Responsibility | Obligation (RCI) |
| United States | 4.6 | 20.7 | 29.7 | 23.3 | 33.9 | 31.8 |
| EU (27) | 7.2 | 21.6 | 27.9 | 15.9 | 20.5 | 24.8 |
| United Kingdom | 0.9 | 3.1 | 4.2 | 2.1 | 2.9 | 3.7 |
| Germany | 1.2 | 4.1 | 5.6 | 3.4 | 4.6 | 5.2 |
| Sweden | 0.1 | 0.5 | 0.7 | 0.3 | 0.3 | 0.5 |
| Japan | 1.9 | 6.1 | 8.1 | 4.6 | 6.2 | 7.4 |
| Russia | 2.0 | 3.2 | 2.9 | 6.3 | 5.9 | 3.9 |
| Brazil | 2.9 | 2.8 | 2.3 | 1.4 | 1.2 | 1.8 |
| China | 19.7 | 12.5 | 5.9 | 15.7 | 7.5 | 6.6 |
| India | 17.2 | 5.2 | 0.8 | 4.2 | 0.7 | 0.8 |
| South Africa | 0.7 | 0.7 | 0.6 | 1.6 | 1.4 | 0.9 |
| LDCs | 12.5 | 1.5 | 0.1 | 0.6 | 0.0 | 0.1 |
| Annex 1 | 18.8 | 57.2 | 75.1 | 56.5 | 73.4 | 74.6 |
| Non-Annex 1 | 81.2 | 42.8 | 24.9 | 43.5 | 26.7 | 25.4 |
| All high income | 15.1 | 55.2 | 75.6 | 50.9 | 71.4 | 74.3 |
| All middle Income | 46.7 | 36.4 | 23.4 | 42.2 | 27.8 | 24.8 |
| All low Income | 38.2 | 8.5 | 1.0 | 6.9 | 0.9 | 0.9 |
| World | 100% | 100% | 100% | 100% | 100% | 100% |

**Calculating National 'Bills'**

Having calculated RCIs, we can now estimate the obligations that would fall to specific countries. How those obligations would best be apportioned within countries is, of course, a different matter, though it would be contrary to the spirit of the GDR system if, at the end of the day, the costs of climate protection were to devolve to those below the development threshold. The challenges here are great, but they are not specific to the GDR system. Any climate regime must ensure that, at a minimum, it neither worsens the overall fairness of the global economy or the overall well-being of the poor. If it does either, it is unlikely to survive.

Our first task, if we are to use our RCIs to estimate national mitigation and adaptation costs, is to generate reasonable estimates of the global costs that must be apportioned, and this despite a background of extreme uncertainty and confusion. (The UNFCCC has just reported its own estimates, which are not wildly different from those used here.[25].) The most widely cited numbers are for stabilization between 500 and 550 ppm $CO_2$-equivalent, and estimate the cost to be about 1 percent of GWP (65 trillion US dollars in 2005) annually, although exactly how this number is defined is often a bit unclear in the literature.[26] Expected costs vary with baseline levels of economic and population growth and with assumptions about the efficiency with which policies will be implemented. And of course differences in basic definitions (what counts as a cost, and to whom?) and modeling assumptions produce different calculated costs, even with the same baseline and policy assumptions (see Chapter 1 of this volume for discussion of the economics of cost assessment).

More important still is the fact that adaptation costs, properly conceived, may turn out to be as large as or even larger than mitigation costs. The burden-sharing literature rarely treats these costs seriously, but estimates in the region of $100 billion per year and higher are being reported, though there's little basis for confidence.[27] To be sure, there is little basis for confidence in the precision of such figures, as discussions about what kinds of adaptation measures are possible and desirable are just beginning, and there has yet to be any coherent proposal as to what kind and degree of adaptation would be 'adequate', or of how 'practical' proposals might be measured against such a standard. Even more importantly, discussions of adaptation have studiously avoided the highly charged issues of liability and compensation. Yet lurking behind images of fresh new seawalls are increasingly clear understandings of the disaster relief and relocation costs, and unalleviated suffering that will accompany future climate-change induced 'impacts' that are now inevitable. Considering these factors, and the impacts that will be visited on both developed and developing countries, it is hardly farfetched to imagine global adaptation and compensation costs exceeding 1 percent of GWP each year.

We will not attempt to resolve the uncertainties here, but will rather proceed by estimating national bills assuming that costs are $1 trillion. This is about 1.5 percent of Gross World Product, which is well within the range of published estimates of the cost of a global climate transition. (Since our concern is to allocate that total burden – adaptation plus mitigation costs – we do not need to parse them out separately.)

The US, with its 31.8 percent of the global RCI, would be obligated to pay $318 billion. Similarly, the EU's share would be $248 billion (24.8 percent of the global RCI). China's share would be $66 billion (6.6 percent), India's share would be $8 billion (0.8 percent), and so on, as shown in Table 4.2. The RCI, in effect, serves as the basis of a progressive global 'climate tax' – not a carbon tax, per se, but a responsibility and capacity tax.

We can make the scale of these national obligations more tangible by considering them in terms of the average annual 'tax' that they imply, as shown in Table 4.3 below.

But first note that national obligations derived from a progressive international framework such as GDR approach should, in principle, be fulfilled within nations in a similarly progressive manner. Above all, individuals below the development threshold – who contribute nothing to national capacity and responsibility and hence nothing to national obligation – should similarly pay nothing toward fulfilling that obligation. Indeed, it would contradict the underlying principles of the GDR framework to pass the national obligation down to them. Thus, the average 'tax' shown in Table 4.3 is calculated by dividing the national obligation among only that subset of the population above the $7,500/year development threshold. Of course, those just above the threshold should similarly bear a much smaller burden than those far above it, but, for simplicity's sake, Table 4.3 presents the personal 'tax' as an average obligation for those above the development threshold.

What is most useful about this analysis is that it supports the notion that equity, a virtue often dismissed as 'unrealistic' in geopolitical matters, is in fact attainable. Even if costs of a rapid climate transition are assumed to be quite high (e.g., one trillion dollars per year), and even if these costs are deemed to be the obligation of the minority of people with incomes above the development threshold (less than one-third of the global population), they would still be quite bearable. The relatively well-off can afford to shield the poor from the costs of combating climate change. They can, in other words, afford to honor a right to development.

*Table 4.3 National income, national capacity and 'taxpayer' bills.*

| | National Income (Billion $) | National Capacity (Billion $) | National Obligation (Billion $) | Population above the development threshold (%) | Average "tax" (for people above the development threshold) ($ per person) |
|---|---|---|---|---|---|
| United States | 14,298 | 11,970 | 318 | 94.7 | 1,065 |
| EU (27) | 14,920 | 11,249 | 248 | 95.5 | 525 |
| UK | 2,149 | 1,688 | 37 | 98.5 | 608 |
| Germany | 2,854 | 2,240 | 52 | 99.2 | 641 |
| Sweden | 333 | 262 | 5 | 99.9 | 555 |
| Japan | 4,227 | 3,271 | 74 | 98.8 | 587 |
| Russia | 2,184 | 1,172 | 39 | 85 | 331 |
| Brazil | 1,900 | 931 | 18 | 37 | 242 |
| China | 8,611 | 2,357 | 66 | 27 | 180 |
| India | 3,559 | 322 | 8 | 6.7 | 95 |
| South Africa | 504 | 258 | 9 | 39 | 465 |
| LDCs | 1,023 | 36 | 0.7 | 0.9 | 83 |
| Annex 1 | 39,556 | 30,265 | 746 | 89 | 650 |
| Non-Annex 1 | 29,550 | 10,024 | 254 | 19 | 245 |
| All High Income | 38,147 | 30,471 | 743 | 97 | 744 |
| All Mid. Income | 25,120 | 9,432 | 248 | 15 | 505 |
| All Low Income | 5,839 | 387 | 9 | 3.8 | 91 |
| World | 69,106 | 40,289 | 1000 | 32 | 458 |

*Note:* The UK, Germany, and Sweden are included in the EU27 figures, and also shown separately. (All figures are based on projections to 2010 in 2005 US dollars, PPP-adjusted)

In response to the obvious objection that these levels of 'climate taxation' are not 'realistic' it is useful to consider what they might appropriately be compared to. Military budgets in particular invite comparison. For example the US military budget, depending on what is included in its definition, is not less than $500 billion a year and, if estimated in a reasonable fashion, considerably more, as much as a third of the total US Federal budget.[28] All other military budgets are smaller, but they still outweigh the climate costs assumed above. The UK's official military budget, for example, is about $51 billion a year, while China's is estimated at $188 billion and India's at $114 billion (all these figures are PPP). These are all conservatively estimated figures, and it is interesting to note that the military expenditures of the top 15 spenders amounts to just over 2 percent of GWP (PPP adjusted).[29] Given this, it is fair to say that an emergency program would entail a 'Keynesian' effort of about the same size as the global military enterprise, though one that, obviously, follows a radically different storyline.

Finally, it is important to put these figures in the context of continuing global economic growth. As Azar and Schneider[30] among others have pointed out, even costs that seem very large – 2 percent of GWP, for example, is well over a trillion dollars – imply a very small delay in the rate at which people become richer. In a developed country growing at 2 percent a year, a two percent national bill would only mean that the year by which today's per capita incomes would have doubled will be delayed from 2042 to 2043. And in a poor country growing at 5 percent annually, a 2 percent national bill would amount to less than a six-month delay in reaching such a milestone, from late 2022 to early 2023.

## A GLOBAL ALLOCATION SYSTEM

So far we have said little about implementation of a global emergency program. In this section, we explore one option: the implementation of the mitigation side of a GDRs system within an international 'cap and allocate' trading system.[31]

The mitigation side of any global climate agreement is virtually guaranteed to involve market mechanisms, particularly in the critical years just ahead.[32] This is so despite the fact that carbon trading systems have had a rather inauspicious beginning. They have, in particular, shown themselves prone to capture by corporations and private traders, and this has in turn legitimated the fear, now extremely widespread, that any global emissions trading system will function as a device by which wealthy countries, corporations, and individuals can 'buy their way out' of inconvenient emissions limitations. Still, such mechanisms have tremendous momentum and a large constituency – including carbon-intensive corporations, CDM project developers and hosts, the World Bank's Carbon Finance Unit, allowance-starved Annex 1 countries and finance-starved developing countries – that fully intend to move quickly into a next and grander phase of carbon trading (see Chapter 11 of this volume). In this context, it seems important to examine a global cap and allocate system which could, if well designed and effectively regulated, help to support an emergency climate program. It could make it possible to achieve reductions more cost-effectively by carrying them out wherever they were least expensive. But most importantly, a workable cap-and-allocate system would make it possible to establish national mitigation obligations without regard to the volume of reductions that are physically (and economically) available within any given country. Trading, in other words, offers a way to implement a global burden sharing system in which countries with high capacity and responsibility are obligated to carry out strenuous reductions at home and also to help pay for decarbonization in poorer countries.

**Cap and Allocate (and Trade)**

How then would we use the GDRs Responsibility and Capacity Indicator to distribute permits under a cap-and-allocate system? The means is fairly straightforward, and requires only three steps:

First, it is necessary to estimate the global mitigation requirement. This is the difference between a global reference trajectory (constructed as a bottom-up aggregation of national reference trajectories) and the 2°C emergency pathway. Graphically, the 'gap' or 'wedge' between these two curves reflects the amount of mitigation work that needs to be done globally.

Second, this global mitigation requirement is allocated among countries as per the GDR burden-sharing framework. That is, it is divided into *national mitigation obligations* where each country – however rich or poor it may be – is allocated a portion of the global mitigation requirement, in proportion to its aggregate national RCI.

Third, each country is assigned a *national emission allocation* equal to its national reference trajectory minus its national mitigation obligation. This determines each country's share of the (rapidly declining) global emissions budget, and makes it possible to assign each country an appropriate allotment of permits allocation (equal to its national emission allocation).

In Figure 4.4, we show a global 'Business as Usual' trajectory, which extrapolates the historical approach to energy conservation, renewables, fossil fuel subsidies, pollution controls, etc.[33] Below it (the lower border of the top wedge) is a so-called 'No Regrets' trajectory, a projection of the global emissions pathway as it would be if many negative- and zero-cost emissions reductions were successfully captured.[34] The top wedge, in other words, represents free and profitable reductions, which are large, though not by any means large enough to bring emissions, all the way down to the global emergency 2°C trajectory (shown by the bottom of the second wedge).

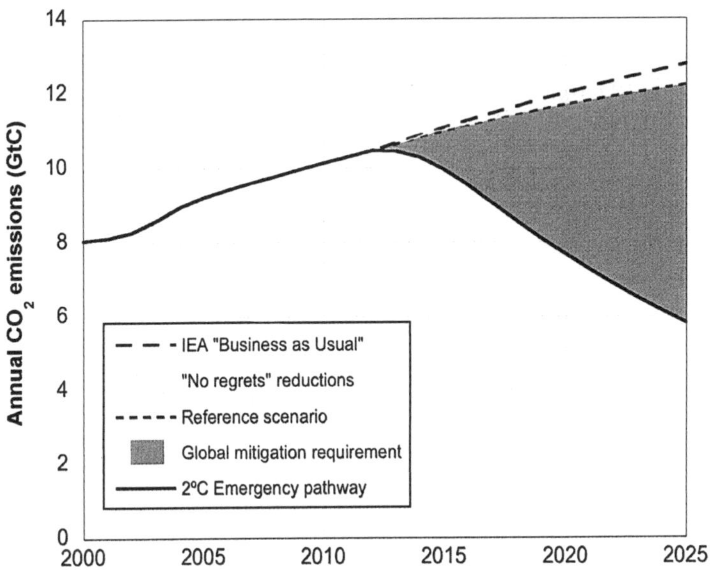


*Note:* The global mitigation requirement (dark wedge) is shown by the difference between the 'no regrets' trajectory and the 2°C 'emergency pathway'.

*Figure 4.4 Global mitigation requirement*

From the perspective of a global burden-sharing framework, these 'no-regrets' reductions should be treated differently from positive-cost options. Because countries can in principle exploit these opportunities to their benefit, one might argue that all nations should be responsible for capturing their own no-regrets reductions, and that only further reductions – those that actually have positive costs – should be considered part of the global mitigation requirement to be allocated among nations within the broader burden-sharing framework. However, in practice, one cannot ignore the barriers preventing countries from achieving all their no-regrets reductions. These barriers are broad and high, and encompass structural, institutional, technological – and even financial – obstacles to otherwise cost-effective options. And while some no-regrets options might face barriers that can be overcome domestically, for example through institutional changes and policy reform, others face barriers that might well be insurmountable without external assistance such as concessionary financing and technological cooperation.

Recognizing these two fundamentally different cases, the GDR framework obliges developing countries to only achieve the more accessible fraction of their no-regrets options, and folds the remainder into the global burden-sharing arrangement. The precise fraction of any country's no-regrets opportunities that might plausibly be achieved through domestic efforts will have to be determined on a country-by-country basis, in a manner that reflects differing national circumstances. For the purposes of our indicative analysis, we crudely estimate that the more accessible no-regrets opportunities amount to 50 percent of the total for non-Annex 1 countries. These are included in their national reference trajectories, and the remainder are added to the global mitigation requirement. (For Annex 1 countries, 100 percent of the estimated no-regrets opportunities are included in the national reference trajectories.) This apportioning of the no-regrets opportunities is reflected in Figure 4.4.

Taking this 'no regrets' definition of the reference trajectory, Figure 4.4 shows the global mitigation requirement associated with the emergency program as the second (darker) wedge. Its width, growing through time, reflects the additional annual emissions reductions required to hold the 2°C line, relative to a world in which countries diligently work to capture the benefits of many no-regrets opportunities. Given our reference projection and our emergency pathway, the global mitigation burden rises to 19 $GtCO_2$-eq of emissions reductions by 2020. This burden is then allocated to each nation in proportion to its share of the global RCI, as shown in Table 4.3 above.

The global mitigation burden is shown further divided into national wedges in Figure 4.5. These wedges are analogous to the technology-based wedges defined by Pacala and Socolow (2004), but instead of showing technologies and the gigatons of reductions that they are projected to deliver, they show countries and the gigatons of reductions they're obligated to pay for. Accordingly, the US's reduction obligation amounts to approximately 32 percent of the mitigation gap (the large striped wedge); the EU's is 25 percent (the slightly smaller solid dark wedge); China just under 7 percent (the dotted wedge); and India less than 1 percent (thin light dark, barely visible). So, for example, the US mitigation obligation is 32 percent of the 19 $GtCO_2$-eq global mitigation requirement in 2020, or about 6 $GtCO_2$-eq.

This gives us the big picture, in a way that set us up to talk, usefully and quantitatively, about individual national situations. For example, we can 'zoom in' on a country to look at its mitigation obligation wedge – its share of the necessary global reductions – and compare this wedge to its national reference trajectory. We can also examine the relationship between a country's plausible rates of domestic emissions reductions and the scale of its total mitigation obligation, and thus specify the international reduction it would need to somehow fund to fulfill its obligations. Depending on the relationship between its reference trajectory and its mitigation obligation, a country might have: (1) an allocation allowing some emissions growth over time; (2) an allocation requiring a rate of emission reductions that can easily be met domestically; or (3) an allocation requiring substantial domestic reductions *as well as* the financing of further reductions abroad. We will show examples illustrating the first and last of these cases.

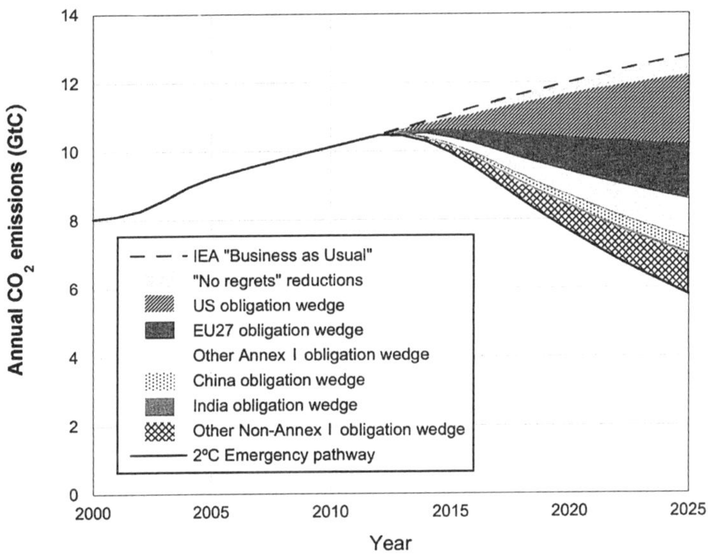


*Note:* The wedges, which reflect national/regional shares of RCI, are labelled in the legend from top to bottom. India's wedge, at roughly 1 percent, is essentially a line.

*Figure 4.5 Total global mitigation requirement, divided into 'reduction obligation wedges'*

## The Example of the United States

In Figure 4.6 we show such a calculation for the United States. The highest line represents the 'Business as Usual' case for the US, while the bottom of the upper wedge indicates a reference trajectory that assumes all 'no-regrets' reductions have been captured. If the US reduction obligation were interpreted literally and achieved entirely through domestic mitigation, it would imply reductions of nearly 140 percent below 1990 levels by 2025, and a US emission level of minus 2 $GtCO_2$-eq by 2025. Obviously, for a mitigation obligation of this magnitude to make sense, the US must not be expected to meet its entire obligation through domestic reductions. Whatever is not accomplished domestically, the US would need to fulfill internationally, by way of supporting reductions in other countries. Figure 4.6 depicts this.

The middle wedge represents an ambitious domestic reduction trajectory that reduces national emissions more than 40 percent below 1990 levels in 2025, and puts the US on course toward emissions 90 percent below 1990 levels in 2050. This mitigation trajectory is more ambitious than even the strictest of the bills now in play in the US Congress: the House of Representative's *Safe Climate Act* and the Senate's *Global Warming Pollution Reduction Act.* Still, even these rapid reductions would satisfy less than half of the US's total obligation. The remainder would have to be met by funding additional international reductions. These are shown with the bottom (hatched) wedge.

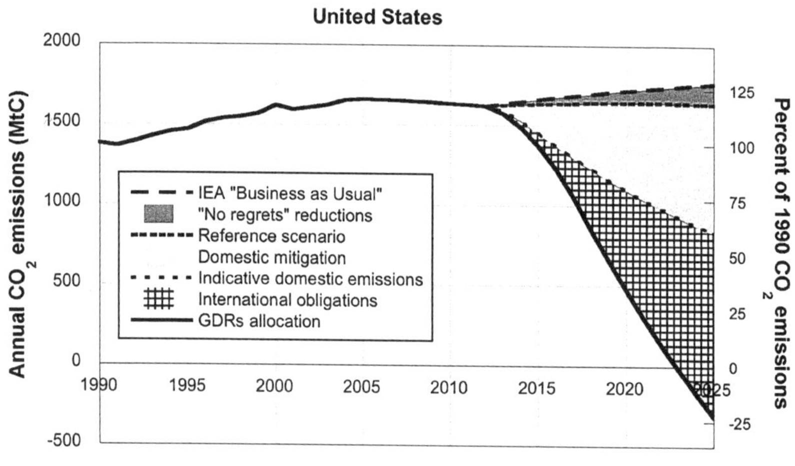


*Figure 4.6 US allocation under GDRs reference case*

A greater rate of domestic reductions would of course reduce the US's need to purchase offshore reductions. And, conversely, the US could, at least in theory, refuse to make any reductions domestically, and to choose instead to purchase all its required reductions internationally. This latter approach, however, would be implausible, or irrational, or both, given that domestic reduction opportunities would accumulate unused while the national expenditure on internationally purchased reductions grew more and more taxing. Still, the possibility is worth considering, for it raises the specter that the US – or any other wealthy nation – could 'buy its way out' of the need to make inconvenient domestic accommodations to the climate crisis. Such a choice would be both ethically problematic and politically dangerous.

What this scenario illustrates – and indeed doing so is a major point of this entire exercise – is that even very steep domestic emissions reductions would only discharge a fraction of the mitigation obligations that, under a reasonable calculation of national responsibility and capacity, would properly fall upon the wealthy countries. This, again, is striking but not surprising. The underlying premise of the Greenhouse Development Rights framework is that the right to development must be safeguarded, and that doing so requires the world's wealthier population to both free up sufficient space for the poorer nations and also support their rapid transition to low-carbon economies. The need for the US to make steep domestic reductions and still pay for major reductions internationally is merely the logical outcome of this foundational premise.

## The Example of China

The complement to the situation illustrated above is the one in the developing world, where mitigation obligations are smaller than the reductions that would be needed to maintain the emergency 2°C trajectory. This situation is well illustrated by the case of China (Figure 4.7).

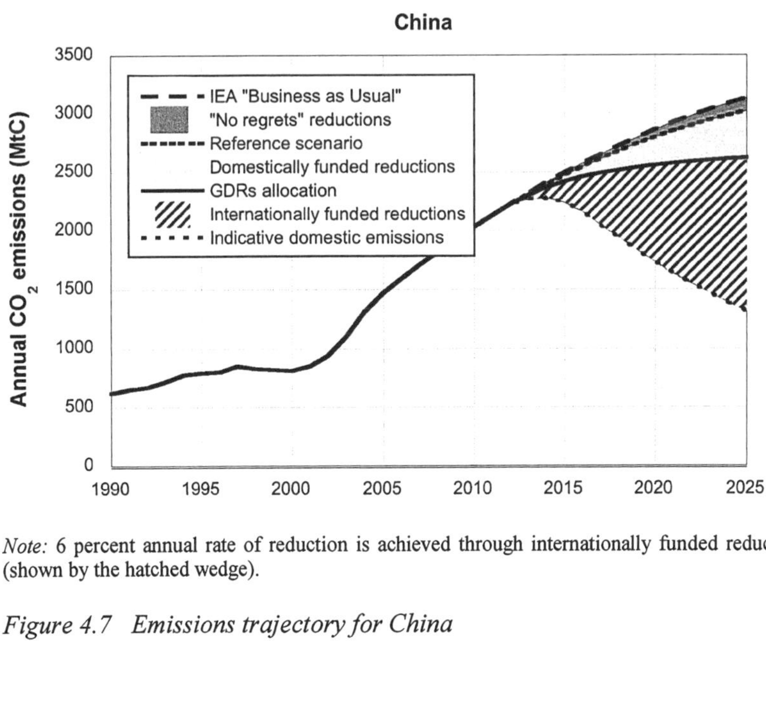


*Note:* 6 percent annual rate of reduction is achieved through internationally funded reductions (shown by the hatched wedge).

*Figure 4.7 Emissions trajectory for China*

In Figure 4.7 we show the results for China, where the highest line represents the 'Business as Usual' case,[35] the upper wedge represents a portion of no-regrets reductions captured by China, and the lower border of that no-regrets wedge is China's reference scenario. Note that China's mitigation obligation (middle wedge), calculated as it is on the basis of China's RCI, is still not particularly large.[36] In particular, it does not come close to making China's emissions consistent with a 2°C emergency pathway. What this requires is substantial additional emissions reductions (the striped wedge) that are made within China, but financed by wealthy countries whose obligations exceed their domestic mitigation potential. These reductions are absolutely necessary, for China's emissions are large, and making full use of its mitigation potential is essential if we are to keep within the emergency 2°C trajectory. Fortunately, under the GDRs framework, there is a strong incentive for China to reduce beyond its national obligation by, in effect, selling mitigation potential to wealthier countries like the US that need it to fulfill their mitigation obligations. Or, to put it another way, in a cap and allocate system, China would in principle be able to sell reductions at an international price that is greater than its marginal cost, and by so doing earn the revenue needed to finance its own required reductions, at least partially and perhaps wholly.

## CONCLUSION

It is time now to act in good faith. Many years have passed since ignorance of the climate problem could honestly be cited as an excuse for inaction. The climate problem is now a climate crisis, and it is time – past time really – to admit it. Prudence no longer means modest, measured and gradual action. Indeed, the only prudent course left to us is an emergency climate stabilization program – one that begins immediately and takes in the whole world.

It is also time to stop pretending that the climate crisis can be solved on its own, and that the development crisis is another matter. Only a regime that structurally encompasses the right to development has any real hope of catalyzing the necessary emergency program. And hard though it may be to admit it, recognizing the right to development inevitably means taking account of inequality within nations as well as inequality between them.

The way out of this problem, as we have argued, is to recognize that the right to development adheres not to nations, but to people, and that the wealthy – whether they happen to live in Washington, or Shanghai, or New Delhi – have no further claim to it at all. The alternative to this realization, and to its operationalization within a global climate regime, is to sit helplessly by as our endless negotiations, designed for a world of idealized and monolithic nations, come finally to failure, delegitimation, and despair.

This is not to claim that the climate regime can solve all the problems of the world. Inequality preceded the climate crisis, and there is little doubt that it will survive past the coming peak in global greenhouse gas emissions. But in a world as bitterly divided as ours, a viable climate regime must at least do no harm, and this means that it must not erect further barriers to the progress of the poor. The key virtue of the Greenhouse Development Rights approach is that it does not do so; indeed it is because it does not that we can claim that the GDR approach is in fact realistic. And if the cost of meeting this condition is that, in the end, both mitigation and adaptation must be financed via a (fairly modest) tax on the luxury consumption of the relatively wealthy – for this is, finally, what GDRs proposes – well what is this but realism about our actual conditions of life on this shared, finite planet?

In the meanwhile, no one should confuse the expediency of the currently possible with the realism demanded by a true emergency program. If we manage to avoid a global climate catastrophe, it is not going to be by much. And the sooner the architecture of the climate regime is aligned to the real structure of the problem the better our chances are going to be.

# NOTES

1. Greenhouse Development Rights has been long in the making, and there are many to thank, including Steve Bernow (now deceased), Andrew Pendleton at Christian Aid, Jörg Haas at the Heinrich Böll Foundation, Simon Rettallack of the UK's Institute for Public Policy Research, Eric Kemp-Benedict of the Stockholm Environment Institute, John Gershman at the Wagner School of Public Policy, Kate Raworth from the Oxfam International Research Department, Matthew Lockwood of the UK's Institute for Public Policy Research, Simon Rettallack of the UK's Institute for Public Policy Research, and Charlie Kronick from UK Greenpeace. We also acknowledge the support of the Stockholm Environment Institute and the Climate Policy Research Program (CLIPORE) of Mistra, the Foundation for Strategic Environmental Research. We also want to acknowledge the climate movement itself, the Climate Action Network in particular, without which we probably wouldn't even have been able to conceive of this effort, and Friends of the Earth International, for its diffuse but indispensable solidarity. The Greenhouse Development Rights framework is more completely documented in Baer et al. (2007).
2. By 'aggressive realist scenarios' we mean for example the recommendations of the Scientific Expert Group (2007) or the Stern Review (2006), both of which put 450 ppm $CO_2$-equivalent as their lowest recommended stabilization target. Yet both acknowledge (following for example Meinshausen, 2006) that 450 ppm $CO_2$-equivalent has at best even odds of keeping below 2°C warming, and something like a 20 percent likelihood of exceeding 3°C warming. And as James Hansen and colleagues (2006, 2007) among others have warned, the destabilization of the Greenland Ice Sheet is possible even before global mean warming reaches the 2°C level, potentially causing up to seven meters of sea level rise, over centuries or, perhaps, much more quickly.
3. See Meinshausen (2006) or Baer and Mastrandrea (2006).
4. As we discuss later, even if Annex 1 countries reached 80 percent below 1990 levels by 2050 through exclusively *domestic* reductions and, at the same time, non-Annex 1

emissions converged to equal them (in per capita terms), global emissions would still be inconsistent with a high likelihood of staying below 2°C. Worse, in most 'realist' proposals, steep Annex 1 reductions are not assumed to be exclusively domestic, but rather to be met, in large part, with purchased offsets.

5. This must be done, of course, even as the impacts of the now inevitable warming intensify the development burden and undercut efforts to alleviate poverty. The disproportionate impact of climate change on poor people and developing countries due to both specific climatic impacts and greater vulnerability is well documented in the report of Working Group II of the IPCC's Fourth Assessment Report. A more political view of the topic, and in particular its likely impacts on development progress and poverty alleviation, can be found in, for example, 'Up In Smoke' (Simms et al., 2004) from the New Economics Foundation (www.neweconomics.org).
6. See for example, Barclays Capital's 'Equity Gilt Study 2007', which argues for the optimistic case with these words: 'If ever the time were ripe for such an energy revolution, it is now. And like all historical adoptions of general purpose technologies, the process should prove immensely stimulative to economic growth. Oddly, the climate change policy debate is couched in terms of the cost to GDP growth. Even the proponents of policy shifts tend to assume a negative effect on growth. This stance is underselling the actual impact of an energy revolution. All of the historical changes in energy supply – from dung to wood to coal to oil – were stimulative for the economy concerned. Every major technological change was accompanied or followed by faster economic growth'. We accept this argument, but believe that it tells far less than the whole story.
7. The UNFCCC famously notes in its preamble that 'the global nature of climate change calls for the widest possible cooperation by all countries and their participation in an effective and appropriate international response, in accordance with their common but differentiated responsibilities and respective capabilities and their social and economic conditions'.
8. This trajectory falls within the 'Category I' range of scenarios considered by the IPCC (IPCC, 2007a; Table 3.5, p. 198).
9. These calculations are based on the model used in Baer and Mastrandrea (2006), cited in Note 2. Because the probability distributions for key parameters such as the climate sensitivity and the behavior of the carbon cycle are not well defined, the probabilistic methodology takes as an input subjective expert opinion about the uncertainty of various parameters. This method accounts for the fact that a range of reasonable assumptions can be made about key parameters by reporting the calculated risk as a range (in which the upper and lower bounds reflect the spread in the scientific opinion). For a discussion of the issues and the model used in these calculations, see the appendix of Baer et al. (2007) or Baer and Mastrandrea (2006).
10. See IPCC (2007b; Box TS.1, p. 23), the IPCC's glossary of probabilistic terms.
11. Perhaps there are even more radical trajectories, in which global emissions actually go negative. These might be possible with 'negative emission' mitigation options, such as biomass-based power coupled with carbon capture and sequestration (Azar et al., 2006), which extract carbon dioxide from the atmosphere. (Coal-based power coupled with sequestration could be close to zero emission, but not negative.) This could open the door to trajectories with higher probabilities of preserving the 2°C line than the most stringent of our emergency trajectories. In theory, it could also open the door to trajectories that slightly delay the necessary emissions peak. In practice, however, such trajectories would require us to bank on debatable assumptions: that we would eventually find these unproven technologies to be feasible, that we would implement them at a sufficiently large scale to reverse our earlier delay, that we would deploy them rapidly enough to avoid a climate catastrophe in the meantime.
12. See Matthews and Caldeira (2008) and Hansen et al. (2008).
13. See, for example, World Bank (2000), UNDP (2002), and UNDP (2005).
14. This is not to imply that poor people are responsible for all or even most land clearing, as opposed to national or international elites; only that land-use emissions must be dramatically reduced, whatever their purpose.

15. All dollar figures in this chapter are given using 2005 US dollars, converted on a purchasing power parity (PPP) basis.
16. Pritchett (2003, 2006) concluded that the use of this line 'is justifiable, more consistent with international fairness, and is a better foundation for the World Bank's organizational mission of poverty reduction' and that 'If the poverty line were defined as the level of income at which people typically achieve acceptable levels of the Millennium Development Goal indicators (such as universal primary school completion), it would be set at about [$16] a day'. Note, this figure is calculated on a purchasing power parity (PPP) adjusted basis, and therefore converts to an appropriately lower income level in a local developing country currency than if converted at market exchange rates. It represents the purchasing power of $16 per day in the US, which is not very much. In terms of energy use, food consumption, medical care, and so forth, it goes only slightly beyond bare necessities. Indeed, in the industrialized countries, persons earning this amount or less not only are typically exempted from income taxes, but are eligible for subsidies of various sorts from the national treasury. Different development thresholds are explored via a sensitivity analysis in Baer et al. (2007).
17. Bill Gates was still listed as the world's richest man in the March 2007 Forbes list of billionaires. However, that title is now held by telecom tycoon Carlos Slim. A Mexican, Slim is a citizen of a country that is not even in the top fifty in terms of per capita national income. ('Mexican tycoon overtakes Bill Gates as world's richest man', by Fiona Walsh, London Guardian, 3 July, 2007).
18. A Brazilian proposal famously allocated obligations, albeit only within Annex I, on the basis of responsibility for global temperature change.
19. Plainly deforestation causes a large fraction of the emissions from tropical countries today. Yet most northern countries were largely deforested centuries ago for the same reasons – for timber, fuel-wood, and agriculture. By one calculation that we have done, per capita emissions from land use change in the US reached 10 tons of carbon (not $CO_2$!) per capita in the mid-19th century. But these forests are now regrowing, perhaps fertilized by increased $CO_2$ concentrations, and even being claimed as carbon-sinks. Clearly a fair treatment of land-use emissions will require consideration of these issues.
20. This distinction between luxury and subsistence emissions has been popularized by Agarwal and Narain (1991); see also Agarwal et al. (1999) of India's Centre for Science and the Environment, and by the philosopher Henry Shue (1993)
21. Benito Müller (2002) also treads this ground
22. Note that the fact that the chart appears to reach a maximum income level at about $20,000 does not mean that there are not people in India with higher incomes. It is rather that the average income of the highest one percent is still fairly low.
23. The World Bank defines countries by income class using per capita income in market exchange rate, not purchasing power parity, terms. The official classes (in 2005 dollars) are low income (below $875), lower-middle ($876–$3465), upper-middle ($3,466–$10,725), and high (over $10,725). We combine lower-middle and upper-middle income groups. In PPP terms, the borders are on the order of $2000, $7000, and $15000. For a list of countries, see the Appendix of Baer et al.(2007).
24. For an approach that is similar to ours in spirit, but significantly different in details, see Oxfam (2007).
25. The UNFCCC secretariat's background paper (UNFCCC Secretariat, 2007) argues that that 'global additional investment and financial flows of USD 200–210 billion will be necessary in 2030 to return GHG emissions to current levels', and that this amount 'is large compared with the funding currently available under the Convention and its Kyoto Protocol, but small in relation to estimated global gross domestic product (GDP) (0.3–0.5 percent) and global investment (1.1–1.7 percent) in 2030'.
26. Some models simply calculate the reduction in GWP versus a presumed baseline GWP in (say) 2050; others estimate a marginal and average cost of emissions reductions and a total amount of reductions to calculate a total cost.

27. The global adaptation need will be even more challenging to calculate than a global mitigation shortfall, for the scope of adaptations reflect choices that are fundamentally social and not economic in nature. But this challenge is by no means unique to the GDRs approach. Any approach that takes the notion of 'polluter pays' seriously requires a cost assessment. To a first order, this assessment can be envisioned as an evolution and generalization of the process that is already underway to develop National Adaptation Plans of Action. See also section 5 of UNFCCC Secretariat (2007).
28. See for example 'Bush's New Defense Budget', by Robert Higgs, 14 February, 2005: Posted at www.independent.org/newsroom/article.asp?id=1464
29. GWP is $46 trillion and military expenditures are $1.2 trillion in 2006 (or approximately 2.5 percent). See: www.sipri.org/contents/milap/milex/mex_trends.html and en.wikipedia.org/wiki/World _ecomomy
30. Christian Azar and Steve Schneider (2002) among others have pointed out that in a world of continuing economic growth at 2 or 3 percent annually, even a 5 percent decrease in GWP in 2050 implies only a delay of two years or so in becoming twice as wealthy. Presumably, most people, if asked whether they would go without raises for two years in order to preserve the planet for their grandchildren, would not hesitate.
31. The term 'cap and allocate' is shorthand for 'cap and allocate and trade', and refers to any principle-based allocation of tradable allowances to countries, under a global cap. It is distinct from the (all too familiar) 'cap and grandfather' systems, and there are many, that continue patterns of historical inequity by formalizing rights to something (close to) historical emissions (for example, phase 1 of the EU's ETS).
32. Adaptation is, at its core, a problem of resilience and adaptive capacity, and thus a development challenge that cannot plausibly be addressed by market-based institutions. So while modeling the mitigation side of a global climate regime makes good sense, and while market institutions are certain to play a role in the mitigation regime, adaptation investments must, for fundamental reasons, be implemented through democratically controlled funds that rely heavily on the involvement of civil society.
33. Based on the 2007 World Energy Outlook of the International Energy Agency (2007).
34. This is estimated from the global mitigation potential data compiled by McKinsey and Company (Enkvist et al., 2007) and IPCC (2007a, Table TS. 15).
35. The size of China's no-regrets wedge is drawn from the same sources as the global curves.
36. Note that China's reduction obligation for the whole 2011–2025 period is proportional to its share of global RCI based on 2010 figures. If its RCI were recalculated in an intermediate year its share would presumably be somewhat larger.

# REFERENCES

Agarwal, A. and S. Narain (1991), *Global Warming in an Unequal World: A Case of Environmental Colonialism*, New Delhi, Centre for Science and Environment.

Agarwal, A., Narain, S., and A. Sharma (eds) (1999), *Green Politics: Global Environmental Negotiations 1*, New Delhi: Centre for Science and the Environment.

Ananthapadmanabhan, G., K. Srinivas and V. Gopal (2007), *Hiding Behind the Poor*, New Delhi: Greenpeace India.

Azar, C. and S.H. Schneider (2002), 'Are the economic costs of stabilising the atmosphere prohibitive?', *Ecological Economics*, **42** (1–2): 73–80.

Azar, C., K. Lindgren, E Larson,and K. Mollersten (2006), 'Carbon capture and storage from fossil fuels and biomass – Costs and potential role in stabilizing the atmosphere', *Climatic Change*, **74** (1–3): 47–79.

Baer, P., T. Athanasiou and S. Kartha, (2007) 'The Right to Development in a Climate Constrained World: The Greenhouse Development Rights Framework' available online at http://www.ecoequity.org/GDRs.

Baer, P. and M. Mastrandrea (2006), 'High Stakes: Designing emissions pathways to reduce the risk of dangerous climate change', London: Institute for Public Policy Research, http://www.ippr.org.

Barclays Capital (2007), *Equity Gilt Study 2007*, London: Barclays Bank.

Brenner, M., M. Riddle and J.K. Boyce (2007), 'A Chinese sky trust? Distributional impacts of carbon charges and revenue recycling in China', *Energy Policy*, 35 (3), 1771–1784.

Enkvist, Per-Anders, Tomas Nauclér and Jerker Rosander (2007) 'A cost-curve for greenhouse gas reduction.' *The McKinsey Quarterly,* 2007(1): 35–45.

Hansen, J., R. Ruedy, M. Sato et al. (2007), 'Dangerous human-made interference with climate: a GISS modelE study', *Atmospheric Chemistry And Physics*, **7** (9): 2287–2312.

Hansen, J., R. Ruedy, M. Sato et al. (2006), 'Global temperature change', *Proceedings of The National Academy of Sciences of the United States of America*, **103** (39): 14288–14293.

Hansen, J., M. Sato, P. Kharecha, D. Beerling, R. Berner, V. Masson-Delmotte, M. Pagani, M. Raymo, D.L. Royer and J.C. Zachos (2008), 'Target Atmospheric $CO_2$: Where Should Humanity Aim?' *Open Atmospheric Science Journal* (arXiv:0804.1135v2 [physics.ao-ph]).

International Energy Agency (2007), *World Energy Outlook 2007*, Paris: OECD/IEA.

IPCC (2007a), *Climate Change 2007: Mitigation*, Contribution of Working Group III to the Fourth Assessment Report of the Intergovernmental Panel on Climate Change [B. Metz, O.R. Davidson, P.R. Bosch, R. Dave, L.A. Meyer (eds)], (TRS?) Cambridge University Press: Cambridge, UK and New York, NY, USA.

IPCC (2007b), *Climate Change 2007: Synthesis Report* Contribution of Working Groups I, II and III to the Fourth Assessment Report of the Intergovernmental Panel on Climate Change [Core Writing Team, R.K Pachauri, and A Reisinger, (eds)], IPCC: Geneva, Switzerland.

Johnson, Jo (2007), 'Worlds collide in India over global warming', *Financial Times*, June 7.

Matthews, H.D. and K. Caldeira (2008), 'Stabilizing climate requires near-zero emissions', *Geophysical Research Letters*, 35, L04705.

Meinshausen, Malte (2006), 'On the Risk of Overshooting 2°C', in H.J. Schellnhuber, W. Cramer, N. Nakicenovic, T. Wigley and G. Yohe (eds), *Avoiding Dangerous Climate Change*, Cambridge, UK: Cambridge University Press.

Metcalf, G. (2007), 'A Proposal for a U.S. Carbon Tax Swap: An Equitable Tax Reform to Address Global Climate Change', Discussion Paper 2007-12, The Hamilton Project, Brookings Institution.

Müller, B. (2002), 'Equity in Climate Change: The Great Divide', Oxford Institute for Energy Studies, EV 31.

Oxfam Briefing Paper 104 (2007), 'Adapting to climate change: What's needed in poor countries, and who should pay', http://publications.oxfam.org.uk//

Pacala, S. and R. Socolow (2004), 'Stabilization wedges: solving the climate problem for the next 50 years with current technologies', *Science*, **305**: 968–972.

Pritchett, Lant (2003), 'Who is not poor? Proposing a higher international standard for poverty', *The Center for Global Development*, **21** (1): 1–23, http://www.cgdev.org/content/publications/ detail/2758.

Pritchett, Lant (2006), 'Who is Not Poor? Dreaming of a World Truly Free of Poverty', The World Bank Research Observer, Working Paper Number 33. http://wbro.oxfordjournals.org/cgi/ reprint/lkj002?ijkey=nfo6au5gH8Lhprd&keytype=ref.

Scientific Expert Group on Climate Change (2007), 'Confronting Climate Change: Avoiding the Unmanageable, Managing the Unavoidable', Research Triangle Park, Sigma Xi and the United Nations Foundation.

Shue, H. (1993), 'Subsistence emissions and luxury emissions', *Law and Policy*, **15** (1): 39–59.

Simms, A., J. Magrath and H. Reid (2004), 'Up in Smoke', New Economics Foundation, London, http:// www.neweconomics.org/gen/z_sys_publicationdetail.aspx?pid=196.

Stern, Nicholas (2006), *The Stern Review: The Economics of Climate Change*, London: HM Treasury, http://www.hmtreasury.gov.uk/independent_reviews/stern_review_economics_climate_change/sternreview_index.cfm.

UNDP (2002), *Energy for Sustainable Development: A Policy Agenda* New York: UNDP/Bureau for Development Policy.

UNDP (2005), *Achieving the MDGs: The Role of Energy Services*, UNDP, New York: UNDP.

UNFCCC Secretariat (2007), 'Analysis of existing and planned investment and financial flows relevant to the development of effective and appropriate international response to climate change', http://unfccc.int/files/cooperation and_support/financial_mechanism/application/pdf/background_paper.pdf.

World Bank (2000), *Energy and Development Report 2000: Energy Services for the World's Poor*, Energy Sector Management Assistance Program, The World Bank.

# PART II

# Macroeconomic Theory Perspectives

# 5. The Economic Fundamentals of Global Warming

**Duncan K. Foley**[1]

---

Human productive activities have significant effects on the global environment. The depletion of the ozone layer by the release of chlorofluorocarbons employed in refrigeration and propellant devices and the threat of global warming as a result of the accumulation of 'greenhouse gases', carbon dioxide and methane, released in agriculture, energy generation, and transportation, are two leading examples. The emergence of these historically unprecedented impacts of human productive activity on a global scale creates an inescapable challenge to economic policy. Policies to foster economic growth, equity, trade, and technological change also have substantial impact on the unfolding of the global environmental scenario, which must therefore be taken into account in evaluating these policies. Even 'doing nothing' once the impacts of economic production on the global environment has been recognized amounts to a policy choice.[2]

The broad framework of economic policy evaluation methods evolved over 150 years of the development of economic thought can inform these policy choices, but public and scholarly discussion of global warming often fails to apply these methods consistently. One deleterious consequence of the failure to analyze the economics of global warming correctly is the widespread, but erroneous, belief that policies to reduce greenhouse gas emission will impose a cost on the current generation, which must be weighed against the benefits future generations will enjoy from mitigation. Because greenhouse gas emissions are an unpriced economic externality, this belief is incorrect. Correcting the externality by imposing a price on greenhouse gas emissions, whether through regulation, taxation, or a system of tradable emissions permits, together with appropriate compensating measures, can increase the consumption of economic goods and services of both future and current generations.[3]

The misperception that addressing the global warming problem involves a trade-off between the standards of living of future and current generations rests on a failure to appreciate that current output, as measured by real GDP, is divided between consumption which affects the welfare of current generations, and investment in productive facilities, technology and knowledge, which increases the ability of future generations to produce. Real resources to make investments in greenhouse gas mitigation can come either from reductions in current consumption, or from reductions in conventional investments. Without some system of mitigation of greenhouse gas emissions, current generations are investing too little in mitigation and too much in conventional forms of capital. If this misallocation of investment is corrected, a net benefit will accrue to future generations, raising their welfare, with no reduction in the consumption of the current generation. In fact, it is possible to share this economic gain between future and current generations by increasing the consumption of the current generation at the same time that it mitigates greenhouse gas emissions, and still benefit future generations.

As a practical matter, this outcome could be achieved by financing investment in greenhouse gas emission reduction, including compensation for the current generation for its reduction in consumption of carbon-intensive energy, through borrowing, which would crowd out the least profitable conventional investments and shift the burden of global warming mitigation to the future generations who will benefit from it.

Once the externality of greenhouse gas emissions has been corrected, whether through regulatory caps, carbon taxes, or a system of tradable emissions permits, global warming policy raises no intergenerational economic issues that are not already inherent in the overall decision to divide current world output between consumption and investment. Thus the question of whether a different discount rate should be applied to investments in greenhouse gas emission than to other forms of investment is economically irrelevant. What is economically relevant is the question of what price in terms of conventional investment future generations would pay for any degree of abatement of global warming, because that price determines the correct price at which current investments in greenhouse gas abatement should be valued. The more we think future generations will value abatement of global warming, the larger should be the share of investments in greenhouse gas abatement the current generation bequeaths to them.

## THE ECONOMIC ANALYTICS OF GLOBAL WARMING

The essential economic elements of the global warming scenario can be expressed in a simple economic model involving four elements: the consumption of the present generation, $C$, the consumption of future generations, $F$, the *conventional capital stock* resulting from the investment of the current generation, $K$, and the *climatological capital stock* representing the reduction in the stock of greenhouse gases in the atmosphere due to investments of the current generation in the mitigation of global warming, $E$. It is reasonable to suppose that there are trade-offs between the consumption of each generation and the capital stocks, so that in mathematical terms $C$ and $F$ are functions of $K$ and $E$. The consumption of the current generation declines with increases in $K$ and $E$ because both conventional and climatological investment require the diversion of real resources from consumption, while the consumption of the future generation (including its ability to make provisions for yet further generations) increases with $K$ and $E$ because the more conventional capital and the lower environmental damage from global warming, the more future generations can produce and consume.

For the moment let us consider the consumption level of the current generation, $C$, as fixed at its actual level $\bar{C}$. There is a menu of combinations of $K$ and $E$ that are consistent with this level of consumption. Since at present the world economy puts close to a zero price on investment in $E$, the level of $E$ it is bequeathing to future generations is very low. Furthermore, the marginal reduction in $K$ required to increase $E$ is very low as well. But if the threat of global warming is real, the consumption of future generations, $F$, could be raised by lowering $K$ and increasing $E$. The marginal cost of increasing $E$ in terms of $K$ foregone is less than the marginal benefit of increasing $E$ and lowering $K$ to the consumption of future generations. Thus it would benefit future generations to divert resources from conventional investment, $K$, to climatological investment, $E$. Such a diversion would leave the consumption of the current generation unchanged, and would increase the consumption of future generations. There is *no trade-off* between $C$ and $F$ until investment in $E$ has reached the point where its marginal cost in terms of $K$ equals its marginal benefit in raising the consumption possibilities of future generations. Figure 5.1 illustrates this point.

The convex production possibilities curve represents combinations of $E$ and $K$ compatible with the present level of consumption of the current generation. Without mitigation of global warming the current generation will bequeath effectively zero climatological capital to future generations represented by the point ($E_{\text{now}}$, $K_{\text{now}}$). The lower concave (social indifference) curve shows the combinations of $E$ and $K$ that would allow future generations to achieve the same level of consumption. Because the marginal cost of mitigation at the original point is zero, but the marginal benefit of mitigation for future generations is positive, the current allocation is inefficient. It would be possible without reducing the consumption of the current generation to move to (or closer to) the efficient allocation of investment, ($E^*$, $K^*$), at which future generations could enjoy a higher level of consumption, represented by the upper concave (social indifference) curve showing the combinations of $E$ and $K$ that would allow future generations to achieve a higher level of consumption. At the efficient point the marginal cost and benefit of mitigation in terms of conventional investment are equal. The straight line represents the price of mitigation in terms of conventional capital at the efficient allocation.

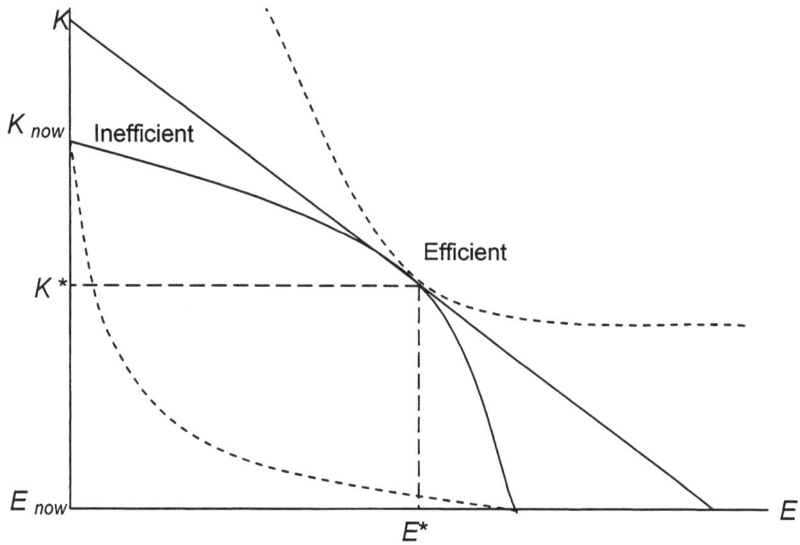


*Figure 5.1 Conventional and environmental investment policies*

## MITIGATION STRATEGIES

The efficient level of investment in mitigation the current generation should aim for is uncertain, due to uncertainties in the costs and benefits of various mitigation strategies (if there is any global warming problem to begin with, however, it is certain that some level of mitigation is called for). Policymakers, in setting a level of carbon taxes or a cap on greenhouse gas emissions, have to estimate how much future generations would be willing to pay in terms of conventional investment to inherit any given level of reduction in global warming. (The timing of investments in mitigation raises more complex technical questions, but does not alter the fundamental economic point that there is no trade-off involved in correcting an existing externality.) There is bound to be controversy over the magnitude of this willingness to pay, but this controversy should not obscure the fact that what is at issue is the distribution of a potential net benefit between generations, not the distribution of a net cost. The problem is to approximate the efficient composition of the investment portfolio the current generation leaves to future generations between conventional and climatological investments.

As long as the real resource costs of mitigation of global warming are paid out of conventional investment, the cost of errors of over- or under-investment in mitigation will be borne by future generations. One way to protect the consumption of the current generation is to finance mitigation, including the cost of compensation to the current generation, by borrowing. Borrowing to finance global warming mitigation will raise interest rates and crowd out marginal conventional investment, thus ensuring that the resources required for mitigation come from conventional investment, not current consumption. The finance of mitigation by borrowing also ensures that the monetary costs of mitigation will be paid by future generations, who will also be the main beneficiaries of climatological investment.

## INTERGENERATIONAL EQUITY AND TIME-DISCOUNTING

Except for the externality that undervalues investment in greenhouse gas reduction, there is no difference between climatological investment and conventional investment in their impact on the distribution of economic welfare between current and future generations. The issue of generational distribution concerns the overall size of the investment the current generation makes. There is nothing special about the investment the current generation might make in global warming abatement that requires a separate intergenerational equity discussion centered on this point.

When the global-warming externality is uncorrected, the world allocation of consumption between current and future generations is inefficient. The correction of the externality permits an increase in consumption of both current and future generations. The exact division of this increase between current and future generations will depend on the value the current generation puts on future generations' consumption. Figure 5.2 illustrates this point.

The convex (intertemporal) production possibilities curve represents combinations of $F$ and $C$ compatible with the technological trade-offs between consumption of current and future generations, taking account of both conventional and environmental investments. Without mitigation of global warming the point representing the consumption of future and current generations is inside this frontier ($F_{now}$, $C_{now}$). Correction of the global-warming externality would move the world to (or closer to) the efficiency frontier. One possible efficient allocation is shown as ($F^*$, $C^*$), where the efficiency frontier is tangent to the highest possible social indifference curve between consumption of current and future generations. The exact division of the benefit of correcting the externality between future and current generations will depend on the marginal valuation current generations put on the consumption of future generations, represented by the slope of the straight line tangent to the efficiency frontier.

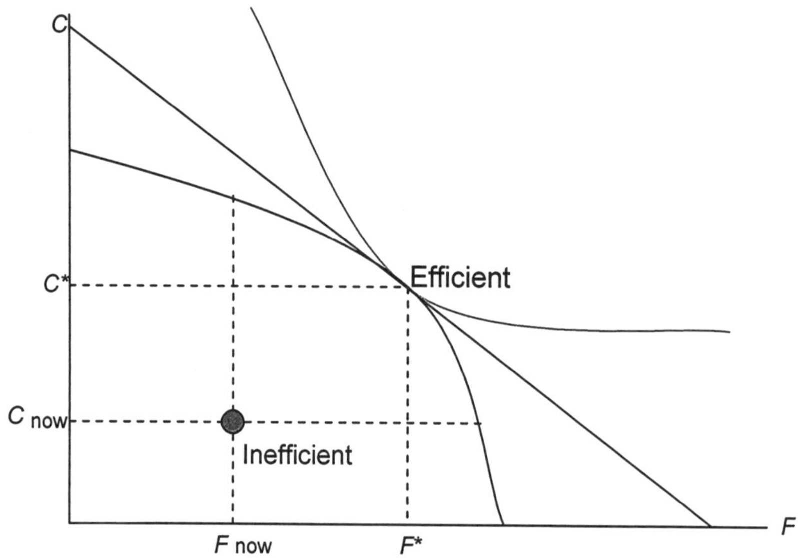


*Figure 5.2 Current and future consumption possibilities*

Many economic discussions of global warming mitigation, including the 'Stern Review' (Stern, 2006) and comments on it (Dasgupta, 2006; Nordhaus, 2006), seem implicitly to consider investment in global warming mitigation as an addition to whatever conventional investment the current generation is making. It is only from this point of view that it makes sense to calculate the balance between intergenerational costs and benefits using a pure inter-temporal discount rate. If the level of current conventional investment is taken as a constraint in deciding global warming mitigation policy, then the resource costs of the investment in greenhouse gas emissions would have to be borne by the consumption of current generations. In this case it would be necessary to consider intergenerational consumption trade-offs. But why should the current level of conventional investment be taken as a constraint in analyzing the mitigation of global warming? This presumption obscures the key point that correcting the greenhouse gas externality can improve the consumption possibilities for future generations without reducing the consumption of current generations at all. In assuming that mitigation must be financed from current consumption, this type of economic analysis implicitly biases its conclusions against climatological investment.

If the correction of the greenhouse gas externality raised the whole future path of world income substantially, there would be a case for redistributing this benefit by overcompensating the current generation for its reduction in emission of greenhouse gases with other types of consumption. Some degree of overcompensation is probably desirable in any case to allow for errors in the compensation scheme and to create political support for mitigation policy. But it would only be in the context of this second-order adjustment that the questions of intergenerational equity and time-discounting would become relevant. Since the allocation of welfare between current and future generations is already affected by conventional investment policy, the global warming problem introduces no novel considerations in this discussion.

## FINANCING CLIMATOLOGICAL INVESTMENT

As the analysis above shows, the key economic point is that the appropriate level of mitigation of global warming can be achieved without cost to the current generation, if the resources used to achieve mitigation come from investment rather than consumption. The fact that the benefits of investment in mitigation of global warming will accrue largely on a timescale longer than the pay-off of most conventional investments makes no difference to this logic. Consider an intermediate generation, which does not benefit much (or at all) from mitigation, between the current generation which invests in mitigation and a distant future generation that benefits from mitigation. If the current generation invests less in conventional capital, the intermediate generation will produce a smaller output than it would have with a larger conventional capital stock, but need not have a lower standard of living if it consumes a larger proportion of that smaller output by restricting its conventional investment. The distant future generation will inherit a smaller conventional capital stock from the intermediate generation, but will be more than compensated by the larger environmental capital representing reduced global warming.

How does this logic play out in terms of actual economic policy and behavior? Whether greenhouse gas emissions are reduced as a result of direct regulation, carbon taxes, or a tradable system of emissions permits, the economic effect of mitigation will be to raise the real price of carbon-intensive energy to current users (and reduce the incomes of owners of carbon-intensive energy resources). This change in and of itself clearly imposes real costs in terms of standard of living and consumption on current users. In order to hold the current generation harmless in the face of this change it is necessary to compensate them with higher consumption of non-carbon-intensive consumption. The political problem is how to fashion such a compensation system and educate the public to realize that they will directly benefit from the combination of greenhouse gas mitigation and the compensation measures. There is no point in refunding the higher price of carbon-intensive energy at the pump, so to speak, since that would remove the incentive effects to reduce emissions which are the point of the policy to begin with. The users of carbon-intensive energy have to be compensated through some other channel.

Economic theory suggests 'lump-sum' transfers as the ideal method of compensation for the costs imposed by correcting a production externality. It would in theory be possible to compensate current energy users for an increase in carbon-intensive energy prices by a combination of increases in public expenditures for education, health care, and transportation combined with general reduction in income, property, sales, and employment taxes, for example. Some methods of reducing carbon-intensive energy, such as a carbon tax, would generate some revenue to offset these expenditure and tax changes. The remaining revenue shortfall could and should be met by borrowing, which would have a solid economic justification as a method of shifting the real costs of mitigation to the future generations that would reap its benefits. The traditional economic argument against debt finance is that borrowing 'crowds out' conventional investment by raising the interest rate. But in the case of global warming mitigation, the crowding out of conventional investment is exactly what is called for. The mitigation of greenhouse gas emissions, far from being a potential drain on the public finances, actually represents a potentially large additional revenue source.

There is no economic logic supporting proposals to link reduction of greenhouse gas emission through an increase in carbon-intensive energy prices to any particular expenditure increase or tax reduction, such as subsidies to non-carbon-intensive energy technologies. If prices of carbon-intensive energy rise to reflect the real opportunity cost of global warming to future generations, this in itself will provide the appropriate incentives for investments in alternative energy technologies.

As a practical political matter, it is desirable that the package of changes in expenditures and taxes that accompanies greenhouse gas mitigation come as close as possible to compensating (or somewhat over-compensating) all the citizens who will be disadvantaged by an increase in carbon-intensive energy prices. There are bound to be 'hardship' cases where the increase in carbon-intensive energy prices imposes unusually high costs on individuals, or even communities. Some safety-valve mechanism for compensating credible hardships is a desirable part of the policy package.

The economic policy discussion on climate change has focused on the undoubtedly important question of mechanisms for controlling greenhouse gas emissions, such as direct controls, a carbon tax, or cap-and-trade markets for emission permits. Because these measures all impose the same real resource costs on current users of carbon-intensive energy to achieve any level of global warming mitigation, they all raise the same broader question of how to compensate the current generation for its environmental investment. In principle compensation can be achieved by diverting resources from conventional investments; the task is to unpack this insight into transparent policy proposals that would convey to politicians and their constituencies the economic substance of the global warming problem.

## POLITICAL RESISTANCE TO COSTLESS ECONOMIC POLICY MEASURES

The widespread resistance on the part of some politicians and pundits to investing real resources in effective mitigation of global warming reminds us that the analysis presented here is not universally understood, and that the premises of the argument are not universally accepted.

The argument for reducing greenhouse gas emissions rests on the twin premises that reduction of atmospheric greenhouse gas concentrations will lower future global temperatures, and that higher future global temperatures will impose real costs on future generations. These two premises imply the conclusion that greenhouse gas emissions are a real uncorrected economic externality that is preventing the world economy from reaching its efficiency frontier. Presumably political opposition to correcting the externality must rest either on a judgment that greenhouse gas concentrations have no predictable effect on global temperatures, or that future generations would be better off with higher global temperatures. The scientific case that there is some impact of greenhouse gases on global warming is very strong. Those who accept this science and still oppose mitigation must therefore believe that global warming is a good thing, which would imply a policy of increasing greenhouse gas emissions.

The possibility of economic misunderstanding by politicians is ever-present, as even a cursory study of economic policy-making will confirm. The resistance to investing in mitigation of global warming is most often expressed on the grounds that the resources diverted to mitigation would reduce 'economic growth'. The present analysis makes clear that this is simply not true. Mitigation changes the composition, but not the aggregate amount, of investment. It is hard to imagine what measure of economic growth would fail to acknowledge the increase in consumption possibilities for future generations made possible by correcting the greenhouse gas externality.

One possible misunderstanding is simply that politicians who talk this way are victims of 'conventional real GDP illusion', in that they have been so mesmerized by economists' fixation on real GDP growth as currently measured that they cannot imagine incorporating the benefits of global warming in their economic thinking. The only cure for this type of illusion is for economists to be more careful in explaining the relationship between particular definitions of real GDP and economic growth and welfare.

Politicians may also be particularly sensitive to the collective action aspect of global warming mitigation. Since any reduction in emissions will reduce the global stock of greenhouse gases, it is true that any one region of the planet benefits substantially from other regions' mitigation efforts. But the basic economic logic of the correction of an externality applies even to individual regions' investments. Any mitigation a region accomplishes will benefit that region to some degree (less, to be sure, than if all other regions made the same effort, but still conferring a positive economic benefit). Thus one would expect that the collective action aspect of the global warming problem might slow, but would not block, individual regional investment in mitigation. (Indeed there are signs that this point has dawned on policymakers in some regions, and even large corporations, which have unilaterally begun to make investments in mitigation, presumably reflecting their private calculation of a net benefit.)

It is also possible that the political system functions badly on this issue, in that disagreements over the distribution of the net gains from correcting the global warming externality will prevent us from achieving any gain at all. The correct economic analysis of the global warming problem, however, suggests that it is not properly speaking a political issue, and that ideology and partisanship have little relevance to it.

The analysis presented here suggests that the prospects for actually doing something about the global warming problem are good. We have recognized the issue in time to do something about it, and we have methods and resources to mitigate global warming. Because the reduction of greenhouse gas emissions financed by an economically appropriate reduction in conventional investments can benefit future generations with no reduction in the overall consumption of the current generation, there is appears to be no real insurmountable political obstacle to a worldwide system of mitigation.

# CONCLUSION

If unpriced emission of greenhouse gases imposes real costs on future generations, both present and future generations can enjoy a higher consumption of economic goods and services through the correction of this unpriced externality. This means that there is no real economic opportunity cost to mitigation of global warming. The misperception that control of global warming is costly rests on the mistaken assumption that the investment allocation of the world economy without mitigation measures is efficient, but in the presence of an externality the world economy is not on its efficiency frontier. Once the externality is corrected, global warming presents no novel issues of the distribution of economic welfare between generations that are not already inherent in other investment choices. The costs of greenhouse gas mitigation can be shifted to future generations by reducing conventional investment, rather than by reducing current standards of living. This suggests financing investments in greenhouse gas emission, including compensation of current generations for the necessary substitution away from carbon intensive energy, through borrowing, thereby 'crowding out' some conventional investment. The question of the appropriate intergenerational discount rate to apply to the benefits of greenhouse gas emission mitigation is irrelevant to global warming policy. The relevant question is the marginal value future generations will put on a lower stock of atmospheric greenhouse gases relative to conventional capital. This value should determine the composition of the entire capital stock that current generations bestow on the future, including the stock of climatological capital represented by the level of greenhouse gas accumulation.

# NOTES

1. Leo Model Professor of Economics, New School for Social Research, 79 Fifth Avenue, New York, NY 10003, foleyd@newschool.edu and External Faculty, Santa Fe Institute. This paper was prepared for the Workshop on the Economics of Global Warming sponsored by the Schwartz Center for Economic Policy Analysis, October 12, 2007. I benefitted from comments and suggestions when I gave an earlier version of this paper at the Santa Fe Institute in June, 2007. The author would like to thank Jonathan Harris, Julie Nelson, Lance Taylor, and Gerard M. Foley for helpful comments on earlier drafts.
2. See Cline (1992), Chichilnisky (1994), Mendelsohn et al. (1994), and Nordhaus (2001) for a sampling of the economic literature on this issue.
3. Throughout this chapter, it will be assumed that any impacts of the policy choices discussed on aggregate demand will be offset by other macroeconomic policies, such as monetary policy, and do not affect the degree of utilization of productive resources.

# REFERENCES

Chichilnisky, Graciela (1994), 'North–South trade and the global environment', *American Economic Review*, **84** (4): 851–74.
Cline, William (1992), *The Economics of Global Warming*, Washington, DC: Institute of International Economics.
Dasgupta, Partha (2006), 'Comments on the Stern Review's Economics of Climate Change', revised 12 December, http://www.econ.cam.ac.uk/faculty/dasgupta/STERN.pdf.
Mendelsohn, R., W.D. Nordhaus and D. Shaw (1994), 'The impact of global warming on agriculture: a Ricardian analysis', *American Economic Review*, **84** (4): 753–71.
Nordhaus, William (2001), 'Global warming economics', *Science*, **294** (5545): 1283–84.
Nordhaus, William (2006), 'The *Stern Review* on the Economics of Climate Change', 17 November, http://nordhaus.econ.yale.edu/SternReviewD2.pdf.
Stern, Nicholas (2006), *The Stern Review: The Economics of Climate Change*, London: HM Treasury, http://www.hmtreasury.gov.uk/independent _reviews/stern _review_economics_climate_change/sternreview_index.cfm.

# 6. Energy Productivity, Labor Productivity, and Global Warming

**Lance Taylor**[1]

Global warming is the consequence of three very strong and increasingly contradictory trends.

First, emission of carbon dioxide, the main driver (for now) of the greenhouse effect, is a direct consequence of using fossil fuels and biomass as the predominant sources of energy for utilization by humans.

Second, people in developing countries worldwide desperately want to increase their real income levels per capita. That necessarily requires growth in real output per unit of labor, or labor productivity. Population growth also enters the equation for overall income (and output) expansion, but if all goes well its energy-use impacts will be less than those of rising per capita incomes.

Mathematically, let $X$ be real output, and assume that the both labor force and population are proportional to a variable $L$ (that is, labor force participation rates are stable). Let

$$\varepsilon_L = \frac{X}{L}$$

be output (or income) per person and a 'hat' over a variable denote its growth rate, for example:

$$\hat{X} = \frac{\frac{dX}{dt}}{X}$$

Then:

$$\hat{X} = \hat{\varepsilon}_L + \hat{L}$$

That is, output growth is the sum of growth rates of per capita income and population. If over the next few decades poor countries do have rising per capita income (the historical rate in rich economies is around 2 percent per year), productivity growth will dominate population expansion.

Third, historically a crucial factor supporting rising labor productivity and per capita income has been increasing use of energy. This is an old idea, widely accepted among ecological economists but never fully taken on board by the professional mainstream. It dates back to the 'energetics' movement of the last half of the 19th century (Martinez-Alier and Schlüpmann, 1987; Mirowski, 1989) but not much further.[2] A slightly overstated paraphrase is 'The currency of the world is not the dollar, it's the joule' (Lewis, 2007).

One can make the linkage between rising labor productivity and increasing energy use a bit more precise by comparing growth rates of average labor and energy productivities and the energy/labor ratio. It is easy to show that the latter two growth rates must sum to the first as an algebraic identity. Let average energy productivity be:

$$\varepsilon_E = \frac{X}{E}$$

with $E$ as energy input. Then;

$$\frac{\varepsilon_L}{\varepsilon_E} = \frac{E}{L} = \lambda$$

It follows that:

$$\hat{\varepsilon}_L = \hat{\varepsilon}_E + (\hat{E} - \hat{L}) = \hat{\varepsilon}_E + \hat{\lambda}$$

Output is measured in real 1990 dollars at market prices, not in terms of purchasing power parity which is macroeconomically meaningless (Rada von Arnim and Taylor, 2008).

## EMPIRICAL RESULTS

To concentrate on global warming, it makes sense to focus on fossil fuels and biomass as the principal energy inputs at a national level. We will assume that energy production from hydro, solar, wind and nuclear power can initially be ignored, since these sources currently represent only a small fraction of global energy use).

Figure 6.1 presents two scatter diagrams of growth rates of the ratio of annual energy use to employment and labor productivity, for the periods 1970–1990 and 1990–2004 for 12 regional groups of developing economies[3] and the rich countries in the OECD. There appears to be a robust relationship between increasing energy use per worker and labor productivity growth, with a steeper slope and a better fit in the later period. Similar results show up when growth rates are compared at the individual country level. The slope of the relationship in 1990–2004 is around 0.6, suggesting a substantial contribution of more energy use per worker to higher productivity.

Table 6.1 presents the data in numerical form for the regions and selected countries. A unit of time is necessarily involved – so we are really considering power usage. The numbers are in units of terajoules per worker-year.[4] In 2004, there was evidently a wide range of energy/labor ratios per year – from 0.01 (77 gallons of gasoline) in sub-Saharan Africa to 0.74 (5700 gallons) in Saudi Arabia. The ratio is 0.58 in the US and less than 0.3 in Western European countries, the Asian Tigers, and Japan.

## IMPLICATIONS FOR GLOBAL WARMING

In the context of global warming, these numbers are not reassuring. For example, if the slope of the relevant future curve as in Figure 6.1 really is 0.6, then 2 percent per capita income growth would require the energy/labor ratio to rise at 1.2 percent per year. Factoring in population growth might raise total energy usage by around 2 percent annually. In fact, the situation is not quite so dire because the largest non-industrialized groups (notably China, the former USSR, South Asia, and the semi-industrialized economies) report relatively high energy productivity growth. But it still makes sense to ask how current growth rates of energy consumption may feed into the atmospheric stock of carbon dioxide.

As background, Tables 6.2a and 6.2b present comparisons of energy consumption per worker and carbon dioxide emission per capita for the world and selected countries in 2004. Emissions per unit of energy are in the range of 65–75 metric tons per terajoule in rich countries and somewhat higher in (some) developing and transition economies.

One implication is that lower emission levels in the latter are mostly due to smaller energy/labor ratios. The numbers for China, Kenya, Brazil, etc. suggest that there is room for reducing worldwide emissions simply by increasing poor countries' efficiency of carbon utilization, but that major benefits can only come from cutting back on energy use per capita and per unit of economic output.[5]

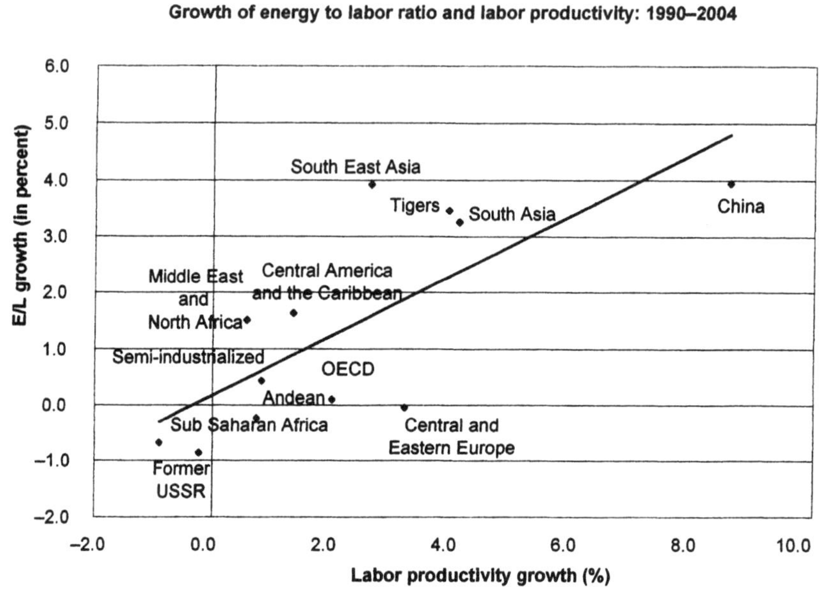


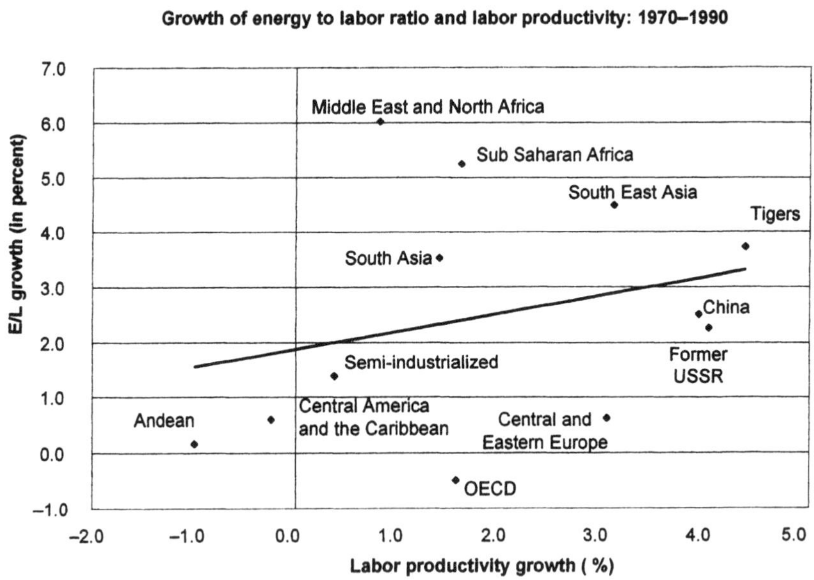


*Figure 6.1 Growth rates of labor productivity and the energy/labor ratio*

*Table 6.1a Growth of energy productivity, labor productivity, and the energy/labor ratio, 1970–1990*

| 1970–1990 | Selected OECD | Central and Eastern Europe | USSR* (1989 end year) | Tigers | South East Asia | China | South Asia | Semi-Industrialized countries | Central America and the Caribbean | Andean | Middle East | Sub-Saharan Africa |
|---|---|---|---|---|---|---|---|---|---|---|---|---|
| Growth Rates Energy Productivity (%) | 2.1 | 2.4 | 1.6 | 0.6 | –1.3 | 1.4 | –2.1 | –1.0 | –0.8 | –1.1 | –4.9 | –3.5 |
| Growth Rates Labor Productivity (%) | 1.6 | 3.0 | 4.0 | 4.4 | 3.1 | 3.9 | 1.4 | 0.4 | –0.2 | –1.0 | 0.8 | 1.6 |
| Growth Rates E/L (%) | –0.5 | 0.6 | 2.3 | 3.7 | 4.5 | 2.5 | 3.5 | 1.4 | 0.6 | 0.2 | 6.0 | 5.3 |
| E/L beginning year (1970) | 0.49 | 0.21 | 0.26 | 0.08 | 0.01 | 0.02 | 0.01 | 0.09 | 0.04 | 0.04 | 0.05 | 0.0048 |
| E/L end year (1990) | 0.45 | 0.24 | 0.40 | 0.17 | 0.03 | 0.04 | 0.02 | 0.12 | 0.05 | 0.04 | 0.16 | 0.0133 |

*Source:* *World Bank Development Indicators* 2005 database; Gronningen Center for Growth and Development database http://www.ggdc.net/.

*Table 6.1b Growth of energy productivity, labor productivity, and the energy/labor ratio, 1990–2004*

| 1990–2004 | Selected OECD | Central and Eastern Europe | USSR* (beginning year) | Tigers | South East Asia | China | South Asia | Semi-Industrialized countries | Central America and the Caribbean | Andean | Middle East | Sub-Saharan Africa |
|---|---|---|---|---|---|---|---|---|---|---|---|---|
| Growth Rates Energy Productivity (%) | 1.9 | 3.2 | 2.1 | 0.4 | –1.3 | 4.5 | 0.8 | 0.4 | –0.3 | 1.0 | –0.9 | –0.2 |
| Growth Rates Labour Productivity (%) | 2.0 | 3.2 | –0.2 | 3.9 | 2.6 | 8.6 | 4.1 | 0.8 | 1.3 | 0.7 | 0.6 | –0.9 |
| Growth Rates E/L (%) | 0.1 | 0.0 | –0.9 | 3.5 | 3.9 | 3.9 | 3.3 | 0.4 | 1.6 | –0.2 | 1.5 | –0.7 |
| E/L beginning year (1990) (%) | 0.45 | 0.24 | 0.41 | 0.17 | 0.03 | 0.04 | 0.02 | 0.12 | 0.05 | 0.04 | 0.16 | 0.01 |
| E/L end year (2004) (%) | 0.45 | 0.24 | 0.37 | 0.27 | 0.05 | 0.07 | 0.04 | 0.12 | 0.06 | 0.04 | 0.19 | 0.01 |

*Source:* *World Bank Development Indicators* 2005 database; Gronningen Center for Growth and Development database http://www.ggdc.net/.

*Table 6.2a* *Carbon emission and energy consumption (world and OECD countries)*

| 2004 | World | US | UK | Sweden | France | Japan |
|---|---|---|---|---|---|---|
| Total $CO_2$ Emission (thousands of metric tons) | 27,245,758 | 6,049,435 | 587,261 | 53,033 | 373,693 | 1,257,963 |
| Total Energy Consumption (thousands of terajoules) | 361,849.00 | 81,762.00 | 8,926.00 | 671.00 | 5,667.00 | 17,094.00 |
| Employment | 2,836,437 | 140,702 | 28,008 | 4,311 | 24,963 | 63,290 |
| Population | 6,411,145 | 293,028 | 60,271 | 8,986 | 60,991 | 127,480 |
| Energy Consumption/Labor | 0.13 | 0.58 | 0.32 | 0.16 | 0.23 | 0.27 |
| $CO_2$ Emission/Energy Consumption | 75.3 | 74.0 | 65.8 | 79.0 | 65.94 | 74 |
| $CO_2$ Emissions/Population | 4.25 | 20.6 | 9.7 | 5.9 | 6.1 | 9.9 |

*Source:* Gronningen Center for Growth and Development database http://www.ggdc.net/; *2004 Energy Statistics Yearbook*, United Nations; Carbon Dioxide Information Analysis Center, United States Department of Energy.

*Table 6.2b* *Carbon emission and energy consumption (developing nations)*

| 2004 | China | India | Argentina | Brazil | Venezuela | South Africa | Kenya | Saudi Arabia | Poland | Russia |
|---|---|---|---|---|---|---|---|---|---|---|
| Total Carbon Emission (thousands of metric tons) | 5,012,377 | 1,342,962 | 141,786 | 331,795 | 172,623 | 437,032 | 10,588 | 308,393 | 307,238 | 1,524,993 |
| Total Energy Consumption (thousands of terajoules) | 51,339 | 14,890 | 2,358 | 4,880 | 2,295 | 4,939 | 119 | 5,715 | 3,745 | 24,355 |
| Employment | 752,000 | 394,612 | 14,329 | 71,058 | 8,855 | 19,092 | 15,110 | 7,675 | 13,855 | 66,407 |
| Population | 1,295,734 | 1,065,071 | 38,984 | 183,169 | 24,765 | 44,448 | 33,973 | 25,796 | 38,580 | 143,508 |
| Energy Consumption/Labor | 0.07 | 0.04 | 0.16 | 0.07 | 0.26 | 0.26 | 0.01 | 0.74 | 0.27 | 0.37 |
| Carbon Emission/ Energy Consumption | 97.6 | 74.0 | 65.8 | 79.0 | 65.94 | 74 | 89.0 | 74.0 | 73.7 | 74.7 |
| Carbon Emissions/ Population | 3.87 | 1.3 | 3.6 | 1.8 | 7.0 | 9.8 | 0.31 | 12.0 | 8.0 | 10.6 |

*Source:* Gronningen Center for Growth and Development database http://www.ggdc.net/; *2004 Energy Statistics Yearbook*, United Nations; Carbon Dioxide Information Analysis Center, United States Department of Energy.

## RICH AND POOR COUNTRY TRADE-OFFS

Assuming that the $CO_2$/energy ratio stays constant, Figure 6.2 illustrates the potential trade-offs.

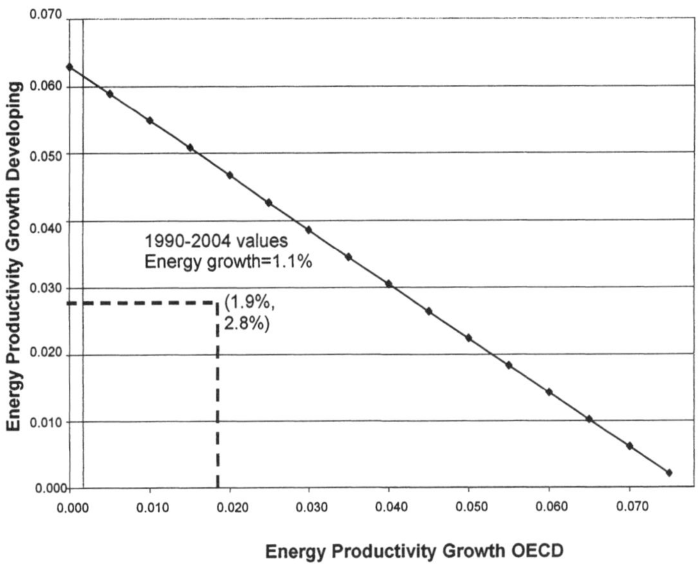


*Figure 6.2 Energy productivity growth rates required to hold overall growth of energy use to zero, 1990–2004.*

In the period 1990–2004, energy productivity rose at 1.9 percent per year in the 'rich OECD' economies and at 2.8 percent in the rest of the world because of high productivity growth rates (noted above) in some of the larger economies. The downward-sloping line is an isocline showing combinations of energy productivity growth rates that would have been needed to hold the growth rate of total energy use to zero. This scenario represents the initial stages of the 'flat path' of carbon emissions that Socolow and Pacala (2006) propose to hold atmospheric $CO_2$ to less than twice its pre-industrial level.

The prospects are not favorable. Had the energy productivity growth rate in poor countries remained stable, a rate of almost 4.5 percent per year would have been required in the developed world to hold energy growth to zero.

Alternatively, with a constant energy productivity growth rate in the rich countries, energy productivity growth of almost 5 percent per year would have been needed in the poor ones. The growth rates of the energy/labor ratio corresponding to these cases for rich and poor countries are −2.5 percent and −2.3 percent respectively. A flat path could also be achieved with a worldwide energy productivity growth rate of about 3.5 percent, (i.e. 3.5 percent in both developed and developing countries). This would imply a growth rate in the energy/labor ratio of about −1.5 percent in rich countries and about −1 per cent in poor countries.

By way of contrast, the Kyoto targets call for (roughly) an annual one percent reduction in energy use for the rich countries, implying that their energy productivity growth rate would have to be about 4 percent. If (hypothetically) the Kyoto targets were met, we can calculate the impact on world energy growth using the following equation for the worldwide growth rate of energy consumption:

$$\hat{E} = \theta(\hat{L}_R + \hat{\varepsilon}_{LR} - \hat{\varepsilon}_{ER}) + (1-\theta)(\hat{L}_P + \hat{\varepsilon}_{LP} - \hat{\varepsilon}_{EP})$$

where the subscripts $R$ and $P$ stand for rich and poor countries respectively, and $\theta$ represents the share of the rich in world energy use (about 45 percent in 2004). The achievement of Kyoto targets would reduce growth of worldwide fossil energy consumption from 1.1 percent to 0.65 percent per year, well above the flat path.

Compared to the historical data summarized in Table 6.1, the rates of change in energy/labor ratios required to achieve a flat path look extremely optimistic. The required changes in growth rates are on the order of 100 percent of the historical growth rates themselves – a large adjustment by any standard! The only countries that are now in the required range of energy/labor growth rates are stagnant with negligible or negative labor productivity growth. And in the recent period, there has been no significant downward trend in energy/labor ratios in rich economies.

It is also possible that $CO_2$/energy ratios could decline, either due to a significantly higher proportion of non-carbon energy sources (solar, wind, hydro, nuclear, etc.) or to the introduction of effective carbon capture and storage technology. Socolow and Pacala (2006) include these possibilities as potential contributors to a flat path of carbon emissions. Unless there are truly dramatic changes in these areas, however, the requirements for changes in energy/labor ratios would not be much less drastic than those outlined above.

On the whole, poor countries import 'modern' technologies previously created in advanced economies. The key policy question is whether in the near future rich country energy/labor ratios can be reduced (or energy productivity increased relative to labor productivity) substantially by technological innovation and social rearrangements.[6] If such innovations work out, then perhaps they can be passed to developing economies soon enough to enable them to maintain positive per capita output growth with only slowly increasing or (better) decreasing energy/labor ratios.

If such a growth pattern does not prove to be possible, then the three contradictory trends mentioned at the outset will inevitably collide. Only 16 percent of the world's population now lives in the rich countries which account for 45 percent of world energy use. Both shares are declining. Unless the advanced economies find the means to reduce their own energy-labor ratios substantially (and unhistorically) and pass the techniques along to the rest of the world, the consequences of colliding income growth, energy use per capita, and global warming trends are unforeseeable but may well be catastrophic indeed.

## NOTES

1. New School for Social Research. Comments by Duncan Foley, Jonathan Harris, Codrina Rada von Arnim, Armon Rezai, and participants at a workshop on the Economics of Global Warming at the Schwartz Center for Economic Policy Analysis at the New School are gratefully acknowledged.
2. Leibnitz proposed the basic concept of energy around 1680 but it did not take its modern form until the 1840s.
3. These groups are described and analyzed extensively in Rada von Arnim and Taylor (2008).
4. One joule is the energy required to lift a small (100 gram) apple one meter against the earth's gravity. One terajoule is roughly equivalent to 7700 gallons of gasoline or 31 tons of coal. Alternatively, one watt equals one joule of energy use per second. Dividing terajoules per year by the number of seconds in a year shows that an American worker utilizes 19.3 kilowatts of power to produce his or her contribution to real GDP. An African uses 300 watts.
5. In any case, switching from the current worldwide mix of fossil fuel energy sources to using natural gas (the least carbon-intensive source) exclusively would reduce carbon emissions by only about 15 percent (see Lewis, 2007).
6. The same observation applies to $CO_2$/energy ratios as well.

## REFERENCES

Lewis, Nathan S. (2007), 'Powering the Planet', *Engineering and Science*, **70** (2): 12–23.

Martinez-Alier, Juan and Klaus Schlüpmann (1991), *Ecological Economics: Energy, Environment, and Society*, Oxford, UK: Basil Blackwell Publishing.

Mirowski, Phillip (1989), *More Heat than Light*, Cambridge, UK: Cambridge University Press.

Rada von Arnim, Codrina and Lance Taylor (2008), 'Growth Rates, Economic Structure, Energy Use, and Sources of Demand', in Philip Arestis and John Eatwell (eds), Issues in Economic Development and Globalization: Essays in Honour of Ajit Singh, London: Palgrave-Macmillan (forthcoming).

Socolow, Robert H. and Stephen W. Pacala (2006), 'A Plan to Keep Carbon in Check', *Scientific American*, **295** (3): 50–57.

# 7. Macroeconomics and Sustainable Development: Applying the Sustainomics Framework

**Mohan Munasinghe**[1]

---

The concept of sustainable development is receiving increasing attention from world decision makers, in their search for new solutions to many critical problems, including issues related to climate change (WCED, 1987; Munasinghe, 1992, 2007; Banuri and Weyant, 2001). In this context, the role of macroeconomic policies has come under increasing scrutiny, because of their powerful and widespread social and environmental impacts (Munasinghe and Cruz, 1994; Reed, 1996; Munasinghe, 2002).

The *sustainomics* framework shows that sustainable development has economic, social and environmental dimensions – see Figure 7.1 (Munasinghe, 1992). It may be defined as a process for improving the range of opportunities that will enable individual human beings and communities to meet their needs, as well as to achieve their aspirations and full potential over a sustained period of time, while maintaining the resilience of economic, social and environmental systems. Each of these systems has its own distinct driving forces and objectives. The economy is geared towards improving human welfare, primarily through increases in the consumption of goods and services. The environmental domain focuses on protection of the integrity and resilience of ecological systems. The social domain emphasizes the enrichment of human relationships and achievement of individual and group aspirations. The goal of sustainomics is to *make development more sustainable* with continuous improvements in the present quality of life at a lower intensity of resource use, thereby leaving behind for future generations an undiminished stock of productive assets (that is, manufactured, natural and social capital) that will enhance opportunities for improving their quality of life (Munasinghe, 1992, 2001). This wider perspective on human well-being is important, since it combines economic principles with the pursuit of environmental and social sustainability – in contrast to most traditional economic policies that focus on maximizing economic output, sometimes at significant environmental and social cost.

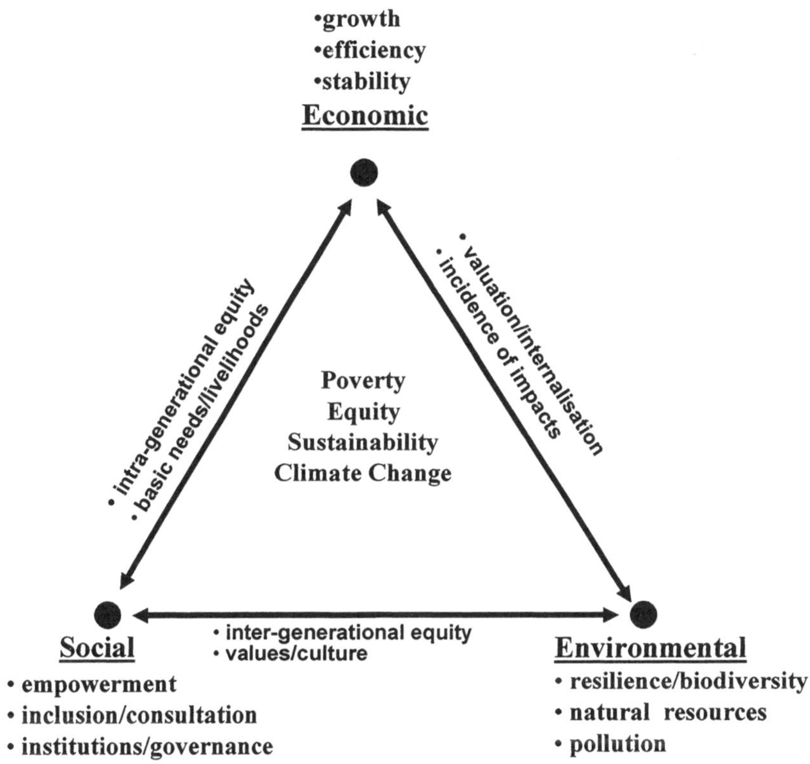


*Source*: Munasinghe (1992).

*Figure 7.1 Key elements of sustainable development and interconnections*

Macroeconomic strategies have widespread effects, ranging from exchange rate, interest rate and wage policies, to trade liberalization, privatization and similar programs. They are coupled with sectoral measures involving various economic instruments like pricing in key sectors (energy or agriculture) and broad sector-wide taxation or subsidy programs (e.g. agricultural subsidies and industrial investment incentives). Such economy-wide policies are often packaged within programs of structural adjustment, stabilization and sectoral reform, aimed at promoting economic stability, efficiency and growth, and ultimately improving human welfare. Although the emphasis is on economic policies, other non-economic measures (such as social, institutional and legal actions) are also relevant.

The next section continues with a brief review of the historical evolution of ideas linking macroeconomic policies and the environment, in the context of sustainomics. Section 7.2 describes more recent empirical evidence, beginning with a discussion of the widespread impacts of structural adjustment programs since the 1980s, and followed by some stylized results. One important conclusion is that it is the combination of growth and economic imperfections that lead to environmental and social damage and unsustainable outcomes. Section 7.3 contains a discussion of some basic analytical frameworks for analyzing the linkages between the macro-economy and the environment. Both micro- and macro-economic models confirm the key conclusions of the previous section. Finally, Section 7.4 sets out the concluding remarks, including directions for future work.

## 7. 1: HISTORICAL EVOLUTION OF IDEAS

Many key ideas on macroeconomics and the environment have been developed within the last two decades, although some historical roots are discernible in several classical papers. We focus below on selected papers describing macroeconomy-environment interactions.

### Tracing Macroeconomy–Environmental Linkages

Early work on such linkages pursued three interwoven lines of enquiry. First, economic activities require natural resources. The crucial role of land scarcities in limiting growth was recognized by Malthus (1798), who stressed impoverishment due to agricultural constraints and exponential population growth. Subsequently, Ricardo (1817) theorized that diminishing returns to land would impose checks on wealth and population. Hotelling (1931) further developed the theory of exhaustible resources.

Koopman's (1973) paper combines exhaustible natural capital in Hotelling's simple 'cake-eating' problem with accumulating manufactured capital, to optimize consumption within a Ramsey type growth model. The macroeconomic interest rate plays a significant role. Subsequent work (Withagen, 1990) explored many ramifications of this approach, leading to recent work by Hartwick (1990) and others (see below). Stiglitz (1974) uses a model with capital, labor and natural resources as substitutes in production, to show that higher consumption levels are sustainable, provided increasing technological progress compensates for declining natural resource stocks.

Daly (1991) points out that getting macroeconomic policies right may ensure optimal resource allocation, but does not address scale issues, as economies grow beyond the environmental carrying capacity. Solow (1993) defines Net National Product (NNP), adjusted to reflect both natural resource depletion and changes in environmental quality, as a measure of maximum consumption that can be sustained forever. These arguments link neoclassical economic theory with earlier work in environmental economics and environmental accounting. England's paper (2000) identifies three conditions which would curtail growth and lead to a steady-state economy – scarcity of natural capital; complementarity (non-substitutability) between manufactured and natural capital in production; and constraints on technological progress that raises productivity of natural capital use. Recent work has focused on the interactions between sustainable development and optimal growth in the long term (Munasinghe et al., 2001, Markandya et al., 2002).

The second historical approach draws on input–output (I-O) analysis developed during the 1930s. Leontief (1970) describes a seminal framework to analyze polluting outputs from productive sectors, and the impact of policies to reduce such externalities in pollution abatement sectors. Many subsequent studies have elaborated on the basic I-O approach, by linking it with vintage models specifying labor demand and capital stock, as well as by endogenized consumer demand based on linear expenditure systems. More sophisticated models made the technical I-O coefficients endogenous and dependent on prices. Present state-of-the-art computable general equilibrium models used for macroeconomic–environmental analysis, as well as the integrated frameworks for environmental–economic accounting, use the I-O approach (see below).

Third, environmental considerations have been incorporated into more conventional macroeconomic models used in policymaking, ranging from extensions of the Keynesian IS-LM type used in analyses of comparative statics, to sophisticated computable general equilibrium (CGE) models that include environmental variables. Environmental considerations are increasingly examined in macroeconomic models, focusing on short-run Keynesian issues such as capacity utilization, unemployment and cyclical movements in the economy. Girma (1992) starts from a conventional macroeconomic modeling framework, and adds an environmental sector to examine key macro policies and their impacts on the environment. Longer run environmental–macroeconomic models for both closed and open economies, are built around supply-side issues like capital accumulation, natural resource depletion, long-run labor supply, discount rate and rate of technological progress.

**Empirical Surveys of Macroeconomy–Environment Linkages**

Grossman and Krueger (1995) analyse the empirical relationship between per capita income and several indicators of air and water pollution. Does environmental pollution vary with income in the shape of an inverted U-shaped 'environmental Kuznets curve', as Grossman and Krueger assert? There is agreement that environmental quality declines with increases in per capita income in the early stages of growth, but it is unclear whether continued growth reverses this trend, since the shape of the curve appears to vary widely by country and form of environmental degradation (*Ecological Economics*, 1998; *Environment and Development Economics* 1997; Stern, 1998; and de Bruyn and Heintz, 1999). In particular, some analysts argue that per capita carbon emissions tend to increase with economic growth, with no 'turning point' evident even for highly industrialized nations (Galeotti et al., 2006; Richmond and Kaufmann, 2006) (see Figure 7.2).

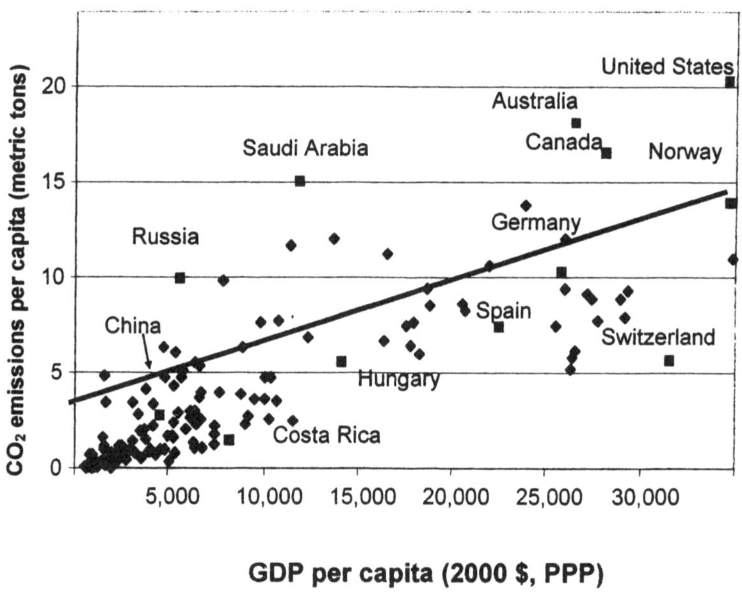


*Source:* World Bank's World Development Indicators database.

*Figure 7.2* $CO_2$ *emissions vs. GDP per capita, 2002*

Opschoor and Jongma's (1996) paper is a comprehensive review of environmental impacts of World Bank and International Monetary Fund structural adjustment and stabilization programs in developing countries. They argue for complementary environmental policies to counteract any adverse impacts of growth-oriented macroeconomic policies as a short-run remedy, but urge a more integrated approach in the long run.

Panaytou and Hupe (1996) point out that structural adjustment programs must pay as much attention to market and institutional failures as they pay to policy failures. Using environmental and social policies as parallel policies to cushion the environmental and social impacts of structural adjustment is second best, compared to full integration of these policies with the economic reforms. Partial reforms or incomplete implementation of reforms may do more harm than good if they are selectively applied without anticipating their social and environmental impacts.

Kessler and Van Dorp's (1998) paper draws attention to the unpredictable nature of impacts of structural adjustment programs, focusing on key indicators relating to soils, water resources and forests. The importance of remediation efforts is emphasized, through ex-ante assessment of the environmental impacts of adjustment policy packages.

## Mathematical Modeling

Jorgensen and Wilcoxon (1990) analyse the economic impact of environmental regulations on the US economy using a computable general equilibrium (CGE) approach that applies intertemporal analysis to a complex disaggregate model of long-term growth impacts. It focuses on critical energy–economy–environment linkages, and estimates the share of abatement costs in total costs for industry and transport. Bergman's (1990) paper also uses a CGE model designed to simulate the effects of environmental regulation and energy policy on the Swedish economy. In this case, the environmental market failure is corrected by creating a market for emission permits, whose costs are incorporated in the cost functions.

Persson and Munasinghe (1995) examine deforestation in Costa Rica. Their CGE model confirms partial equilibrium analyses, showing that establishing property rights tends to decrease deforestation, whereas higher interest rates promote deforestation. Glomsrod et al. (1998) also use a CGE model to study the impacts of structural adjustment policies on deforestation in Nicaragua. Improving the fiscal balance by reducing public expenditure or through sales tax reform promotes economic growth and conserves forests. Some polices increase deforestation in the near term, but ease pressure on forests in the longer term.

A paper by Holden et al. (1998) simulate six types of village economies in Zambia, to show that structural adjustment policies have significant adverse impacts on the environment. The removal of policy distortions does not necessarily lead to well functioning markets, because of high transactions costs and imperfect information in remote areas. The model results are consistent with empirical findings.

Useful qualitative insights about the environmental consequences of macro policy reforms may be gained with CGE models (Devarajan, 1990; Robinson, 1990; Persson and Munasinghe 1995). Islam et al. (2003) examine the sustainability of optimal growth. Their model analyses economic–ecological interactions, including resource depletion, pollution, irreversibility, and uncertainty. Key socioeconomic issues include savings, investment, technical progress, substitutability of productive factors, intergenerational efficiency, and equity. Many policy options emerge that could make growth more sustainable.

## Trade and Environment

Steininger's (1999) paper provides a comprehensive review of trade–environment models, including Heckscher–Olin, statistical–econometric, and applied general equilibrium models, that can address a variety of issues such as leakage, distribution, policy feedback effects, inter-linkages between production and markets, and specialization patterns.

Batabyal (1994) traces impacts of domestic environmental policies on international trade. His theoretical study shows that a large developing country might be worse off by pursuing environmental policies unilaterally. The government could use market power to set (second best) optimal pollution taxes to correct for domestic economic distortions, and thereby capture trade gains. Goldin and Roland-Host's (1997) paper examines the converse question – how growth in international trade might affect the local environment in Morocco. In their CGE simulation, trade liberalization alone promotes export-led growth, but also increases water stress. When complementary water price increases are simultaneously undertaken with trade liberalization, growth benefits are retained, while water stress improves.

Mani and Wheeler (1998) analyse data during 1960–95 for a variety of industrial sectors, in a wide range of countries, to determine whether pollution-intensive industries seek havens in countries with lax environmental standards. They conclude that trade does not generally increase production of pollution-intensive goods, since production takes place primarily for domestic markets rather than exports.

## Green National Income Accounting

Hartwick (1990) derives net national product (NNP) as the current value Hamiltonian for an optimal growth problem, including conventional economic inputs and natural resources. To derive NNP, drawdown of natural resource stocks should be netted out of gross national product (GNP), like depreciation of economic capital. Repetto et al. (1989) show how Indonesia's conventionally measured economic output could keep rising, while its natural resource base is being degraded, unless use of natural resource stocks is netted out. Hultkrantz (1992) provides monetary estimates of changes in timber stocks, production of non-marketed and non-timber products, and depletion of other natural assets in Sweden.

Bartelmus et al. (1991) integrated environmental and resource accounting into the standard system of national accounts (SNA) through the System of Environmental and Economic Accounting (SEEA) (UN, 2000). Atkinson et al. (1997) describe methods of adjusting SNA to account for environmental effects, including social accounting matrices. The concept of green national product or GNP (that is, conventional GNP revised to include changes in environmental services and resources) is extended, to develop the idea of 'genuine savings' (that is, national savings that include environmental effects). Persistent negative genuine savings provides a danger signal.

Aronsson and Lofgren's (1998) paper reviews recent developments on the subject. Their theoretical framework summarizes the consensus concerning the current state of knowledge, and sets out some areas of uncertainty and key questions for further research.

## 7.2: EMPIRICAL EVIDENCE

### Environmental Impacts of Structural Adjustment

During recent decades, structural adjustment programs (SAPs) have emerged as a powerful form of macroeconomic intervention in the developing world. Many developing countries experienced economic hardship during the 1980s. Domestic mismanagement and external economic factors caused the 'debt crisis'. The major oil price increases of 1974 and 1979 were a significant shock to oil-importing countries. Furthermore, restrictive monetary policies adopted by Western countries to curtail their own inflation, caused real interest rates to rise and made debt-service difficult for developing countries. Consequently, developing countries experienced balance of payment problems, which made them even more reliant on foreign donors. Economic growth rates declined and unemployment worsened.

The International Monetary Fund (IMF) and World Bank (WB) agreed to provide financial assistance to help countries service their debt, provided they adopted broad reforms called structural adjustment programs (SAP). These stringent economic and fiscal reform policies, which were designed to restore growth, also had adverse environmental and social impacts.

Stabilization policies sought to reduce pressure on foreign reserves by reducing domestic demand. Balance of payment problems were addressed by controlling inflation and reducing imports with contractionary fiscal policies and tight money supply. Simultaneously, currency devaluation aimed to improve the terms of trade and make exports more competitive. Adjustment policies focused on the supply side and addressed inefficiencies of the internal economic structure, including public sector reforms, to accelerate economic recovery and export growth. Parallel policies were adopted to improve the efficiency of resource allocation and competitiveness of markets at the sectoral level. Unfortunately, these reforms often had recessionary effects, resulting in significant loss of jobs and livelihoods – before the promised export-led growth could materialize. Furthermore, budget cutting pressures often forced governments to abandon social 'safety-net' programs, thereby causing further hardship to low income groups.

Reform programs have not always achieved even their economic goals. Furthermore, where macroeconomic gains have been realized through adjustment, environmental and social problems have worsened. The sustainable development literature is seeking to identify and remedy development strategies that lead to the unsustainable use of natural resources. Often, the very economic policies aimed at alleviating economic problems may undermine the environmental resources and social fabric on which national long-term development will ultimately depend (Munasinghe 2001).

## Some Stylized Results

Many case studies exist of environmental and social impacts of countrywide policies (Reed, 1992, 1996; Munasinghe and Cruz, 1994; Abaza, 1995; Young and Bishop, 1995; Munasinghe, 1996; et al. Opschoor and Jongma, 1996; Cruz et al., 1997; and Warford et al., 1997; *Environment and Development Economics*, 1999). However, generalizing about environmental and social impacts of economy-wide policies is difficult, because the linkages are complex and country specific. Even the purely economic impacts of structural adjustment programs are difficult to trace comprehensively (Tarp, 1993). Nevertheless, we attempt to summarize the main lessons learned from recent studies, below.

Economy-wide policy reforms aim to achieve major economic objectives (e.g., macroeconomic stability, efficiency, growth and poverty alleviation). Their environmental and social consequences fall into three broad categories – beneficial, harmful and unknown. First are the so-called 'win–win' policies, where it is possible to achieve simultaneous gains in all three areas of sustainable development (that is, economic, social and environmental). The second category recognizes important exceptions where such potential gains cannot be realized unless the macro-reforms are complemented by additional measures which protect both the environment and the poor. The third group consists of impacts that are unpredictable, because of the complex linkages involved, and long-run time perspective.

**Beneficial Impacts**

Several studies indicate that liberalizing reforms (like removing price distortions, promoting market incentives and encouraging trade), often contribute to both economic and sustainability gains. For example, reforms that improve the efficiency of industrial- or energy-related activities could reduce economic waste, increase the efficiency of natural resource use and limit environmental pollution. Similarly, improving land tenure rights and access to financial and social services will yield economic gains, promote better environmental stewardship and help the poor.

Analogously, shorter-run policy measures aimed at restoring macroeconomic stability will generally yield economic, social and environmental benefits. For example, price, wage and employment stability encourage firms and households to take a longer-term view, thereby encouraging environmentally sustainable activities. Lower inflation rates not only clarify price signals and enhance investment decisions, but also protect fixed income earners and the poor.

Studies of macroeconomic policies in Zimbabwe and Mexico (Munasinghe and Cruz, 1994), and Thailand (Panayatou and Susangkarn, 1991) illustrate win–win situations, with both economic and environmental gains. Birdsall and Wheeler (1992) argue that open trade policies in Latin America have promoted both economically productive and environmentally benign modern technologies. Other studies of environmental impacts of macroeconomic adjustment policies have been done for Sub Saharan Africa (Stryker et al., 1989), Thailand, Ivory Coast and Mexico (Reed, 1992), and Philippines (Cruz and Repetto, 1992).

Country case studies involving win–win outcomes of sectoral policy reforms cover energy and industry in Mexico (Munasinghe and Cruz, 1994), and Sri Lanka (Meier et al., 1995); water and sanitation in Brazil, China and India (World Bank, 1992b,1992c, 1993a); and land use in Tunisian rangelands (Munasinghe and Cruz, 1994), Zambian farms (World Bank, 1992d), Brazilian forests (Mahar, 1988; Schneider, 1993), Sudanese forests (Larson and Bromley, 1991), and Botswana pastures (Perrings, 1993).

Macroeconomic stabilization policies to control inflation lead to more sustainable logging in Costa Rica (Persson and Munasinghe, 1995), and sustainable farming in South America (Southgate and Pearce, 1988; Schneider, 1994).

**Avoiding Harmful Impacts**

Typical economy-wide reform programs are implemented in stages, with the initial adjustment package targeting the most important macroeconomic issues. Often, some unaddressed distortions (policy, market or institutional imperfections), will combine with an adjustment program to cause environmental or social harm (Munasinghe and Cruz, 1994; Abaza, 1995). Adverse social and environmental impacts may be avoided by implementing additional complementary measures that remove such distortions, without necessarily reversing the original reforms. Examples include:

*Policy distortions:* Promotional measures that increase profitability of exports might encourage excessive extraction of an underpriced natural resource (e.g., deforestation of open access areas due to subsidized timber stumpage fees). Similarly, trade liberalization could lead to expansion of wasteful energy-intensive activities, in a country where subsidized energy prices persisted.

*Market failures:* Successful adjustment may be associated with severe environmental damage – e.g., if external environmental effects of economic expansion (like air or water pollution), are not adequately reflected in market prices. In Indonesia, liberalization policies and industrial promotion accelerated growth in the modern sector, and reduced pollution. However, the scale of expansion increased pollution externalities, requiring complementary pollution taxes and environmental regulations (Munasinghe and Cruz, 1994).

*Institutional constraints:* Unaddressed institutional problems (like poor accountability of indebted state-owned enterprises, weak financial intermediation, or inadequately defined property rights), undermine incentives for sustainable resource management and worsen equity. Thus, reform of regulations and institutions should not lag behind economic restructuring, as shown in the case of energy pricing and institutional reforms in Poland (Bates et al. 1995; Kassenberg, this volume). In Peru, economy-wide reforms could have potentially increased harvesting pressures on over-exploited fisheries, without complementary regulations to protect various fishing grounds included within the adjustment program (World Bank, 1993b).

*Short-term stabilization*: Unless government budget cuts to bring inflation under control are carefully targeted, they may disproportionately penalize critical expenditures on environmental protection or poverty safety nets (ECLAC, 1989; Miranda and Muzondo, 1991; Cornia et al., 1992). Other examples include increases in air pollution in Thailand and Mexico due to reduced infrastructure expenditures (Reed, 1992), adverse impacts on low income groups in Africa (especially women and children) caused by lowered government spending in areas like health (Nzomo, 1992), and underfunding of forest protection activities (World Bank, 1994). Another adverse linkage is the possible short-term recessionary impact of adjustment on poverty and unemployment, whereby the migratory poor are forced to increase their pressures on fragile lands and 'open access' natural resources. The remedy would be to expand economic opportunities elsewhere.

**Long-term and Less Predictable Effects**

Finally, economy-wide policies may have unpredictable and counter-intuitive longer term effects on sustainability. Some of these effects may be traced through a general equilibrium framework that captures both direct and indirect links. The Costa Rica CGE model captures indirect effects on deforestation, to show that economic and environmental implications of wage restraints in structural adjustment are different from the results of partial equilibrium analyses (Persson and Munasinghe, 1995).

Adjustment often succeeds in generating new economic opportunities and livelihoods, thereby alleviating poverty and breaking the vicious cycle of environmental degradation and poverty (World Bank, 1992a). Higher incomes increase the willingness-to-pay for better environmental protection. However, while such growth is important for poor nations, it will increase overall pressures on environmental resources. At the same time, properly valuing resources, increasing efficiency and reducing waste, will reshape the structure of economic growth and limit undesirable environmental impacts. The long-run economic and environmental consequences of adjustment programs depend on the mobility of capital and labor. Finally, environmental policies themselves could have impacts on income distribution and employment.

Inequitable access to land and rapid population growth exacerbate rural unemployment and income inequality, thereby forcing the poor to depend increasingly on marginal resources for their livelihood (Feder et al., 1988; Lele and Stone, 1989; Cruz and Gibbs, 1990; *Environment and Development Economics*, 2004). The result is more pressure on fragile environments. A Philippines case study (Munasinghe and Cruz, 1994) evaluates the policy determinants of long-term changes in rural poverty and unemployment that have worsened lowland to upland migration, and conversion of forest lands to unsustainable agriculture. Shifting cultivation and grazing could worsen land degradation, where capital and technical change are limited, and population growth is rapid (Cleaver and Schreiber, 1991). Important long-term links between adjustment programs, trade and agriculture have been analysed by Goldin and Winters (1992).

## 7.3: FRAMEWORK FOR ANALYSIS

### A Microeconomic View of Environmental Harm – Magnitude and Structure of Growth

The *magnitude of growth* which may cause environmental damage could be moderated by policy measures that *restructure growth* – to make it less resource intensive and polluting. Munasinghe (1995) analyses the interplay of price and income effects in an initially stagnant economy which has open access forests, to clarify how economic reforms could combine with neglected economic distortions, to cause environmental harm.

The downward sloping curve $D_0$ in Figure 7.3 depicts demand for timber, which is assumed to depend on both price $p$ and income $Y$ (that is, $D = D(p, Y)$). At the effective (subsidized) price $p_S$ representing the marginal cost of logging, the initial deforestation rate is $Q_0$. Suppose $Q_L$ is the safe limiting rate of deforestation beyond which serious ecological damage occurs. If $Q_0 < Q_L$, the situation may continue undetected and uncorrected.

Clearly, the remedy is not to stop growth, but rather to introduce complementary measures that establish proper timber prices. First, property rights could be re-established in open access areas and 'efficient' stumpage fees imposed – to eliminate the economic subsidy (*ES*) and correctly reflect the opportunity cost of the timber. The resulting efficient price ($P_{ec}$) would reduce the logging rate to $Q_{ec}$, which still exceeds $Q_L$. Second, an additional environmental externality cost (*EE*) may be charged, to reflect loss of biodiversity or watershed damage, and thereby establish the full environmentally adjusted price ($P_{en}$). The deforestation rate now falls to $Q_{en} < Q_L$.

Exactly analogous reasoning would apply if we considered fuel prices and polluting emissions from urban transport or industry. In this case, $p_S$ might be a subsidized diesel price, $p_{ec}$ the equivalent trading opportunity cost, $p_{en}$ the full price including taxes to cover air pollution externality costs, and $Q_L$ the health-determined safety standard. One special case of air pollution would be carbon dioxide emissions, which worsen climate change.

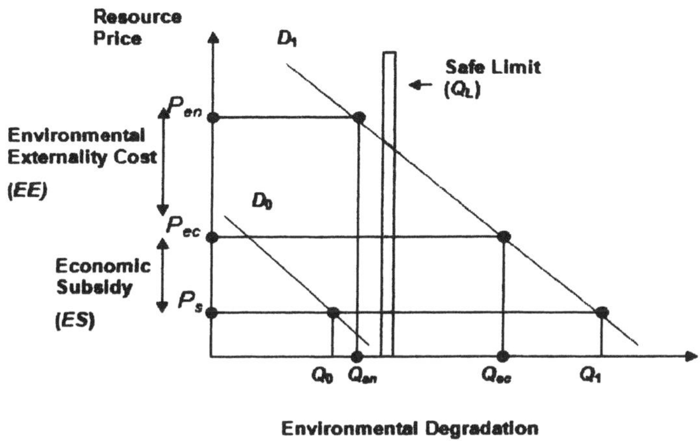


*Source*: Munasinghe (1995).

*Figure 7.3 Restructuring growth to reduce environmental degradation*

## A Macroeconomic View of Environmental Harm

In this section, we examine whether macroeconomic policies might be directly tailored to satisfy environmental considerations, without using additional complementary measures.

### The Role of Second-Best Policies

Maler and Munasinghe (1996) developed a theoretical model, showing that first-best macroeconomic policies which seek a Pareto optimum will not maximize welfare, if an environmental externality exists. Hence second-best macroeconomic policies ought to be pursued, to trade-off broad macroeconomic goals against environmental damage. Their model confirms both empirical evidence and microeconomic analysis presented earlier, that environmental damage is indeed caused by the interaction of growth-inducing economy-wide policies with residual imperfections. Therefore, the first-best solution would be to correct the imperfections using complementary policies while pursuing the original macroeconomic reforms. However, if political or other constraints prevent or delay introduction of complementary measures, then second-best macroeconomic policies may be justified – especially in cases where environmental harm could be significant.

Second-best options are also relevant to the dynamics of policy reform processes. For example, such reforms might be gradually intensified (instead of being suddenly imposed), thereby allowing further time to phase out residual imperfections that degrade the environment.

**The Timing and Sequence of Policy Reforms**

Could the timing and sequencing of economic reforms affect the extent of environmental damage? Some insights emerge from recent literature on the timing and sequencing of adjustment measures to achieve economic goals (Edwards, 1992).

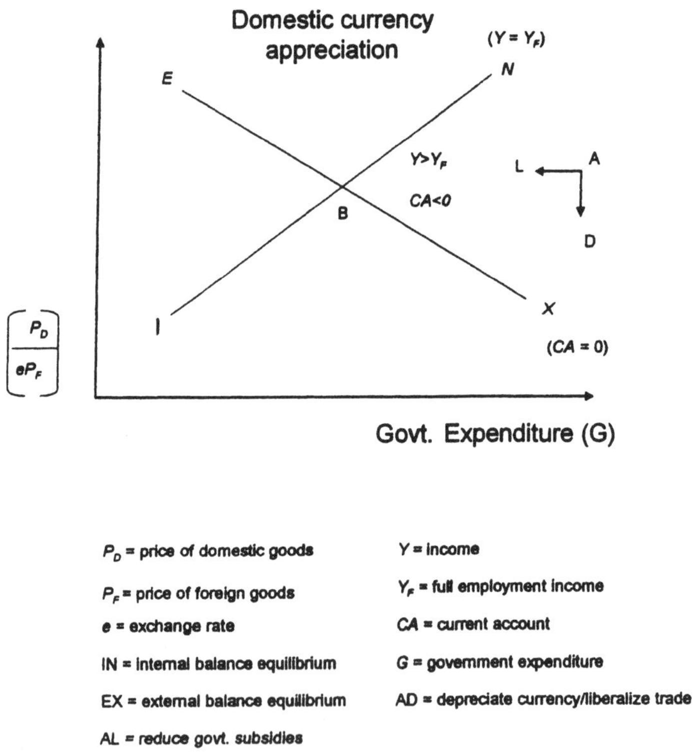


*Figure 7.4* *Timing and sequencing of economic policies to make development more sustainable*

In Figure 7.4, the $x$ axis indicates aggregate expenditure in a national economy (for example, government expenditure) and the $y$ axis reflects the effects of domestic currency appreciation (for example, ratio of domestic goods prices to foreign goods prices weighted by exchange rate). Point A represents the initial state of the economy – below the line of internal balance *IN* (representing an economy producing at the full employment level *YF*), and above the line of external balance *EX* (representing a zero current account, *CA*). Typically, macro-policymakers would seek to move the economy towards equilibrium point B by reducing both the current account deficit (since $CA < 0$) and excess demand (since $Y > YF$).

A downward movement AD is achieved by currency devaluation and removal of trade barriers, while a leftward shift AL occurs if government subsidies were eliminated (for example, raising subsidized energy prices). Suppose that reforms affecting AD could be achieved first and AL somewhat later (for example, delayed by powerful transport or industrial lobbies). Then, economic liberalization represented by AD alone might lead to greater foreign investment and expansion of energy-intensive industries which were attracted by low energy prices. However, this apparent gain would also result in wasteful use of (subsidized) energy and more environmental pollution. A coordinated elimination of subsidies together with currency devaluation would have better effects from the point of view of both conservation and environmental protection.

This simple, static analysis provides useful insights, although restraint and good judgment are required to resist making major changes in economy-wide policies merely to achieve minor environmental (and social) gains. Once again, policy options that achieved 'win–win' gains would be the most desirable.

## Extending the Conventional IS-LM Analysis to Include the Environment

Next, we examine environmental concerns, based on the well-known IS-LM framework used in comparative static analysis of macro-economic policies (Heyes, 2000). In Figure 7.5, the familiar IS-LM curves are plotted in $(r, y)$ space, where $r$ is the interest (discount) rate and $y$ is aggregate demand.

The IS curve is derived from aggregate demand and supply identity, representing equilibrium in the goods market:

$$y = [c(y) + i(r) + g] = [c(y) + s(y) + t.y] \qquad (7.1)$$

or equivalently

$$[i + g] = [s + t]$$

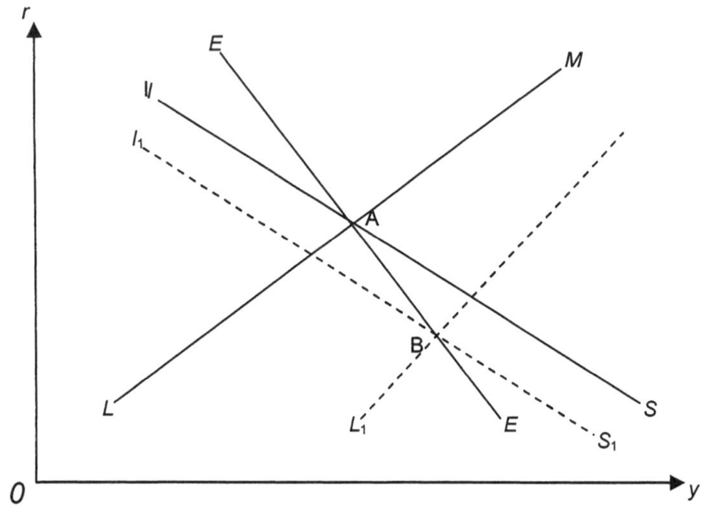


*Figure 7.5 Extending conventional IS-LM analysis to include the environment*

In this equation, $c$ is consumption, $i$ is investment, $g$ is government spending, $s$ is saving, and $t$ is the tax rate. Simple calculus yields the basic *IS* curve in the equation below, which is downward sloping:

$$[dr/dy]IS = [t + ds/dy] / [di/dy] \quad (7.2)$$

The *LM* curve is derived from the corresponding money market equilibrium:

$$M/p = L(r, y) \quad (7.3)$$

In this equation, $M$ is (fixed) money supply, $p$ is the price level and $L$ is money demand. Simple differentiation yields the basic *LM* curve, which is upward sloping:

$$[dr/dy]LM = -[dL/dy] / [dL/dr] \quad (7.4)$$

Environmental variables could be introduced into the familiar $(r, y)$ space, by examining the variation of environmental capital over time:

$$[d(KE)/dt] = [e(r).y + k.KE] \quad (7.5)$$

In this equation, *KE* is the stock of environmental assets, *t* is time, *e* is the environmental intensity of economic activity (or pollutants emitted per unit of economic output), and *k* is the rate of environmental self-renewal in the natural state. In a steady state economy, *d(KE)/dt* is zero, and implicit differentiation yields:

$$[dr/dy]EE = -[e] / [y.(de/dr)] \tag{7.6}$$

Assume that environmental intensity increases with capital cost, that is, $(de/dr) > 0$. Therefore, $[dr/dy]EE$ is downward sloping. The *EE* curve is drawn steeper than the *IS* curve, assuming that *e* is relatively insensitive to *r*. Suppose that *e* is also a function of some regulatory framework parameter *Z*, which determines how effectively polluters are obliged to pay for environmental externalities. If $(de/dZ) < 0$, then *EE* would shift leftward as regulatory enforcement improves.

To demonstrate the pedagogic value of this approach, consider an economy initially at equilibrium, with the *IS*, *LM* and *EE* curves intersecting at point A. Expansionary monetary policies would cause a shift from *LM* to $L_1M_1$ . Restoring the tripartite equilibrium at point B, would now require contractionary fiscal policies that yields the countervailing shift *IS* to $I_1S_1$ (assuming the *EE* curve is stable). Many similar policy exercises may be conducted, involving changes in various parameters and curves.

## Action Impact Matrix (AIM): A Tool for Policy Analysis, Formulation and Coordination

The Action Impact Matrix (AIM) is a sustainomics tool that portrays an integrated viewpoint, meshing development decisions with priority economic, environmental and social impacts. Table 7.1 shows a simple AIM, although an actual one would be larger and more detailed (Munasinghe and Cruz, 1994). The far left column lists key development interventions (both policies and projects), while the top row indicates major sustainable development issues. Thus the matrix cells: (a) explicitly identify critical linkages; (b) focus attention on valuation and other methods of analyzing the most important impacts; and (c) suggest action priorities. The organization of matrix also facilitates the tracing of impacts, as well as coherent articulation of links among various development actions – that is, policies and projects. This AIM-building process has helped to harmonize views among economists, environmentalists and others in several countries, thereby improving prospects for successful implementation.

*Table 7.1a Simplified preliminary action impact matrix, Part I*

| Activity/policy | Main objective | Impacts on key sustainable development issues | | | |
|---|---|---|---|---|---|
| | | Land degradation | Air Pollution | Resettlement | Others |
| Macroeconomic and Sectoral Policies | Macroeconmic and sectoral improvements | Positive impacts due to removal of distortions Negative impacts mainly due to remaining constraints | | | |
| Exchange Rate | Improve trade balance and economic growth | (-H) (deforest open-access areas) | | | |
| Energy Pricing | Improve economics and energy use efficiency | | (+M) (energy efficiency) | | |
| Others | | | | | |

*Source:* Munasinghe and Cruz (1994).

## Screening and problem identification

The AIM-based process facilitates early screening and problem identification – by preparing a preliminary matrix that identifies broad relationships, and providing a qualitative idea of policy impacts. Thus, the preliminary AIM helps to prioritize key linkages between policies and their sustainability impacts. For example, in the top row of Table 7.1a, a currency devaluation aimed at improving the trade balance may make timber exports more profitable but lead to deforestation of open access forests. The remedy involves complementary measures to strengthen property rights and restrict access to forest areas.

Another example involves increasing energy prices closer to marginal costs – to improve energy efficiency and decrease pollution (second row of Table 7.1a). Adding pollution taxes to marginal energy costs (to further reduce pollution), is the complementary measure. Increasing public sector accountability will reinforce favorable responses to these price incentives, by reducing the ability of inefficient firms to pass on cost increases to consumers or to transfer their losses to government.

In the third example, a major hydroelectric project (shown in Table 7.1b), has two adverse impacts – inundation of forested areas and villages, and one positive impact – replacement of thermal power generation (thereby reducing air pollution). A re-afforestation project coupled with adequate resettlement efforts will address both negative impacts.

*Table 7.1b Simplified preliminary action impact matrix, Part II*

| Activity/ policy | Main objective | Impacts on key sustainable development issues | | | |
|---|---|---|---|---|---|
| | | Land degradation | Air pollution | Resettlement | Others |
| Complementary Measures | Specific/local social and environmental gains | Enhance positive impacts and mitigate negative impacts (above) of broader macroeconomic and sectoral policies | | | |
| Market based | Reverse negative impacts of market failures, policy distortions and institutional constraints | | (+M) (pollution tax) | | |
| Non-Market Based | | (+H) (property rights) | (+M) (public sector accountability) | | |
| Investment Projects | Improve efficiency of investments | Investment decisions made more consistent with broader policy and institutional framework | | | |
| Project 1 *(Hydro Dam)* | Use of project evaluation (cost benefit analysis, environmental assessment, multi-criteria analysis, etc.) | (-H) (inundate forests) | (+M) (displace fossil fuel use) | (-M) (displace people) | |
| Project 2 *(Re-afforest and relocate)* | | (+H) (replant forests) | | (+M) (relocate people) | |
| Project N | | | | | |

*Source:* Munasinghe and Cruz (1994).

*Note:* A few examples of typical policies and projects as well as key environmental and social issues are shown. + and – signify beneficial and harmful impacts, while H and M indicate high and moderate intensity.

The AIM therefore encourages systematic articulation and coordination of policies and projects to achieve sustainable development goals, using readily available data. Social impacts, especially those affecting the poor, need to be incorporated into the AIM, using the same approach.

## Analysis and Remediation

*Analysis and remediation* is the next stage, where more detailed analyses are carried out for matrix elements representing high priority linkage between economy-wide policies and environmental impacts. Such analyses range from simple methods to fairly comprehensive system or multi-sector modeling efforts (for instance, CGE models including environmental and social variables), depending on planning goals and available data and resources. Economic valuation of environmental and social impacts is a key (and often difficult) step, in integrating these concerns into conventional economic cost-benefit analysis (Munasinghe, 1992; Freeman, 1993). When such valuation is problematic, other techniques like multi-criteria analysis may need to be used.

Sectoral and partial equilibrium analyses are more useful to identify direct impacts, whereas CGE modeling provides a more comprehensive but aggregate view with insights into indirect linkages. This process would lead to a more detailed AIM, which helps quantify impacts and formulate additional policy measures to enhance positive linkages and mitigate negative ones.

## Environmental Kuznets Curve (EKC)

The structure of economic growth is an important determinant of environmental degradation. Figure 7.6 shows the much-debated 'environmental Kuznets curve' or EKC, representing the relationship between economic progress (for example, GNP per capita) and environmental risk (for example, $CO_2$ emissions per capita) (Munasinghe, 1995). This approach is not concerned with empirically estimating the EKCs for any single country. Instead, it focuses on identifying policies to delink environmental degradation and growth.

Point C might represent an industrial country, whereas a developing country would be at point B. Ideally, the industrial country (which has exceeded safe limits) should increase environmental protection efforts and follow the future growth path CE. Developing countries which learn from past experiences of the industrialized world, could adopt measures permitting them to 'tunnel' through BDE – preferably below the safe limit indicating where environmental damage (like climate change or biodiversity loss) could become irreversible.

Such a tunnel also corresponds to a more economically optimal path, and resembles 'turnpike' growth paths which appeared in past literature (Burmeister and Dobell, 1971).

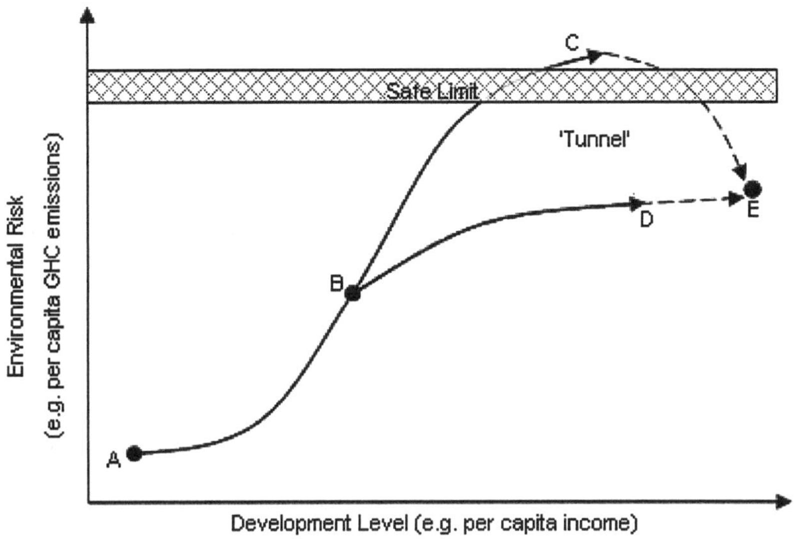


*Source*: adapted from Munasinghe (1995).

*Figure 7.6 Tunneling through to reduce environmental risk*

The highly peaked path ABCE could result from economic imperfections that make private decisions deviate from socially optimal ones. Corrective policies would help to reduce such divergences and permit movement through the tunnel BDE. Developing countries could thereby avoid severe environmental degradation along conventional development paths of industrial economies (ABCE).

The following actions might help decision-makers in finding such a 'tunnel':

1. Actively seeking 'win–win' policies that simultaneously yield both economically and environmentally (and socially) sustainable paths.
2. Pre-empting excessive environmental (and social) harm through ex-ante environmental (and social) assessment of projects and policies, introducing remedies that eliminate imperfections (like policy distortions, market failures and institutional constraints), and strengthening capacity for environmental protection.
3. Considering the fine-tuning of growth inducing economy-wide policies (such as altering their timing and sequencing), especially where severe environmental (and social) damage could occur.

In the specific case of climate change, Figure 7.6 would indicate a promising way forward for collaboration between industrial (i.e., Annex I) and developing countries (Munasinghe, 2008). Industrial countries (exceeding safe limits for 'dangerous' climate change) should mitigate along the path CE by restructuring their development patterns to delink carbon emissions and economic growth. Developing countries could adopt innovative policies to 'tunnel' through (along BDE). They would be assisted financially and technically by industrial nations – to simultaneously develop (and grow) more sustainably, follow a less carbon-intensive growth path, and reduce their climate vulnerability.

## Macroeconomic Performance Measurement Issues

To better include sustainability concerns in macroeconomic analyses, the conventional system of national accounts (SNA) must be improved, and new measures of environmental and social progress developed. Gross domestic product (GDP) is the common market-based measure which influences macroeconomic policy. Its shortcomings include neglect of income distributional concerns, non-market activities and environmental effects. Current SNA measures do not adequately reflect either the depletion of natural resource stocks (like deforestation), or environmental damage (due to pollution) (USBEA 1995).

Several countries have explored different environmental adjustments to the SNA. Various measures of national product and wealth are under consideration, including natural resource (stock) accounts, resource and pollutant flow accounts, environmental expenditure accounts, and alternative national accounts aggregates (Atkinson et al., 1997). However, no countries have formally altered their SNA to reflect environmental concerns, beyond the 1993 revision to the SNA (UNSO, 1993).

The United Nations Integrated System of Environmental and Economic Accounting (SEEA) is a pioneering step towards standardizing various accounting approaches (UN, 2000). It adds satellite accounts to the conventional SNA (without modifying the core accounts), involving disaggregation of the standard accounts to highlight environmental relationships, linked physical and monetary accounting, imputations of environmental costs, and extensions of the SNA production boundary.

The SEEA framework may be used to estimate various national accounts aggregates such as 'green GNP' – which are adjusted downward to reflect the costs of net resource depletion and environmental pollution. Green NNP is a Hicks–Lindahl measure of potentially sustainable income (Hicks, 1946). However, it cannot indicate whether the rate of saving is sufficient to maintain this income indefinitely and typically does not measure potential consumption if the economy were actually on a constant-utility path.

'Genuine savings' is a better measure of macro-sustainability (Atkinson et al., 1997).

Total wealth per capita is a useful indicator of sustainability, if the SNA measures total national wealth including the value of stocks of manufactured capital, as well as living and non-living resources. For total wealth $W$ and population $P$, development is (weakly) sustainable, when:

$$S = [d(W/P)/dt]/[W/P] \geq 0 \tag{7.7}$$

This index has several desirable properties – for instance, separately accounting for changes in natural assets having low substitution possibilities.

Some researchers have computed composite indices of human welfare to show that the relationship between 'true' welfare and conventional income per capita is positive in the early stages of development, but becomes negative later on – in contrast to the EKC effect (Daly and Cobb, 1989; Max-Neef, 1995). One such measure called Index of Sustainable Economic Welfare (ISEW), has already peaked in the 1970s or 1980s and is now declining for the US, UK, Germany, Austria and Netherlands. Poverty alleviation remains a dominant social objective (Sen, 1984). Thus, recent work is seeking to expand the social accounting matrix (SAM) to include the distributional impacts of environmental damage across income groups (Munasinghe, 2002)

## 7.4: CONCLUDING REMARKS

The sustainomics framework shows how macroeconomic reforms could make development more sustainable through simultaneous economic, social and environmental gains. Unintended adverse environmental and social impacts may occur when such reforms are undertaken while other policy, market or institutional imperfections persist. The remedy involves additional complementary measures that remove such imperfections, while maintaining the original economy-wide reforms. While growth is essential in poor countries, the magnitude of growth will intensify pressures on environmental resources. Increasing efficiency, reducing waste, and properly valuing resources, will restructure growth and reduce environmental damage. Strategies to make development more sustainable must be devised on a country-specific basis, based on local conditions, resource endowments and social needs.

The Action Impact Matrix (AIM) is a sustainomics tool that provides a systematic framework for identifying and addressing the most important environmental and social impacts of economy-wide policy reforms. The process for avoiding environmental (and social) damage includes:

- AIM-based analysis to identify, prioritize and analyse the most serious economic sustainability linkages;
- Specific *ex-ante* complementary measures to limit environmental and social harm, before economy-wide reforms are implemented;
- Contingency plans and carefully monitoring of sustainability issues, to deal with them *ex-post*;
- Reviewing the timing and sequencing of economy-wide policies and complementary measures, to minimize environmental and social damage.

Developing countries seeking sustainable development paths, could learn from the experience of the industrialized countries and avoid making the same mistakes. Economic imperfections that make private decisions deviate from socially optimal ones, exacerbate environmental damage along EKC growth paths. Tunneling through the EKC is possible, by:

- adopting 'win–win' policies that provide simultaneous economic, environmental and social gains;
- using complementary measure to address harmful impacts on sustainability; and
- reshaping economy-wide policies in cases where environmental and social damage was serious enough.

Better sustainable development indicators, including environmentally adjusted national accounts, will improve macroeconomic decision making.

**Areas for Further Work**

More country-specific case studies are required in tracing the environmental and social implications of economy-wide policies, especially in areas like trade and privatization. Exploring the sustainability of long-run growth is important, especially in the context of worsening natural resource scarcities, including degradation of the global environment and firm evidence of climate change due to anthropogenic emissions of greenhouse gases. Better practical models and analytical tools are required, based on approaches familiar to practicing macroeconomists (such as extended IS-LM framework).

Distributional, political economy and institutional issues also need to be addressed in future work. The cross-linkages between environmental and social impacts of economy-wide policies needs to be further explored. Better environmental and social indicators should be developed, including environmentally adjusted national accounts, and improved techniques for valuing environmental impacts. Where economic valuation of environmental and social impacts is difficult, techniques like multi-criteria analysis (MCA) can usefully supplement conventional cost-benefit analysis (CBA).

# NOTE

1. Munasinghe Institute for Development (MIND), Colombo, Sri Lanka.

# REFERENCES

Abaza, H. (1995), 'UNEP/World Bank Workshop on the Environmental Impacts of Structural Adjustment Programmes – New York, 20–21 March 1995', *Ecological Economics*, **14** (1): 1–5.

Aronsson, T. and K.G. Lofgren (1998), 'Green Accounting: What Do We Know and What Do We Need to Know?' in T. Tietenberg and H. Folmer (eds), *International Yearbook of Environmental and Resource Economics* 1998/99, Cheltenham, UK and Northampton, MA, USA: Edward Elgar, chapter 6.

Atkinson, G., R. Dubourg, K. Hamilton, Mohan Munasinghe, D. Pearce, and C. Young (1997), *Measuring Sustainable Development*, Cheltenham, UK and Lyme, USA: Edward Elgar.

Banuri, T. and J. Weyant (2001), 'Setting the Stage: Climate Change and Sustainable Development', in Bert Metz et al. (eds), *Climate Change 2001, Vol. 3: Mitigation*, Cambridge, UK: Cambridge University Press, published for the Intergovernmental Panel on Climate Change, chapter 1.

Bartelmus, P., C. Stahmer and J. van Tongeren (1991), 'Integrated Environmental and Economic Accounting: Framework for a SNA Satellite System', *Review of Income and Wealth*, **37** (2): 111–148.

Batabyal, A.A. (1994), 'An Open Economy Model of the Effects of Unilateral Environmental Policy by a Large Developing Country', *Ecological Economics*, **10** (3): 221–232.

Bates, R., J. Cofala and M. Toman (1995), 'Alternative Policies for the Control of Air Pollution in Poland', Environment Paper No. 7, Washington, DC: World Bank.

Bergman, L. (1990), 'Energy and Environmental Constraints on Growth: A CGE Modeling Approach', *Journal of Policy Modeling*, **12** (4): 671–691.

Birdsall, N. and D. Wheeler (1992), 'Trade Policy and Industrial Pollution in Latin America: Where are the Pollution Havens?', in P. Low (ed.), *International Trade and the Environment*, World Bank Discussion Paper No. 159, Washington, DC: World Bank.

Burmeister, E. and R. Dobell (1971), *Mathematical Theories of Economic Growth*, New York: Macmillan.

Cleaver, K. and G. Schreiber (1991), 'The Population, Environment, and Agriculture Nexus in Sub-Saharan Africa', Africa Region Technical Paper, Washington, DC: World Bank.

Cornia, G.A., R. Jolly and F. Stewart (1992), *Adjustment with a Human Face: Protecting the Vulnerable and Promoting Growth*, Oxford: Clarendon Press.

Cruz, W. and C. Gibbs (1990), 'Resource Policy Reform in the Context of Population Pressure, and Deforestation in the Philippines', *American Journal of Agricultural Economics*, **72** (5).
Cruz, W. and R. Repetto (1992), *The Environmental Effects of Stabilization and Structural Adjustment Programs: The Philippines Case*, Washington, DC: World Resources Institute..
Cruz, W., M. Munasinghe and J. Warford (1997), *The Greening of Economic Policy Reform, vol. 1 (Principles) and vol. 2 (Case Studies)*, Washington, DC: World Bank.
Daly, H.E. and W. Cobb (1989), *For the Common Good: Redirecting the Economy Toward Community, the Environment and a Sustainable Future*, Boston: Beacon Press.
Daly, H.E. (1991), 'Elements of Environmental Macroeconomics', in R. Costanza (ed.), *Ecological Economics: The Science and Management of Sustainability*, New York: Columbia University Press, chapter 3.
De Bruyn, S. and R.J. Heintz (1999), 'The Environmental Kuznets Curve Hypothesis', in J.C.J.M. van den Bergh (ed.), *Handbook of Environmental and Resource Economics*, Cheltenham, UK and Northampton, MA, USA: Edward Elgar, chapter 46.
Devarajan, S. (1990), 'Can Computable General Equilibrium Models Shed Light on the Environmental Problems of Developing Countries?', Paper prepared for WIDER conference the Environment and Emerging Development Issues, Helsinki, September.
*Ecological Economics* (1998), Special Issue on the Environmental Kuznets Curve, **25**.
Economic Commission for Latin America and the Caribbean (ECLAC) (1989), 'External Debt, Macroeconomic Policies, and Their Relation to the Environment in Latin America and the Caribbean', Meeting on Regional Co-operation in Environmental Matters in Latin America and the Caribbean, United Nations Environmental Programme, Brasilia.
Edwards, Sebastian (1992), 'Structural Adjustment and Stabilization: Issues on Sequencing and Speed', EDI Working Papers, Economic Development Institute, Washington DC: World Bank.
England, R.W. (2000), 'Natural Capital and the Theory of Economic Growth', *Ecological Economics*, **34** (3): 425–431.
*Environment and Development Economics* (1997), Special Issue on Environmental Kuznets Curve, **2**, Part 4.
*Environment and Development Economics* (1999), Special Issue on Structural Adjustment and the Environment, **4**, Part 1.
*Environment and Development Economics* (2004), Special Issue on Poverty and Forest Degradation, **9**, Part 2.
Feder, G., T. Ochan, Y. Chalamwong and C. Hongladarom (1988), *Land Policies and Farm Productivity in Thailand*, Baltimore, MD: Johns Hopkins University Press.
Freeman, A.M. (1993), *The Measurement of Environmental and Resource Values: Theory and Methods*, Washington, DC: Resources For the Future.
Galeotti, M, A. Lanza and P. Francesco (2006), 'Reassessing the Environmental Kuznets Curve for CO2 Emissions: A Robustness Exercise', *Ecological Economics*, **57** (1): 152–163.
Girma, M. (1992), 'Macropolicy and the Environment: A Framework for Analysis', *World Development*, **20** (4): 531–540.

Glomsrod, S., M.D. Monge and H. Vennemo (1998), 'Structural Adjustment and Deforestation in Nicaragua', *Environment and Development Economics*, **4** (1), 19–43.

Goldin, I. and A. Winters (1992), *Open Economies: Structural Adjustment and Agriculture*, Cambridge, UK: Cambridge University Press.

Goldin I. and D. Roland-Host (1997), 'Economic Policies for Sustainable Resource Use in Morocco', in W. Cruz, M. Munasinghe and J. Warford (eds), *The Greening of Economic Policy Reform, Vol. II: Case Studies*, Washington, DC: World Bank, chapter 3.

Grossman, G.M. and A.B. Krueger (1995), 'Economic Growth and the Environment', *Quarterly Journal of Economics*, **110**: 353–377.

Hartwick, J.M. (1990), 'Natural Resources, National Accounting and Economic Depreciation', *Journal of Public Economics*, **43**: 291–304.

Heyes, A. (2000), 'A Proposal for the Greening of Textbook Macroeconomics: IS-LM-EE', *Ecological Economics*, **32**(1): 1–8.

Hicks, J. (1946), *Value and Capital*, 2nd edition, Oxford, UK: Oxford University Press.

Holden, S.T., J.E. Taylor and S. Hampton (1998), 'Structural Adjustment and Market Imperfections: A Stylized Village Economy-wide Model with Non-separable Farm Households', *Environment and Development Economics*, **4** (1): 69–87.

Hotelling, H. (1931), 'The Economics of Exhaustible Resources', *Journal of Political Economy*, **39** (2): 137–175.

Hultkrantz, L. (1992), 'National Account of Timber and Forest Environmental Resources in Sweden', *Environmental and Resource Economics*, **2** (3): 283–305.

Islam, S., M. Munasinghe and M. Clarke (2003), 'Making Long-term Economic Growth More Sustainable: Evaluating the Costs and Benefits', *Ecological Economics*, **47** (2–3): 149–166.

Jorgensen, D.W. and P.J. Wilcoxon (1990), 'Intertemporal General Equilibrium Modeling of U.S. Environmental Regulation', *Journal of Policy Modeling*, **12** (4): 715–744.

Kessler J.J. and M. Van Dorp (1998), 'Structural Adjustment and the Environment: The Need for an Analytical Methodology', *Ecological Economics*, **27** (3): 267–281.

Koopmans, T.C. (1973), 'Some Observations on Optimal Economic Growth and Exhaustible Resources', in H.C. Bos, H. Linnemann and P. de Wolff (eds), *Economic Structure and Development: Essays in Honour of Jan Tinbergen*, New York, NY: American Elsevier Publishing Company, pp.239–255.

Larson, B. and D. Bromley (1991), 'Natural Resource Prices, Export Policies, and Deforestation: The Case of Sudan', *World Development*, **19** (10): 1289–1297.

Lele, U. and S. Stone (1989) 'Population Pressure, the Environment, and agricultural Intensification: Variations on the Boserup Hypothesis', MADIA Discussion Paper No. 4, Washington, DC: World Bank.

Leontief, W. (1970), 'Environmental Repercussions and the Economic Structure: An Input-output Approach', *Review of Economics and Statistics*, **52** (3): 262–271.

Mahar, D. (1988), 'Government Policies and deforestation in Brazil's Amazon Region', Environment Working Paper No. 7, Environment Department, Washington, DC: World Bank.

Maler, K.G. and M. Munasinghe (1996), 'Macroeconomic Policies, Second-best Theory, and the Environment', *Environment and Development Economics*, **1** (2): 149-164.

Malthus, T. (1798), *On Population*, New York, NY: Random House.

Mani, M. and D. Wheeler (1998), 'In Search of Pollution Havens? Dirty Industry in the World Economy, 1960–1995', in *Trade, Global Policy, and the Environment*, World Bank Discussion Paper No. 402, Washington DC: World Bank, chapter 8.

Markandya, A., P. Harou, L.G. Bellu and V. Cistoulli (2002), *Environmental Economics for Sustainable Growth*, Cheltenham, UK and Northampton, MA, USA: Edward Elgar Publishing for the World Bank, Washington, DC.

Max-Neef, M. (1995), 'Economic growth and quality of life: a threshold hypothesis', *Ecological Economics*, **15**: 115–118.

Meier, P., M. Munasinghe and T. Siyambalapitiya (1995), 'Energy Sector Policy and the Environment: A Case Study of Sri Lanka', in M. Munasinghe (ed.), *Environmental Impacts of Macroeconomic and Sectoral Policies*, Washington, DC: World Bank.

Miranda, K. and T. Muzondo (1991), 'Public Policy and the Environment', *Finance and Development*, **28** (2): 25–27.

Munasinghe, M. (1992), 'Environmental Economics and Sustainable Development', Paper presented at the United Nations Earth Summit, Rio de Janeiro, Brazil and reprinted by the World Bank, Washington DC.

Munasinghe, M. (1995), 'Making Growth more Sustainable', *Ecological Economics*, **15**: 121–124.

Munasinghe, M. (1996), 'An Overview of the Environmental Impacts of Macroeconomic and Sectoral Policies', in M. Munasinghe (ed.), *Environmental Impacts of Macroeconomic and Sectoral Policies*, Washington, DC: World Bank.

Munasinghe, M. (2001), 'The Sustainomics Trans-disciplinary Meta-framework for Making Development More Sustainable: Applications to Energy Issues', *International Journal of Sustainable Development*, **5** (1–2): 125–182.

Munasinghe, M., ed. (2002), *Macroeconomics and the Environment*, Cheltenham, UK and Northampton, MA, USA: Edward Elgar Publishing.

Munasinghe, M. (2007), *Making Development More Sustainable*, Munasinghe Institute for Development (MIND), Colombo, Sri Lanka: MIND Press.

Munasinghe, M. (2008), 'Rising Temperatures, Rising Risks', *Finance and Development*, March: 37–41.

Munasinghe, M. and W. Cruz (1994), *Economywide Policies and the Environment: Lessons from Experience*, Washington, DC: World Bank.

Munasinghe, M., O. Sunkel and C. de Miguel (eds), (2001), *The Sustainability of Long-term Growth: Socioeconomic and Ecological Perspectives*, Cheltenham, UK and Northampton, MA, USA: Edward Elgar Publishing.

Nzomo, M. (1992), 'Beyond Structural Adjustment Programs: Democracy, Gender, Equity, and Development in Africa, with Special Reference to Kenya', in J. Nyang'oro and T. Shaw (eds), *Beyond Structural Adjustment in Africa – The Political Economy of Sustainable and Democratic Development*, New York, NY: Praeger.

Opschoor, J.B. and S.M. Jongma (1996), 'Structural Adjustment Policies and Sustainability', *Environment and Development Economics*, **1**: 183–202.

Panayatou, T. and K. Hupe (1996), 'Environmental Impacts of Structural Adjustment Programs: Synthesis and Recommendations', in M. Munasinghe (ed.), *Environmental Impacts of Macroeconomic and Sectoral Policies*, Washington, DC: World Bank, chapter 3.

Panayatou, T. and C. Susangkarn (1991), 'The Debt Crisis, Structural Adjustment and the Environment: The Case of Thailand', Paper prepared for the World Wildlife

Fund Project on the Impact of Macroeconomic Adjustment on the Environment, Washington, DC.
Perrings, C. (1993), 'Pastoral Strategies in Sub-Saharan Africa: The Economic and Ecological Sustainability of Dryland Range Management', Environment Working Paper No. 57, Environment Department, Washington, DC: World Bank.
Persson, A. and M. Munasinghe (1995), 'Natural Resource Management and Economywide Policies in Costa Rica: A Computable General Equilibrium (CGE) Modeling Approach', *World Bank Economic Review*, **9** (2): 656–677.
Reed, D. (ed.) (1992), *Structural Adjustment and the Environment*, Boulder, CO: Westview Press.
Reed, D. (1996), *Structural Adjustment, the Environment and Sustainable Development*, London, UK: Earthscan Publishers.
Repetto, R., W. Magrath, M. Wells, C. Beer and F. Ossini (1989), 'The Need for Natural Resource Accounting', in *Wasting Assets: Natural Resources in the National Income Accounts*, Washington, DC: World Resources Institute, chapter 1.
Ricardo, D. (1817), 'Principles of Political Economy and Taxation', in P. Sraffa and Maurice H. Dobb (eds), *The Works of David Ricardo*, Cambridge, UK: Cambridge University Press.
Richmond, A. and R. Kaufmann (2006), 'Energy Prices and Turning Points: The Relationship between Income and Energy Use/Carbon Emissions', *Energy Journal*, **27** (4): 157–180.
Robinson, S. (1990), 'Pollution, Market Failure, and Optimal Policy in an Economywide Framework', Working Paper No. 559, Department of Agricultural and Resource Economics, University of California at Berkeley.
Schneider, R. April (1993), 'Land Abandonment, Property Rights, and Agricultural Sustainability in the Amazon', LATEN Dissemination Note No. 3, Washington, DC: World Bank.
Schneider, R. (1994), 'Government and the Economy on the Amazon Frontier', Latin America and the Caribbean Technical Department, Regional Studies Program. Report No. 34, Washington, DC: World Bank.
Sen, A.K. (1984), *Resources, Values and Development*, Oxford, UK: Blackwell Publishing.
Solow, R. (1993), 'An Almost Practical Step Toward Sustainability', *Resources Policy*, **19** (3): 162–172.
Southgate, D. and D.W. Pearce (1988), 'Agricultural Colonization and Environmental Degradation in Frontier Developing Economies', Environment Working Paper No. 9, Environment Department, Washington, DC: World Bank.
Stiglitz, J. (1974), 'Growth with Exhaustible Natural Resources: Efficient and Optimal Growth Paths', *Review of Economic Studies*, **41**, Special Symposium Issue: 123–137.
Steininger, K.W. (1999), 'General Models of Environmental Policy and Foreign Trade', in J.C.J.M. van den Bergh (ed.), *Handbook of Environmental and Resource Economics*, Cheltenham, UK and Northampton, MA, USA: Edward Elgar Publishing, chapter 28.
Stern, D.I. (1998), 'The Rise and Fall of the Environmental Kuznets Curve', *World Development*, **32** (8): 1419–1439.
Stryker, J.D., et al. (1989), 'Linkages between Policy Reform and Natural Resource Management in Sub-Saharan Africa', Fletcher School, Tufts University, Medford, MA, and Associates for International Resources and Development.

Tarp, F. (1993), *Stabilization and Structural Adjustment: Macroeconomic Frameworks for Analyzing the Crisis in Sub-Saharan Africa*, New York, NY: Routledge.

United Nations Statistical Office (UNSO) (1993), *System of National Accounts 1991*, New York, NY: United Nations.

United Nations Department of Economic and Social Affairs, Statistics Division (2000), *Integrated Environmental and Economic Accounting*, New York, NY: United Nations.

United States Bureau of Economic Analysis (USBEA) (1995), 'Natural Resource and Environment Accounting', USBEA Conference Proceedings, Washington, DC.

Warford, J., M. Munasinghe and W. Cruz (1997), *The Greening of Economic Policy Reform, 1 (Principles),* Washington, DC: World Bank.

Withagen, C. (1990), 'Topics in Resource Economics', in F. van der Ploeg (ed.), *Advanced Lectures in Quantitative Economics*, London, UK: Academic Press, pp. 381–420

World Bank (1992a), *World Development Report 1992: Development and the Environment*, Oxford, UK: Oxford University Press.

World Bank (1992b), *Water Quality and Pollution Control Project in Brazil*, Staff Appraisal Report, Washington, DC: World Bank.

World Bank (1992c), *The Changchun Water Supply and Environmental Project in China*. Staff Appraisal Report, Washington, DC: World Bank.

World Bank (1992d), *The Zambia Marketing and Processing Infrastructure Project*, Staff Appraisal Report, Washington, DC: World Bank.

World Bank (1993a), *The Karnataka Rural Water Supply and Environmental Sanitation Project in India*, Staff Appraisal Report, Washington, DC: World Bank.

World Bank (1993b), Peru: Privatization Adjustment Loan, report no. P-5929-PE. Washington, DC: World Bank.

World Bank (1994), *Adjustment in Africa: Reforms, Results and the Road Ahead*, World Bank Policy Research Report, Washington, DC.

World Commission on Environment and Development (WCED) (1987), *Our Common Future*, Oxford, UK: Oxford University Press.

Young, C.E.F. and J. Bishop (1995), 'Adjustment Policies and the Environment: A Critical Review of the Literature', CREED Working Paper Series No. 1, IIED, London, UK.

# 8. Ecological Macroeconomics: Consumption, Investment and Climate Change

**Jonathan M. Harris**

In February 2008, two separate scientific research articles analyzed climate models that included deep-sea warming, and reached the conclusion that carbon dioxide emissions must fall to near zero by the mid twenty-first century to prevent temperature increases in the range of 7° Fahrenheit by 2100 (Schmittner et al., 2008; Matthews and Caldeira, 2008). These results were consistent with, though somewhat stronger than, those of the Fourth Assessment Report of the Intergovernmental Panel on Climate Change (IPCC, 2007b), which indicates that a reduction of 50–85 per cent in carbon emissions by 2050 is needed to limit the likelihood of temperature increases in excess of 2°C (3.6°F). Also in the spring of 2008, the Earth Policy Institute reported that 'global carbon dioxide ($CO_2$) emissions from the burning of fossil fuels stood at a record 8.38 gigatons of carbon (GtC) in 2006, 20 percent above the level in 2000. Emissions grew 3.1 percent a year between 2000 and 2006, more than twice the rate of growth during the 1990s' (Moore, 2008).

The cognitive disconnect between scientists' warnings of potential catastrophe if carbon emissions continue unchecked on the one hand, and the political and economic realities of steadily increasing emissions on the other, defines the outstanding economic problem of the twenty-first century. Can economic growth continue while carbon emissions are drastically reduced? Addressing this issue necessarily refocuses attention on the meaning of economic growth itself.

The debate over economic growth and the environment has a long history, and involves many issues other than climate change. Theorists have considered possible growth limits associated with population, agriculture, energy, renewable resource systems and waste generation (see Harris and Goodwin, 2003). Ecological economists have suggested that environmental and resource constraints imply limits on economic scale, and thus limits to growth (Daly, 1996). Mainstream neoclassical economics, however, has generally rejected the concept of growth limits. The contrast between these two perspectives has remained unresolved so long as no immediate issues of urgent growth constraints at the macroeconomic level have come to the fore. Areas in which ecological capacities are clearly being overstressed – such as declining fisheries, degraded agricultural systems, or ecosystems loss – have been recognized as important problems, but are not usually seen as serious threats to the continuation of global economic growth. Global climate change, by contrast, has a clear and direct relationship to economic growth both in industrialized and developing nations.

The challenge of reducing global carbon emissions by 50–85 per cent by the year 2050, which is suggested by the Intergovernmental Panel on Climate Change (2007a) as a target compatible with limiting the risk of a more-than-2°C temperature increase, clearly conflicts with existing patterns of economic growth, which are heavily dependent on increased use of fossil fuel energy. While it is theoretically possible to conceive of economic growth being 'delinked' from fossil fuel consumption, any such delinking would represent a drastic change from economic patterns of the last 150 years.

Macroeconomic theory is heavily oriented towards an assumption of continuous, exponential growth in GDP. Fluctuations in economic activity – expansions and recessions – are presumed to occur as deviations from a stable long-term economic growth path (Figure 8.1). Indeed, the economic history of the past 150 years can be described as being consistent with this growth-oriented worldview, despite periodic interruptions of which the most serious was the Great Depression of the 1930s. But the record of global economic growth is strongly correlated with a parallel record of increasing fossil energy use and $CO_2$ emissions (Figures 8.2 and 8.3).

Is it possible to visualize the emissions trend shown in Figure 8.2 being reversed without drastic interruption in economic growth? Figure 8.4 shows the emissions patterns suggested by the IPCC as consistent with atmospheric stabilization of $CO_2$ at levels of 450 and 550 ppm. Even these stabilization levels represent a near-doubling over pre-industrial $CO_2$ levels, with a probable associated global temperature increase of around 2–3° C. To achieve these stabilization paths, global emissions must stop growing by 2020–2030, following which emissions patterns must shift to a rapid decline. Given existing patterns of population and economic growth, this almost certainly implies that emissions in currently industrialized nations must stop growing and start declining before 2020, with developing country emissions starting to decline after 2020 (see Chapter 4, this volume). What does this mean for economic growth, on global and national levels?

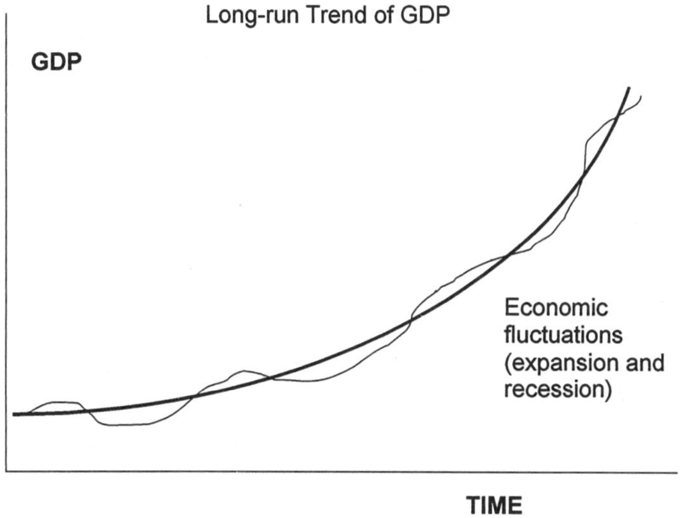


*Figure 8.1 The standard conception of long-term macroeconomic growth*

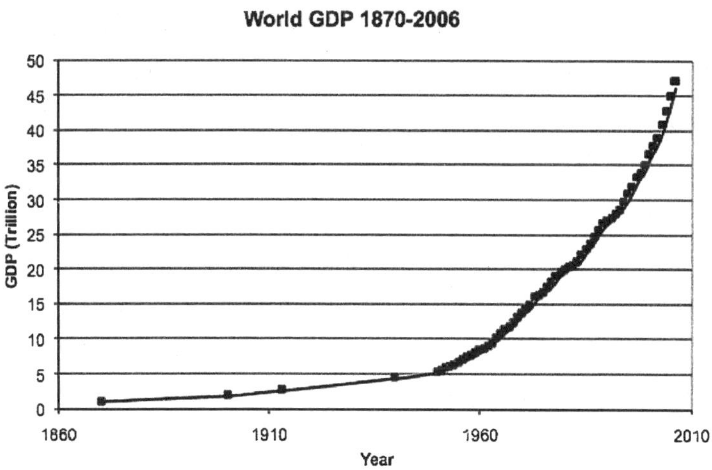


*Source:* Maddison, 2008.

*Figure 8.2 The record of long-term global economic growth, 1870–2006*

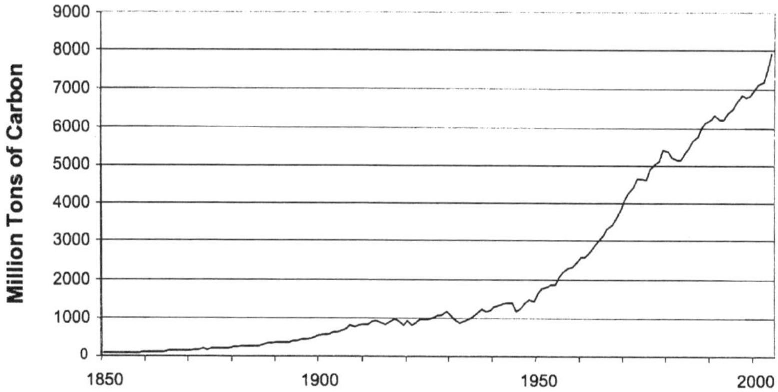


*Source:* Carbon Dioxide Information Analysis Center (CDIAC), http://cdiac.ornl.gov/.

*Figure 8.3 Carbon dioxide emissions from fossil fuel burning, 1850–2004*

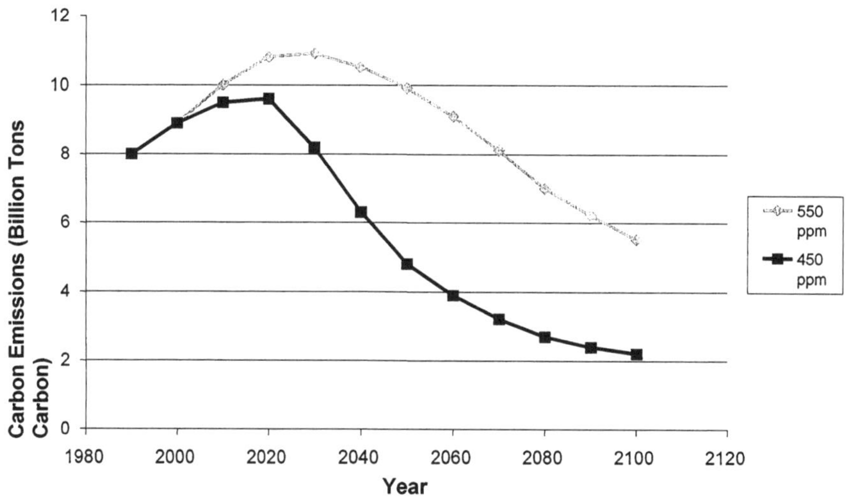


*Source:* Based on IPPC (2001).

*Figure 8.4 Carbon emission stabilization paths for 450 and 550 ppm*

## Some Possible Growth Outcomes

We can conceive of different ways in which the necessity of a rapid reduction in carbon emissions could affect economic growth:

1. If technologies, investment and consumption patterns remain similar to those of the present day, limiting carbon emissions could imply a drastic constraint on economic growth, leading to widespread recession and unemployment, and consigning much of the developing world to a state of stagnation.
2. A rapid change in energy technology and industrial patterns could permit a continuation of economic growth, but oriented strongly towards energy efficiency and non-carbon-based energy sources. This would require the transformation of much of the world's energy, industrial and building infrastructure.
3. Growth could be moderated, but less painfully than in the first option, through demand-side reductions in consumption. This would involve population stabilization and modification of consumption patterns towards greater use of services provided primarily by human capital, including education and health care. In addition, leisure time and household production would be emphasized instead of increased goods production.
4. Growth as a goal could be replaced entirely for richer nations, with an orientation instead to sustainable but moderate consumption levels and greater equity. ('Moderate consumption levels' would probably imply a reduction from today's levels, at least for certain kinds of consumption – more on this below). For developing nations, the goal would be the attainment of these 'global middle class' consumption levels, but no more. The focus of economic progress could then be on improved social and cultural life.

The last of these option sounds like the future envisioned in much utopian literature, and harks back to the 'stationary state' economy conceived of by J.S. Mill in the nineteenth century, and currently advocated by Herman Daly as the 'steady state' (Daly, 1991b). This is represented in Figure 8.5 as a radical alternative to the standard conception of exponential economic growth over time (the upper curve in Figure 8.4 essentially repeats the 'long-term growth trend' from Figure 8.1). In between these two options, there is a wide range of possibilities denoted by a question mark in Figure 8.4, and representing some combination of options (2) and (3) above. If we accept the necessity of reducing carbon emissions, but wish to avoid the unpleasant future of option (1), then future economic growth must follow some pattern of this sort. But how can standard economic theory adapt to these changes? Can the goal of drastically reduced carbon emissions be achieved without worsening unemployment, increased conflict between 'haves' and 'have-nots', or reduced well-being? The answers to these questions depend partly on technological potential, partly on social willingness to alter consumption goals, but also significantly on the approach we take to macroeconomic theory.

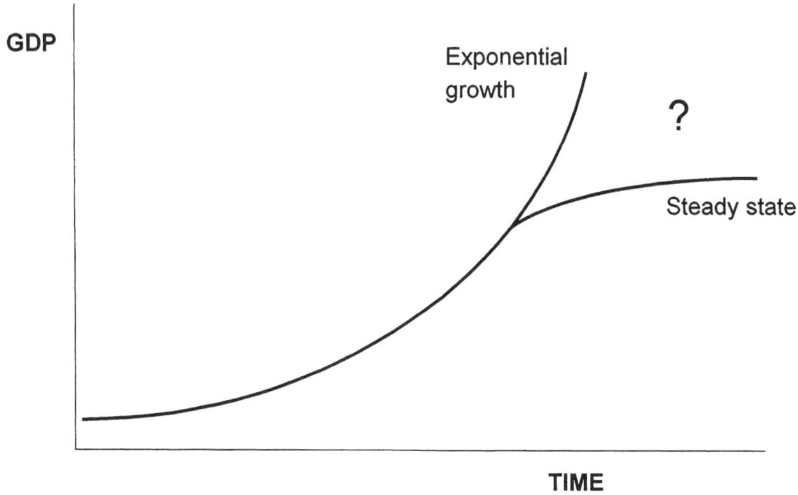


*Figure 8.5 Differing views of the future of economic growth*

## THREE DILEMMAS: ECONOMIC, DEMOGRAPHIC AND ECOLOGICAL

An ecological approach to macroeconomics requires recognition of physical limits to growth. As we have noted, the climate change issue brings this question most urgently to the fore, but climate change is part of an inter-related group of environmental issues associated with growth limits. These include population, agriculture, resource management and industrial ecology. As the public focus on climate issues has intensified, the linkages among these issues have become clearer.

Population growth is clearly a driver of climate change. Population growth in the United States, for example, is about 1 per cent per year, approximately the same as the rate of increase in carbon emissions since 1990. This implies that a stable US population would have had little or no net increase in carbon emissions over this period. Projections for global population growth by 2050 range from an additional 1.6 billion to an additional 3 billion people over 2000 levels, an increase of between 26 per cent and 49 per cent (United Nations, 2007). This clearly increases the pressures leading to higher energy consumption and carbon emissions, and makes achievement of a reduction path significantly more difficult than it would be with a stable population.

Increasing agricultural production is also a driver of climate change, resulting from both energy use and methane production from rice paddies, livestock and agricultural wastes. Agriculture in turn is impacted by policies to respond to climate change, such as expanded production of biofuels. A reduced rate of agricultural land expansion is already an important constraint on agricultural production growth, raising issues of agricultural carrying capacity (Harris and Kennedy, 1999), and significant land demands for biofuels increase pressures on the agricultural system as well as on conversion of forest lands to agriculture.

Other environmental issues such as freshwater limits and species loss are also exacerbated by climate change. Loss of glacial and snowmelt water resulting from warming temperatures worsen the situation in areas where water limits are already a major problem, such as the Western United States and areas of India and Bangladesh that are dependent on Himalayan runoff. Changing temperature gradients affect species habitat, increasing pressures for species extinction. As noted, combined food and fuel demands promote conversion of wild lands to agricultural production.

Recent rising food and fuel prices serve as a partial economic indicator of these interrelated environmental limits, but the ecological damage is much greater than reflected in the economic system, since most of the environmental losses are not internalized into prices. If ecological impacts were to be even partly internalized through a carbon tax or similar policy, prices for food, fuel and energy-intensive goods would increase further.

## The Problem of Consumption

The recognition of physical and environmental limits implies the need for a modified approach to consumption. Consumption represents the largest component of an expenditure approach to GDP, and is also the basis for more ecologically oriented measures such as the Genuine Progress Indicator (GPI).[1] But physical consumption, according to the principle of limited macroeconomic scale set forth by Daly (1991a), cannot grow without limit. 'Throughput', or the combination of resource inputs and product and waste outputs, must be controlled to avoid excessive resource depletion and damage to ecosystems. This raises an essential dilemma for ecological macroeconomics. Standard macroeconomic models envision ever-growing consumption, with investment ideally serving the function of maximizing consumption over time, according to the so-called 'golden rule' of capital accumulation.[2] But if an ecological perspective implies limits on consumption, what happens to investment?

If resources are shifted from consumption to investment, this implies an even greater potential for consumption growth over time. But if investment is reduced, there is a danger of rising unemployment. This dilemma can only be resolved by forms of investment which improve well-being but do not contribute to greater consumption of material goods and non-renewable energy. These might include investment in human capital, in natural capital, or in factors contributing to energy-efficient infrastructure and overall energy efficiency. Price incentives may encourage the choice of such forms of investment through the market mechanism, depending on price incentives, but in many cases (such as improved public transportation systems and other infrastructure) large-scale public investment will be essential.

## The Population Dilemma

Another dilemma concerns stabilizing population. The ecological principle of carrying capacity implies some limits on population. While there has been extensive debate over the extent to which human ingenuity and technology can stretch these limits, there is now a broad consensus that continued rapid growth in population will be damaging both to the planetary environment and to economic well-being.[3] Both normative and positive perspectives (population policy as well as spontaneously declining fertility rates) suggest a stabilizing of global population by the mid twenty-first century. A stabilizing population is a 'graying' population, with an increased elderly dependence ratio. Growing populations increase pressure on resources, but stabilized populations demand high social expenditures with a reduced work force. Similarly, increasing life expectancy improves human well-being, but further boosts social and medical expenditures. Thus a development which is apparently desirable from ecological and well-being perspectives will impose significant macroeconomic strains on both developed and, eventually, developing economies.

This population-related dilemma is evident in the current debate in the United States over Social Security, and similar conflicts over the future of the European welfare state. A large component of this debate has to do with demographic factors: the growing percentage of elderly who, with greater longevity, require higher social security and medical expenditures. These pressures will only increase with time, according to most budget projections. Russia, Germany and various East European nations are already experiencing declining populations. The comparable stresses predictable in the not-so-distant future for developing nations will be much larger in absolute terms. China is on the verge of a transition to a stable or declining population, with a significantly larger proportion of elderly people, and other large developing nations will soon follow (Population Resource Bureau, 2007). Some analysts suggest that the economic costs of aging populations argue against population stabilization policies (Longman, 2004). But policies that maintain or increase birth rates merely shift the problem later in time, while increasing absolute numbers, and therefore environmental pressures, as well as ultimate economic costs.

**Environmental and Social Investment**

A third dilemma has to do with the costs of environmental conservation. Goals such as stabilizing atmospheric carbon accumulations require large investments in conservation, renewable energy, and new technologies such as carbon capture and storage. These investments must take place in the short and medium term, for very long-term returns. The current short-term bias of macroeconomic policies makes it difficult to justify such investments. In addition to climate-related investments, there are other environmentally-related areas such as biodiversity conservation, water and sanitation, disease control, transportation and urban infrastructure, in which current global investment clearly falls dramatically short of what would be needed to address the problems.

- *Responses to global climate change.* The economic costs of modest action to prevent climate change, such as the emissions cuts mandated in the Kyoto Protocol, are low, and indeed may even provide a net economic benefit (Repetto and Austin, 1997; Nordhaus and Boyer, 2000; Cline, 2002; Stern, 2006). However, the measures ultimately needed to stabilize atmospheric greenhouse gases are significantly more drastic, requiring cuts of 50–85 per cent in global emissions at costs of hundreds of billions (IPCC, 2007a), According to the Stern Review analysis (see Chapter 2, this volume) the current economic costs of such a program are justified by the eventual economic and environmental benefits. Foley (Chapter 5, this volume) provides a different economic justification, in terms of the appropriate choice of investment to benefit future generations. Regardless of the eventual benefits, the current investment requirements are huge. They would involve restructuring presently industrialized nations to increase energy efficiency by 50 per cent or more, shifting from fossil to renewable fuels, and promoting massive technology transfer to enable presently developing nations to take high-efficiency, non-carbon energy paths. Clearly this requires major public and private investment expenditures, well beyond any now taken or contemplated.

- *Biodiversity conservation.* The global destruction of forest, wetland, coastal and ocean ecosystems continues at a steady, increasing, or only slightly diminished pace, depending on the particular ecosystem, as noted in numerous reports by international environmental organizations (UNEP, 2007;

Millennium Ecosystem Assessment, 2005), Commercial interests including agriculture, ranching, mining, logging, fishing and aquaculture create increasing economic pressures which greatly outweigh private and public conservation efforts. In some cases market-based reforms, such as individual transferable quotas in fisheries, can redirect commercial efforts in a way that is more consistent with ecosystem conservation. But in many cases 'economically rational' solutions are environmentally destructive, as when old-growth forests are logged for short-term profit. The interests of ecosystem survival, a classic case of a public good, can only be represented through public policy measures, including mobilization of public investment capacity. While this principle has been recognized through the establishment of international agencies such as the Global Environment Facility, the scope of the existing effort is tiny relative to the problem.

• *Global public health, nutrition, and basic education.* Some of the most productive areas for investment in human well-being are the areas of public health, nutrition, and basic education, which often have an environmental component. Provision of clean water, sanitation, and prevention or cure of widespread killer diseases, both 'old' like malaria and 'new' like AIDS, is generally beyond the capacity of poorer developing nations, and international aid is insufficient. Climate change will accentuate the importance of this issue, creating threats to water availability and agricultural productivity in tropical areas, while also promoting increased spread of tropical diseases (Epstein and Mills, 2006). In more rapidly developing and developed nations, market priorities often mean that public health and education are insufficiently funded, so that health care, access to water, or basic education is available only at high cost, creating life-and-death class distinctions based on income, and privileging luxury consumption over basic health needs. Any economic theory that identifies human well-being as the ultimate aim of economic systems must address this paradox at the macroeconomic level, where it involves both distribution of income and provision of social investment.

Thus the three dilemmas are: the balancing of consumption and investment while maintaining high employment as well as limits on material consumption; the provision of adequate social and health expenditures, including the added expenditures necessary for a 'graying' population with greater longevity; and sufficient investment in the maintenance of critical natural capital systems including ecosystems and atmosphere. These are essential macroeconomic issues for the twenty-first century.

# A PROPOSED RESOLUTION OF THE DILEMMAS

The first dilemma can be expressed in terms of balancing the well-known macroeconomic aggregate equation:

$$Y = C + I + G + (X - M) \tag{8.1}$$

in a situation where $C$ must be limited, at least insofar as it represents material consumption. This implies either limits on output $Y$ (the 'steady-state' solution advocated by Daly), a change in the nature of $C$, or an increase in $I$ or $G$. On a global scale, no solution to the problem can be found in the foreign trade sector $(X - M)$, since foreign trade balances must sum to zero overall. Increases in $I$ are problematical, because in a profit-driven economy they can only be motivated by the prospect of increased sales (i.e. increases in $C$). Conceivably $Y$, and employment levels, might be maintained or increased through increasing the size of $G$, but this will certainly generate resistance to an expanding role for 'big government', and increasing $G$ can also have significant environmental impacts.

The second two dilemmas discussed above may contribute to resolving the first. They define the need for large investment expenditures which are not directly related to increasing material consumption. Rather than being a burden or threat, the need for such expenditures may be the solution to maintaining full employment with limited consumption.

To capture this logic in terms of macroeconomic aggregates, it is necessary to break them down more specifically as follows:

$C_g$ = consumption of non-durable goods and energy-intensive services
$C_s$ = consumption of human-capital-intensive services[4]
$C_m$ = household investment in consumer durables
$I_{me}$ = investment in energy-intensive manufactured capital
$I_m$ = investment in energy-conserving manufactured capital
$I_n$ = investment in natural capital[5]
$I_h$ = investment in human capital
$G_g$ = government consumption of non-durable goods and energy-intensive services
$G_s$ = government consumption of human capital-intensive services
$G_{me}$ = government investment in energy-intensive manufactured capital
$G_{mc}$ = government investment in energy-conserving manufactured capital
$G_n$ = government investment in natural capital
$G_h$ = government investment in human capital

Thus the basic equation of macroeconomic balance can be restated as:

$$Y = (C_g + C_s + C_m) + (I_{me} + I_{mc} + I_n + I_h) + (G_g + G_s + G_{me} + G_{mc} + G_n + G_h) + (X - M) \quad (8.2)$$

This formulation gives us more to work with. While ecological principles imply limits on $C_g$, $I_{me}$, $G_g$ and $G_{me}$, the other terms in the equation can grow over time without significant negative environmental impact, and indeed with a positive effect in the case of natural capital or energy-conserving investment.[6] The equation can be rearranged to distinguish between macroeconomic aggregates that we wish to limit, and those that we wish to encourage:

$$Y = (C_g + I_{me} + G_g + G_{me}) + (C_s + C_m + I_{mc} + I_n + I_h + G_s + G_n + G_{mc} + G_h) + (X - M) \quad (8.3)$$

To satisfy sustainability criteria, the terms in the first set of brackets should be stabilized or reduced over time, but the terms in the second set of brackets can be expanded. This should give plenty of scope for macroeconomic policy aimed at the maintenance of full employment. Regarding the foreign sector term, a trade surplus or deficit might be acceptable depending on the situation of a given country, though very large trade imbalances linked to excessive consumption (as in the case of the United States) or perverse capital flows (as in the case of developing nation debt service) should be avoided.

The second and third dilemmas become more tractable once it is recognized that expansion of the terms in the second set of parentheses in equation (8.3) is desirable from the points of view of employment, social well-being and environmental sustainability. Viewed from this perspective, the large investments necessary to provide for public health, nutrition and education, environmental protection, support for the elderly, and transition to a non-carbon energy system, appear as economic benefits rather than costs. This is in keeping with the original Keynesian insight that increasing aggregate demand in an underemployed economy confers net benefits both through the original spending and through multiplier effects. It also offers greater scope for 'green' taxes. To the extent that such taxes reduce aggregate demand, their revenues can be recycled to promote spending in the more socially and environmentally beneficial sectors of the economy.

## New Forms of Keynesian Policy

This approach also returns to the Keynesian focus on the need to compensate for the limitations of the market system at the macro level (Harris, 2007). An enduring myth of neoclassical economics is that the economy has a 'growth path', as shown in Figure 8.1, from which it may deviate in the short term, possibly requiring macroeconomic stabilization policy, but to which it will return in the long term. The more complex formulation above makes clear that there are many potential growth paths, which might be conceptualized as lying between the exponential and steady-state growth paths shown in Figure 8.4, but which might also be thought of as moving in different dimensions from the one-dimensional money measure of GDP. Furthermore, government policy plays an essential role not just in stabilization but in determining which growth path will be followed. The set of paths that is suggested here represents what Daly (1996) has called 'development' rather than 'growth' – but if economists and the public are committed to 'growth', this approach offers a different kind of growth, in which macroeconomic aggregates grow but throughput does not. The original Keynesian approach has often been distorted to promote 'growthmania' but there is nothing about the true Keynesian model that necessarily links full employment to increased *material* consumption.

Equation (8.3) suggests that the standard Keynesian policy tools of fiscal and monetary policy need to be refined or complemented with other tools. 'Green' taxes or equivalents such as cap-and-trade with auction are effective mechanisms to shift expenditure from the first bracketed set of terms to the second. The revenues generated by such policies offer significant fiscal potential for promoting income equity or for social investment (both traditional Keynesian goals). In contrast to the 'blunt instruments' of demand management that simply seek to adjust overall consumption levels, this 'green' Keynesianism also aims at redistributing demand towards environmentally sounder areas of spending.

Internalizing environmental externalities has a sound basis in standard economic theory, but an ecological version of Keynesianism conceptualizes internalization at the macroeconomic rather than microeconomic level. On the expenditure side, not all government expenditure on health, education and environment needs to be considered as an expansion of 'big government'. Systems for decentralizing grants, encouraging community initiatives and providing microlending can provide for social investment controlled and directed at the local level. Tax rebates for purchases such as hybrid vehicles or solar systems effectively combine macro policy with microeconomic incentives. Overall, the use of tax policy to promote energy efficiency and renewables would imply a dramatic shift towards taxing negative externalities, and away from payroll and income taxes (see Chapter 9, this volume).

Monetary policy, also, can be 'greened'. Standard monetary policy raises or lowers interest rates, also a 'blunt instrument' since the impacts of Federal Reserve policy affect all investment and loans on an equal basis. But creative monetary policy could promote preferential interest rates for investments in energy efficiency and renewables. Quasi-public entities like Fannie Mae and Freddie Mac, whose importance to the credit markets for good or ill became evident in the credit crisis of 2008, could be retooled to help promote the necessary transition to hyper-efficient buildings and vehicles through offering low-interest loans for clean energy investments.

Some may object that this approach puts too much power in the hands of government, and that it would be better to rely primarily on market-mediated private investment. But these are not government policies of direct control or 'picking winners'. Rather, they are ways of setting ground rules for markets that both promote stability and encourage environmentally sound investment. Some investments, such as in mass transit and rail infrastructure, are necessarily public, but in many cases what is needed is general guidance for private investment through internalization of environmental costs into prices, or by incentives for environmentally sound investment (see Chapter 10, this volume). In addition, there is a well-established phenomenon whereby government infrastructure investment can 'lock in' patterns of private investment that persist for many years, for example by developing road or rail networks that determine transportation patterns and industry location in ways that can be environmentally beneficial or harmful. The extensive existing network of implicit or explicit government subsidies could also be redirected to promote sustainable development paths.[7]

At the root of the issue is the unquestionable fact that per capita economic growth is based on productivity growth. Keynes saw that such productivity growth, in the absence of sufficient aggregate demand, could become a social problem and lead to persistent unemployment. To this insight we must add the current problem that growth of labor productivity, which has historically been supported by an increase in the proportion of material and energy inputs to labor inputs, can lead to increased environmental degradation. The macroeconomic policy challenge is to manage and direct productivity growth in ways that benefit human well-being and the environment.

Viewed this way, there is a lot of scope for solving problems that otherwise appear intractable. Suppose, for example that labor productivity grows at 2 per cent per annum, a rate consistent with recent and projected US productivity growth rates, which are actually slightly higher (Jorgensen et al., 2004). This implies a doubling of per capita output in about 35 years. Thus over this period consumption levels could be maintained, or slightly increased, while providing trillions of dollars of productive capacity for social investment. At the same time, material and energy 'throughput' could be substantially reduced through investment in increased efficiency (i.e., increased productivity of material and energy inputs).

This places problems such as rising Social Security or Medicare expenses, or the infrastructure investment required to avert global climate change, in a different light. These areas can provide the needed Keynesian stimulus to maintain 'economic growth' – though a different kind of growth from that commonly understood. The problem is to redirect policy towards these ends, and to do so with as much emphasis as possible on decentralization, local initiative, and individual choice. An extensive array of both government and market-based policies are available to this end, so that both public and private sectors can be redirected towards a more sustainable economic system.

## CONCLUSION

Macroeconomic policy traditionally aims at stabilization of economic systems, avoiding excessive inflation or recession. A broader view of macroeconomics takes into account other goals: ecological sustainability, provision of basic social needs such as education and health care, and distributional equity.

This is consistent with the original intent of Keynes, who wrote that 'the outstanding faults of the economic society in which we live are its failure to provide for full employment and its arbitrary and inequitable distribution of wealth and incomes' (Keynes, 1964 [1936]). Keynes did not focus on issues of ecological sustainability, but from the standpoint of the first decade of the twenty-first century, it certainly seems reasonable to include environmental degradation as one of the 'outstanding faults' of the economic system.

The implementation of ambitious programs for social investment and redirection of the macroeconomy towards sustainability will be essential for preserving economic systems in the twenty-first century. It will, however, require a turn away from conventional macroeconomics. The current state of macroeconomic thought is somewhat paradoxical. Keynesianism is out of favor, and predominant economic theory argues against the effectiveness of government policy intervention – yet as soon as trouble threatens, political leaders uniformly reach for Keynesian policy tools such as tax cuts or interest rate cuts to deal with recessionary threats. The credit crunch and economic slowdown of 2007–2008 quickly led to across-the-board tax rebates, and the Fed moved into new areas of lending to inject funds into a troubled financial sector.

This general practical acceptance of Keynesian principles suggests that the barrier to the implementation of the kind of expanded Keynesianism sketched out in this chapter is not any inherent theoretical weakness, nor any problems of policy implementation. Rather, it is a political and cultural adherence to the 'old' view of material-based, energy-intensive, market-driven economic growth as the only route to prosperity.

Economists bear significant responsibility for perpetuating this outdated world-view by promoting the myth that government intervention, with limited exceptions, is likely to interfere with efficient market operations and create a drag on growth. If economists were instead to adopt the position that social choices regarding long-term growth paths are essential, and acknowledge the importance of public investment in determining our ability to respond to current problems, that would not guarantee that politicians would turn away from 'market-friendly' policies that often reinforce negative directions in the economy. But it would remove at least one rationale: that economics tells us we can't .... (alleviate global warming, eliminate malnutrition, provide adequate Social Security and Medicare, etc.). In order to promote the contrary perception – that we can, if we choose, respond adequately to the problems that threaten the planetary future – economists must reorient growth theory to be consistent with ecological sustainability. Old and new policy tools can then be combined create economic institutions that can achieve a rapid reduction in carbon emissions while promoting investment in human and natural capital.

## NOTES

1. The GPI is a linear descendant of the Index of Sustainable Economic Welfare (ISEW) introduced by Daly and Cobb (1984). Recent data for the GPI is available at Redefining Progress, http://www.rprogress.org.
2. See Phelps (1961) for the original formulation of the 'golden rule' regarding the level of savings and investment necessary to maximize consumption over time.
3. See e.g. Kelley (1998) and Birdsall (1994) for analysis of the destructive effects of rapid population growth, viewed within a standard economic paradigm.
4. In GDP accounting, the term 'services' refers to a wide range of activities including health care, education and information services, as well as transportation and utility services. Here we divide services into more energy-intensive types such as transportation and more human-capital-intensive types such as education.
5. The concept of 'natural capital' has been promoted by ecological economists to emphasize the importance of healthy ecosystems and natural resources to economic production and human well-being. Investment in natural capital preserves or improves these resource functions – for example, conserving forests and wetlands or rebuilding soils. See e.g. Ekins (2003).
6. Not all services are environmentally benign, but many services such as education and health care typically have less environmental impact than goods production. This formulation also assumes that investment in natural capital is wisely managed; for example, replacement of natural forest with plantation forest would not count as investment in natural capital.
7. See Myers and Kent (2001), for an extensive analysis of current environmentally damaging subsidies in agriculture, forestry, fisheries, energy, water and transportation.

# REFERENCES


Birdsall, Nancy (1994), 'Government, Population, and Poverty: A Win–Win Tale', Kerstin Lindahl-Kiessling and Hans Landberg (eds) *Population, Economic Development, and the Environment*, New York and Oxford: Oxford University Press.

Cline, William R. (2002), *Global Warming: The Economic Stakes*, Washington, DC: Institute for International Economics.

Daly, Herman E. (1991a), 'Elements of Environmental Macroeconomics', Chapter 3 in Robert Costanza (ed.), *Ecological Economics: The Science and Management of Sustainability*, New York: Columbia University Press.

Daly, Herman E. (1991b), *Steady-State Economics*, Washington, DC: Island Press.

Daly, Herman E. (1996), *Beyond Growth: The Economic of Sustainable Development*, Boston: Beacon Press.

Daly, Herman, and John B. Cobb Jr. (1994), *For the Common Good: Redirecting the Economy Toward Community, the Environment, and a Sustainable Future*, Boston: Beacon Press.

Ekins, Paul et al. (2003), 'A Framework for the Practical Application of the Concepts of Critical Natural Capital and Strong Sustainability', *Ecological Economics*, **44** (2003): 165–185.

Epstein, Paul and Evan Mills (eds) (2006), *Climate Change Futures: Health, Ecological and Economic Dimensions*, Center for Health and the Global Environment, Harvard Medical School, http://chge.med.harvard.edu/publications /index.html.

Harris, Jonathan M. (2007), 'Reorienting Macroeconomic Theory towards Environmental Sustainability,' Chapter 2 in John M. Gowdy and John D. Erickson (eds), *Frontiers in Ecological Economic Theory and Application*, Cheltenham, U.K. and Northampton, MA: Edward Elgar.

Harris, Jonathan M. and Neva R. Goodwin (2003), 'Reconciling Growth and Environment', Chapter 11 in Jonathan M. Harris and Neva R. Goodwin (eds), *New Thinking in Macroeconomics*, Cheltenham, UK and Northampton, MA, USA: Edward Elgar.

Harris, Jonathan M. and Scott Kennedy (1999) 'Carrying Capacity in Agriculture: Global and Regional Issues', *Ecological Economics*, **29**, 3 (June).

Intergovernmental Panel on Climate Change (IPCC) (2007a), *Climate Change 2007: Mitigation.* Contribution of Working Group III to the Fourth Assessment Report of the Intergovernmental Panel on Climate Change, Cambridge, United Kingdom and New York, NY, USA: Cambridge University Press. Also available at http://www.ipcc.ch/.

Intergovernmental Panel on Climate Change (IPCC) (2007b), *Climate Change 2007: Synthesis Report*, Contribution of Working Groups I, II and III to the Fourth Assessment Report of the Intergovernmental Panel on Climate Change, Cambridge, United Kingdom and New York, NY, USA: Cambridge University Press. Also available at http://www.ipcc.ch/.

Longman, Phillip (2004), 'The Global Baby Bust', *Foreign Affairs*, May/June.

Jorgensen, Dale W., Mun S. Ho and Kevin J. Stiroh (2004), 'Will the U.S. Productivity Resurgence Continue?' *Current Issues in Economic and Finance* **10**, 13 (December), Federal Reserve Bank of New York.

Kelley, Allen C. (1998), 'Economic Consequences of Population Change in the Third World', *Journal of Economic Literature*, 26 (December): 1685–1728.

Keynes, John M. (1964 [1936]), *The General Theory of Employment, Interest, and Money*, New York: Harcourt, Brace (original publication London: Macmillan).
Maddison, Angus (2008), *Historical Statistics for the World Economy*, available at http://www.ggdc.net/maddison/
Matthews, H.D., and K. Caldeira (2008), 'Stabilizing Climate Requires Near-zero Emissions', *Geophysical Research Letters*, 35, 27 February.
Millennium Ecosystem Assessment (2005), *Ecosystems and Human Well-Being: Synthesis*, Washington, DC: Island Press.
Moore, Frances C. (2008) 'Carbon Dioxide Emissions Accelerating Rapidly', Earth Policy Institute, April 9, http://www.earthpolicy.org/Indicators/CO2/2008.htm.
Myers, Norman and Jennifer Kent (2001), *Perverse Subsidies: How Tax Dollars can Undercut the Environment and the Economy*, Washington, DC: Island Press.
Nordhaus, William D. and Joseph Boyer (2000), *Warming the World: Economic Models of Global Warming*, Cambridge, MA: MIT Press.
Phelps, Edmund S. (1961), 'The Golden Rule of Accumulation', *American Economic Review*, **51**: 648–53.
Population Resource Bureau (2007), *World Population Data Sheet*, http://www.prb.org.
Repetto, Robert and Duncan Austin (1997), *The Costs of Climate Protection: A Guide for the Perplexed*, Washington, DC: World Resources Institute.
Schmittner, A., A. Oschlies, H.D. Matthews and E.D. Galbraith (2008), 'Future Changes in Climate, Ocean Circulation, Ecosystems, and Biogeochemical Cycling Simulated for a Business-as-usual CO2 Emission Scenario until Year 4000 AD', *Global Biogeochemical Cycles*, 22, 14 February.
Stern, Nicholas (2006), *The Stern Review: The Economics of Climate Change*, London: HM Treasury. Available at: http://www.hm-treasury.gov.uk/sternreview_index.htm
United Nations Department of Economic and Social Affairs (2007), Population Division, *World Population Prospects: The 2006 Revision*, http://esa.un.org/unpp.
United Nations Environmental Programme (UNEP) (2007), *Global Environmental Outlook (GEO 4): Environment for Development*, Nairobi: UNEP.

# PART III

# Policy Options for Responding to Climate Change

# 9. Cap and Dividend: How to Curb Global Warming While Promoting Income Equity

**James K. Boyce and Matthew Riddle**[1]

The time is coming when the United States government will enact policies to curb emissions of carbon dioxide and other greenhouse gases, joining the efforts of other nations to confront the historic challenge of global warming. When this happens, a key question – from the standpoints of both fairness and political feasibility – will be how to protect the incomes of American families.

The Clinton administration signed the 1997 Kyoto Protocol, which envisioned a 7 percent cut in US carbon emissions from their 1990 level by the year 2012. But the Senate refused to ratify the agreement, and when the government of George W. Bush came to power it announced it had 'no interest' in the accord.

Political winds in the country are now shifting. At the Group of Eight summit meeting in Germany in June 2007, the Bush administration agreed to re-enter international climate negotiations and to 'seriously consider' a European plan to cut greenhouse gas emissions in half by 2050. A legislative proposal unveiled in August 2007 by US senators Joseph Lieberman and John Warner goes further, calling for a 70 percent reduction by 2050. While the proposal was defeated by filibuster in the Senate in June 2008, it gained 54 votes; similar legislation, or a stronger proposal being considered by the House, will certainly be on the agenda in 2009. It now seems possible, even likely, that the US will adopt a serious emissions-reduction policy early in the post-Bush administration.

Any policy to curb carbon emissions will raise prices of fossil fuels – coal, oil, and natural gas – and the prices of other goods and services in proportion to the use of fossil fuels in supplying them. These price increases will reduce the real incomes of Americans in general, and low-income and middle-class

American households in particular. But for every dollar paid by consumers in higher prices, someone else receives a dollar in additional income. Recycling this money to the public would protect real incomes of the majority of Americans. This paper examines how this can be done by a cap-and-dividend policy that distributes carbon revenues equally to all. Similar policies could of course be applied in any country, or even globally (see Chapter 4, this volume) but this chapter focuses on domestic US policy.

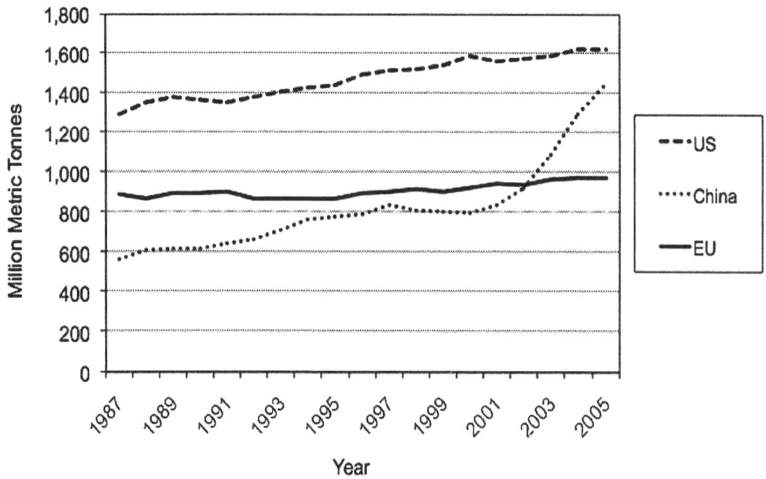


*Source:* US Energy Information Administration (2007, Table H.1).

*Note:* EU includes the fifteen member states of the European Union as of 1995. Emissions for Germany prior to German reunification in 1990 are the total for West Germany and East Germany.

*Figure 9.1a Carbon emissions of the US, China, and EU-15, 1987–2005*

## THE CARBON ECONOMY

The United States is the world's top emitter of carbon dioxide ($CO_2$), the most important greenhouse gas. The burning of fossil fuels in the US released 1.6 billion metric tons (mt) of carbon (5.9 billion mt of $CO_2$) in 2005. This is 12 percent more than China, the second-largest emitter, and 65 percent more than the EU-15 (see Figure 9.1a). As of 2008, China is close to surpassing the US in total emissions, but in per capita terms, US emissions are five times higher than China's and more than double those of the EU-15 (see Figure 9.1b).

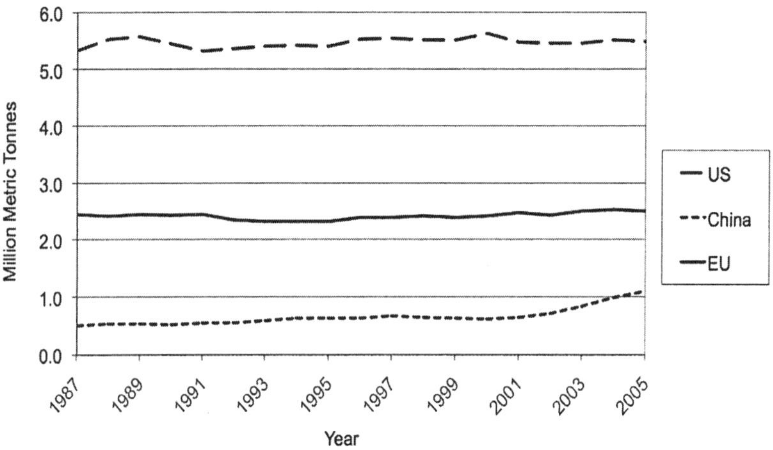


*Source:* US Energy Information Administration (2007, Table H.1c).

*Figure 9.1b Carbon emissions per capita of the US, China, and EU-15, 1987–2005*

The composition of US carbon dioxide emissions across fuels and sectors is shown in Table 9.1. Petroleum accounts for roughly 44 percent of emissions, coal for 36 percent, and natural gas for 20 percent. Electricity generation using these fuels accounts for 39 percent of the total, with coal-fired plants accounting for more than four-fifths of this amount. Transportation accounts for roughly one-third of total emissions, industry for a further 29 percent, residential energy use for 20 percent, and commercial energy use for 18 percent.

The 'carbon footprint' of individual American households – the amount of carbon emissions generated in supplying the goods and services they consume – varies depending on their total expenditure and its composition. Table 9.2 shows how expenditure patterns varied across households in 2003, ranging from the poorest tenth of the population, whose annual per capita expenditure was under $2,000, to the richest tenth, whose per capita expenditure was close to $30,000.[2]

The carbon content of various categories of consumption items can be calculated from input–output accounts. These provide detailed data on the inputs used by each industry, making it possible to trace the price effects of a change in fossil fuel prices from industry to industry (capturing not only the fuels used directly by each industry but also those used indirectly in production of other inputs). For this purpose we rely on calculations by Metcalf (1999), updating his measure to reflect 2003 prices.[4] The results are presented in Table 9.3. As one would expect, the most carbon-intensive categories of consumption are electricity, household fuels (primarily heating oil and natural gas) and car fuels, each of which generates more than two metric tons of carbon per $1000 expenditure. The least carbon-intensive category is services, for which the corresponding figure is 80 kilograms.

*Table 9.1 Carbon dioxide emissions by fuel source and sector, 2004 (millions of metric tons of $CO_2$)*

| Fuel Source | Petroleum | Coal | Nat Gas | Other | Total | % via electricity |
|---|---|---|---|---|---|---|
| Sector: | | | | | | |
| Residential | 141.6 | 695.4 | 372.8 | 4.1 | 1213.9 | 69.4 |
| Transport | 1902.7 | 3.8 | 32.7 | 0.0 | 1939.2 | 0.2 |
| Industrial | 465.4 | 747.4 | 519.9 | 3.3 | 1736.0 | 38.1 |
| Commercial | 88.2 | 669.0 | 272.9 | 3.9 | 1034.1 | 77.4 |
| Total | 2597.9 | 2115.6 | 1198.3 | 11.3 | 5923.2 | 39.0 |
| (%) | (43.9) | (35.7) | (20.2) | (0.2) | (100) | |

*Notes:* a. 'Other' includes emissions from electricity generation from municipal solid waste and geothermal energy.
b. Industrial emissions from coal include net coke imports.

*Source:* Calculated from US Energy Information Administration's Historical Data Series.[3]

Combining the information in Tables 9.2 and 9.3, we can examine the average carbon emissions from US household consumption across the range of per capita expenditure. The results are presented in Table 9.4. The consumption of the average American, with per capita expenditure of about $10,000, generates approximately 3.7 metric tons of carbon emissions.[5] Direct energy use in the form of car fuels, residential electricity, and household fuels (mainly heating oil and natural gas) accounts for roughly three-fifths of these emissions. Indirect use, via carbon emissions generated in producing other goods and services consumed by the household, account for the remaining two-fifths.

As one might expect, households with higher expenditure generally have bigger carbon footprints. As shown in the final column of Table 9.4, carbon emissions per person in the richest decile (tenth) of the population are more than double the national average, and more than eight times higher than those in the lowest decile.

*Table 9.2 Consumption patterns by expenditure decile, 2003*

| Per capita expenditure decile | Per capita expenditure ($) | Average per capita expenditures by consumption category ($) | | | | | | | |
|---|---|---|---|---|---|---|---|---|---|
| | | Food | Industrial goods | Services | Electricity | Household fuels | Car fuels | Air transport | Other transport |
| 1 | 1927 | 659 | 225 | 729 | 128 | 52 | 124 | 3 | 8 |
| 2 | 3521 | 1118 | 426 | 1418 | 227 | 83 | 226 | 11 | 13 |
| 3 | 4736 | 1361 | 638 | 2001 | 278 | 113 | 304 | 23 | 18 |
| 4 | 5991 | 1621 | 904 | 2559 | 341 | 144 | 375 | 28 | 19 |
| 5 | 7380 | 1813 | 1188 | 3351 | 349 | 164 | 444 | 45 | 27 |
| 6 | 8847 | 2051 | 1795 | 3849 | 380 | 186 | 489 | 67 | 30 |
| 7 | 10711 | 2297 | 2219 | 4901 | 415 | 211 | 537 | 83 | 46 |
| 8 | 13228 | 2559 | 3343 | 5880 | 459 | 214 | 614 | 105 | 54 |
| 9 | 17178 | 3081 | 4821 | 7489 | 519 | 273 | 735 | 177 | 83 |
| 10 | 29943 | 4292 | 10908 | 12363 | 642 | 334 | 888 | 367 | 149 |
| Total | 10346 | 2085 | 2647 | 4454 | 374 | 177 | 474 | 91 | 45 |

*Source:* Authors' calculations from *Consumer Expenditure Survey* (data for 2002–2003).

*Table 9.3 Carbon emissions per dollar expenditure by consumption category*

| Consumption category | tC per $1000 (2003 dollars) |
|---|---|
| Food | 0.15 |
| Industrial goods | 0.14 |
| Services | 0.08 |
| Electricity | 2.82 |
| Household fuels | 2.64 |
| Car fuels | 2.08 |
| Air transport | 0.56 |
| Other transport | 0.30 |

*Source:* Calculated from Metcalf (1999); see text for details.

Carbon emissions *per dollar* decline, however, as household expenditure rises. In the top decile, one dollar of expenditure on average generates 0.27 kilograms (kg) of carbon emissions; in the lowest decile the corresponding figure is 0.50 kg. The reason lies in their consumption patterns, as can be seen in Table 9.3: the poor spend a larger fraction of their household budget on electricity and fuels, while more affluent households spend a larger fraction on services and industrial goods. It so happens that necessities, which account for a larger share of the expenditure of the poor, are more carbon-intensive than luxuries, which account for a larger share of the expenditure of the well-to-do. As a result, carbon emissions rise with household expenditure at a diminishing rate (see Figure 9.2). As discussed in the next section, this concave relationship has important implications for the distributional effects of public policies to reduce carbon emissions.

## THE CASE FOR A CAP-AND-DIVIDEND POLICY

The most reliable way to reduce carbon emissions is to establish a 'cap', a limit on the total amount of fossil-fuel carbon that enters the US economy in a given year. The cap can gradually be lowered over time to meet targets for emissions reductions in future years.

Based on the cap, a fixed number of annual permits are issued to suppliers of fossil fuels, including both domestic producers and importers. Whether these permits are sold or given away, they represent a claim on a scarce resource – the US share of the biosphere's capacity to absorb and recycle carbon – and as such they have economic value.

*Table 9.4 Carbon emissions by expenditure decile (metric tons of carbon per year)*

| Per capita expenditure decile | Per capita expenditure ($) | Average per capita carbon emissions by expenditure category | | | | | | | | Total carbon emissions per capita |
|---|---|---|---|---|---|---|---|---|---|---|
| | | Food | Industrial goods | Services | Electricity | Household fuels | Car fuels | Air transport | Other transport | |
| 1 | 1927 | 0.10 | 0.03 | 0.05 | 0.36 | 0.15 | 0.26 | 0.002 | 0.002 | 0.96 |
| 2 | 3521 | 0.18 | 0.06 | 0.10 | 0.64 | 0.23 | 0.47 | 0.006 | 0.004 | 1.69 |
| 3 | 4736 | 0.21 | 0.09 | 0.15 | 0.79 | 0.32 | 0.63 | 0.013 | 0.005 | 2.21 |
| 4 | 5991 | 0.25 | 0.13 | 0.21 | 0.96 | 0.39 | 0.78 | 0.016 | 0.006 | 2.74 |
| 5 | 7380 | 0.27 | 0.17 | 0.27 | 0.99 | 0.46 | 0.92 | 0.025 | 0.008 | 3.11 |
| 6 | 8847 | 0.30 | 0.27 | 0.32 | 1.07 | 0.51 | 1.02 | 0.037 | 0.009 | 3.53 |
| 7 | 10711 | 0.34 | 0.33 | 0.41 | 1.17 | 0.58 | 1.12 | 0.047 | 0.014 | 4.01 |
| 8 | 13228 | 0.37 | 0.50 | 0.50 | 1.30 | 0.59 | 1.28 | 0.059 | 0.016 | 4.60 |
| 9 | 17178 | 0.44 | 0.72 | 0.64 | 1.47 | 0.75 | 1.53 | 0.099 | 0.025 | 5.66 |
| 10 | 29943 | 0.59 | 1.63 | 1.08 | 1.81 | 0.91 | 1.85 | 0.206 | 0.044 | 8.13 |
| Total | 10346 | 0.31 | 0.39 | 0.37 | 1.06 | 0.49 | 0.98 | 0.051 | 0.013 | 3.67 |

*Source:* Authors' calculations using data in Tables 9.2 and 9.3.

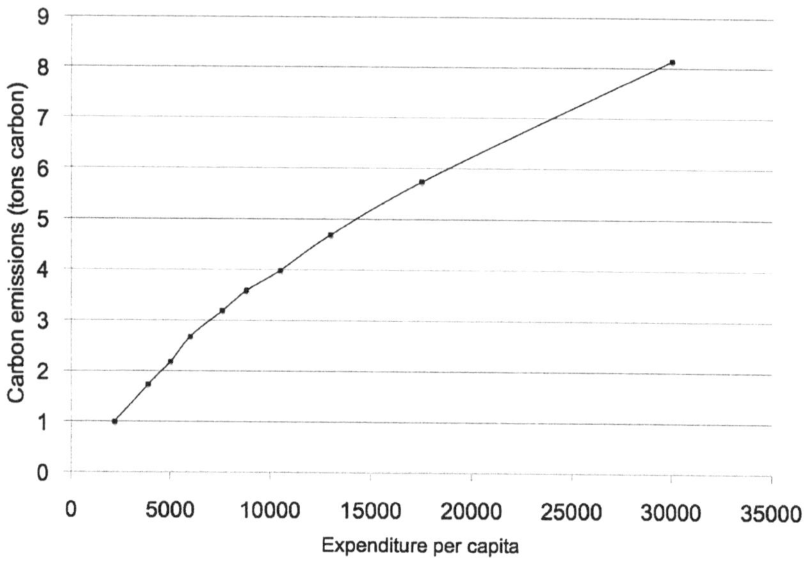


*Source:* See Table 9.4.

*Figure 9.2 Carbon emissions and household expenditure, 2003*

The net effect of emission-reduction policies on household incomes depends on:

(i) how the household is impacted by higher prices for fossil fuels, and
(ii) how the economic value represented by carbon permits is distributed.

If the permits are given away, a key issue is who gets them. If they are sold, a key issue is who gets the money. If the permits are given free-of-charge to energy companies – based, for example, on their historic levels of sales of fossil fuels – the result is a windfall gain to these firms, or more precisely, to their shareholders.[6] If the permits are auctioned to the highest bidder and the proceeds are retained by the government, the revenue is similar to that from a tax, and the money can be used to increase government spending and/or cut other taxes. In this chapter we analyze a third option, in which the permits are auctioned and the revenue is rebated to the public on an equal per capita basis, a policy sometimes termed a 'sky trust' (Barnes 2001).[7] We refer to these three policy options as 'cap-and-giveaway', 'cap-and-spend', and 'cap-and-dividend', respectively (see Figure 9.3).

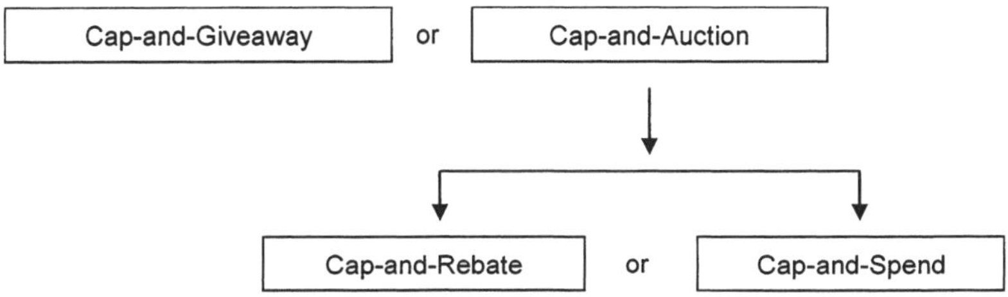


*Figure 9.3 Three policy options for carbon permit allocation*

**From Open Access to Common Wealth**

The enactment of policies to curb carbon emissions is tantamount to the creation of property rights to the sky, or more precisely, to the carbon-absorptive capacity of the biosphere. In the absence of such policies, this is an 'open access' resource, in principle freely available to all but in practice disproportionately available to those with the wealth and power to claim it: those who burn the most fossil fuel.[8] Government regulations, carbon taxes, and carbon permits all assert the right to regulate access to this resource, effectively converting it into a form of property.

The question then becomes, who are the rightful owners of this property? If we believe that the gifts of creation are held by all of us in common, rather than being the property of private owners or the government, then the answer is clear: it belongs equally to every woman, man, and child in the country.

A cap-and-dividend policy would transform the US share of the Earth's carbon-absorptive capacity from an open-access resource into the common wealth of all Americans. As a way to curb US carbon emissions, this policy has four attractive features:

- First, the cap-and-dividend policy puts into practice the principle of common ownership of nature's wealth: rights to benefit from the carbon-absorptive capacities of the biosphere are allocated equally to all.
- Second, the cap-and-dividend policy protects the real incomes of the majority of the population in the face of higher prices for fossil fuels, surmounting a major political impediment to the adoption of policies to curb global warming.
- Third, the cap-and-dividend policy results in a progressive redistribution of income, the scale of which depends on the level of the carbon charges

and how the carbon intensity of household expenditure varies with income.

- Fourth, unlike carbon taxes or a cap-and-spend policy, the cap-and-dividend policy's favorable distributional outcome does not hinge on the willingness and ability of the government to do 'the right thing' – however this may be defined – with present and future carbon revenues.[9]

**How Would a Cap-and-Dividend Policy Work?**

The cap-and-dividend policy would deposit the revenues from auction sales of carbon permits into a trust fund, an autonomous institution apart from the government budget, akin to the Social Security Trust Fund. These revenues would then be rebated to individuals on an equal per person basis.

Carbon revenues would be most easily collected 'upstream', at the mine heads, oil refineries, natural gas pipelines, and ports where fossil fuels enter the US economy. Nationwide there would be roughly 2000 such collection points (Kopp et al., 1999; US Congressional Budget Office (CBO), 2001). The costs of collecting the revenue would represent a very small fraction of the amount collected; the administrative costs of petroleum taxes and excise duties currently range from 0.12 to 0.25 percent of revenue (Smulders and Vollebergh, 2001, p. 116).[10]

A fixed number of carbon permits would be auctioned (monthly, quarterly, or annually), with the number determined by the national carbon cap at any given point in time. Permit holders would be entitled to bring fossil carbon into the economy within a specified time (say, one year from the date of purchase of the permit). A secondary market in permits would emerge, in which permit holders who decide not to use their carbon allotment could sell it to others. With frequent auctions and limited permit life spans, this market would likely be small relative to the total number of permits, but if permit periods were longer, the secondary market would play a more important role in determining permit prices.

The number of permits issued would diminish over time, as the cap on carbon emissions is gradually tightened. Issuing a fixed number of permits rather than setting a fixed carbon charge (a 'carbon tax') would guarantee that the nation's emission-reduction objectives are achieved. The price of the permits would depend on demand and supply. When the economy is booming, for example, higher demand for permits will lead to a higher price than when the economy is sluggish. Similarly, if higher fossil fuel prices and other policies spark rapid improvements in energy efficiency and development of renewable energy sources, the carbon permit price would be lower than if these occur more slowly. In contrast, setting a fixed price instead of a fixed number of permits would allow the quantity of carbon emissions to vary depending on these and other factors. Given the uncertainties as to the extent of emission reductions, the price-setting approach also could be more vulnerable to erroneous forecasts or political manipulations that undermine emission-reduction goals.

Revenues from the sale of carbon permits would be paid out equally to every man, woman, and child in the country. One way to distribute these dividends would be to issue 'Sky Trust cards' that could be used at automatic teller machines (ATMs) to withdraw cash. If permit auctions are held quarterly, the balances in every individual's account would be topped up quarterly, too. As with bank accounts, individuals could check their balances online, as well as at the ATM. The administrative costs of issuing Sky Trust cards would be no greater than the current cost of issuing Social Security cards; in fact, after the initial distribution to existing holders of Social Security cards, the two operations could be combined.

In the case of children, an alternative way to distribute carbon revenues would be to accumulate their dividends in individual development accounts (IDAs) until they reach the age of eighteen. They could withdraw funds as they enter adulthood, perhaps with rules or incentives to encourage investment in further education or purchases of homes or businesses.

The introduction of carbon permits would alter relative prices throughout the economy. Fossil fuels, and goods and services whose supply relies heavily on them, would become more expensive, strengthening incentives to invest in energy efficiency and non-fossil energy sources. The energy investment playing field, which is currently tilted in favor of fossil fuels by the implicit subsidy resulting from free use of the Earth's finite capacity to recycle emissions, would become more level. The playing field could be further levelled by ending the explicit government subsidies currently given to fossil-fuel industries in the form of tax breaks and royalty-free access to public lands. Redirection of subsidies to public investment in energy efficiency and renewable energy would complement the stimulus to private investment arising from the realignment of relative prices.

The redirection of private investment is crucial for any strategy to curb global warming. The Intergovernmental Panel on Climate Change (2007, p. 13), which foresees future energy investments totalling more than $20 *trillion* worldwide between now and 2030, observes that limiting global carbon emissions to 2005 levels by 2030 'would require a large shift in the pattern of investment, although the net additional investment required ranges from negligible to five to ten percent'.

As documented below, a cap-and-dividend policy would protect the real incomes of the majority of American families in the face of rising fossil fuel prices. But households and communities that currently depend on employment in fossil-fuel-intensive industries, such as coal mining, would nevertheless see income losses. To protect these vulnerable sectors, a fraction of the revenue from the sale of carbon permits could be earmarked initially for transitional adjustment assistance. For example, Barnes (2001) proposes a transition fund that initially would recycle 25 percent of the revenue and gradually be phased out over a ten-year period.

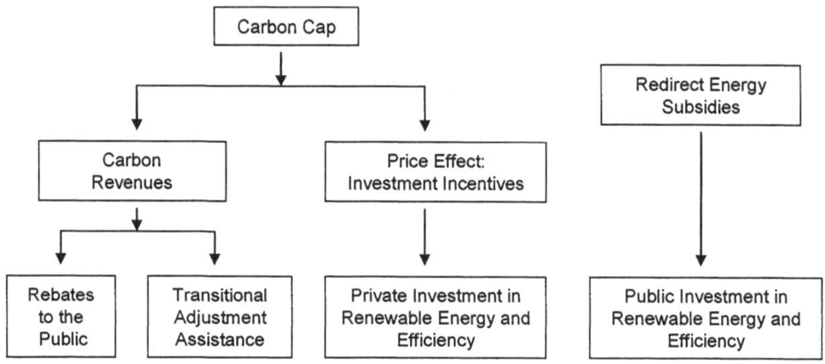


*Figure 9.4 Cap-and-dividend policy*

Figure 9.4 summarizes the basic features of a cap-and-dividend policy: cap carbon emissions; auction permits to bring fossil carbon into the economy; distribute revenues from permit sales to the public, with a fraction initially earmarked for transitional adjustment assistance; realign incentives for private investment; and redirect government subsidies to public investments in energy efficiency and renewable energy.

In the next section, we analyze how a cap-and-dividend policy would affect the distribution of income in the United States. Before doing so, we briefly review prior studies on the distributional impacts of higher fossil fuel prices and carbon revenue recycling.

**Distributional Impact of Higher Fossil Fuel Prices**

Carbon emission-reduction policies – whether in the form of regulations, carbon taxes, or caps and permits – will raise the price of fossil fuels, at least in the foreseeable future. The increased price is the flip side of reduced use. The higher cost of coal, oil, and natural gas in turn alters relative prices of goods and services throughout the economy in proportion to the carbon embodied in their production and distribution. In the end, the price increases are passed along to consumers (although producers may absorb part of the cost via lower profit margins, a possibility to which we return below).

The result of higher prices, in terms of absolute dollars, is that those who consume more fossil fuels directly in the form of energy, and indirectly in the form of other goods and services whose supply uses fossil fuels, pay more. Since the rich generally consume more of most things than the poor, they pay more (although how much any specific household pays depends on its consumption decisions). Relative to total expenditure, however, the poor pay more as noted above. This means that carbon emission-reduction policies have a regressive impact on income distribution – unless coupled with revenue-recycling policies that protect the real incomes of the poor and middle classes.

Based on the data in Table 9.4, for example, we can calculate that a $200/ton price for carbon would translate into a $215 rise in the cost of living for the average person in the poorest decile, equivalent to more than 10 percent of annual expenditure. The cost of living in richest decile would rise by $1,475 per person, but this would be equivalent to less than 5 percent of annual expenditure.

Previous studies have reached similar conclusions. The US Congressional Budget Office (CBO), in an analysis of the distributional impacts of carbon permits, estimated that the price effects would reduce real incomes in the lowest quintile of the income distribution by 3.3 percent, almost twice the 1.7 percent reduction in the highest quintile (CBO, 2000, p. 21). In a follow-on study, Dinan and Rogers (2002, p. 212) report an even sharper disparity: reductions of 6.6 percent and 1.7 percent for the poorest and richest quintiles, respectively. In estimates based on a higher carbon price, Barnes and Breslow (2003, p. 144) report the cost for the lowest decile to be equivalent to 16.8 percent of income, whereas the cost for the top decile is equivalent to 2.5 percent of income.

Studies in other industrialized countries generally support the conclusion that carbon charges are regressive – taking a bigger slice in percentage terms from low-income households than from high-income households – or, at best, distributionally neutral or mixed. An analysis by Symons et al. (1994) found that a carbon tax in the United Kingdom would be 'severely regressive'. In Canada, Hamilton and Cameron (1994) concluded that a carbon tax would be 'moderately regressive'. Cornwell and Creedy (1996) likewise found that a carbon tax in Australia would be regressive. Symons et al. (2000) reported regressive effects in Germany, France, and Spain, a mixed effect in the UK, and a neutral effect in Italy. Klinge Jacobsen et al. (2003) and Wier et al. (2005) found that Denmark's existing carbon taxes are regressive, and Brännlund and Nordström (2004) reported that increases in carbon taxes in

Sweden would be regressive.[11] Summarizing studies from a number of OECD countries, Cramton and Kerr (1999, p. 261) conclude: 'The weak regressivity of carbon regulation appears to hold across countries and modelling techniques.'[12]

## Carbon Revenue Recycling

When consumers pay higher prices for goods and services, in proportion to the fossil carbon embodied in them, a great deal of money changes hands. The net effect of carbon charges depends crucially on where this money goes.

Recognizing that carbon charges could generate annual revenues of 'tens or hundreds of billions of dollars', the US Congressional Budget Office (2000) compared two methods of allocating carbon emission allowances: selling them through an auction, or giving them away free-of-charge to the energy companies that produce and import fossil fuels. The CBO also compared two methods of revenue recycling: reducing corporate taxes or rebating an identical lump-sum amount to each household. The only policy mix found to have a progressive distributional effect was the 'sky trust' combination of permit sales and lump-sum redistribution of the revenues.[13] In this case, the regressive effect of fossil-fuel price increases was outweighed by the progressive effect of equal payments to each household. With a carbon charge of $100/ton, the CBO estimated that after-tax incomes in the lowest quintile of the income distribution would rise by 1.8 percent, while those of the top quintile would decrease by 0.9 percent. In an extension of the CBO analysis, Dinan and Rogers (2002) reported somewhat stronger redistributive impacts: a 3.5 percent rise in incomes for the lowest quintile, coupled with a 1.6 percent decline for the top quintile.[14]

Both of these studies assumed that carbon charges create 'deadweight losses' by reducing fossil fuel consumption (and also, in the Dinan and Rogers study, by lowering real returns to labor and capital and thereby reducing factor supplies). For example, when consumers curtail fuel consumption in response to higher prices, they experience welfare losses in the form of 'the discomfort associated with keeping their house cooler in the winter or the loss in satisfaction that would result from cancelling a vacation because of high gasoline prices' (CBO, 2003, p. 3). The studies add these losses to the monetary costs borne by consumers in the form of higher prices for the fossil fuels that they continue to consume.

Neither study accounted, however, for the welfare *gains* that would result from reduced use of fossil fuels. These include benefits from the mitigation of climate change and 'co-benefits' from reduced emissions of other pollutants, including airborne particulates and sulfur dioxide, that are released by burning fossil fuels.[15] Yet the rationale for policies to reduce carbon emissions is precisely that the welfare gains to society exceed the welfare losses. A comprehensive analysis of the welfare impacts of carbon emission-reduction policies would allocate these gains across households, too. In the absence of such an accounting, the incorporation of 'deadweight losses' from carbon caps gives a misleading picture of net effects: it counts the cost of reducing carbon emissions without counting the benefits.

The effect of this one-sided treatment of welfare effects is that the total costs of carbon charges (from higher prices plus 'deadweight losses') exceed the total amount of revenue to be recycled (from higher prices alone). This understates the cap-and-dividend policy's positive impact on incomes of low-income households, and overstates its negative impact on those of high-income households.

In this chapter, we adopt the simpler – and, in our view, more appropriate – procedure of estimating the monetary impacts of carbon charges and revenue recycling alone, without attempting to incorporate other welfare effects. Barnes and Breslow (2003) followed this procedure in a third analysis of the distributional impact of a cap-and-dividend policy.[16] They find that the bottom decile would receive a net benefit equal to 5.1 percent of income, while the top decile would bear a net loss of 0.9 percent. Roughly 70 percent of the population sees net gains, getting more back in dividends than they pay in higher fuel prices. Insofar as public policy is guided by majority rule, this augurs well for the political feasibility of a cap-and-dividend policy for curbing carbon emissions.

## DISTRIBUTIONAL IMPACTS OF A CAP-AND-DIVIDEND POLICY

In this section we provide new estimates of the impacts of a cap-and-dividend policy on the distribution of income in the United States, taking into account both the impact of higher prices on consumers and the recycling of carbon revenue via equal per capita dividends.

Apart from using more recent data for these calculations, our analysis differs from prior studies in several respects. We stratify households on the basis of expenditure rather than income, on the grounds that expenditure is a better proxy for lifetime income. Since households differ in size, we use expenditure per person rather than expenditure per household, on the grounds that this is a better measure of relative income. In addition to our baseline estimate of the net impact of a cap-and-dividend policy, the next section examines how the results change when some fraction of the carbon revenue is allocated initially to other uses, such as transitional adjustment assistance. In the appendix, we also show how the results are affected if we assume that some fraction of the cost of carbon permits is absorbed by producers via lower profit margins, instead of being entirely 'passed through' to consumers.

**What Price for Carbon?**

The amount of money that will be generated by the sale of carbon permits depends on both the quantity of permits sold and their price. The quantity is set by the carbon emission cap. The price depends on the price elasticities of demand for fossil fuels, which translate changes in quantity into changes in prices.

No one can be certain as to the precise magnitude of these elasticities, particularly in the long run when induced technological changes are taken into account. The Intergovernmental Panel on Climate Change (2007, p. 19), for example, reports that carbon prices of \$20–295 per ton (\$5–80 per ton of $CO_2$) in the year 2030 would be consistent with a trajectory for eventual stabilization of atmospheric concentrations in the year 2100. This wide price range illustrates why setting a cap on the quantity of permits and letting market forces determine their price is preferable to setting a price on permits (or levying a carbon tax) and letting market forces determine the quantity of emissions. If our central aim is to meet a timetable for emissions reductions, fixing the quantity guarantees that we will hit the target. Fixing the price does not.

While we do not know the precise magnitude of the price elasticity of demand for fossil fuels, we do know that it is inelastic, particularly in the short run; that is, the percentage change in price exceeds the associated percentage change in quantity demanded. With a price elasticity of –0.2, for example, a 2 percent reduction in quantity requires a 10 percent increase in price. This means that the lower the quantity of emissions permitted under the cap (and the higher the price of the permits), the greater the total amount of revenue.

We base the calculations that follow on a permit price of \$200 per ton of carbon (tC). This is near the middle of the range of carbon price scenarios used in the literature reviewed by Barnes and Breslow (2003, pp. 142–143). It is also close to the initial price of \$180/tC (\$50/t$CO_2$) that a recent study by the MIT Joint Program on the Science and Policy of Global Change reckons is needed to achieve an 80 percent reduction in emissions by the year 2050, with the price gradually rising to \$730/tC by that year (Paltsev et al., 2007). While the price we use for our calculations affects the magnitudes of costs and benefits, it does not affect their distributional pattern across households:

if the permit price were higher, then the costs, dividends, and net benefits would rise; if the price were lower, they would be smaller.[17]

*Table 9.5 Impacts of $200/ton carbon charge on fossil fuel prices*

| Fuel | Price (2006)[a] | Carbon charge | Price increase (%) |
|---|---|---|---|
| Gasoline | $2.53/gallon | $0.53/gallon | 21 |
| Heating Oil | $2.42/gallon | $0.71/gallon | 29 |
| Natural gas (residential) | $13.76/1000 cu. ft. | $3.26/1000 cu. ft. | 24 |
| Coal (delivered to electric utilities) | $31.22/short ton | $116/short ton | 371 |
| Electricity | 9.45 cents/kwh | 3.68 cents/kwh | 39 |

*Note:* a. Coal and electricity prices refer to the year 2005.

*Sources:* Price data from US Energy Information Administration (EIA).[18]

Table 9.5 shows how a $200/tC charge would change energy prices, assuming the cost to be entirely passed through into the price to end-users. Price increases for gasoline, heating oil, and natural gas are in the 20–30 percent range. The price of coal rises much more steeply, due to its relatively low price and high carbon content, and electricity prices rise by nearly 40 percent.

To calculate how these price increases impact households, we use the data on consumption patterns and the carbon content of goods and services reported in Tables 9.2 to 9.4. To incorporate the response of consumers to changes in relative prices, we use estimates drawn from other studies of the price elasticities of demand for the various consumption categories.[19] These are reported in Table 9.6.

We estimate that a $200 per ton carbon charge would reduce US emissions by approximately seven percent. Put differently, if a cap on annual carbon emissions is set at seven percent below current levels, and the corresponding number of carbon permits is auctioned to fossil fuel suppliers, we estimate that the market price for these permits will be approximately $200/tC. At this price, the total amount of revenue generated by permit sales is $198 billion per year.[20]

**Baseline Scenario**

In Table 9.7, we present the distributional impacts of a cap-and-dividend policy, with the entire cost of carbon permits passed through to consumers and the entire revenue from the sale of permits recycled to the public in the form of equal per capita dividends. The amount per person that households pay in higher prices is reported in the 'charge' column. This amount rises with per capita household expenditure, from $215/person/year in the poorest decile to $1,475/person/year in the richest decile.

*Table 9.6 Price elasticities of demand*

| Consumption category | Price elasticity of demand |
|---|---|
| Food | 0.60 |
| Industrial goods | 1.30 |
| Services | 1.00 |
| Electricity | 0.20 |
| Natural gas | 0.20 |
| Heating oil | 0.27 |
| Car fuels | 0.26 |
| Air transport | 0.25 |
| Other transport | 0.25 |

*Note:* Short-run own price elasticities of demand.

The dividend is the same across all households: $678 per person. For the bottom six deciles, this exceeds the amount paid in higher prices; for the top four deciles the charge exceeds the dividend. In other words, roughly 60 percent of Americans come out ahead in sheer monetary terms from the cap-and-dividend policy, while 40 percent pay more in higher prices than they get back in their share of the dividends.

The poorer the household, the larger the net benefit; the richer the household, the larger the net cost. The policy increases net incomes in the poorest decile by 24 percent, while net incomes in the richest decile decline by 2.7 percent.

These estimates are decile averages. But for any individual household, the net impact of the cap-and-dividend policy depends on its consumption pattern and how much it responds to changing relative prices by shifting from more carbon-intensive to less carbon-intensive consumption. Any households that curtails its direct and indirect consumption of fossil fuels to a level below the national average comes out ahead, receiving more money in dividends than it pays in higher prices, regardless of its expenditure decile. The policy rewards 'good behavior' – reductions in carbon emissions – across the income spectrum.

*Table 9.7 Distributional impact of a cap-and-dividend policy (based on a carbon charge of $200/tC, with 100% recycling to individuals)*

| Per capita expenditure decile | Per capita expenditure ($) | Average household size | Per capita incidence ($) | | | As percentage of expenditures | | |
|---|---|---|---|---|---|---|---|---|
| | | | Charge | Dividend | Net benefit | Charge % | Dividend % | Net benefit % |
| 1 | 1927 | 3.4 | 215 | 678 | 463 | 11.2 | 35.2 | 24.0 |
| 2 | 3521 | 3.3 | 338 | 678 | 341 | 9.6 | 19.3 | 9.7 |
| 3 | 4736 | 3.2 | 424 | 678 | 254 | 9.0 | 14.3 | 5.4 |
| 4 | 5991 | 2.7 | 514 | 678 | 164 | 8.6 | 11.3 | 2.7 |
| 5 | 7380 | 2.6 | 576 | 678 | 102 | 7.8 | 9.2 | 1.4 |
| 6 | 8847 | 2.5 | 649 | 678 | 30 | 7.3 | 7.7 | 0.3 |
| 7 | 10711 | 2.3 | 732 | 678 | –53 | 6.8 | 6.3 | –0.5 |
| 8 | 13228 | 2.1 | 837 | 678 | –158 | 6.3 | 5.1 | –1.2 |
| 9 | 17178 | 2.0 | 1024 | 678 | –346 | 6.0 | 3.9 | –2.0 |
| 10 | 29943 | 1.8 | 1475 | 678 | –797 | 4.9 | 2.3 | –2.7 |

*Source:* Authors' calculations (see text for details).

## Cap-and-Dividend versus Cap-and-Giveaway

The cap-and-dividend distributional outcome differs radically from what would happen under a cap-and-giveaway policy in which carbon permits are distributed free-of-charge to fossil-fuel firms. Both policies would increase the prices of fossil fuels, and of other goods and services in proportion to the use of fossil fuels in their supply, but instead of capturing the 'rent' from permit sales and rebating it to the public on an equal per person basis, the cap-and-giveaway policy would generate windfall profits for fossil-fuel firms. These profits would flow to shareholders in the form of higher dividends and capital gains, benefiting households in proportion to their ownership of corporate stock. In the words of a recent report of the US Congressional Budget Office (2007, p. 2), a giveaway strategy 'would transfer income from energy consumers – among whom lower-income households would bear disproportionately large burdens – to shareholders of energy companies, who are disproportionately higher-income households'.[21]

Data on the distribution of stock ownership by income decile are presented in Table 9.8.[22] Stock ownership is concentrated in upper-income households, with the top tenth owning nearly 65 percent of the total, and the top two-tenths owning 77 percent. Using these figures, we can approximate the distributional effects of a cap-and-giveaway policy.[23]

*Table 9.8 Distribution of stock ownership*

| Per capita income decile | Stock ownership | Share of total stock ownership |
|---|---|---|
| 1 | 7437 | 0.8% |
| 2 | 4564 | 0.5% |
| 3 | 8697 | 0.9% |
| 4 | 16069 | 1.7% |
| 5 | 23066 | 2.4% |
| 6 | 40296 | 4.2% |
| 7 | 54571 | 5.7% |
| 8 | 67427 | 7.0% |
| 9 | 116542 | 12.1% |
| 10 | 626335 | 64.9% |

*Source:* Calculated from 2004 Survey of Consumer Finances.

Table 9.9 summarizes distributional outcomes under these two policy scenarios. In contrast to cap-and-dividend, the cap-and-giveaway policy results in a regressive redistribution of income and imposes net costs on the majority of American households: the bottom nine deciles pay more as a result of higher fuel prices than they receive in higher stock dividends and capital gains. The contrast between the distributional outcomes of the two policies is depicted graphically in Figure 9.5, with the deciles combined into quintiles for simplicity.

In the absence of revenue recycling, the price increases arising from a carbon cap that yields a $200/tC permit price would raise the cost of living of the median American family by about $1,570 per year.[24] It is unlikely that the public would welcome such belt-tightening, particularly if they see the money going from their pockets into windfall profits for energy companies. Whether the public would be much happier if the money instead went to the government, as would occur with a cap-and-spend policy (or a carbon tax) is an open question. In contrast to these other policies, cap-and-dividend protects the real incomes of middle-class and low-income households. The political implications of these differences among policy outcomes should be evident.

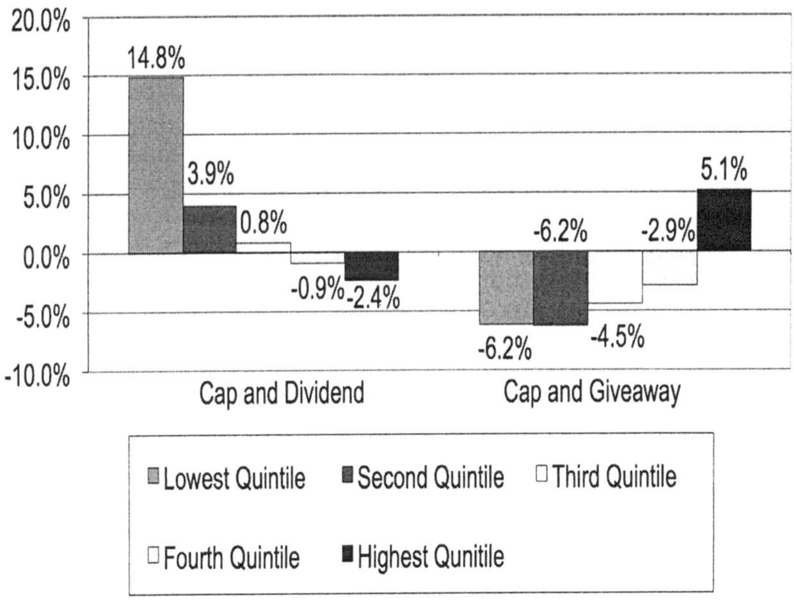


*Figure 9.5 Cap-and-dividend versus cap-and-giveaway*

*Table 9.9 Cap-and-giveaway versus cap-and-dividend (based on a carbon charge of $200 per tC)*

| Per capita expenditure decile | Per capita expenditure ($) | Household size | Cap-and-Giveaway | | Cap-and-Dividend | |
|---|---|---|---|---|---|---|
| | | | Net benefits per capita ($) | As % of total expenditures | Net benefits per capita ($) | As % of total expenditures |
| 1 | 1927 | 3.4 | –91 | –4.7 | 463 | 24.0 |
| 2 | 3521 | 3.3 | –244 | –6.9 | 341 | 9.7 |
| 3 | 4736 | 3.2 | –309 | –6.5 | 254 | 5.4 |
| 4 | 5991 | 2.7 | –355 | –5.9 | 164 | 2.7 |
| 5 | 7380 | 2.6 | –377 | –5.1 | 102 | 1.4 |
| 6 | 8847 | 2.5 | –342 | –3.9 | 30 | 0.3 |
| 7 | 10711 | 2.3 | –336 | –3.1 | –53 | –0.5 |
| 8 | 13228 | 2.1 | –360 | –2.7 | –158 | –1.2 |
| 9 | 17178 | 2.0 | –231 | –1.3 | –346 | –2.0 |
| 10 | 29943 | 1.8 | 2645 | 8.8 | –797 | –2.7 |

*Source:* Authors' calculations (see text for details).

## FIVE CAVEATS

Like all models of the distributional impacts of public policies, the estimates presented in Table 8.7 rest on a number of simplifying assumptions. We want to note five caveats in particular: (i) the assumption that the cost of carbon permits is passed through fully to consumers, rather than part of the cost being absorbed by producers via lower profit margins; (ii) the assumption of constant price elasticities of demand across expenditure deciles; (iii) the omission of welfare effects from our calculations; (iv) the omission of fossil fuel uses not tied to household consumption; and (v) the omission of sectoral employment impacts.

### 'Pass-Through' to Consumers

Studies of environmental policies – whether in the form of regulations, pollution taxes, or marketable pollution permits – typically assume that the costs these policies impose on firms are fully passed through to consumers in the form of higher prices. We have followed this conventional practice. It is plausible, however, that some fraction of the costs of carbon permits will be absorbed by producers via reduced profits – a possibility that may help to explain why producers often oppose environmental protection policies.

One reason why some firms might not shift the entire cost of carbon charges forward to consumers is that they are competing with other firms that are not equally impacted by the charges. Production costs of firms using less carbon-intensive technologies will rise less than those of firms in the same industry that use more carbon-intensive technologies.[25] To defend their market shares, the latter may trim profit margins rather than increasing prices to consumers enough to cover the full cost of their carbon permits. The ability of firms to absorb permit costs would be enhanced if they have been earning above-normal profits (for example, due to oligopolistic market power).

Households would bear the cost of any profit squeeze in proportion to their ownership of corporate stock. As noted above, this is highly unequal. With less-than-100 percent pass-through, some of the carbon revenue would come out of corporate profits, instead of all of it coming from higher prices paid by consumers. The effect would be to reduce the regressivity of carbon charges and enhance the progressivity of the cap-and-dividend policy. In the Appendix, we report calculations on distributional outcomes based on varying assumptions as to the actual extent of pass-through.

### Constant Price Elasticities

In our calculations we assume that all households respond identically to price changes; that is, the price elasticity of demand does not vary across the expenditure spectrum. But there are plausible reasons to think that price elasticities may vary with income. For example, lower-income households may tend to respond more strongly to higher prices than upper-income households: with less money, they have a stronger incentive to economize.[26] In one of the few empirical studies of this question, West and Williams (2004) find that the lower-income households are more responsive to changes in the price of gasoline: in the poorest quintile they estimate the price elasticity of demand to be –0.73 (in other words, a 10 percent price rise leads to a 7.3 percent decline in demand), whereas in the richest quintile the price elasticity is only –0.18. If this pattern could be generalized, it would imply that our estimates overstate the impact of carbon charges on lower-expenditure households and hence understate the progressivity of a cap-and-dividend policy.[27]

### Welfare Effects

Our calculations refer only to the real-income effects of carbon charges and revenue recycling. As noted above, we do not attempt to take into account the positive and negative welfare effects arising from reduced use of fossil fuels. But it bears repeating that the underlying rationale for policies to curb carbon emissions is that the benefits of doing so outweigh the costs. In an analysis of welfare effects that excludes benefits from reduced global warming, De Canio (2007) concludes that the distribution of carbon revenues has much stronger effects on household incomes than the macroeconomic effects of the carbon cap, and that an egalitarian distribution of carbon revenues 'will improve the material well-being of a majority of the agents, even without taking into account the environmental benefits of the emissions reductions'.

Our analysis also does not take into account the diminishing marginal utility of income, the eminently plausible proposition that a dollar is worth more to a poor person than to a rich one. A cap-and-dividend policy would transfer dollars from richer households, where the marginal utility of a dollar is relatively low, to poorer ones, where the marginal utility of a dollar is relatively high. The incorporation of such 'interpersonal comparisons' into a welfare-based accounting of distributional impacts would further reinforce the progressivity of the cap-and-dividend policy's outcome.

## Non-Household Users of Fossil Fuels

The Consumer Expenditure Survey (CEX) data on which we rely for our calculations omit non-household end-users of fossil fuels and other goods and services. According to the national income accounts (NIA), consumption represented 71 percent of US GDP in 2003 (the remaining items are investment, net exports, and government spending).[28] This is fairly close to the ratio of our CEX-based measure of carbon emissions reported in Table 11.4 (3.67 mt/person/year) to total US emissions reported in Figure 9.1b (5.46 mt/person/year).[29]

Carbon permits will raise prices to non-household end-users, too. For simplicity, we have omitted these from our calculations of both revenue and dividends, but the distributional outcome is not greatly affected by the omission. Assuming that carbon charges associated with investment are passed to consumers in the same way as variable input costs, the inclusion of investment would simply increase the magnitudes of revenue and dividends without altering substantially the distributional pattern of net benefits.[30] Since carbon permit charges are levied on exports but not imports, omission of trade effects leads to a modest understatement of net benefits to US households: part of the revenue rebated to them comes from foreign consumers, while the permit charges do not raise import prices.[31]

In the case of government, there are two ways to offset the impacts of higher fossil-fuel prices on real expenditure while providing the governments with an incentive to improve energy efficiency and shift to alternative energy sources. The first is to earmark a share of total carbon revenues to be directly recycled to federal, state and local governments, according to a formula based on their expenditures. Assuming this share equals what they pay in increased costs as a result of higher fossil-fuel prices, our calculations of net benefits would be unaffected. The second option is to rebate all of the carbon revenue to households, and let governments recoup their higher costs through taxation. Assuming this is accomplished through progressive taxes, this would enhance the progressivity of net benefits from the cap-and-dividend policy.

## Employment Effects

Finally, our calculations do not include the short-run impacts of carbon emission-reduction policies on employment. These include both negative impacts on fossil-fuel-based sectors of the economy and positive impacts on other sectors, notably those involving alternative energy sources. Since the shift in relative prices raises labor demand in some sectors while lowering it in others, there is no obvious reason to expect a substantial impact on aggregate employment. But insofar as alternative energy sectors are more labor-intensive than fossil-fuel industries – and there is some evidence that this is the case – the change may generate net increases in employment, particularly if investments are channeled into communities with high unemployment rates.[32]

Labor does not move costlessly across industries and sectors, however. As we have noted, workers in fossil-fuel-intensive industries could experience income losses as a result of policies that curtail carbon emissions. These adverse impacts could be offset by the provision of transitional adjustment assistance to the affected households and communities, an issue to which we turn in the next section. It is worth noting, however, that this issue arises with *any* public policy to reduce carbon emissions, not only a cap-and-dividend policy. Indeed, from the standpoint of displaced workers, cap-and-dividend at least has the advantage of offsetting the impact of higher fossil fuel prices on their real incomes, in the absence of which they would face a double blow from price effects as well as employment impacts.

## EARMARKS FOR NON-DIVIDEND USES

In this section we examine how the distributional outcome of a cap-and-dividend policy would differ if part of the revenue from carbon permits is earmarked initially for other uses, such as transitional adjustment assistance, rather than being entirely recycled as individual dividends.

The baseline results reported above assumed that all of the carbon revenues are recycled to individuals in the form of equal per capita dividends. It is possible, however, that policymakers will decide to earmark part of the revenue from the sale of carbon permits for other uses, particularly during the first few years of the policy's implementation. For example, part of the revenue might be devoted to transitional adjustment assistance for workers and communities that suffer employment losses as a result of the reduced production and consumption of fossil fuels.

Other possible uses of carbon revenues include spending on public goods (such as investments in renewable energy), cuts in other taxes, aid to promote 'decarbonized' economic development in lower-income countries, and what might be termed transitional adjustment assistance to corporations (for example, via give-aways of a fraction of the carbon permits free-of-charge). Each of these may have its own attractions on political grounds, but there are economic and political costs to devoting more than a modest share of carbon revenues to them for reasons explained below.

The effects of withholding carbon revenues for other uses are shown in Table 9.10. We vary the percentage withheld from 0 to 25 percent in five percentage-point increments, to show the sensitivity of our results to alternative assumptions. As the percentage earmarked for other uses goes up, net benefits to households go down and the percentage of households who come out ahead (in purely monetary terms) decreases. Whereas the bottom six deciles receive positive net benefits when 100 percent of the revenue is distributed in individual dividends (our baseline scenario, reproduced in the first column), only the bottom half receive positive net benefits with 10 percent of the revenue earmarked for other uses. With 20 percent earmarked for other uses, only the bottom four deciles come out ahead.

*Table 9.10 Effect of withholding carbon revenues for other uses*

| Per capita expenditure decile | Per capita expenditure ($) | Net benefit/expenditure with different withholding percentages | | | | | |
|---|---|---|---|---|---|---|---|
| | | 0% | 5% | 10% | 15% | 20% | 25% |
| 1 | 1927 | 24.0 | 22.3 | 20.6 | 18.9 | 17.2 | 15.5 |
| 2 | 3521 | 9.7 | 8.7 | 7.8 | 6.8 | 5.9 | 5.0 |
| 3 | 4736 | 5.4 | 4.7 | 4.0 | 3.3 | 2.6 | 1.9 |
| 4 | 5991 | 2.7 | 2.2 | 1.6 | 1.1 | 0.5 | 0.0 |
| 5 | 7380 | 1.4 | 0.9 | 0.5 | 0.0 | −0.4 | −0.9 |
| 6 | 8847 | 0.3 | 0.0 | −0.4 | −0.8 | −1.2 | −1.5 |
| 7 | 10711 | −0.5 | −0.8 | −1.1 | −1.4 | −1.8 | −2.1 |
| 8 | 13228 | −1.2 | −1.5 | −1.7 | −2.0 | −2.2 | −2.5 |
| 9 | 17178 | −2.0 | −2.2 | −2.4 | −2.6 | −2.8 | −3.0 |
| 10 | 29943 | −2.75 | −2.8 | −2.9 | −3.0 | −3.1 | −3.2 |

*Source:* Authors' calculations.

Note that these results refer only to the net impact of higher fossil fuel prices and individual dividends, without taking into account the distributional effects of other uses of carbon revenues. The latter would depend, of course, on precisely what these other uses are. If the other uses benefit lower-income and middle-income households, their losses from lower dividends could be offset and the distributional progressivity of the overall result possibly enhanced. On the other hand, if the other uses primarily benefit upper-income households, this would reduce their losses and diminish the progressivity of the policy mix.

In our view, there are good economic and political reasons to minimize the extent of non-dividend uses of carbon revenues:

- *First,* the scale of other uses must be limited if we are to meet the central policy goal of reducing carbon emissions while protecting the real incomes of lower-income and middle-income households. We regard income protection as a crucial ingredient of climate policy: any policy that instead puts the economic burden on the poor and middle class risks a political backlash that could fatally undermine public support for curbing carbon emissions.
- *Second,* greater investment in energy efficiency and renewable energy sources will be induced by raising the price of fossil fuels and eliminating the implicit subsidy these now receive by virtue of the zero-pricing of carbon emissions. Such investment could – and, we believe, should – be boosted further by redirecting explicit subsidies from fossil fuels to renewables. Currently, federal subsidies for the fossil-fuel industry in the form of tax breaks and royalty-free access to public lands are worth $24 billion per year (Andrews, 2007).[33] Reorienting these would dramatically increase federal support for energy efficiency and renewables without tapping the revenue from sales of carbon permits.
- *Third,* every dollar of revenues that is devoted to other uses is deducted equally from the dividends of all Americans, rich and poor alike. In other words, it is equivalent to a head tax: by taking a fixed amount from each person, it takes a higher percentage of income from the poor than from the rich. In effect, this would be one of the most regressive taxes in the country, a retreat from the principle of using progressive taxation to fund social expenditures.
- *Fourth,* using carbon revenues to make an equivalent cut in payroll taxes – as former vice-president Al Gore has advocated [34] – would fail to protect the real incomes of lower-income and middle-income population who do not pay these taxes, including the elderly, the disabled and the unemployed. It would also tie the future of Social Security and Medicare to a funding source that ultimately will shrink as the transition to a post-fossil fuel economy moves forward.
- *Finally,* if carbon revenues are used to finance government expenditures or tax cuts, there is no guarantee as to what these uses will turn out to be. Instead of a cut in payroll taxes, for example, we could see a cut in corporate income taxes; indeed, this is the alternative to the cap-and-dividend policy that was analyzed in the CBO studies. Instead of financing expenditures on renewable energy or mass transit, we could see increased government spending on subsidies for fossil fuel corporations. We live with the administrations we have, not necessarily those we want. A policy in which the revenues are dedicated to individual dividends comes as close as possible to building a 'locked box' that is not vulnerable to political vicissitudes in future years.

## CONCLUSIONS

A cap-and-dividend policy would combine an effective means to curb US carbon emissions from burning fossil fuels with protection of real incomes of lower-income and middle-income Americans from the consequences of higher fossil fuel prices.

Any policy that reduces carbon emissions will raise the prices of fossil fuels: higher prices are the handmaiden of lower demand. Higher prices for oil, coal, and natural gas will mean higher prices for goods and services produced with them. As documented in this study, these higher prices will hit the real incomes of lower-income and middle-income households harder than those of upper-income households.

But higher prices for fossil fuels are only one side of the story. The other side is summed up by the question, 'Who gets the money?' If the money is recycled to the public on an equal per capita basis, via cap-and-dividend, the impact of the emissions-reduction policy on the distribution of incomes is transformed: lower-income and middle-income households come out ahead in monetary terms, both absolutely and relative to upper-income groups.

A cap-and-dividend policy has three basic steps:

- *First,* US carbon emissions are capped at a level that gradually declines over time. For example, if we reduce emissions at a rate of 4 percent per year starting in 2010, we will cut emissions to 20 percent of their 2010 level by the year 2050.
- *Second,* based on the cap in a given year, permits are auctioned to firms that bring fossil carbon into the economy (whether through domestic extraction or imports). The supply of permits in a given year is fixed by the cap; their price depends on the demand for them.
- *Third,* the revenue from the sale of permits is deposited into a trust fund and paid out to all individuals on an equal per person basis. In addition, some fraction of the revenue initially may be earmarked for other uses, such as transitional adjustment assistance.

A cap-and-dividend policy has several attractive features. It asserts the principle of common ownership of nature's wealth: rights to benefit from the US share of the Earth's capacity to absorb carbon are allocated equally to all Americans. It protects the real incomes of the majority of the population, overcoming a crucial political hurdle to the adoption of effective policies to curb global warming. It results in a progressive redistribution of income, a result that does not hinge on the propensity of present and future governments to use the revenues for egalitarian purposes.

At a permit price of $200 per ton of carbon, the annual revenue from the sale of permits would amount to roughly $200 billion. If this revenue is recycled to individuals equally, the majority of households will receive positive net benefits: their dividends exceed the amount they pay as a result of higher fossil fuel prices. The net impact ranges from a 2.7 percent loss for the richest 10 percent of households to a 24 percent gain for the poorest 10 percent.

This 'baseline scenario' assumes that 100 percent of the cost of carbon permits is shifted to consumers. If the extent of pass-through to consumers is less than 100 percent, and some of the cost is absorbed via lower profit margins, then the distributional progressivity of the outcome is enhanced and the percentage of American families who come out ahead increases.

Allowing a modest fraction of the carbon revenues to be earmarked initially for other uses, such as transitional adjustment assistance, could further enhance the political appeal of the cap-and-dividend policy. Our results indicate that up to 10 per cent of the carbon revenues can be dedicated to other uses while maintaining positive net benefits for roughly 50 percent of households; withholding carbon revenues beyond the 10 percent threshold pushes the net beneficiary share of the population below half.

In sum, a cap-and-dividend policy is a 'win–win' option for the majority of Americans, maintaining or increasing real incomes while curbing global warming and hastening the US economy's transition towards the energy sources of the future. Not only is it an attractive policy on environmental, economic, and political grounds; it is, as far as we know, the only policy that combines these virtues in a realistic proposal. If the American public engages actively in shaping the nation's climate policies, the cap-and-dividend policy could become not just an attractive idea but a historic breakthrough.

## NOTES

1. James K. Boyce is professor of economics at the University of Massachusetts, Amherst, where he directs the program on development, peacebuilding, and the environment at the Political Economy Research Institute. Matthew Riddle is a PhD candidate in Economics at the University of Massachusetts. We are grateful to Jonathan Harris, Marcellus Andrews, Peter Barnes, Jonathan Teller-Elsberg and Laurie Johnson for useful comments on earlier versions of this chapter.
2. The data in Table 9.2 are drawn from the Consumer Expenditure Survey, conducted quarterly for the US Bureau of Labor Statistics by the Census Bureau. We pooled annual consumption data for households that began participating in the survey from the 3rd quarter of 2002 through the 2nd quarter of 2003.
3. Emissions resulting from electricity use a re allocated across fuel sources on the basis of total emissions from the electric power sector. Emissions by sector: http://www.eia.doe.gov /emeu/aer/ pdf/pages/sec12_5.pdf. Emissions from electricity generation by fuel source: http://www.eia.doe.gov/emeu/aer/pdf/pages/sec12_16.pdf.

4. We calculated separate price impacts for air transport and 'other transport' (including trains and mass transit), categories combined in Metcalf's study, using data from the 1992 input–output accounts (Lawson, 1997).
5. The higher per capita emissions shown in Figure 9.1b (5.5 tC) include carbon emissions from other sources, such as government expenditure, in addition to those associated with household consumption.
6. This is what happened when the European Union introduced carbon permits for electric power generation and gave them free-of-charge to utility companies. For accounts, see Ball (2006) and Dutzik et al. (2007, p. 22). As Paltsev et al. (2007, p. 5) note, if regulated utility markets were to prevent price rises (and windfall profits), this would dissipate the incentive for consumers to curb consumption.
7. This is an extension of the 'feebate' concept, whereby fees are paid according to the extent of individual resource use, and the proceeds rebated equally to all use-rights holders. This idea has been applied to a variety of environmental problems; see, for example, Puig-Ventosa (2004). For an early application to gasoline taxes, see Shepard (1976).
8. The so-called 'tragedy of the commons' – in which unrestricted access to a scarce resource leads to its overuse – is more accurately termed the tragedy of open access, since communities often devise rules to protect common-property resources. Open access often leads to a second tragedy, too: those who reap most of the short-run benefits from open access are the wealthy and powerful, while those most severely impacted by the long-run costs are the poor, who are relatively powerless. For discussion, see Boyce (2002, pp. 7–8).
9. It is possible to design alternative uses of carbon-charge revenues that are superior, at least in theory, to lump-sum redistribution on efficiency or distributional grounds (see Zhang and Baranzini 2004, pp. 511–2). In practice, however, these alternatives would be subject to the vagaries of fiscal politics. Moreover, unlike the cap-and-dividend policy, they would not affirm the fundamental principle of equal rights to nature's common wealth.
10. For discussion of administrative costs, see also Fisher et al. (1998). As the CBO (2001, p. 19) notes, administrative costs would increase if charges were levied not only on fossil fuels, but also on imports of carbon-intensive products (such as aluminum) so as to avoid placing domestic producers at a disadvantage in the absence of similar carbon policies in the exporting countries. Presumably these cost increases would be offset by the additional revenue collected.
11. A recent study of Italy's carbon tax (Tiezzi, 2005) finds that it has a progressive incidence, however, by virtue of the facts that it is designed to hit transport fuels harder than domestic fuel use and that higher-income Italian households were less responsive to higher prices.
12. In assessing distributional impacts, researchers often stratify households on the basis of expenditure rather than income, on the grounds that expenditure is a better proxy for lifetime income and less subject to transitory shocks. We do the same in this chapter. If incidence instead is calculated on the basis of income data, carbon charges generally appear to be even more regressive because expenditure-to-income ratios typically decline as incomes rise. For discussion, see Metcalf (1999).
13. The give-away option, sometimes referred to as 'grandfathering', was the main method adopted when sulfur dioxide emission permits were introduced in the US in the 1990s. Insofar as the resulting windfall profits are taxed, this method generates some government revenue (albeit less than if the permits were sold by auction). In an analysis of the effects of grandfathered carbon emissions permits with profits taxed at the rate of 35 percent, Parry (2004) likewise finds that the distributional impact is regressive even when coupled with lump-sum redistribution of the revenues recouped by taxation, due to the skewed distribution of profit income.
14. The stronger distributional effects in the Dinan and Rogers study arise mainly from (i) use of a lower value for average income in the lowest quintile, and (ii) incorporation of an estimated 'deadweight loss' in factor markets due to the impact of higher carbon prices on real returns to capital and labor.

15. For a tool for calculating co-benefits, see Mulholland (2007). For estimates of damages from releases of particulates, sulfur dioxide, and nitrogen oxides in the US, see Muller and Mendelsohn (2007).
16. The authors assume that dividends are distributed equally per person, rather than equally per household as in the CBO (2000) and Dinan and Rogers (2002) studies.
17. A doubling of the permit price would not quite double total revenue and net benefits, because it would entail reduced demand and fewer permits.
18. Sources for specific price data:
Gasoline:http://tonto.eia.doe.gov/dnav/pet/hist/mg_rco_usA.htm;
Heating oil: http://tonto.eia.doe.gov/dnav/pet/hist/mhoreus4m.htm;
Natural gas: http://tonto.eia.doe.gov/dnav/ng/hist/n3010us3a.htm
Coal: http://www.eia.doe.gov/cneaf/coal/page/acr/table34.html
Electricity: http://www.eia.doe.gov/cneaf/electricity/epa/epat7p4.html
Carbon charge for fuels calculated using carbon emission coefficients from EIA:
http://www.eia.doe.gov/oiaf/1605/coefficients.html
http://www.eia.doe.gov/emeu/aer/txt/ptb0702.html
Carbon charge for electricity (at existing source composition) calculated using emissions and generation data from EIA: http://www.eia.doe.gov/neic/quickfacts/quickelectric.html.
19. For energy sectors, the elasticities are based on the literature review by Dahl (1993). For food, services, and industrial goods, we use Williamson's (2006) 'stylized facts of demand'.
20. This falls near the middle of the $50–300 billion/year range (in 2007 dollars) that the US Congressional Budget Office (2007, p. 2) reports as the likely value of carbon emission permits in 2020, based on a review of the existing literature and the range of emission-reduction goals currently being debated.
21. One rationale sometimes offered for a cap-and-giveaway strategy is that it would compensate shareholders of fossil-fuel companies for declines in stock values arising from lower sales. At the same time, however, shareholders of renewable-energy companies would be expected to experience increases in stock values due to higher sales. Some shareholders win, others lose. We see no compelling reason for the public to insure the shareholders of polluting firms against the risk that society will adopt policies to curb pollution. In any event, as the US Congressional Budget Office (2007, p. 5) notes, compensation to adversely affected shareholders would require only a 'small fraction' of the total value of carbon permits. Goulder (2002) estimates that a cap-and-giveaway policy with permits rising from a modest initial price of $25/tC to a final price of $50/tC would lead to a sevenfold increase in stock values for coal companies and to a doubling of stock values for oil and gas firms.
22. The deciles in Table 9.8 are grouped by per capita income rather than per capita expenditure. (The difference between the two probably explains the anomalous finding that the bottom decile owns somewhat more stock than the second lowest decile.) We have not found comparable data for expenditure deciles. These stock ownership data include both direct ownership of stocks and indirect ownership through mutual funds and other sources. For discussion, see Bucks et al. (2006).
23. For simplicity, we assume that all windfall profits are recycled to US households in proportion to their stock ownership. In practice, some profits would 'leak' out of the country in returns to foreign owners of stock in fossil-fuel companies, diminishing net benefits of the cap-and-giveaway policy to US households. Some profits might also be withheld from shareholders and instead used to increase executive compensation. For both reasons, the cap-and-giveaway results presented in Table 9.9 can be regarded as a 'best-case' approximation that, if anything, understates net costs for the majority of households.
24. This is the average per capita charge for the 5th and 6th deciles, multiplied by the average household size in these deciles, as reported in Table 9.7.
25. A similar situation could arise for tradable goods producers who face competition from foreign firms not covered by the carbon permit mandate. All else equal, the introduction of carbon permits in the US economy would make imports more competitive and exports less

competitive. In industries where these trade effects are significant, there is a case for corrective policies: tariffs on imports (based on fossil carbon emissions in their production) and rebates on exports. Careful research is needed to assess needs for such compensating policies. We note, however, that many foreign competitors (notably in Europe) now pay higher prices for fossil fuels than US producers, due to government environmental and taxation policies. In these cases, it would be difficult to argue that introducing carbon permits would place US firms at an unfair disadvantage. More generally, trade competitiveness depends on many factors – including exchange rates, labor costs, taxation, and the pace of technological innovation – and these are likely to overshadow the effects of environmental policies, which empirical studies generally find to be quite small (for discussions, see Goodstein, 1999 and Ackerman, 2006).

26. To be sure, lower-income households devote a higher proportion of their expenditure to necessities than to luxuries, and from this it is sometimes inferred that they tend to be less responsive, for example, to changes in the price of gasoline (Kayser, 2000). But the same reasoning applies to non-fuel expenditures by lower-income households: not cutting gasoline consumption in response to higher prices would imply bigger cutbacks in other necessities such as food and health care. A more plausible reason to expect greater price responsiveness among upper-income households is that in some cases (such as buying more energy-efficient vehicles), cutbacks in fuel consumption require investments in expensive durable goods.
27. Other studies of price elasticity differences across the income spectrum have produced mixed results. West (2004) and Archibald and Gillingham (1980) also find that lower-income US households are more responsive to gasoline prices than are upper-income households, while Kayser (2000) reports a contrary finding. In a study in the United Kingdom, Dargay and Vythoulkas (1999) also find greater price-responsiveness among lower-income households: the long-run elasticity of car ownership with respect to running costs is –0.92 for low-income groups, –0.51 for middle-income groups, and –0.38 for high-income groups (see also UK Department for Transport, 2006). In a study of Denmark, Brännlund and Nordstrom (2004) find little variation across income groups in the price elasticities of demand for gasoline and other goods.
28. Unlike the CEX, the NIA consumption measure includes expenditures by non-profit institutions serving households, which account for roughly 11 percent of consumption, or 8 percent of GDP (based on 1993 data cited by Garner et al. 2006, p. 22). Subtracting this from the NIA measure, household consumption represented roughly 63 percent of national income.
29. Another possible source of discrepancy between the two figures is under-reporting of consumption in the CEX. The CEX-based estimate of total consumption in the United States, derived from household surveys, is roughly 60 percent of the National Income Accounts-based estimate of aggregate consumption, derived primarily from economic censuses of firms (for discussion, see Garner et al., 2006). In part, this disparity arises from definitional differences (for example, the latter includes consumption by many non-profit institutions whereas the CEX does not), and in part from measurement errors in one or both instruments. Insofar as under-reporting in the CEX accounts is to blame, this would affect the pattern of distributional impacts reported here only if the under-reporting were uneven across expenditure deciles. Since we lack adequate data on which to assess this possibility, we make do with the data at hand. If the degree of any under-reporting in the CEX is roughly constant across deciles, then its only effect on the distributional impacts of a cap-and-dividend policy reported in Table 9.7 would be on absolute magnitudes, not on the pattern of relative impacts across deciles.
30. If investment per unit output and carbon emissions per dollar investment are roughly the same across sectors, inclusion of investment-related emissions would somewhat reduce the disparities in carbon content across consumption categories reported in Table 9.3. Since low-carbon categories account for a larger share of expenditure by upper-income households, this would reduce the regressivity of carbon charges and enhance the progressivity of the cap-and-dividend outcome.

31. In some cases, however, trade policies may compensate for these effects; see note 22.
32. For a comparison of the employment impacts of alternative energy sources and fossil fuels, see Pollin and Garrett-Peltier (2008).
33. To put this number in perspective, in 2005 public expenditure on research and development for wind energy, fuel cells and photovoltaics combined was about $250 million (Kammen and Nemet, 2005, p. 86).
34. See 'Solving the Climate Crisis', speech by Al Gore at New York University, 18 September 2006, available at http://www.nyu.edu/community/gore.html. See also Metcalf (2007).

## REFERENCES

Ackerman, Frank (2006), 'The Unbearable Lightness of Regulatory Costs', *Fordham Urban Law Journal*, May.

Andrews, Edmund L. (2007), 'Democrats Press Plan to Channel Billions in Oil Subsidies to Renewable Fuels', *The New York Times*, June 18.

Archibald, Robert and Robert Gillingham (1980), 'An Analysis of the Short-Run Consumer Demand for Gasoline Using Household Survey Data', *Review of Economics and Statistics*, **62** (4), 622–628.

Ball, Jeffrey (2006), 'For German Firms, New Emission Caps Roil Landscape', *The Wall Street Journal*, 11 September 2006.

Barnes, Peter (2001), *Who Owns the Sky? Our Common Assets and the Future of Capitalism*, Washington, DC: Island Press.

Barnes, Peter and Marc Breslow (2003), 'The Sky Trust: The Battle for Atmospheric Scarcity Rent', in James K. Boyce and Barry G. Shelley (eds), *Natural Assets: Democratizing Environmental Ownership*, Washington, DC: Island Press, pp. 135–149.

Boyce, James K. (2002), *The Political Economy of the Environment*, Cheltenham UK and Northampton, MA, USA: Edward Elgar.

Brännlund, Runar and Jonas Nordstrom (2004), 'Carbon Tax Simulations Using a Household Demand Model', *European Economic Review*, **48**: 211–233.

Bucks, Brian K., Arthur B. Kennickell and Kevin B. Moore (2006), 'Recent Changes in US Family Finances: Evidence from the 2001 and 2004 Survey of Consumer Finances', *Federal Reserve Bulletin*, **92**: A1–A38.

Cornwell, Antonia and John Creedy (1996), 'Carbon Taxation, Prices and Inequality in Australia', *Fiscal Studies*, **17** (3): 21–38.

Cramton, Peter and Suzi Kerr (1999), 'The Distributional Effects of Carbon Regulation: Why Auctioned Carbon Permits are Attractive and Feasible', in Thomas Sterner (ed.), *The Market and the Environment*, Cheltenham, UK and Northampton, MA, USA: Edward Elgar, pp. 255–271.

Dahl, Carol (1993), 'A Survey of Energy Demand Elasticities in Support of the Development of the NEMS', US Department of Energy, National Energy Modeling System (NEMS), Contract No. DE-AP01-93EI23499.

Dargay, Joyce M. and Petros C. Vythoulkas (1999), 'Estimation of a Dynamic Car Ownership Model: A Pseudo-Panel Approach', *Journal of Transport Economics & Policy*, **33**(3): 287–302.

De Canio, Stephen J. (2007), 'Distribution of Emissions Allowances as an Opportunity', *Climate Policy*, **7** (2): 91-103.

Dinan, Terry M. and Diane Lim Rogers (2002), 'Distributional Effects of Carbon Allowance Trading: How Government Decisions Determine Winners and Losers', *National Tax Journal*, **55**: 199–222.

Dutzik, Tony, Rob Sargent and Emily Figdor (2007), 'Cleaner, Cheaper, Smarter: The Case for Auctioning Pollution Allowances in a Global Warming Cap-and-Trade Program', Boston: US PIRG Education Fund, http://www.uspirg.org/uploads/Ma/3Q/Ma3Qikh9OWao1QdkyV9bHw/Cleaner-Cheaper-Smarter-USPIRG.pdf.

Fisher, Carolyn, Suzi Kerr and Michael Toman (1998), 'Using Emissions Trading to Regulate US Greenhouse Gas Emissions: Design and Implementation Issues', *National Tax Journal*, **51** (3): 453–464.

Garner, Thesia I., George Janini, William Passero, Laura Paszkiewicz and Mark Vendemia (2006), 'The CE and the PCE: A Comparison', *Monthly Labor Review*, **129** (9): 20–46.

Goodstein, Eban (1999), *The Trade-Off Myth: Fact and Fiction about Jobs and the Environment*, Washington, DC: Island Press.

Goulder, Lawrence H. (2002), 'Mitigating the Adverse Impacts of $CO_2$ Abatement Policies on Energy-Intensive Industries', Washington, DC: Resources for the Future, Discussion Paper 02–22.

Hamilton, Kirk and Grant Cameron (1994), 'Simulating the Distributional Effects of a Canadian Carbon Tax', *Canadian Public Policy*, **20** (4), 385–399.

Intergovernmental Panel on Climate Change (IPCC) (2007), 'Summary for Policymakers', in *Climate Change 2007: Mitigation*, Contribution of Working Group III to the Fourth Assessment Report of the Intergovernmental Panel on Climate Change, http://www.ipcc.ch/SPM040507.pdf.

Kammen, Daniel M. and Gregory F. Nemet (2005), 'Reversing the Incredible Shrinking Energy R&D Budget', *Issues in Science and Technology*, **22** (1): 84–88.

Kayser, Hilke A. (2000), 'Gasoline Demand and Car Choice: Estimating Gasoline Demand Using Household Information', *Energy Economics*, **22**: 331–348.

Klinge Jacobsen, H., K. Birr-Pedersen and M. Wier (2003), 'Distributional Implications of Environmental Taxation in Denmark', *Fiscal Studies*, **24** (4): 477–499.

Kopp, Raymond, Richard Morgenstern, William Pizer and Michael Toman (1999), 'A Proposal for Credible Early Action in US Climate Policy', Washington, DC: Resources for the Future, http://www.weathervane.rff.org/features/feature060.html.

Lawson, Ann M. (1997), 'Benchmark Input–Output Accounts for the US Economy, 1992', *Survey of Current Business*, **77**(11): 36–82.

Metcalf, Gilbert E. (1999), 'A Distributional Analysis of Green Tax Reforms', *National Tax Journal*, **52** (4): 655–681.

Metcalf, Gilbert (2007), *A Green Employment Tax Swap: Using a Carbon Tax to Finance Payroll Tax Relief*, Washington, D.C: World Resources Institute, available at http:// www.wri.org/publication/green-employment-tax-swap

Mulholland, Denise (2007), 'Estimating and Valuing Human Health Effects of State and Local Emissions Reductions: The Co-Benefits Risk Assessment (COBRA) Screening Model', Washington, DC: US Environmental Protection Agency.

Muller, Nicholas Z. and Robert Mendelsohn (2007), 'Measuring the Damages of Air Pollution in the United States', *Journal of Environmental Economics and Management*, **54** (1): 1–14.

Paltsev, Sergey et al. (2007), 'Assessment of US Cap-and-Trade Proposals', Cambridge, MA: Massachusetts Institute of Technology Joint Program on the Science and Policy of Global Change, Report No. 146, http://web.mit.edu/globalchange/www/MITJPSPGC_Rpt146.pdf.

Parry, Ian W.H. (2004), 'Are Emissions Permits Regressive?', *Journal of Environmental Economics and Management*, **47**: 364–387.

Pollin, Robert and Heidi Garrett-Peltier (2008), 'A Unified Approach to Job Creation and a Clean Energy Economy', Amherst, MA: Political Economy Research Institute.

Puig-Ventosa, Ignasi (2004), 'Potential Use of Feebate Systems to Foster Environmentally Sound Urban Waste Management', *Waste Management*, **24**: 3–7.

Shepard, Lawrence (1976), 'The Short-Run Incidence of a Gasoline Tax Rebate Plan', *Journal of Economic Issue*, **10** (1), 169–172.

Smulders, Sjak and Herman R.J. Vollebergh (2001), 'Green Taxes and Administrative Costs', in Carlo Carraro and Gilbert E. Metcalf (eds), *Behavioral and Distributional Effects of Environmental Policy*, Chicago: University of Chicago Press, pp. 92–129.

Symons, Elizabeth, John Proops and Philip Gay (1994), 'Carbon Taxes, Consumer Demand and Carbon Dioxide Emissions: A Simulation Analysis for the UK', *Fiscal Studies*, **15** (2), 19–43.

Symons, Elizabeth, Stefan Speck and John Proops (2000), 'The Effects of Pollution and Energy Taxes across the European Income Distribution', Keele University Economics Research Paper No. 2000/05.

Tiezzi, Silvia (2005) 'The Welfare Effects and the Distributive Impact of Carbon Taxation on Italian Households', *Energy Policy*, **33**: 1597–1612.

UK Department for Transport (2006), 'Generalized Cost Elasticities and Income Level: Literature Review', http://www.dft.gov.uk/foi/responses/2006/jul/aandrsternreview/informationregardinganalyses2737.

US Congressional Budget Office (2000), 'Who Gains and Who Pays Under Carbon-Allowance Trading? The Distributional Effects of Alternative Policy Designs', Washington, DC: Congressional Budget Office.

US Congressional Budget Office (2001), 'An Evaluation of Cap-and-Trade Programs for Reducing US Carbon Emissions', Washington, DC: Congressional Budget Office.

US Congressional Budget Office (2003), 'Shifting the Cost Burden of a Carbon Cap-and-Trade Program', Washington, DC: Congressional Budget Office.

US Congressional Budget Office (2007), 'Trade-Offs in Allocating Allowances for $CO_2$ Emissions', *CBO Economic and Budget Issue Brief*, 25 April 2007.

US Energy Information Administration (2007), 'Energy Information Annual 2005', Washington, DC: US Department of Energy, http://www.eia.doe.gov/emeu/iea/carbon.html.

West, Sarah E. (2004), 'Distributional Effects of Alternative Pollution Control Policies', *Journal of Public Economics*, **88**: 735–757.

West, Sarah E. and Robertson C. Williams III (2004), 'Estimates from a Consumer Demand System: Implications for the Incidence of Environmental Taxes', *Journal of Environmental Economics and Management*, **47**: 535–558.

Wier, Mette, Katja Birr-Pedersen, Henrik Klinge Jacobsen and Jacob Klok (2005), 'Are $CO_2$ Taxes Regressive? Evidence from the Danish Experience', *Ecological Economics*, **52**: 239–251.

Williamson, Jeffrey G. (2006), *Did British Capitalism Breed Inequality?* London: Routledge.

Zhang, Zhongxiang and Andrea Baranzini (2004), 'What Do We Know about Carbon Taxes? An Inquiry into their Impacts on Competitiveness and Distribution of Income', *Energy Policy*, **32**: 507–518.

# 10. Policies for Funding a Response to Climate Change

**Brian Roach**

## INTRODUCTION

Global emissions of carbon dioxide, the primary greenhouse gas, have risen about 30 percent since 1990. Projections indicate that in the absence of effective climate change policies global $CO_2$ emissions could increase a further 60 to 70 percent by 2030, with continued growth in emissions beyond that (International Energy Agency, 2005; US Department of Energy, 2006a; US Environmental Protection Agency, 2006). It is becoming increasingly clear that the global growth of $CO_2$ emissions needs to be halted and eventually reversed during the 21st century in order to avoid potentially catastrophic effects from global climate change. The recent much-publicized *Stern Review on the Economics of Climate Change* notes that climate stabilization at an atmospheric concentration of 550 parts per million $CO_2$-equivalent would require global emissions to peak in the next ten to twenty years and then fall to 25 percent below current levels by 2050, with further declines thereafter (Stern, 2006). Climate stabilization even at this level could result in significant negative effects including reduced crop yields, increased water shortages, and ecological damages.

Thus there exists a large 'mitigation gap' between projected carbon emissions and the emissions level needed to achieve climate stabilization that moderates the risk of adverse climate change. Closing this gap will require significant, coordinated, and wide-ranging policy action. However, the most comprehensive policy response to climate change to date, the Kyoto Protocol, will produce only a limited beneficial impact, especially since the United States has withdrawn from the treaty. The US is the world's largest emitter of greenhouse gases, yet current federal policy does not place any limits on emissions of $CO_2$. The George W. Bush administration has instead pursued voluntary and incentive-based programs, while US emissions of $CO_2$ continue to increase. US Department of Energy projections estimate a 36 percent increase in total $CO_2$ emissions between 2006 and 2030 (US Department of Energy, 2006b).

An effective global response to climate change will require much stronger policy efforts in the US. The Bush administration has tended to focus on the potential of technological advances, using policy to 'encourage research breakthroughs that lead to technological innovation' (Office of the Press Secretary, 2001). In his 2007 State of the Union speech, the President stated the importance of diversifying US energy supply and that 'the way forward is through technology'. While significant progress on reducing carbon emissions will undoubtedly require much more sweeping measures, such as comprehensive carbon cap-and-trade legislation, technological innovations are clearly a critical component of an adequate response to the challenge of global climate change. This chapter argues that a significant increase in US public funding for climate change research and development (R&D) is needed. While additional public R&D funding alone is unlikely to provide a sufficient policy response, it is a critical policy component in an effective long-run strategy. Different possibilities for generating additional public revenues for R&D funding are considered. The analysis demonstrates that quite modest taxes on carbon emissions or gasoline could fund a significant increase in public R&D funding for clean energy. As an alternative to tax instruments, the chapter also considers a program of voluntary retirement contributions to a clean energy fund.

## PUBLIC POLICY RESPONSES TO CLIMATE CHANGE

Two types of market failure prevent an adequate response to climate change from unregulated private markets (US Congressional Budget Office, 2006). First, the negative externalities associated with carbon emissions are not reflected in market prices. The most common proposal to address this market failure is carbon taxation at a level that reflects the social costs of carbon emissions, or a cap-and-trade system with comparable effects on carbon pricing. The second market failure is an insufficient level of private research and development on clean energy technologies because the benefits of such innovations cannot be fully captured by the innovating firm. This market failure suggests the need to supplement private R&D with public R&D funding for technologies that could potentially promote climate stabilization.

The emphasis of most policy proposals to address climate change is on carbon pricing. Economic models estimating the relative effectiveness of carbon taxation and R&D subsidies suggest that pricing policies alone are much more cost effective than R&D subsidies alone but that overall cost effectiveness is achieved by a combination of both policies (US

Congressional Budget Office, 2006). While public R&D funds promote the development of new technologies, in the absence of higher carbon prices there may not exist any incentive to adopt those technologies (Popp, 2004).

Even in the presence of a socially optimal price for carbon, private R&D on clean energy technology will still be undersupplied. One problem is that in the case of climate change the benefits of private investment may accrue outside of the short-term planning horizon of most firms. Thus many technologies that could make a significant contribution to carbon mitigation in the long term may fail to be commercialized without determined policy intervention (International Energy Agency, 2006b).

Second, the benefits of innovations do not fully accrue to the innovating firm. Beneficiaries also include other firms and society as a whole. Research suggests that the social rates of return on R&D investments can be in the range of 30 to 50 percent while private rates of return fall in the range of 7 to 15 percent (Popp, 2004). The gap between social and private rates of return is likely to be greatest in the case of basic research:

> Federal support would probably be most cost-effective if it went toward basic research on technologies that are in the early stages of development. Such research is more likely to be underfunded in the absence of government support because it is more likely to create knowledge that is beneficial to other firms but that does not generate profits for the firm conducting the research. (US Congressional Budget Office, 2006, p. 2)

Similarly, a review article by Salter and Martin (2001) states that 'the limited evidence gathered to date indicates that publicly funded basic research does have a large positive payoff' (p. 514) although they note methodological difficulties in estimating the benefits quantitatively.

A third problem is that there exists considerable uncertainty regarding which technologies will prevail in a low-carbon society. Given that some technologies will fail for technical or economic reasons, a portfolio approach to clean energy investment is required. Directed public R&D investments could ensure research on the widest range of technologies, not just those that present the greatest possibility of short-term profits. Numerous technological advances will be required for a sustainable future and a portfolio approach will greatly reduce the risks should some technologies fail (International Energy Agency, 2006a).

The Stern Review advocates a complementary approach of higher carbon taxes and increased public R&D funding. The report notes that despite growing concern over climate change, both private and public energy R&D is generally declining. Public energy R&D funding by the 26 industrial nations of the International Energy Agency (IEA) peaked at about $18 billion annually (in 2004 dollars) in 1980 in response to the energy crises of the

1970s. Funding by these countries has since fallen to about half this level. The Stern Review promotes a doubling of public R&D funding for low-carbon technologies as an initial step (Stern, 2006).

Public energy investment should be seen as complementary to, rather than competitive with, private investment. In particular, public R&D should focus on clean energy technologies that are currently far from market feasibility but that offer the greatest potential for substantial carbon reductions. Private investment, particularly in the presence of higher carbon prices, will tend to focus on technologies that offer near-term market profitability. For example, private R&D might focus on the development of more efficient gas–electric hybrid engines while public R&D would concentrate on the development of hydrogen fuel cells as a replacement power plant for vehicles. This complementary process is already occurring as energy market liberalization has motivated private firms to concentrate more on short-term R&D while government research shifts towards a longer-term focus (International Energy Agency, 2003a).

The IEA notes that a future scenario of rapid technological development does not necessarily imply reduced economic growth. In a scenario of significant technological change responding to environmental concerns:

> Growth would be slower at the beginning in developed countries, due to the increased costs of providing energy in a more environmentally compatible way. However, as the system responds and technology advances, the net increase in energy prices may not be that big. Furthermore, technological innovation by creating successful new industries and environment-friendly products would foster new economic growth. (International Energy Agency, 2003b, p. 92)

In this IEA scenario, governments aim to improve technologies through a 'mix of government–industry partnerships in R&D and regulation'. Again, a long-term perspective is required that stresses basic research on a broad range of technological options. Even if a concerted technology push were to begin immediately, successful new technologies might not be introduced into the market until at least 2020. A simulation model by Edenhofer et al. (2005) produces similar results regarding the relationship between economic growth and climate policy – investment in technological change in the renewable energy and carbon capture sectors significantly reduces the costs of climate protection and allows ambitious climate goals to be met, while still permitting stable economic growth.

In the IEA scenario referred to above, the US is not expected to participate in the Kyoto process in the near term. Yet if the US adopts a long-term climate change policy emphasizing aggressive technological development, it may be able to speed up the introduction of new technologies that will eventually bring down the price of carbon mitigation and lead to a more successful international accord subsequent to the Kyoto Protocol. Countries that have ratified the Kyoto Protocol, meanwhile, may face greater pressure to take short-term measures to meet their Kyoto targets. Thus, the US refusal to participate in the Kyoto Protocol could, ironically, offer it a unique opportunity to take a leadership role in developing long-term technological innovations to address climate change.

## PUBLIC AND PRIVATE ENERGY R&D FUNDING

In 2006 public energy R&D funding in the IEA countries was $10.9 billion (in 2006 dollars). As seen in Figure 10.1, R&D funding among industrial countries is dominated by Japan and the United States. In the United States, public R&D energy funding peaked in 1979 at $8.5 billion (in 2006 dollars) but in 2006 stood at only 37 percent of this amount, or $3.2 billion. Since the early 1990s Japan has been the world's leader in public R&D energy funding, with a 2006 total of $3.6 billion. In 2006 Japan and the United States accounted for 62 percent of the total public R&D energy funding among the 26 nations of the IEA. Only a few industrial countries are consistently increasing R&D energy funding. The IEA country with the greatest recent increase in funding is South Korea, which increased its public R&D energy funding by 258 percent between 2002 and 2006.

The decline in energy research funding in the United States is even more pronounced for private R&D. Between 1985 and 1999 private R&D energy expenditures declined by 66 percent in real terms, from $4.1 billion to $1.4 billion (World Energy Council, 2001). Dooley (1998) suggests that energy market deregulation is driving the decline in private R&D in the US. In a deregulated market, private energy companies are directing their remaining R&D towards proprietary technologies with the potential for short-term payback. Thus there is likely to be little private investment in such technologies as advanced solar and wind energy since few firms are currently profitable enough to maintain research programs on these technologies without public funding assistance. Dooley also indicates the importance of continuity in funding energy research. A crash public program to develop low-carbon energy technologies is unlikely to produce satisfactory results because of its dependency on a wide range of scientific disciplines.

Public R&D funding appears to be particularly important with respect to renewable energy. For example, of 14 key innovations in the field of photovoltaic energy where the funding source could be identified, nine were developed totally with public funding, four as a result of public–private partnerships, and only one solely from private funding (Norberg-Bohm, 2000). A strength of public US R&D funding for photovoltaic energy has been the attention paid to a wide range of research activities, including basic research. But progress has been limited partly due to the inconsistency of funding.

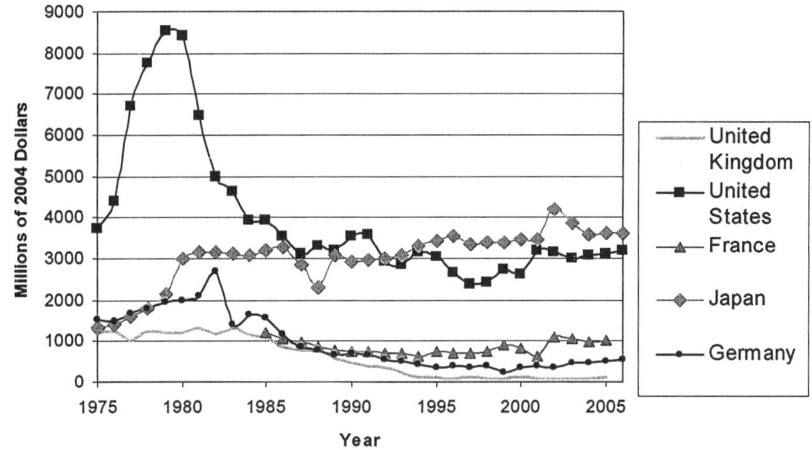


*Source:* Online IEA R&D Statistics Database, 2007 edition.

*Figure 10.1 Public R&D energy funding, selected IEA countries, 1975–2006*

## THE ROLE OF TECHNOLOGY AND R&D FUNDING IN US CLIMATE POLICY

Under the George W. Bush administration the United States set a goal of reducing greenhouse gas intensity by 18 percent by 2012 as compared to 2002 levels. Greenhouse gas intensity is measured as total emissions divided by economic output. Reducing greenhouse gas intensity does not imply actually reducing emissions. Instead, it merely implies that emissions grow less rapidly than economic output. Analysis by the Pew Center on Global Climate Change (2002) indicates that the administration's plan would allow actual emissions to increase 12 percent over the 2002–2012 period. Further, given that greenhouse gas intensity fell by 21 percent during the 1980s and by 16 percent in the 1990s, the plan essentially amounts to a business-as-usual approach.

The United States has developed a strategic plan on the role of technology in addressing climate change (US Climate Change Technology Program, 2006). The climate change response of the United States 'places special emphasis on the fundamental importance of science and technology as a means of achieving climate goals' (p. 2). Like the IEA scenarios, the strategic plan also recognizes the compatibility of technological advancement and economic growth:

> accelerated advances in technology have the potential to facilitate progress towards meeting climate change goals and, under certain assumptions, to significantly reduce the cost of such progress over the course of the 21st century, compared to what otherwise would be the case without accelerated advances in technology. Further, it is expected that the new technologies would create substantial opportunities for economic growth. (US Climate Change Technology Program, p. 7)

Among the goals set forth in the plan is the objective of increasing basic scientific research, including innovating research that offers the potential for breakthrough technologies. The strategic plan recognizes the need for a portfolio approach that hedges against risk by investing in a wide array of technologies. In addition, the plan seeks to 'encourage further formation of public-private partnerships as a common mode of conducting R&D portfolio planning and program execution' (p. 215). However, in contrast to the recommendations of the Stern Review and the IEA, the US strategic plan does not specifically call for an increase of public R&D funding.

The President's Council of Advisors on Science & Technology (PCAST) under President Clinton did call for an increase in R&D funding related to environmental threats:

> *PCAST believes that the United States is underinvesting in the R&D needed to understand, anticipate, adapt to, and mitigate emerging environmental threats.* In addition to sustaining or increasing its own R&D investments, the Federal government will need to forge new partnerships with the many businesses, industries, and nongovernmental organizations that are working today to advance sustainable development through substantial R&D investments, strategic planning, effective environmental management systems, and outreach programs. (PCAST, 1997, original emphasis)

The bipartisan National Commission on Energy Policy (2004) has recommended a doubling of US public funding of energy R&D while promoting effective private–pubic partnerships. Nemet and Kammen (2007) conclude that increasing public energy R&D by a factor of two or more is necessary and feasible in light of previous large-scale government R&D efforts such as the Manhattan Project and Apollo Program.

## Scenario for Increased US Public R&D Funding for Climate Change

The case for a significant increase in US public R&D funding to address climate change appears compelling. If we accept that the US is under-investing in climate change R&D, by how much should funding levels be increased? This chapter considers three alternative funding levels. First, following the recommendations of Stern and the National Commission on Energy Policy, a doubling of US public R&D funding would require an additional $3.2 billion per year. Second, returning to the peak US annual investment in energy R&D achieved in 1979 would require a $5.0 billion/year increase in funding. Finally, we consider an ambitious scenario in which the US unilaterally commits to undertake the global recommendation of the Stern Review – doubling global R&D funding – with an increased expenditure of $11.0 billion/year. We now consider alternatives for raising the additional funds for each of these funding increases.

Before considering alternatives for raising the necessary funds under these different scenarios, it is worthwhile to place these values in context. Additional federal spending of $3.2–$11.0 billion annually is quite minor when compared to total federal spending ($2,568 billion in 2006) and spending for other priorities (for example, the war in Iraq cost over $90 billion in 2006 according to the Congressional Budget Office). A relatively minor adjustment of federal spending priorities could shift an additional $3.2–$11.0 billion towards climate change R&D. Another approach would be to obtain the additional funds with a broad-based but small tax increase. For example, raising an additional $3.2 billion in taxes would equate to an additional $28 annually per US household. Or, as discussed below, the funds could be obtained through voluntary retirement contributions.

## Increasing R&D Funding Using Environmental Taxes

One option for generating additional R&D funding is carbon taxation, either as a direct carbon tax or as revenue from the auctioning of carbon permits under a cap-and-trade scheme. Numerous studies have provided estimates of the socially optimal level of carbon taxation by calculating the present value of damages from carbon emissions. A literature review by Tol (2005) found large variance in carbon damage estimates. Based on 28 studies, the mean carbon damage estimate was $93 per ton but the median was only $14/ton, and the 90 percent confidence interval was –$10 to $350/ton.[1] The primary reason for the large difference in carbon damage estimates was the variation in researchers' choice of a discount rate. Tol concludes that it 'is unlikely that the marginal damage costs of carbon dioxide emissions exceed $50/tC and are likely to be substantially smaller than that' (Tol, 2005, p. 2073). This conclusion has been disputed by other analysts (see Ackerman, this volume). The Stern Review, for example, estimates the social cost of carbon at over \$300/ton. To put these figures in context, a carbon tax of \$10/ton would increase the price of oil by about 1 per cent, the price of natural gas by about 3 per cent, and the price of coal by about 23 per cent (Harris and Roach, 2007).

Carbon taxation has met with considerable resistance in the US, and instituting a significant broad carbon tax appears unlikely in the immediate future. This analysis considers whether a less ambitious carbon tax could raise the funds necessary to permit a dramatic increase in public funding for energy R&D. Total carbon dioxide emissions in the US in 2006 were 5.9 billion tons (US Department of Energy, 2008). Assuming all carbon emissions could be taxed, a doubling of US energy R&D funding could be met with a carbon tax of only about 50 cents per ton (see Table 10.1). Even in the most ambitious scenario, where the US alone doubles global energy R&D funding, a tax of only \$1.87/ton of carbon dioxide would be necessary. Thus even a relatively small tax on carbon emissions in the US, well below most estimates of the socially efficient carbon tax, could be used to fund a large increase in public funding for climate change research.

For reasons of practicality and administration, it may not be feasible to tax all carbon emissions. Table 10.1 also considers the effect of taxing only commercial and industrial emissions, currently about 2.7 billion tons annually. Again, the carbon tax levels necessary to raise additional R&D funds are relatively modest, and significantly below most estimates of carbon damages.

*Table 10.1 Cost of increased public energy R&D funding*

| Policy Option | Funding Increase of \$3.2 Billion | Funding Increase of \$5.0 Billion | Funding Increase of \$11.0 Billion |
|---|---|---|---|
| Tax all $CO_2$ emissions | \$0.54/ton $CO_2$ | \$0.85/ton $CO_2$ | \$1.87/ton $CO_2$ |
| Tax all commercial and industrial emissions | \$1.17/ton $CO_2$ | \$1.83/ton $CO_2$ | \$4.02/ton $CO_2$ |
| Tax on only gasoline | 2.3 cents/gal. | 3.5 cents/gal. | 7.8 cents/gal. |

The final policy option considered in Table 10.1 is a tax solely on gasoline. Unlike carbon taxation, a tax on gasoline would not require monitoring of all carbon emissions. The current federal tax on gasoline is 18.4 cents per gallon, with state taxes ranging from six to 42 cents per gallon (American Petroleum Institute, 2006). Total gasoline consumption in the US in 2006 was 9,233 thousand barrels per day, or 142 billion gallons annually (US Department of Energy, 2007). Thus US funding of energy R&D could be doubled with a new gasoline tax of only about two cents per gallon. Alternatively, the US could effectively double global R&D funding with a gasoline tax of 7.8 cents per gallon. As with carbon taxation, an additional gas tax of two to eight cents per gallon would still leave gas taxes in the US well below socially efficient levels (Parry and Small, 2004).

## CLEAN ENERGY RETIREMENT ACCOUNTS

The estimates cited above suggest that a dramatic increase in public funding for climate change R&D in the US could be paid for with relatively minor taxes applied to carbon emissions or gasoline. Of course, any of these new taxes could be countered by a decrease in existing taxes to make the policy revenue neutral. But recognizing the political difficulties of instituting new taxes in the US, we will consider a final option for raising the necessary revenue to permit an increase in public R&D funding for climate change research. The proposal is that individuals could voluntarily set up clean energy retirement accounts (CERAs) similar to existing Individual Retirement Accounts (IRAs). Like IRAs, contributions to CERAs would offer tax advantages and provide retirement income. But while IRA contributions are made using various private investment instruments such as stocks and mutual funds, contributions to CERAs would be made to the federal government. The revenue raised would then be used solely to address global climate change. CERAs would also offer individuals a simple opportunity to increase personal savings, something that is particularly needed given the recent decline in savings in the US.

Most Americans indicate that climate change is a serious problem and that the country is currently not doing enough to address the problem. In a January 2007 poll by CBS News, 70 percent of Americans stated that they believed climate change is an environmental problem currently having a serious impact (pollingreport.com, 2007). In a March 2006 ABC News poll, 68 percent of Americans said that 'the federal government should do more than it's doing now to try to deal with global warming'. The public is overwhelmingly in favor of federal policies promoting R&D on issues related to climate change. In a March 2006 Gallup poll, 85 percent favored spending government money to develop alternative fuel sources for automobiles and 77 percent favored spending government money to develop solar and wind power. In a January 2007 UPI-Zogby International poll 55 percent of respondents said that 'increased government investment in looking into alternative sources would be the best way to encourage development of renewable forms of energy' (United Press International, 2007). Another 27 percent of respondents to this survey favored tax breaks to small business or individuals who purchase a hybrid vehicle as the best way to encourage renewable energy development.

These surveys suggest that broad support exists for public funding of climate-change-related R&D, but people are less enthusiastic when it comes to paying higher taxes to support such funding – in the ABC News poll mentioned above only 19 percent approved of addressing climate change with higher electricity taxes and 31 percent approved of setting higher gasoline taxes. CERAs offer an opportunity to raise additional revenue for climate-change-related R&D without raising current taxes or shifting federal spending priorities.

## CERA Revenue Potential

Some idea of the amount of revenue that could be generated from CERAs can be obtained by looking at charitable contributions in the US. In 2003 charitable contributions to environmental causes totaled $7 billion (US State Department, 2005) and in 2005 environmental contributions grew by 16 percent, faster growth than most other sectors (Giving USA, 2006). Public willingness to pay to avert significant climate change may actually be much higher than these figures imply. In a 1997–98 contingent valuation survey by Cameron (2005), average willingness to pay to prevent noticeable climate change, in terms of higher prices and/or taxes, was $228 per month. In another contingent valuation survey by Berrens et al. (2004), households were willing to pay an average of $200 to $1,760 annually, depending on the sample and modeling approach, in terms of higher energy and gasoline prices to support US ratification of the Kyoto Protocol. These surveys suggest that the willingness to pay to prevent climate change among US citizens is well above the $3.2–$11.0 billion assumed in the three scenarios proposed here for increasing energy R&D funding. Of course, these surveys only present costs to respondents while the proposed CERA program would offer the potential for financial gains.

It is also useful to consider how much US taxpayers currently contribute to voluntary retirement programs. According to IRS statistics, in 2000 contributions to IRA plans, including traditional IRAs, Roth IRAs, and SEP IRAs, totaled $36.5 billion (Sailer and Nutter, 2004). In 2001 payments to defined contribution plans, such as 401(k)s and 403(b)s, exceeded $200 billion (US Census Bureau, 2007). The evidence also suggests that IRA plans are significantly underutilized. In 2000 less than ten percent of all tax filers who were eligible for IRA contributions actually made contributions (Sailer and Nutter, 2004). IRA participation rates are particularly low for lower-income and young taxpayers. Only 6 percent of those with adjusted gross incomes below $50,000 contributed to an IRA in 2000. The contribution rate for tax payers under age 40 was 7 percent.

The underutilization of IRAs reflects a broader trend towards reduced personal savings. The personal savings rate in the United States has been less than 1 percent, or even negative, since early 2005 (US Bureau of Economic Analysis, 2008). About 44 percent of American households did not save in 2004, up from 41 percent in 2001 (Bucks et al., 2006). The lack of sufficient voluntary savings for retirement may be exacerbated in the future as a result of a projected shortfall in Social Security payments beginning in 2040 (US Social Security Administration, 2006). All these data suggest an important need to increase retirement savings, particularly for lower- and middle-income households (Duflo et al., 2005).

CERAs present a retirement-savings instrument that could offer several unique features. First, unlike other retirement plans, a CERA would be oriented around a public policy issue with broad support. While CERAs would offer the opportunity for financial returns, as discussed in more detail below, contributions to the plan would also be an investment in long-term environmental quality. In recent years there has been a growing interest in investments screened for social and environmental performance. Socially-responsible investments have become an increasing share of total US mutual fund assets (Social Investment Forum, 2006). CERAs would represent another option for savers to integrate their financial objectives with their personal values.

The CERA program should be structured to offer an uncomplicated opportunity for investing. With existing IRA and voluntary supplemental retirement programs, participation rates may be adversely affected by administrative requirements. Consider the results of one study showing that participation rates in a large company's 401(k) went from around 50 percent to 90 percent when the company switch from voluntary enrollment to automatic enrollment with an opt-out, without changing any other characteristics of the plan (Madrian and Shea, 2001). Participation rates in CERAs could be maximized by allowing contributions through automatic deductions from one's paycheck and/or direct allocations when completing one's federal income tax form.

A CERA program could appeal to both ends of the political spectrum. The plan offers individuals the opportunity to maintain personal accounts to supplement Social Security – a concept that many conservatives endorse. Of course, CERA contributions would be used to combat climate change rather than invested in the stock market. But CERAs still offer individuals an additional personal choice regarding their retirement portfolio. Another appealing feature to conservatives is that the plan does not require an increase in current taxes. Conservatives have also tended to prefer a technology-based approach to responding to climate change as opposed to an approach based on carbon pricing. On the other hand, the CERA program should appeal to environmentalists seeking to increase the US response to climate change. CERAs could move the US into an international leadership role in planning for a future based on renewable energy sources.

As proposed here, the CERA program would have a limited duration. The objective would be to advance low-carbon technologies to the point of financial competitiveness with fossil fuels or sufficient market penetration to put the US well along a path of lower overall carbon emissions. Eventually CERA contributions would be phased out, but since CERAs are retirement plan instruments, payments to CERA holders would still need to be made beyond the point when contributions cease. As with IRAs, withdrawals from CERAs would not be permitted without penalty until the account holder reaches a specific age. For example, withdrawals from IRAs are generally not permitted without penalty until the holder reaches age 59½. Thus in the early years of a CERA program, payments to account holders would be negligible, but then gradually increase as account holders reached retirement age.

## CERA Financial Returns

Participation rates in a CERA program would depend on the possibility of positive financial rates of return. One way to encourage participation would be to guarantee a minimum rate of return, essentially transferring most risk from the investor to the federal government. As one example, the minimum return could be set equal to the implicit rate of return on Social Security taxes. Implicit nominal rates of return for current retirees are around 4 percent but rates vary widely according to one's income level and demographic characteristics (US Government Accountability Office, 1999). Another approach would be to set the minimum rate of return equal to the interest rate on long-term government bonds, about 4.5 percent in nominal terms as of early 2008. Younger savers could be targeted by offering them slightly higher minimum rates of return as compared to older savers.

The program should also offer the possibility of rates of return above any minimum guaranteed levels. The possibility for higher rates of return would depend on the potential for public investments in clean energy technologies to generate future government revenues. The government would use the money contributed to CERAs solely to address climate change but the money would not simply expand existing R&D programs. Two particular uses of CERA funds offer the potential to yield financial returns that could then be used to fund payments to CERA holders when they retire. One possibility is that CERA revenue could be used to provide low-interest loans to existing or start-up private companies pursing climate mitigation technologies. These loans would ideally allow long payback periods, and possibly grace periods. Once the loans are repaid, the money would then be used to provide payments to CERA holders when they retire.

But the greater potential for the CERA program to generate positive financial returns may rest with the success of public–private partnerships. As mentioned above, the US strategic plan on climate change emphasizes the role of public–private partnerships, broadly defined as the joint provision of goods or services by collaboration between public and private entities. In certain circumstances, public–private partnerships will lead to greater social benefits than would occur solely as a result of private investment (Scott, 2000). These circumstances include the development of infrastructure, research on generic technologies, projects with a large potential for spillover benefits, and the pursuit of social, rather than purely market-based, goals.

Unfortunately, there is little empirical evidence regarding the benefits of public–private partnerships. A noteworthy exception is a study by Audretsch, et al. (2002) which evaluates the effectiveness of the US Department of Defense's Small Business Innovation Research (SBIR) program. They find that the SBIR program clearly led to firms undertaking research that would not have taken place without the program. In reference to the funded projects, firms reported an expected present value rate of return in the absence of SBIR support of 25 percent, a rate below their reported minimum private return hurdle of 33 percent. In other words, in the absence of SBIR funding the firms would not have deemed the projects financially viable. However, firms that received SBIR support reported an ex post average rate of return of 76 percent for the supported projects, well above the hurdle point. The large gap between the ex post rate of return and minimum acceptable rate (76 percent versus 33 percent) suggests that even if the government received some payback in cases when public support produced profitable outcomes, private firms would still receive net benefits from public support.

While the SBIR results cannot be considered representative of all public R&D investments, they suggest that large financial and social gains can accrue. Thus public R&D funding related to climate change using public–private partnerships may ultimately produce financial rates of return well above the minimum levels necessary to attract firms to such partnerships. Given this possibility, a condition of the partnership could be that the government will share in the financial returns that accrue as a result of partnership. The situation could be likened to a venture capitalist firm that funds risky business opportunities in order to receive a financial return. Not all investments would yield a positive return but others would likely be highly profitable. In fact, private venture capital investments in clean energy are growing rapidly and could comprise 10 percent of all venture capital investments by 2009, up from 1 to 3 percent during 1999–2001 (Parker and O'Rourke, 2006). Government investments from CERAs should be designed to complement, rather than crowd out, private investments.

## Management of CERA Funds

To ensure an efficient use of CERA funds (and limit cronyism), it is recommended the distribution of funds be managed by an independent panel comprised of experts with backgrounds in such fields as energy technology, climate science, and socially responsible investing. The government would eventually sell its stock holdings in private equity markets to fund retirement payments to CERA holders. Thus in the long run the government would phase out all ownership of equities.

The potential for CERA investment to yield positive rates of return will depend on the ability of low-carbon energy technologies to compete with fossil fuel energy in the future. The analysis by Anderson (2006) indicates that even in the long run (more than 20 years) most low-carbon technologies will not be directly competitive with fossil fuel energy sources. Only in the presence of substantial carbon pricing would low-carbon technologies gain a competitive advantage. Other results, however, suggest that some renewable technologies may already be competitive with fossil fuel energy. The Nuclear Energy Agency et al. (2005) estimates the current costs of generating electricity from wind power to be \$35–\$95 per Mwh, overlapping with the costs of coal (\$25–\$50) and gas (\$37–\$60). Analysis by the American Wind Energy Association (2001) also shows wind energy to currently be cost competitive with higher-carbon electricity technologies.

While loan repayments and public–private partnerships can provide funds to make payments to retired CERA holders, it is possible that the program will not be self-funding and additional revenue will need to be raised to make payments to CERA holders when they retire. Rather than raising the revenue for any shortfall from income or other broad taxes, a reasonable suggestion is that the gap be filled by future taxes on carbon-based energy. Any necessary taxes would be minimal towards the start of the CERA program but then gradually increase as more CERA holders retire. The idea that carbon taxes should gradually increase over time is widely accepted in the economics literature (Nordhaus, 2006).

# CERA SIMULATION MODEL

This section of the chapter explores the potential costs of the CERA program over time using a simple simulation model. The simulation estimates the annual withdrawals made by CERA holders over time. Most withdrawals are made once CERA holders retire, although some withdrawals are made prior to retirement as described below.

Analysis of the CERA program must consider the age of those who contribute. Following published IRS data on IRA contributions, US taxpayers are divided into age-based cohorts of five years each (less than 15 years old, 15–20 years old, etc.). Within each age cohort, all individuals are assumed to contribute into a CERA at the mid-point age in the cohort. The maximum age at which contributions to a CERA are permitted is assumed to be 59½ years. Similar to IRAs, it is assumed that CERA holders can withdraw funds at any time but that withdrawals made before age 59½ are generally subject to a 10 per cent penalty.

Real rates of return are assumed fixed for CERA contributions made by each age cohort but vary across cohorts in order to attract younger investors. For the simulation, only the scenario of a $5 billion in additional R&D funding is analyzed. As mentioned above, a CERA program of limited duration is anticipated. It is assumed that the program attracts $5 billion (in real terms) in investment each year for 25 years, after which no further contributions are allowed. The allocation of the $5 billion annual investment across cohorts is based on the distribution of IRA contributions by age group (Sailer and Nutter, 2004) but is slightly modified to represent a younger distribution of investors. Table 10.2 indicates the percentage of annual CERA contributions received from investors in each age cohort. The table also shows the assumed real rates of return applied to each cohort, ranging from two to three percent in real terms.

The withdrawal of funds by CERA holders of different ages is developed based on IRS statistics on the withdrawal of IRA funds (Sailer and Nutter, 2004). As shown in Figure 10.2, about 25–30 per cent of IRA withdrawals are made by those younger than age 59½, which in most cases incurs a 10 percent penalty. The simulation model includes withdrawals made prior to retirement age, adjusted for each age cohort based on the IRS data. The penalties for early withdraw are returned to the CERA program. Figure 10.2 also shows that only about 1 percent of IRA withdrawals are made by those over age 80. In the simulation it is assumed that all CERA accounts are depleted by age 85. The simulation is run until all payments to CERA account holders have been made, which is 97 years from the start of the program (the youngest investors are age 12 at the start of the simulation; such investors contribute for each year until Year 25, then they withdraw CERA funds until they reach age 85).

*Table 10.2 Assumptions of CERA simulation*

| Age Cohort | Percentage of Annual Contributions | Annual Contributions (Millions) | Real Financial Rate of Return % |
|---|---|---|---|
| Under 15 | 1 | 50,000 | 3.0 |
| 15–20 Years | 1 | 50,000 | 3.0 |
| 20–25 Years | 4 | 200,000 | 3.0 |
| 25–30 Years | 7 | 350,000 | 3.0 |
| 30–35 Years | 12 | 600,000 | 2.7 |
| 35–40 Years | 14 | 700,000 | 2.7 |
| 40–45 Years | 18 | 900,000 | 2.3 |
| 45–50 Years | 18 | 900,000 | 2.3 |
| 50–55 Years | 15 | 750,000 | 2.0 |
| 55–60 Years | 10 | 500,000 | 2.0 |
| Total | 100 | 5,000,000 | |

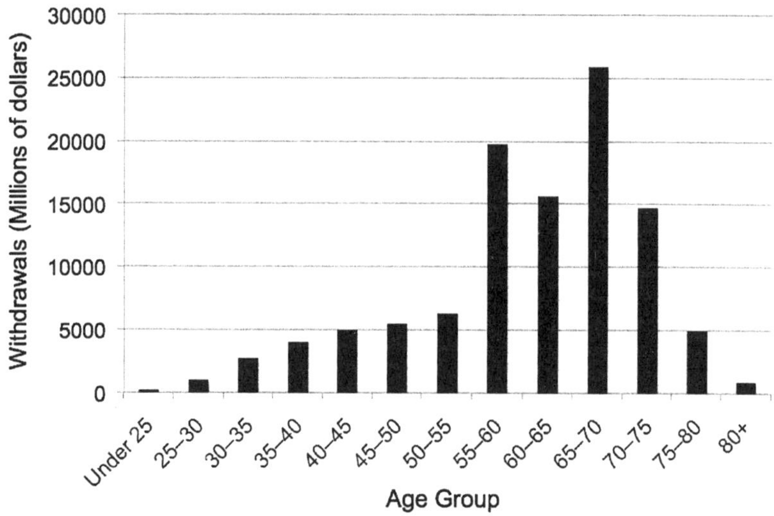


*Source:* Sail and Nutter (2004).

*Figure 10.2 IRA withdrawals by age cohort, 2000 data*

The results are presented in Figure 10.3. Total withdrawals start off low as most CERA contributors are less than retirement age. Withdrawals reach $2.0 billion after 13 years, $3.0 billion after 18 years, and $4.0 billion after 23 years. Recall that the simulation assumes annual contributions of $5.0 billion for 25 years. By the time contributions cease annual withdraws are approximately $4.7 billion. Thus at the end of the 25 years withdrawals are nearly equal to annual CERA contributions. When contributions cease in the

25th year, withdrawals continue to increase, reaching $4.8 billion in the 32nd year. Then withdrawals steadily decline, falling below $1.0 billion in the 65th year and reaching zero in the 98th year. Total withdrawals by CERA holders over the entire simulation period are $200 billion in real terms.

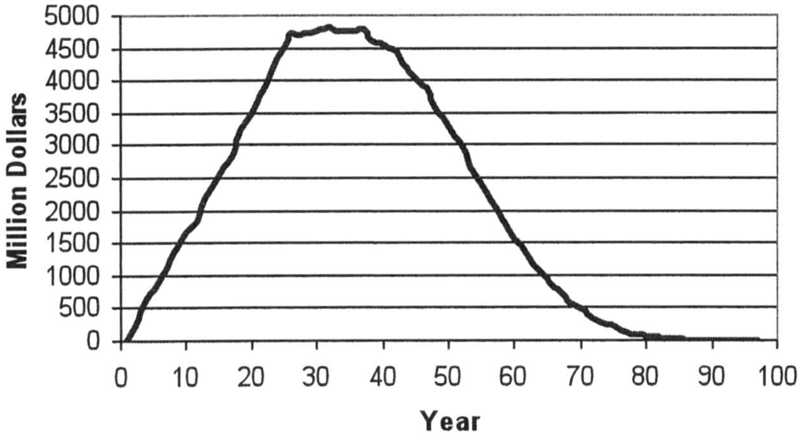


*Figure 10.3* *Simulated annual withdrawals from CERA program (millions of real dollars)*

As mentioned previously, revenues from loan repayments and public–private partnerships are expected to at least partially fund payments to CERA holders. The analysis now considers how much revenue could be generated under different assumptions. It is assumed that revenue from these two sources would begin only after a lag period to allow time for new technologies to be introduced to markets and become profitable. A lag period of ten years is assumed between the time CERA contributions are made and the time returns begin to be generated from those contributions. Also, it is assumed that not all the public–private ventures begun as a result of the CERA program will be viable – some ventures will fail and generate no future revenues. This analysis considers three revenue scenarios:

1. returns on 30 percent of CERA contributions; rate of return of 5 percent for 15 years
2. returns on 50 percent of CERA contributions; rate of return of 10 percent for 15 years
3. returns on 60 percent of CERA contributions; rate of return of 12 percent for 20 years

For example, in the second scenario a return of 10 percent is obtained on half of a CERA contribution of $5 billion made in Year 1 beginning in Year 11 and continuing until Year 25 ($250 million per year). Note that the returns are calculated as a percentage of the initial CERA contribution and that the calculations do not include repayment of any principal. Thus the rate of return in the first two scenarios does not even reflect a return sufficient to payback the original investment. Figure 10.4 displays the revenue streams generated under each of these three assumptions, along with the estimated withdrawals copied from Figure 10.3

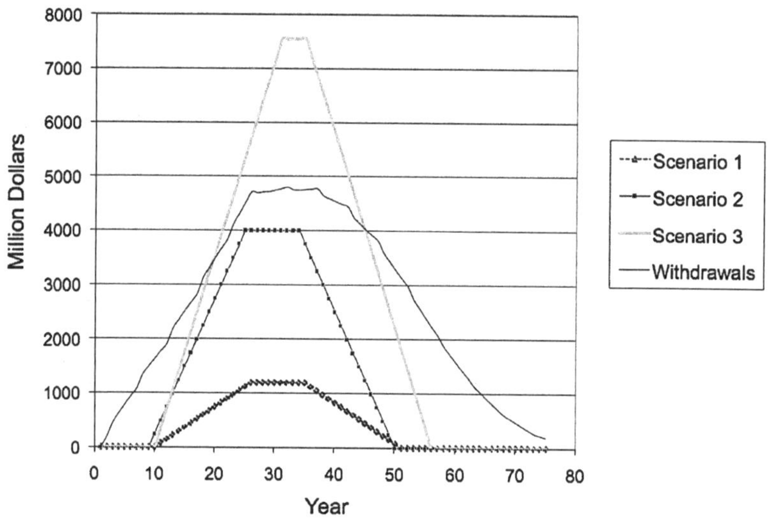


*Figure 10.4 CERA revenues under alternative assumptions*

Figure 10.4 illustrates that the first two revenue scenarios clearly do not fully fund CERA withdrawals by account holders. In the first scenario, revenues from loan repayments and public–private partnerships fund only about 15 percent of CERA payments. In the second scenario, revenues are sufficient to fund half of CERA obligations throughout the life of the program. Yet in the third scenario, with the most optimistic revenue assumptions, CERA payment obligations are fully met with the generated revenues and the program is essentially self-funding. Note that in the third scenario withdrawals exceed revenues during the first 19 years of the program, then revenues exceed withdrawals for years 20–44, and withdrawals exceed revenues beyond the 44th year. Thus the government would need to borrow against future revenues for the early years of the program but then be able to invest excess revenues in the middle years of the program, creating a 'trust fund' that would then be used to fund CERA payments towards the latter years of the program.

In the first two revenue scenarios other revenue sources would be required to meet the estimated shortfall. Again, this analysis considers taxes on carbon emissions or gasoline. One possibility is to estimate the required taxes as a constant rate throughout the duration of the program. However, given that the ability of the CERA program to generate revenues through loan repayments and public–private partnerships would be unknown at the beginning of the program, any tax set at inception would most likely need to be adjusted once actual returns were known. Instead, the required tax rates are calculated each year as the amount necessary to close the gap between CERA revenues and withdrawals in Figure 10.4. In addition to the two scenarios above which would require closing a funding gap, a worst-case scenario is considered in which the CERA program generates no revenues at all from loan repayments and public–private partnerships. For simplicity, the analysis holds carbon emissions and gasoline consumption constant at current levels.

Table 10.3 displays the results. The maximum tax is the required tax rate at the largest annual gap between withdrawals and revenues. The average tax is calculated over the 97-year duration of the CERA program.

*Table 10.3 Required taxes to fund CERA shortfall under alternative assumptions*

| | Tax All Carbon Emissions | | Tax Industrial and Commercial Carbon Emissions | | Tax Solely on Gasoline | |
|---|---|---|---|---|---|---|
| Scenario | Max. Tax | Average Tax | Max. Tax | Average Tax | Max. Tax | Average Tax |
| No CERA returns | \$0.82/ ton $CO_2$ | \$0.35/ ton $CO_2$ | \$1.72/ ton $CO_2$ | \$0.74/ ton $CO_2$ | 3.4¢/ gallon | 1.5¢/ gallon |
| Returns on 30% of contributions; 5% rate of return for 15 years | \$0.61/ ton $CO_2$ | \$0.30/ ton $CO_2$ | \$1.35/ ton $CO_2$ | \$0.63/ ton $CO_2$ | 2.7¢/ gallon | 1.3¢/ gallon |
| Returns on 50% of contributions; 10% rate of return for 15 years | \$0.55/ ton $CO_2$ | \$0.17/ ton $CO_2$ | \$1.17/ ton $CO_2$ | \$0.37/ ton $CO_2$ | 2.3¢/ gallon | 0.7¢/ gallon |

These estimates can be compared to the taxes required to fund a $5 billion annual increase in R&D without the CERA program shown in Table 10.1. Of course, the tax rates in Table 10.3 are lower than those in Table 10.1 because of the long duration of the program. Under the worst-case scenario in which no CERA returns are generated, the required carbon taxes average well below $1.00 per ton $CO_2$ and the average gas tax is only 1.5 cents per gallon. In the scenarios with some CERA returns, the required taxes are quite low – if the shortfall were met through a tax on all gasoline consumption, an average tax of only around one cent per gallon would be necessary.

## CONCLUSIONS

One component of an adequate US response to climate change would be a significant increase in public R&D funding related to climate change. This chapter has demonstrated the financial feasibility of at least doubling such R&D funding. One approach to raising the necessary public revenue would be to institute a tax on carbon emissions or to increase gasoline taxes. The tax levels required to fund a dramatic increase in climate change R&D would still be well below most estimates of socially efficient tax levels.

An alternative to raising current taxes would be to institute a program of Clean Energy Retirement Accounts. Through voluntary contributions to CERAs individuals could boost savings for retirement while supporting US efforts to combat climate change. An appealing aspect of the CERA program is that most of the costs, in terms of payments made to retirees, are deferred until the future. Most economic analyses of climate change suggest little deviation from a business-as-usual strategy because even relatively low discount rates diminish future climate change damages while costs must be paid now (Ackerman and Finlayson, 2006). The CERA program allows costs to be distributed over a longer time horizon. While the CERA program might eventually require minor taxes on carbon emissions or gasoline, those taxes would be paid by those directly benefiting from efforts to reduce climate change, and more likely to have access to low-carbon technologies.

The CERA program may be considered an unnecessary bureaucratic complication compared to, for example, simply raising gas taxes a few cents per gallon or obtaining the revenue out of general tax funds. But another potential advantage of a CERA program is that it gives individuals a direct stake in the success of climate change efforts. Given that CERA returns will depend on the success of ventures funded by the program, those who invest in CERAs will have an incentive to support clean energy technologies when they are introduced to markets. A CERA program can also be viewed as a means of increasing democratic participation by empowering citizens to direct resources towards a specific public concern. Similar to the concept of participatory budgeting, whereby public budget allocations are determined by a democratic exchange of stakeholders rather than by elected officials,[2] a CERA program would create a new public arena for active citizenship.

The evidence that humanity needs to reverse the increase in carbon emissions is compelling. Global efforts to address climate change have so far been inadequate to the task. Breakthrough technologies that could significantly reduce global emissions of carbon do not appear to be forthcoming in the immediate future. The time lag between basic scientific research and the widespread commercial availability of alternatives to high-carbon technologies is likely to be measured in decades. Thus an intensified search for low-carbon alternatives is needed immediately. A country that takes the lead in the development of low-carbon technologies will likely be in an enviable competitive position in a future which is characterized by higher carbon prices, whether driven by carbon reduction policies or by market developments including depletion of oil reserves. The analysis presented here indicates that the US could take such a leadership position at surprisingly little cost.

## NOTES

1. Note that a tax of $14/ton of carbon would equate to a tax of $3.81/ton of $CO_2$.
2. See Novy and Leubolt (2005) for an application of participatory budgeting in Brazil.

## REFERENCES

Ackerman, Frank and Ian Finlayson (2006), 'The Economics of Inaction on Climate Change: A Sensitivity Analysis', *Climate Policy*, **6** (5): 509–526.

American Petroleum Institute (2006), *State Motor Fuel Excise Tax Rate Report*, October 2006.

American Wind Energy Association (2001), 'Comparative Costs of Wind Energy and Other Energy Sources', http://www.awea.org/pubs/factsheets/Cost2001.PDF.

Anderson, Dennis (2006), 'Cost and Finance of Abating Carbon Emissions in the Energy Sector', paper commissioned as part of *The Stern Review on the Economics of Climate Change*.

Audretsch, David B., Albert N. Link and John T. Scott (2002), 'Public/Private Technology Partnerships: Evaluating SBIR-supported Research', *Research Policy*, **31**: 145–158.

Berrens, Robert P., Alok K. Bohara, Hank C. Jenkins-Smith, Carol L. Silva and David L. Weimer (2004), 'Information and Effort in Contingent Valuation Surveys: Application to Global Climate Change using National Internet Samples', *Journal of Environmental Economics and Management*: **47** (2): 331–363.

Bucks, Brian K., Arthur B. Kennickell, and Kevin B. Moore (2006), 'Recent Changes in U.S. Family Finances: Evidence from the 2001 and 2004 Survey of Consumer Finances', *Federal Reserve Bulletin*, 22 March.

Cameron, Trudy Ann (2005), 'Individual Option Prices for Climate Change Mitigation', *Journal of Public Economics*, **89** (2 –3): 283–301.

Dooley, J. J. (1998), 'Unintended Consequences: Energy R&D in a Deregulated Energy Market', *Energy Policy*, **26** (7): 547–555.

Duflo, Esther, William Gale, Jeffrey Liebman, Peter Orzag and Emmanuel Saez (2005), 'Savings Incentives for Low- and Middle-Income Families: Evidence from a Field Experiment with H&R Block', National Bureau of Economic Research Working Paper 11680, September 2005.

Edenhofer, Ottmar, Nico Bauer and Elmar Kriegler (2005), 'The Impact of Technological Change on Climate Protection and Welfare: Insights from the Model MIND', *Ecological Economics*, **54** (2–3): 277–292.

Giving USA (2006), 'Charitable Giving Rises 6 Percent to More than $260 Billion in 2005', Press Release, June 19, 2006.

Harris, Jonathan M. and Brian Roach (2007), *The Economics of Global Climate Change*, http://www.ase.tufts.edu/gdae/education_materials/modules.html.

International Energy Agency (2003a), 'Integrating Energy and Environmental Goals', Report prepared for the Italian government by the IEA for the Ninth Conference of the Parties of the UNFCCC.

International Energy Agency (2003b), *Energy to 2050: Scenarios for a Sustainable Future*. Paris, France.

International Energy Agency (2005), *30 Key Energy Trends*.

International Energy Agency (2006a), *Energy Technology Perspectives: Scenarios and Strategies to 2050.*

International Energy Agency (2006b), *World Energy Outlook 2006*, Paris, France.

Madrian, Brigitte C. and Dennis F. Shea (2001), 'The Power of Suggestion: Inertia in 401(k) Participation and Saving Behavior', *Quarterly Journal of Economics*, **116** (4): 1149–1187.

Nemet, Gregory F. and Daniel M. Kammen (2007). 'U.S. Energy Research and Development: Declining Investment, Increasing Need, and the Feasibility of Expansion', *Energy Policy,* **35**: 746–755.

Norberg-Bohm, Vicki (2000), 'Creating Incentives for Environmentally Enhancing Technological Change: Lessons from 30 Years of U.S. Energy Technology Policy', *Technological Forecasting and Social Change*, **65** (2): 125–148.

Nordhaus, William (2006), 'The Stern Review on the Economics of Climate Change,' NBER Working Paper 12741, December 2006.

Novy, Andreas, and Berhnhard Leubolt (2005), 'Participatory Budgeting in Porto Alegre: Social Innovation and the Dialectical Relationship of State and Civil Society', *Urban Studies* **42** (11): 2023-2036.

Nuclear Energy Agency, International Energy Agency and Organisation for Economic Co-operation and Development (2005), *Projected Costs of Generating Electricity, 2005 Update*, Paris, France.

Office of the Press Secretary (2001), 'President's Statement on Climate Change', 13 July 2001, http://www.whitehouse.gov/news/releases/2001/07/20010713-2.html.

Parker, Nicholas and Anastasia O'Rourke (2006), 'The Cleantech Venture Capital Report – 2006'.

Parry, Ian W.H. and Kenneth A. Small (2004), 'Does Britain or the United States Have the Right Gasoline Tax?', RFF Discussion Paper 02-12, September 2004.

Pew Center on Global Climate Change (2002), 'Analysis of President Bush's February 14th Climate Change Plan', February 2002, Pew Center website, http://www.pewclimate.org/policy_center/analyses/response_bushpolicy.cfm.

pollingreport.com (2007), Environment web page, http://www.pollingreport.com/enviro.htm.

Popp, David (2004), 'R&D Subsidies and Climate Policy: Is There a Free Lunch?', NBER Working Paper 10880, October 2004.

President's Committee of Advisors on Science and Technology (1997), *R&D Priorities for Sustainable Development,* January 1997.

Sailer, Peter J. and Sarah E. Nutter (2004), 'Accumulation and Distribution of Individual Retirement Arrangements, 2000', *IRS Statistics of Income Bulletin,* Spring 2004.

Salter, Ammon J. and Ben R. Martin (2001), 'The Economic Benefits of Publicly Funded Basic Research: A Critical Review', *Research Policy,* **30** (3): 509–532.

Scott, John T. (2000), 'Strategic Research Partnerships: What Have We Learned?', Dartmouth College Working Paper 00-21, November 2000.

Social Investment Forum (2006), *2005 Report on Socially Responsible Investing Trends in the United States*, January 24, 2006.

Stern, Nicholas (2006), *The Economics of Climate Change: The Stern Review.*

Tol, Richard S.J. (2005), 'The Marginal Damage Cost of Carbon Dioxide Emissions: An Assessment of the Uncertainties', *Energy Policy*, **33**: 2064–2074.

United Press International (2007), 'UPI Poll: More R&D on Alternative Energy', January 24, 2007 press release.

United States Bureau of Economic Analysis (2008), *Personal Savings Rate*, http://www.bea.gov/briefrm/saving.htm.

United States Census Bureau (2007), *The Statistical Abstract of the United States, 2007.*

United States Climate Change Technology Program (2006), *Strategic Plan*, September 2006.

United States Congressional Budget Office (2006), *Evaluating the Role of Prices and R&D in Reducing Carbon Dioxide Emissions*, September 2006.

United States Department of Energy, Energy Information Administration (2006a), *International Energy Outlook 2006.*

United States Department of Energy, Energy Information Administration (2006b), *Annual Energy Outlook 2006 with Projections to 2030.*

United States Department of Energy, Energy Information Administration (2007), *Annual Energy Review 2006*, June 2007.

United States Department of Energy, Energy Information Administration (2008). Online U.S. Greenhouse Gas Emissions Data.

United States Environmental Protection Agency (2006), *Fast Facts: The U.S. Greenhouse Gas Emissions Inventory.*

United States Government Accountability Office (1999), *Social Security: Issues in Comparing Rates of Return with Market Investments*, August 1999.

United States Social Security Administration (2006), *The 2006 Annual Report of the Board of Trustees of the Federal Old-Age and Survivors Insurance and Federal Disability Insurance Trust Funds*, 1 May 2006.

United States State Department (2005), 'U.S. Charitable Contributions Top $240 Billion in 2003', USINFO, 17 February 2005.

World Energy Council (2001), 'Energy Technologies for the 21st Century', report by a study group of the World Energy Council, August 2001.

# 11. The New EU Emissions Trading Scheme: A Blueprint for the Global Carbon Market?

**Christian Egenhofer**[1]

## INTRODUCTION

Tackling climate change has been identified by the EU as one of the world's greatest challenges, recognizing that climate change is likely to have major negative consequences for the environment, the economy and societies at large. The EU has repeatedly confirmed its position that an increase in the global annual mean surface temperature should not exceed 2°C above pre-industrial levels. After the withdrawal of the United States from the Kyoto Protocol, the EU has found itself being catapulted into global leadership on climate change. While few had predicted at the time that the Kyoto Protocol would survive, Japan, Canada and Russia ratified the Protocol to bring it into force in 2005, at least in part due to active EU diplomacy. To implement the Protocol, the EU has adopted numerous laws to fulfil its commitments and also to prepare the path for a new follow-up post-Kyoto agreement, when commitments expire in 2012. Among them have been a host of policies to support renewable energy, improve energy efficiency in buildings and transport. The centerpiece of EU climate change policy, however, has been the EU Emissions Trading Scheme (EU ETS) that started in 2005.

Implemented in 2005 with a 3-year pilot phase from 2005 to 2007, the EU ETS suffered from a number of teething problems such as significant delays of registries and National Allocation Plans (NAPs), inconsistency of installation definitions, issues related to monitoring, reporting and verification, and data collection questions. The original EU ETS Directive has a number of deficiencies, essentially stemming from a high degree of decentralization. The main effects have been overallocation of allowances, leading to a price collapse in 2006, distortion of competition for firms operating in the EU internal market, high transaction costs, lack of transparency and finally, windfall profits for the power sector. As a result, the

European Commission has proposed a review of the EU ETS Directive, which is pending adoption by the Council of Ministers and the European Parliament. The objective of this review has been to improve the scheme based on experiences so far, to ensure a cost-effective achievement of the EU greenhouse gas (GHG) reduction commitments during the second phase of the ETS, from 2008 to 2012. Other goals include enhancing the predictability and certainty of long-term emission reductions, and contributing to international carbon markets and encouraging action globally. If efficient and effective, the EU ETS could become a 'docking station' for other schemes to link to, or even become a global standard for GHG emissions trading.

This chapter will review experiences of the EU ETS so far, assess the proposed reform to evaluate whether the new EU ETS can become the 'open system promoting global innovation' that the EU – according to the European Commission website – had in mind when adopting it. The chapter is structured as follows:

1. A brief sketch of the origins and the political context.
2. A review of the initial experiences in phase one and phase two.
3. An assessment of the Commission proposal to reform the ETS.
4. An analysis of the ETS's role in the context of international and domestic climate change policy.
5. A discussion of competitiveness and carbon leakage.
6. Conclusion on EU ETS prospects as part of a global carbon market.

## ORIGINS AND POLITICAL CONTEXT

Prior to adoption of the EU ETS, experience with tradable permits has largely been confined to the United States, which introduced such schemes in the 1970s. Among them was the successful US $SO_2$ trading program, which has become the reference point for emissions trading globally (e.g. Klaassen 1996). While there is little doubt that the EU ETS has strongly been influenced by the US $SO_2$ trading program and the NOx Budget Trading Program,[2] EU and US schemes differs in several important aspects. The principal difference is the high level of decentralization in the EU and the significant degree of discretion for member states in the implementation phase, even if compared to the NOx Budget Trading Program.

### EU Decentralization

A decentralized approach is consistent with the makeup of the EU political system, based on sovereign member states with their own legal systems, traditions, and languages, within which the EU layer of governance (the

Council of Ministers and the European Parliament) agrees on the framework and member states enjoy a high level of discretion in implementation in their respective jurisdictions.[3] As there are as many jurisdictions as member states, one-size-fits-all policies seldom are an option.[4] Consistency across member states is sought by so-called Comitology Committees, consisting of European Commission and member state officials who are responsible for the harmonization of implementation provisions. The mandate (and hence the limit) of Comitology Committees are set both by the relevant provisions in the Directive and EU primary, secondary and case law such as EC internal and competition law.

Despite the fact that the EU exhibits elements of a federal system, one would miss the very essence of the diversity within the EU if one perceived it as a federation. The high degree of decentralization is – at least partly – also the result of consensual decision-making in the EU.[5] As the EU is made up of sovereign states, effective implementation of EU laws by member states is best ensured if legitimate member states' concerns are taken into account during the negotiations in the Council of Ministers when the laws are formulated. As a result, initially the EU tends to choose decentralized options, followed by steps to establish and coordinate a common approach among member states. But initial experiences usually feed into a formal review, which in many cases – including for the EU ETS – is built into the legislation.

## Increasing Use of Market-Based Solutions

Market solutions have in many instances proven easier than harmonization across 27 or more national jurisdictions, which display major differences in legal systems, enforcement cultures and administrative capacities. In the case of the EU ETS, EU legislation has been initiated by nationally proposed legislation. European Commission action towards an emissions trading scheme has – at least partly – been triggered by the establishment of national emissions trading schemes in Denmark and the UK, and the associated risks of 'proliferation' of such schemes in other member states (see e.g. Zapfel and Vainio, 2002). At the same time companies such as BP and Shell, the EU electricity sector and industrial associations such as Entreprises pour l'environnement started to promote emissions trading schemes for greenhouse gases (e.g. Egenhofer 2003; Philibert and Reinaud 2004).

Ultimately, the EU ETS has been promoted on the basis of a mixture of economic, environmental and EU internal market arguments. First, emissions trading offers the prospect of meeting environmental goals in the most cost-effective way by ensuring that the market price of carbon is equal to the lowest marginal abatement cost amongst all controlled sources. Ultimately, it provides a mechanism by which emitters – factory operators, oil refineries, power plants etc. – can identify the most cost-effective ways to reduce their emissions, and thus factor carbon-reduction strategies into day-to-day business decisions. A second potential advantage is that the resulting carbon price should improve long-term predictability, a crucial factor for business to make efficient investment decisions. Thirdly, a cap-and-trade system such as the EU ETS provides environmental certainty by capping the overall emission level from the covered sources. Fourthly, emissions trading can be expected to minimize the distortions to competition in the EU market as it imposes an EU-wide carbon price for all industries alike (see Delbeke, 2006).

Another strand of the literature associates the rise of emissions trading with the 'entrepreneurial role' that DG Environment of the European Commission has played (Christiansen and Wettestad, 2003; Skjærseth and Wettestad, 2008). One could also hold that there was something inevitable about the EU ETS, as all other tools to address greenhouse gas emissions in the context of the Kyoto Protocol at the EU level of governance had failed. Most spectacularly, the 1992 carbon/energy tax proposal by the European Commission failed to be adopted and was later withdrawn. Under the EC treaty – the relevant part of the EU primary law – taxation measures need to be adopted unanimously, meaning de facto that each member state has a veto on taxation. Taxation for environmental purposes has therefore been confined to member states (see e.g. Fujiwara et al., 2006). Similarly, voluntary agreements or 'negotiated environmental agreements' have made very little impact at the EU level of governance, again mainly due to institutional reasons. Since voluntary agreements are negotiated between the European Commission and the industry concerned, the European Parliament has been opposed to such agreements since effectively their content is withheld from parliamentary scrutiny and approval. The conclusion of voluntary agreements is also complicated because of a lack a suitable interlocutors at EU industry level (ten Brink et al., 2003).

## INITIAL EXPERIENCES

The EU ETS has been the result of rigorous consultation on the part of the European Commission with stakeholders both before, during and after the European Climate Change Programme (European Commission, 2001), followed by intensive discussions within and between the Council of Ministers and the European Parliament. The EU ETS was adopted unanimously by the Council of Ministers and by a very large majority in the European Parliament. In general, business was favorably disposed to the scheme, as were environmental NGOs.

Under the EU ETS cap-and-trade scheme, the covered sectors must monitor and annually report their $CO_2$ emissions, and are obliged every year to surrender an amount of EU emission allowances (EUAs) to the government that is equivalent to their $CO_2$ emissions in that year. The scheme covers electricity and heat generation, cement production and pulp and paper production, which initially represent a total of some 40 percent of total EU $CO_2$ emissions. Additional sectors include other industries (e.g. refining, coke ovens), iron and steel, glass, ceramics, paper and board. The EU ETS was to cover about 46 percent of total EU $CO_2$ projected emissions in 2010, equivalent to 38 percent of the EU's total greenhouse gases in 2010. For an authoritative overview on design, see Meadows (2006) and Vis (2006). Credits from the Kyoto Protocol's project mechanisms, the Clean development mechanism (CDM) and Joint Implementation (JI),[6] can be used for compliance within certain limits (Lefevere, 2006).

In order to ensure support from member states and industry to ensure fast adoption the European Commission had to offer a number of concessions, One such concession is free allocation of allowances of up to 95 percent for phase one (2005–07) and up to 90 percent for the second phase (2008–12). The principal reason for free allocation was to 'buy' industry acceptance. As long as allowances are given for free, companies receive additional revenues to partly or entirely offset higher production costs as a result of the EU ETS.

Another necessary concession – this time to member states – has been to leave the allocation *process* in the hands of member states. Although this is in line with the general EU practice of leaving implementation to member states, the high degree of decentralization was the price that had to be paid for both member state and industry support. Member states are reluctant to cede influence on the energy and energy-related industries. And most of the industries felt more comfortable with allocation undertaken at member state rather than at EU level. During the negotiations between Council and European Parliament, for example, attempts by the European Parliament to reduce member state discretion failed due to member states' reluctance to cede 'too much' influence – as they perceived it – to the European Commission on allocation. As a result, the EU could not even agree on a common methodology for allocation, except that the main method of allocation should be free of charge.[7] Discretion of member states is constrained, however, by EC competition law, notably Articles 87–88 on state aid, which are the relevant rules to ensure that free allocation does not amount to state aid.

## Teething Problems

The fact that the ETS was been adopted in record time to implement the EU's determination to tackle climate change posed great challenges to governments and industry in preparing for it. There were a number of significant delays. Most importantly, member states registries and National Allocation Plans (NAPs) were delayed in some cases by more than a year. Delays were also caused by the need to adapt many national laws. Further 'teething problems' included inconsistency of installation definitions, issues related to monitoring, reporting and verification, and insufficiently operating CDM and JI programs. Finally, the absence of the International Transaction Log, to be set up by the UN system to verify the validity of emissions transactions governed by the Kyoto Protocol, meant that credits from CDM could only be traded as forward transactions (see Egenhofer, 2007).

The initial phase also saw volatility, a phenomenon often observed in new trading schemes. In the initial phase, only the power sector engaged in active trading with other participating companies. Rising gas prices and falling coal prices had compelled power plants to burn more coal, which in return meant more emissions. The power sector therefore had been generally short (of allowances). This gave market participants the false impression that there was a real shortage in the market, pushing EU allowances prices to a record price of €30 per tonne despite the overall market being in oversupply. Market participants from those countries with less tight allocation, including but not limited to potential sellers from the new EU member states, had not yet engaged in trading, both as a lack of registries and, in some cases, the absence of installation level allocation.

There were also questions on data. Data collection issues were most apparent when member states started to allocate (basically) for free as the Directive foresaw. Only three member states could rely on verified data. In other member states, data collection was a 'voluntary' effort by all stakeholders, leading to an intensive government–industry dialogue. While member states were cross-checking data they received from industry, this took time with no guarantee that data was accurate. This was compounded by the inclusion of small installations, which has led to overall high administrative burdens on both governments and small installations. Small installations emitting less than 10,000 tonnes $CO_2$/year make up 32 percent (or about 3400 participants) of all EU ETS installations and account for about 1 percent of all emissions. Installations emitting under 25,000 tonnes $CO_2$/year make up 55 percent of all installations while emitting only 2.4 percent of all EU ETS emissions (Worrel and Woosen, 2005). Hence, by excluding 55 percent of the smallest installations, the total number of covered installations could have been reduced to around 4,700 while covered emissions would remain as high as 97.6 percent of the current coverage.

Still, although there have been plenty of 'rough edges', the EU ETS managed to deliver 'a transparent and widely accepted price for tradable $CO_2$ emissions allowances' as well as the necessary 'infrastructure of market institutions, registries, monitoring, reporting and verification' (see Ellerman and Joskow, 2008). The significant allowance price of up to €30 for 18 months is expected to have measurable effects for operation of installations. Ellerman and Buchner (2008) conclude that between 2005 and 2006 there has been abatement of 'probably between 50 and 100 million tons in each of these years'. This would amount to between 2–5 percent of total covered emissions. However as recent work (e.g. Delarue et al., 2008a and b) shows, the relationship between abatement and $CO_2$ prices seems to be too complex to allow for the identification of standard patterns or averages of abatement.

Most importantly, the EU ETS has introduced carbon management systems within companies. The fact that the EU ETS created a price for carbon makes carbon management both a legal necessity, requiring monitoring, reporting and verification of emissions and the registration of allowances in the registry, and a management priority. Investors will want to know about performance, liability and risks. Managers will try to exploit opportunities through better management and participation in the trading market. In some cases, better carbon management can reveal hitherto unnoticed reduction potentials (Browne, 2004).

**Design Flaws**

These successes should not hide the reality that the original EU ETS Directive and its implementation in the first phase had a number of deficiencies including notably overallocation, distorting allocation between member states, windfall profits for the power sector, and the risk of deferred investment.[8] Overallocation has been largely a result of two factors: an excessive degree of de-centralization of the EU ETS, and the absence of a hard constraint. In their National Allocation Plans (NAPs), member states pitched their caps somewhere between 'less than the business as usual' and moving towards a 'path consistent with the Kyoto Protocol'. Most NAPs foresaw modest caps and high dependence on projections. It turned out that most if not all projections were largely inflated (LETS Update 2006). This combination of modest cuts and inflated projections has led to overallocation of as much as 97Mt of $CO_2$ out of a total of about 2.2 billion annual EU allowance, i.e. almost 5 percent of total annual allowances (Kettner et al., 2007).

The experience of allocation in the first phase has been that each member state has developed its own rules, notably for allocation to new entrants and closures and that these rules varied considerably between member states. This high degree of discretion for member states has increased complexity, administrative burdens and transaction costs while decreasing transparency. Moreover, industry has been able to put pressure on governments not to hand out fewer allowances than other governments (e.g. Zetterberg et al., 2004; Matthes et al., 2005).[9]

In Europe's liberalized (regional) wholesale power market, prices are set by the marginal production costs, including the value of emissions in the allowance market. If the marginal producer is a (high-carbon) coal power generator, the power price can increase significantly as a result of the EU ETS. Low carbon electricity generators such as hydro, nuclear or renewables receive substantial gains from generally higher power prices without incurring extra costs. This effect was intended. However power companies were able to receive considerable windfall profits. Power generators operating essentially in a domestic EU market find it easy to pass on additional $CO_2$ cost. The windfall effect occurred as a result of free allocation, as power generators could pass on the full $CO_2$ costs while having received allowances for free. Windfall profits have been estimated to amount to as much as €13 billion annually (e.g. Keats and Neuhoff, 2005).

Another criticism has been that the EU ETS discourages rather than encourages investment in new and low-carbon technologies as a result of uncertainty. Although a fair degree of uncertainty is due to international indecision on a post-2012 agreement, some of the causes for deferral of investment are closer to home. Initial allocation periods provide certainty for only three, and then five years – periods that are far shorter than those associated with investment cycles. Other uncertainty stems from possibly perverse effects from new allocation methodologies, notably new entrants and closure rules or the possible depletion of New Entrants Reserves (the amount of EUAs handed out to new investors). National new entrants and closure rules have been markedly different across the EU, which has created distortions between member states and in some cases perverse incentives (e.g. Reinaud, 2005; Matthes et al., 2005; European Commission and Ecofys, 2006).

**Phase Two Improvements**

The second round of National Allocation Plans (NAPs) in the period from 2008 to 2012 has seen some improvements in the implementation by EU member states and the EU. Member states have less leeway on allocation as a result of the need for consistency towards the Kyoto path. Most importantly, overallocation has been avoided since the European Commission can impose a formula to assess member states' allocation plans and thereby de facto impose an EU-wide cap. For all NAPs-2, the European Commission has used explicit 'objective' projections based on 2005 verified emissions across the board for all member states.[10] As a result, the European Commission could shave off 10 percent of member states' proposed allocations, leaving the ETS sector allowances about 5 percent short of expected emissions in a business-as-usual scenario. Phase two allowances are currently trading at around €25 (as of June 2008).

## THE NEW EMISSIONS TRADING SCHEME

Experiences from the initial phases and design flaws have been the basis for the European Commission to propose radical changes to the EU ETS including. Principal proposed changes include:

- A single EU-wide cap, decreasing annually to 2020 and beyond in a linear way, starting in 2013, to reach 1.720 million tonnes of $CO_2$ in 2020, leading to an overall cap 21 percent lower than 2005 verified emissions;
- EU-wide harmonized allocation rules; full auctioning to sectors that can pass through their costs, e.g. the power sector, partial free allocation to industry based on EU-wide harmonized benchmarks. Overall, this would translate into 60 percent auctioning, which would generate about €33 billion per annum in revenues at a price of €30 per tone of $CO_2$;
- Partial free allocation to industry as a transitional measure (to be phased out by 2020). Free allocation is proposed as a measure to cope with the risk of carbon leakage (discussed further below);
- The use of left-over CDM/JI credits from 2008 to 2012 until 2020; according to the European Commission this amounts to 1.4 billion allowances or one-third of total reduction effort;
- 10 percent of the overall auctioning rights would be re-distributed to lower per capita member states. As auctions in one member state are open to operators across the EU, this redistribution does not trigger distortions of competition across the EU market;
- In case of a global climate change agreement, the EU ETS cap will be adjusted downwards in line with the EU's 30 percent target. The ceiling for CDM/JI credits would increase accordingly.

In addition, the European Commission has proposed to extend the scheme to the chemicals and aluminum sectors, to other GHGs (e.g. nitrous oxide from fertilizers and perfluorocarbons from aluminum). Under a separate proposal, pending adoption, the European Commission wants to include aviation in the EU ETS as of 2011 or 2012. This proposal has raised major disputes with the US administration on trade matters including assessment of responsibility for aviation emissions.

There is a very strong likelihood that these changes will be formally adopted – possibly with minor adjustments – by early 2009. Outstanding issues are: i) the ceiling of CDM and JI credits; ii) the inclusion of forestry; iii) the addition of international shipping; iv) carbon leakage and competitiveness; and v) criteria that a global agreement must meet to trigger the 30 percent GHG emissions target.

## The Role of the New ETS in Climate Change Policy

The EU ETS review must be seen in the broader context of EU climate change policy and the new integrated climate and energy policy for which formal legislative proposals have been published on 23 January 2008. Principal elements are:

- A binding absolute emissions reduction commitment of 30 percent by 2020 compared to 1990, conditional on a global agreement, and a 'firm independent commitment' to achieve at least a 20 percent reduction by 2020. At the same time, the EU advocated that industrialized countries reduce their emissions collectively by 60 percent to 80 percent by 2050 compared to 1990. The European Parliament in its resolution has insisted that the EU should unilaterally commit to 30 percent;
- 20 percent reduction of primary energy consumption by 2020 compared to projections;
- A binding target of 20 percent of renewable energy in total energy consumption by 2020;
- A binding minimum target of 10 percent biofuels for all transport fuels by 2020;
- A commitment for up to 12 large-scale carbon capture and storage (CCS) power plants.

While dealing with climate change, the scope of EU policy is wider than that, attempting to address Europe's energy challenges in general. The integrated energy and climate package has made the link between energy and climate in a systematic way, not least due to changing conditions. The EU's resources are dwindling at the same time that government intervention in the energy industry is on the rise in precisely those countries that potentially could fill the gap, creating doubts as to whether the necessary investment will happen. Many countries that supply oil and other energy resources seem unable to increase production. And even if the necessary investments were made, the fact that supplies are tightly controlled by governments in the exporting countries raises the specter of 'excessive' leverage by supplier countries, some of which are hostile towards the West or politically unstable.[11]

Many reserves will take years to develop due to problems of access, investments and physical conditions. A prolonged tight market might increase political tension and possibly some sort of 'resource nationalism'. The EU has finally realized that success in integrating Russia into a strategic energy partnership is very unlikely. Despite an institutionalized energy dialog (since 2000) and some recent foreign investments in the Russian energy sector, the strategy aimed at opening the Russian market to European and other western enterprises and thus to gain large-scale access to Russian gas and oil reserves has largely failed, and should be expected to continue to do so.

In such a scenario, the EU and its member states have been examining domestic and external policy options to move to a more sustainable and secure energy supply, including: investment in renewable energy sources; promoting carbon capture and storage techniques; and, for those member states that so choose, investment in nuclear energy. Externally, the objective is to diversify (away from Russia). Energy security and climate change now forms part of foreign policy. According to the European Commission, the integrated climate and energy package is expected to bring additional benefits:

- The renewable policy can provide technological leadership in sun-rise technologies;
- Renewable electricity can reduce long-term electricity price and price and price volatility;
- Substitution of fossils combined with renewables may reduce pricing power by Russia (notably on gas); and
- Finally, the introduction of the EU $CO_2$ Emissions Trading Scheme (or taxation measures) will effectively retain some of the economic rents from producer countries, including Russia.

To offset the higher prices both for industry and domestic customer, energy efficiency is a central element of the policy, certainly for a transition period until new technologies and new fuels become available. Reducing consumption while prices increase gives a reasonable prospect of keeping energy bills constant.

There has been an additional aspect of the targets that is often overlooked. The first phase of the EU ETS has shown that setting a hard cap in the EU is next to impossible unless some sort of legally binding constraint exists. In a scenario of a post-2012 agreement without absolute caps, it is indeed difficult to see how the EU ETS could continue to exist in a meaningful way.

## Economics of the ETS and the Climate Change Package

Hard targets for the EU ETS and the non-ETS sectors as well as for renewables have been set on the basis of an 'efficiency approach', i.e. reflecting a least-cost approach for the EU as a whole, but with some adjustment to ensure that in per capita terms, costs for member states remain roughly similar. Note that GDP per capita differences (in PPP) between EU member states are significant. In 2006 differences ranged from somewhat below 40 percent to more than 250 percent of the EU27 per capita average of around €25,000 (excluding the richest member state, Luxembourg, as an outlier with per capita GDP of €70,440, more than twice as high as the other rich member states).

- GHG reduction target: Countries with a low GDP per capita will be allowed to emit more than they did in 2005 in non-EU ETS sectors, reflecting projected higher emissions due to higher economic growth mainly in transport. According to European Commission modelling, this increases overall EU compliance costs for GHG reduction targets by 0.03 percent of total EU GDP.

- Renewables targets: half is calculated based on a flat-rate increase in the share of renewable energy and half weighted by GDP, modulated to take into account national starting points and efforts already made.
- In the EU ETS sector, where an EU-wide cap would be set, and allocation among member states would be based on EU-wide allocation methodologies, 10 percent of the overall auctioning rights will be redistributed to lower per capita member states.

According to European Commission calculations in the Integrated Impact Assessment (European Commission, 2008a and b), the total cost of the package in the form of increased energy and mitigation costs is around 0.61 percent of 2020 GDP, or some €90 billion. GDP growth is reduced by approximately 0.04–0.06 percent between 2013 and 2020, or by some 0.5 percent of GDP in 2020 compared to the baseline. Higher global oil prices than the ones upon which the calculations were based, i.e. $61 per barrel, would reduce costs, as would a more extensive use of CDM. The calculations do also not take into possible macroeconomic benefits as a result of recycling of auctioning revenues.

## Carbon Leakage

The EU ETS has triggered a debate on 'competitiveness' (of industry) and carbon leakage, documented in a sizable body of literature. Carbon leakage is one of the critical issues for the EU ETS review. Several studies (e.g. Carbon Trust, 2004; Demailly and Quirion, 2005; Reinaud, 2005; European Commission, McKinsey and Ecofys, 2006; Grubb and Neuhoff, 2006; Smale et al., 2006; Matthes and Neuhoff, 2007; Climate Strategies, 2007) tend to confirm that the EU ETS could lead to market share losses and, as a result, to carbon leakage, especially if the indirect effects owing to the inclusion of carbon in the power price are realised.

Potential losses in market share, however, depend on the extent to which EU producers can pass on the extra cost to consumers and suppliers. A second element is how quickly non-EU producers can increase their production in the short term. Therefore it is most likely that negative effects on competitiveness will not fully come into play in the short term. This is even truer as long as investors assume that over a reasonable period other countries will gradually become subject to carbon constraints. Most studies agree that there are only a few products among a small number of sectors (e.g. aluminum, steel, chemicals, paper and pulp, cement) that may be negatively affected by the EU ETS.

The European Commission has identified (in the ETS draft directive) a hierarchy of three possible measures to address carbon leakage:

- Free allocation, which in fact constitutes a subsidy;
- A global sectoral approach or agreement, i.e. a global sectoral policy for one or all of the vulnerable sectors;
- Border-measures, e.g. imposing carbon costs on importers.

While the choice of the first option (free allocation) is a pragmatic approach of 'taking the heat out' of a potentially poisonous debate, it allows only for compensation of direct effects, i.e. costs arising due to the fact that emissions need to be covered by an allowance. It does not address the vulnerabilities of those sectors that experience indirect effects through higher input costs, notably higher power prices as a result of the ETS (e.g.. aluminum, basic chemicals, paper and pulp). Therefore, it should not be expected that debate on the other two options will continue.

Under the leadership of the Enterprise and Industry Directorate General, the European Commission has launched a process involving industry, member states, research and stakeholders to assess as exactly as possible the vulnerability of sectors and sub-sectors. Industry has submitted very detailed data for the European Commission to assess the degree of vulnerability. The Commission is not willing to hand out allowances for free to those sectors that can in fact pass through all or parts of the carbon costs. Thereby it is hoped to avoid another round of windfall profits, this time for industry rather than for the power sector. The Commission has set itself a deadline to complete this analysis in such a timeframe as to come out with a decision for the extent of free allocation by 2011 at the latest. Most likely this deadline will be brought forward.

Nevertheless, there are voices from some member states, notably France and some companies, in favour of border measures. So far, these voices are few and there is an overwhelming consensus among EU industry that border measure for an export-dependent economy like the EU would be self-defeating. However, it is clear that border measures as spelled out in the proposed ETS review directive are seen by the EU as a possible legitimate means to put pressure on potential free-riders to sign up to a post-2012 agreement. There appears to be a consensus that a multi-lateral approach towards border measures in a post-2012 agreement is sensible or necessary to address free-riding.

## A BLUEPRINT FOR A GLOBAL CARBON MARKET?

European heads of governments at the Spring 2008 Council have endorsed the package, and the Council of Ministers and the European Parliament are currently negotiating to reach a political agreement towards the end of 2008 – possibly before the Poznan climate change negotiations (COP14) – and final adoption in early 2009. It should be expected that this package will be adopted. All EU governments have given full support to the package. Reopening any of the key elements by one member state would almost certainly lead to an unravelling of the full package, a price too high for any member state to pay, not only because of peer pressure in EU institutions but also due to the high public support that climate change policy enjoys. Nevertheless, a number of issues will be debated within the Council of Ministers and the European Parliament (EP) including:

- Costs and distribution of costs across member states, especially for renewables;
- Trading rules for renewable electricity quotes; some member states with very aggressive targets and electricity utilities argue for more flexibility in trade, while other member states fear a rush to the cheapest source, thereby crowding out certain technologies;
- New calculations seem to suggest that application of EU sustainability criteria will make achievement of EU biofuels targets very difficult;
- Funding of the up to 12 CCS demonstration projects is still unresolved;
- There is a more fundamental debate on the relationship between the EU ETS and other sectoral targets (e.g. renewables and biofuels) and commitments such as on energy efficiency.

One of the critical factors that will shape the outcome of the negotiations on the EU climate and energy package and the EUETS is the debate on competitiveness. If the Commission manages to hold the line that any policy dealing with carbon leakage must be based on facts rather than on political pressure, then the New ETS is most likely to look very much like the Commission proposal, with only minor adjustments. By new design choices, notably an EU-wide cap, EU-wide allocation methodologies, and expanding the scope of coverage, the European Commission has incorporated the lessons from the experiences of the first phases. With the new ETS covering about half of the EU's emissions, a failure of the EU ETS reform would become a failure of EU climate change policy.

Could the New ETS become a blueprint for the global carbon market? The original EU ETS directive allowed for linking the EU ETS with other emissions trading schemes by international agreement. The proposed new directive goes a step further. It foresees different types of linking arrangements, e.g. via a treaty, an international agreement as foreseen under EU law, or through reciprocal commitments applied through domestic policies. The latter provision is innovative, both internally and internationally, as it would allow schemes to be linked through administrative decisions. In essence, this could mean that over time non-EU emissions trading schemes could be linked to the EU ETS, the notion being the EU ETS as a 'docking station' for the global carbon market.

Trading schemes in different jurisdictions may have widely divergent designs,[12] including such aspects as banking rules, coverage of sectors, and which gases are included. Nonetheless, linking schemes does not necessarily run into fundamental problems as long as technical fixes such as gateways or restrictions are put into place. Such fixes, however, generally reduce the efficiency through additional transaction costs, market fragmentation or through perverse effects and trade distortions (Baron and Bygrave, 2002; Haites, 2003; Blyth and Bosi, 2004). This will be an even more significant problem if linking of schemes is seen as a substitute for – and not a complement to – a post-2012 regime on climate change. While linking might lead to some sort of a post-2012 climate change regime, the emerging market would be likely to be inefficient.

We should also expect political obstacles to linking as a result of potential distributional impacts. When two schemes are linked, the market price will be higher than the pre-link price in one of the trading schemes and lower than the pre-link price in the other zone, thereby creating winners and losers. The winners will be net sellers in the low price scheme, as the price will go up for them, and net buyers in the high price scheme, as prices will go down for them. The reverse is true for net buyers in the low price scheme and net sellers in the high price scheme (Bode, 2003; Haites, 2003).

While formal linking through an international agreement may be an option for the long term, a global carbon market may yet emerge as participants of different emissions trading schemes search for arbitrage possibilities between different carbon markets or commodities. Such arbitrage is highly probable as most national or regional climate change policies or ET schemes foresee the use of project type of mechanisms either in the form of the Kyoto Protocol projects (CDM/JI) or comparable mechanisms. As long as domestic or regional emissions trading schemes allow for the use of credits from such projects, and there is sufficient volume, carbon prices will converge.

A third option for an emerging global carbon market would be to move towards sectoral agreement on an international scale (e.g. Ellis and Baron, 2005; Mathy and Hourcade, 2006; Egenhofer and Fujiwara, 2008) as opposed to linking domestic schemes that include a variety of sectors. This would have the benefits of combining similar sectors or 'carbon commodities' with similar characteristics. Whichever path is pursued, the EU ETS will almost certainly play a significant role in the shaping of global carbon markets.

## NOTES

1. Christian Egenhofer, Senior Fellow, Centre for European Policy Studies (CEPS); Jean-Monnet Lecturer, Centre for Energy, Petroleum and Law and Policy (CEPMLP), University of Dundee, Scotland/UK and Lecturer MBA Programme, Solvay Business School, Brussels.; Christian.Egenhofer@ceps.eu; CEPS, Place du Congrès 1, B - 1000 Brussels, Tel. +32 2 229 3960, Fax. +32 2 219 4151.

2. For example, note the 1999 study by the Center for Clean Air Policy (CCAP, 1999) commissioned by DG Environment of the European Commission. Similarities include particularly the choice of a cap-and-trade model, grandfathering, emphasis on monitoring, reporting and verification, transparency and public involvement (see also Kruger and Pizer, 2004).
3. Law that is adopted by the EU needs to be implemented and enforced by member states. This is among other laid out in the principle of Community loyalty in Article 10 of the EC Treaty that guides the EU.
4. In some cases, implementation of a EU law goes even beyond EU member states and may include non-EU countries grouped in the so-called European Economic Area (EEA). The concept of the EEA has been developed for those countries that do not wish to share the political objectives of the European Union such as progressive political integration but want to benefit from economic integration. It allows for the full (and legally binding) integration of countries into the EU internal market without being member. This approach is currently being applied to Iceland, Liechtenstein and Norway (see for example, Emerson et al. (2002).
5. Although the EU ETS as almost all other internal market-related legislation can be adopted by a qualified majority, voting is used only in exceptional cases. This is even more true for important laws, such as the EU ETS.
6. The Clean Development Mechanism (CDM) and Joint Implementation (JI) are arrangements under the Kyoto Protocol allowing industrialized countries with a greenhouse gas reduction commitment and their established companies to invest in emission reducing projects in developing countries (i.e. CDM) or other industrialized countries (i.e. JI) as an alternative to what is generally considered more costly emission reductions in their own countries.
7. The European Commission has published non-binding 'Guidance Documents' (European Commission, 2003, 2005) on Annex III in the form of a Commission Communication to ensure the necessary consistency between the different allocation processes.
8. For details, see also e.g. Matthes et al., (2005); Swedish Energy Agency (2006); Ellerman et al. (2007); Egenhofer (2007); Ellerman and Joskow (2008).
9. For example under phase one rules, a new natural gas combined heat and power plant – producing both electricity and heat – would in Germany receive allowances corresponding to 130 percent of its expected emissions. The corresponding figures are 120 percent for Finland, 90 percent for Denmark and 60 percent for Sweden. For a new natural gas combined cycle electricity production unit (no heat) the differences are even larger. In Germany the installation would receive 105 percent of the required allowances. In Finland 100 percent, in Denmark 82 percent and in Sweden 0 percent – Sweden does not give allowances for non-combined heat and power (Zetterberg et al., 2004).
10. The projections are based on verified 2005 ETS emissions × GDP growth rates for 2005–2010 × carbon intensity improvements rate for 2005–2010 + adjustment for new entrants and other changes, for example in ETS coverage.
11. Russia plays the single biggest role in European energy imports with being responsible for EU27 45 percent of gas, 30 percent of oil and 21 percent of hard coal imports.
12. Emissions trading schemes such as the Regional Greenhouse Gas Initiative (RGGI) in the North-east of the US, in California, or the various proposals for a US cap-and-trade scheme in the US Senate or in Australia exhibit very different design features from the EU ETS with regard to sector coverage, commitments, allocation and even monitoring, reporting and verification. The design of these emissions trading schemes is driven by the domestic political economy with little or no concern for effects on linking.

# REFERENCES

Baron, R. and S. Bygrave (2002), *Towards International Emissions Trading: Design Implications for Linkages*, OECD/IEA information paper, COM/ENV/EPOC/IEA/SLT (2002)5.

Blyth, W. and M. Bosi (2004), *Linking Non-EU Domestic Emissions Trading Schemes with the EU Emissions Trading Scheme*, 17 June, COM/ENV/EPOC/IEA/SLT (2004)6.

Bode, S. (2003), *Implications of Linking National Emissions Trading Schemes Prior to the Start of the First Commitment Period of the Kyoto Protocol*, Hamburg Institute of International Economics: HWWA. HWWA Discussion Paper 214

Browne, J. (2004), 'Beyond Kyoto', *Foreign Affairs*, **83** (4), 20–32, July/August.

Carbon Trust (2004), *The European Emissions Trading Scheme: Implications for Industrial Competitiveness*, The Carbon Trust, UK, June.

CCAP (1999), *Design of a Practical Approach to Greenhouse Gas Emissions Trading Combined with Policies and Measures in the EC*, Center for Clean Air Policy, Washington, DC, Study prepared for the European Commission, November 1999.

Climate Strategies (2007), *Differentiation and Dynamics of EU ETS Industrial Competitiveness Impacts.* (Authors: Jean-Charles Hourcade, Damien Demailly, Karsten Neuhoff and Misato Sato with contributing authors, Michael Grubb, Felix Matthes and Verna Graichen).

Christiansen, A.C. and J. Wettestad (2003), 'The EU as a frontrunner on greenhouse gas emissions trading: how did it happen and will the EU succeed?' *Climate Policy*, **3** (1), 3–18.

Delarue, E., W. D'heaseleer and K. Voorspools (2008a), 'Fuel switching in the electricity sector under the EU ETS: review and prospective', *Journal of Energy Engineering* ASCE, **134** (2), 40–46.

Delarue, E., D. Ellerman and W. D'haeseleer (2008b), *Short-term Abatement in the European Power Sector*, Working Paper (unpublished).

Delbeke, J. (ed.) (2006) *The EU Greenhouse Gas Emissions Trading Scheme* EU Energy Law, Volume IV, Leuven: Clays & Casteels.

Demailly, D. and P. Quirion (2005), *The Competitiveness Impact of CO2 Emissions Reductions in the Cement Sector*, OECD, COM/ENV/EPOC/CTPA/CFA (2004)68/FINAL.

Egenhofer, C. (2003), The compatibility of the Kyoto mechanisms with traditional environmental instruments, in C. Carraro and C. Egenhofer (eds), *Firms, Governments and Climate Policy: Incentive-Based Policies for Long-Term Climate Change*, Cheltenham, UK and Northampton, MA, USA, Edward Elgar.

Egenhofer, C. (2007) 'The making of the EU emissions trading scheme: status, prospects and implications for business', *European Management Journal*, **25** (6), 453-463, December.

Egenhofer, C. and N. Fujiwara (2008), *Global Sectoral Industry Approaches to Address Climate Change: The Way Forward*, CEPS Task Force Report (April)

Ellerman, D. and B. Buchner (2008), 'Overallocation or abatement: a preliminary analysis of EU ETS based on the 2005–06 emissions data', *Environmental and Resource Economics*, **39**.

Ellerman, A.D., B. Buchner and C. Carraro, 2007. *Rights, Rents and Fairness: Allocations in the European Emissions Trading Scheme.* Cambridge University Press, UK.

Ellerman, D. and P. Joskow (2008), *The European Union's Emissions Trading System in Perspective,* Pew Center on Global Climate Change, May.

Ellis, J. and R. Baron. (2005), *Sectoral Crediting Mechanisms: An Initial Assessment of Electricity and Aluminium*, OECD/IEA COM/ENV/EPOC/IEA/SLT(2005)8.

Emerson, M., M. Vahl and S. Woolcock (2002), *Navigating by the Stars: Norway, the European Economic Area and the European Union*, CEPS Paper, Brussels, Centre for European Policy Studies.

European Commission (2001), *European Climate Change Programme: Report*, Brussels, June.

European Commission (2003), 'Communication from the Commission on guidance to assist Member States in the implementation of the criteria listed in Annex III to Directive 2003/87/EC establishing a scheme for greenhouse gas emission allowance trading within the Community and amending Council Directive 96/61/EC, and on the circumstances under which force majeure is demonstrated', Brussels, 7 January, 2004 COM (2003) 830 final.

European Commission (2005), 'Communication from the Commission on further guidance on allocation plans for the 2008–12 trading period of the EU Emissions Trading Scheme', 22.12.05, COM (2005) 703 final.

European Commission (2008a), 'Impact Assessment – Accompanying document for amending Directive 2003/87/EC so as to improve and extend the EU greenhouse gas emission allowance trading system', Commission Staff Working Document, SEC (2008)52, 21.01.2008

European Commission (2008b), 'Impact Assessment – Accompanying document for package of implementation measures for the EU's objective on climate change and renewable energy for 2020.

European Commission and Ecofys (2006), *The Approach to New Entrants and Closures in the EU ETS*, Brussels and Utrecht, December.

European Commission, McKinsey and Ecofys (2006), *EU ETS Review: Report on International Competitiveness*, Brussels and Utrecht, December.

Fujiwara, N., J. Nunez-Ferrer and C. Egenhofer, 'The political economy of environmental taxation in European Countries', CEPS Working Document #245.

Grubb, M. and K. Neuhoff (2006), 'Allocation and competitiveness in the EU emissions trading scheme: Policy overview', *Climate Policy*, **6** (1), 7–30.

Haites, E. (2003), 'Harmonisation between national and international tradable permit schemes: CATEP synthesis paper (document 2)', paper prepared for OECD global forum on sustainable development: CATEP country forum (17–18 March), 12 March.

Keats, K. and K. Neuhoff (2005), 'Allocation of carbon emissions certificates in the power sector: how generators profit from grandfathered rights', *Climate Policy*, **5** (1), 61–78.

Kettner, C., A. Köppl, S. Schleicher and G. Thenius (2007), 'Stringency and distribution in the EU emissions trading scheme – the 2005 evidence', *Nota di Lavora*, 22.2007, Fondazione Eni Enrico Mattei.

Klaassen, G. (1996), *Acid Rain and Environmental Degradation: The Economics of Emissions Trading*, Cheltenham, UK and Northampton, MA, USA: Edward Elgar.

Kruger, J., and W. Pizer (2004), 'Greenhouse gas trading in Europe: the new grand policy experiment', *Environment*, **46** (8), 8–23.

Lefevere, J. (2006), 'The EU ETS linking Directive explained', Delbeke (ed.), *The EU Greenhouse Gas Emissions Trading Scheme.* EU Energy Law, Volume IV, Leuven: Clays & Casteels, pp. 117–151.

LETS Update (2006), 'Decision Makers Summary', *LETS/LIFE Emissions Trading Scheme*, report produced for the LETS Update Partners, AEA Technology Environment and Ecofys, UK.

Mathy, S. and J.C. Hourcade (2006), 'An international co-ordination regime come what may', in Colombier and Loup (eds), *Bringing Developing Countries into the Energy Equation, Analyses No. 02/2006 Changement Climatique*, Paris: IDDRI, pp. 53–60.

Matthes, F. and K. Neuhoff (2007), 'Auctioning in the European Union Emissions Trading Scheme', Report to the WWF, Öko-Institut, Freiburg.

Matthes, F., V. Graichen and J. Repenning (2005), 'The environmental effectiveness and economic efficiency of the European Union Emissions Trading Scheme: structural aspects of allocation', Report to the WWF, Öko-Institut, Freiburg.

Meadows, D. (2006), 'The emissions allowance trading directive 2003/87/EC explained', in J. Delbeke (eds), *The EU Greenhouse Gas Emissions Trading Scheme*, EU Energy Law, Volume IV, Leuven: Clays & Casteels, pp. 63–115.

Philibert, C. and J. Reinaud (2004), *Emissions Trading: Taking Stock and Looking Forward*, IEA/OECD, Paris: COM/ENV/EPOC/IEA/SLT(2004)3.

Reinaud, J. (2005), *Industrial Competitiveness Under the European Union Emissions Trading Scheme*, International Energy Agency Information Paper.

Skjærseth, J. and J. Wettestad (2008), *EU Emissions Trading*, Aldershot: Ashgate.

Smale, R., M. Hartley, C. Hepburn, J. Ward and M. Grubb (2006), 'The impact of $CO_2$ emissions trading on firm profits and market prices', *Climate Policy*, **6** (1), 31–48.

Swedish Energy Agency (2006), *The EU Emissions Trading Scheme after 2012,* Swedish Energy Agency and the Swedish Environmental Protection Agency.

Ten Brink, P. et al. (2003), 'Negotiated agreements and climate change mitigation', in C. Carraro and C. Egenhofer (eds), *Firms, Governments and Climate Policy: Incentive-Based Policies for Long-Term Climate Change*, Cheltenham, UK and Northampton, USA: Edward Elgar.

Vis, P. (2006), 'Basic design options for emissions trading', in Delbeke (ed.), *The EU Greenhouse Gas Emissions Trading Scheme*, EU Energy Law, Volume IV, Leuven: Clays & Casteels, pp. 39–62.

Worrel, E. and S. Woosen (2005), *Small Installations Within the EU Emissions Trading Scheme – Summary*, Ecofys, Utrecht, April

Zapfel, P. and M. Vainio (2002), 'Pathways to European greenhouse gas emissions: history and misconception', *Nota di Lavora,* 85.2002, Fondazione Eni Enrico Mattei (FEEM).

Zetterberg, L., K. Nilsson, M. Åhman, A.-S. Kumlin and L. Birgersdotter (2004), *Analysis of National Allocation plans for the EU ETS*, IVL report B1591.

# 12. Implementation of Sustainable Development in Poland

**Andrzej Kassenberg**[1]

---

This analysis was written on the basis of the experiences of the Institute for Sustainable Development (ISD), which has for more than 17 years monitored political, economic, social and natural developments taking place in Poland as a result of the change of its political system in 1989. Following an agreement between the Communist authorities and Solidarity, that year saw the beginning of a process of democratic transition, the building of civic society and the introduction of a market economy. The purpose of the present analysis is to show the extent to which principles of sustainable development have been implemented over this period, and the extent to which there was a departure from them.

The point at issue is Article 5 of the Constitution of the Republic of Poland, which provides that the State is obliged to solve environmental problems in a manner consistent with the principle of sustainable development.[2] Under the Environmental Law, sustainable development means 'socio-economic development which involves the process of integrating political, economic and social actions, while maintaining the natural equilibrium and the sustainability of the life support natural system, in order to guarantee that the basic needs of particular communities or citizens, of both the contemporary and future generations, can be satisfied'.[3]

The chapter includes, first, a historical review of events since 1989, then an analysis of the sustainability of economic development divided into the following four areas: politics and governance, the economy, the social system, and the environment. The fundamental processes taking place in each of these areas are described, with an assessment of which aspects are favorable and which unfavorable for the implementation of the principles of sustainable development.

## TRANSFORMATION AND SUSTAINABLE DEVELOPMENT

A look at Poland in the 1980s from the viewpoint of the ideas and principles of sustainable development shows above all the totalitarian system of governance where ideology dominated human activity and the functioning of the economy. Decisions were taken without regard to economic realities and without the participation of representatives of the public in this process. Authentic leaders were eliminated from public life and opportunists were depended upon, who – taking care of their interests – applauded the ideological forms of public life. Such a mode of governance did not contribute to the consideration of environmental factors in the decision-making process. Local policies failed to take into account impacts on the natural world, while the ecological debt in the form of unsolved environmental problems rose to a terrifying extent and was in fact shifted onto future generations.[4]

In the period preceding the transformation of its economy, Poland was highly ineffective and partly backward. Natural resources, particularly energy, were wasted. Its consumption per unit production or service was several times higher than that in Western countries. Heavy industry and the coal-based energy sector dominated. Farm output was relatively low, with limited modernization of agriculture. However, small-scale agricultural production and low doses of fertilizer and pesticides permitted the conservation of the traditional landscape and biodiversity to a much greater degree than in Western Europe. Given heavy reliance on public transport, the transportation sector was environmentally relatively sound, although it could be regarded as undeveloped and inefficient. The favorable situation in terms of sustainable development in agriculture and transportation arose because the totalitarian state could not afford any other solutions, rather than from any concern for the environment.

In 1989, the decisions taken at the Roundtable, an agreement between the Communist authorities and Solidarity, started a period of political, social, and economic transition which has lasted until today. From the viewpoint of the implementation of sustainable development, the period of 17 years can be divided into several significant periods.

### Positive Effects of the Roundtable Talks: Environment on the Agenda

The achievements of independent environmental activities carried out in the 1980s, which could not make their effects felt in the economic and social sphere in the light of the system then dominating, were rewarded with the establishment of a separate Sub-table on the Environment in the course of the

Roundtable Talks. The 27 proposals adopted at that time created a new approach to environmental protection, oriented towards a principle of sustainability. They referred to environmentally sound directions of economic development, the introduction of modern legal solutions, the use of market-based instruments for environmental protection, the strengthening of environmental protection services, and the empowerment of the public to solve these issues.

It is important to emphasize that the breakthrough period in question gave rise to many environmental organizations which emerged spontaneously with different programs and ideas. The transformation released huge reservoirs of human activity and the issues of environmental protection were among the dominating problems. The milestone concluding this initial period of transformation was the National Environmental Policy, adopted in May 1991 by the Lower House and then the Upper House of the Parliament of the Republic of Poland.[5] The document represented a significant step forward, as it was based on the philosophy of sustainable development; still, it was not effectively translated into the economic and social processes underway in the country.

## Shock Therapy: Hard Times for All

The political transformation in Poland was received by society with high hopes, although with serious fears and concerns. The majority of Poles were against the continuation of a state based on Communist ideology; on the other hand, future goals were not clear. Most Poles believed that following the change in the political system improvements would come 'overnight' and they would live better. Rapid improvement in welfare, particularly measured by the amounts of purchased goods, was to become the measure of the purposefulness and success of the transformation.

The developments initiated in 1990 were unprecedented in the economic history of the world. In a very short time the planned, command and allocation-based economic system was to change into a market economy, capable of coping with international competition. The option of so-called 'shock therapy' was applied. It provided for the introduction of market mechanisms into the economy as rapidly as possible, along with privatization, with the goal of minimizing the duration of the painful social costs that resulted. The resulting transition was wrenching and very painful for society; particularly so as in the initial phase there was a drastic drop of living standards in many families and high unemployment emerged.

The hope was that 'shock therapy' would soon lead to a stronger economy. Also, at the beginning of a new system of governance in Poland, exercised by politicians originating from the Solidarity movement, there were hopes that the Roundtable provisions concerning environmental issues would be achieved.

**Realities of Transformation: A Lost Opportunity for Sustainability**

In its initial phase, the transformation brought an economic recession, which lasted for a short time, as a result of the application of shock therapy. Starting in 1992, a resumption of economic growth could be observed. In 1995, it reached a level of as much as 7 percent annually. Continued privatization, as well as the development of small and medium-sized enterprises, greatly enhanced the importance of the private sector. The launch of market mechanisms was particularly important. Along with economic growth, the direction of exports was changed: after a breakdown of the Eastern market, the Polish producers of goods and services were forced to compete on the Western market – and in many cases they were successful. The economic recession, privatization (to a limited extent), the market mechanism, and strong competition in the Western markets cut the use of natural resources and reduced pollutant emissions.

The elements of the transformation which were favorable for environmental protection came along with negative elements associated with economic strategies and policies that ignored the provisions of the 1991 National Environmental Policy. This was the case with the strategy for economic development, as well as with transport, energy, industrial and agricultural policies. For the most part, they were based on the principle of economic growth, sometimes with pollutant emission reductions, but with no reference whatsoever to any environmental standards or the provisions of international conventions. Efficient use of resources was not emphasized. At the same time, there was a significant loss of environmentally sound solutions, particularly in transport, where shipments by rail and the role of the public transport in cities declined. Due to economic development, some businesses, municipal enterprises and households became economically strong enough that it would have been possible to apply to them a full range of market-based environmental policy instruments, as envisaged in the National Environmental Policy. However, this was not done, further reducing the opportunity for using the transformation process to implement the principles of sustainable development.

In reaction to the immediate 'shock therapy' effects of poverty and lower living standards, it is important to point out that a new consumption model, based on the Western models, took shape. In a very short time, shops filled with a variety of goods and it became possible for the public, which had become 'famished' over the years of Communism, to taste the flavor of being a high-consuming society.

The transformation period contributed to the restoration of self-government at the local level. On the one hand, this made people interested in putting their own place in order (for example, water supply, solving the problems of wastewater or solid waste); but, on the other hand, given scarce financial resources and unemployment-related problems, there was a lack of attention to resource conservation.

## EU Enlargement Process: Environmental Policy but not Sustainability

In 1998, Poland began the negotiations on its accession to the European Union (EU). In the course of the negotiations, emphasis was given to issues related to the construction of environmental protection infrastructure so that Poland could meet the requirements of EU environmental law. This process was important, because it served to introduce a basic minimum level of environmental protection in Poland, but was not sufficient to ensure progress towards sustainable development.

The negotiations did not have a fundamental or strategic nature. There was no discussion on whether Poland, as a country which had not reached the consumption levels of the EU Member States, was to copy the model of a high-consuming society in material terms, or whether, starting from a position of 'backwardness', Poland should aim to build a society of moderate individual consumption, utilizing the spiritual values inherent in our society to promote non-material consumption goals (such as family ties and local social ties). The negotiations focused narrowly on a timetable for the transfer of EU measures into Polish legislation.

Issues of particular importance from the viewpoint of sustainable development, including development models for transport or agriculture, and the related issue of the protection of natural resources, were not the subject of in-depth negotiations. An automobile-centered model of transportation has led to pollution and excessive energy use in Western countries; unfortunately, this model was adopted by Poland without modification. The EU Common Agricultural Policy, tending to promote industrialized agriculture based on chemical inputs and high energy consumption, poses problems for Polish agriculture, creating a conflict between integration of EU agriculture and the sustainable development of rural areas.

At the same time, very little attention was paid to the possibilities for conserving natural resources and correcting past patterns of squandering resources. For example, energy conservation could reduce total energy use by one-third, instead of building new power plants; similarly, since losses in drinking water supply from water supply systems amount to as much as 30–40 percent, more efficient water use would greatly reduce the need for new drinking water supplies. In other areas of resource use also, demand side management could achieve lower costs and promote more rapid application of modern technologies.

**Poland as a Member of the EU: Building a Western European Style of Economy and Society**

In addition to the fall of Communism, Poland's accession to the EU on May 1, 2004 became a milestone of transition. In a short period of less than 15 years, Poland had become part of an economic system of world significance and, along with its earlier entry into NATO, it had reached political stability on the international scene.

When it became a member of the EU, Poland gained access to substantial resources within the framework of the Structural Funds and the Cohesion Fund. From 2004 to 2006, EUR 11.4 billions (Ministry of Economy, 2003) was committed for such assistance, and more than EUR 80 billion is expected to be acquired from 2007 to 2013; along with the matching funds, this is more than EUR 100 billion. The commitment of such large resources will contribute to basic changes in the economy and the functioning of society. This raises the issue of how these resources will be used.

The objective which the government set for themselves is 'to create the conditions for improving competitiveness of the economy based on knowledge and entrepreneurship, ensuring enhanced employment and higher levels of social, economic and spatial cohesion' (Ministry of Regional Development, 2006). GDP growth was adopted as the basic measure of achievement, with a view to catching up with the least developed members of EU15. The strategy as a whole and the related operational programs are not guided by the principle of sustainable development (see 'Our vision of Poland', 2005), primarily failing to discern the significance of:

- natural capital;
- demand-side management in relation to particular resources and services;
- an alternative philosophy of investing, where increased production is the last rather than first solution;
- enhanced resource productivity and dematerialization of production and consumption;

Some elements of the funding are envisaged to support for example: a higher share of energy generated from renewable sources, improved energy efficiency of the economy, promotion of 'environmentally sound' means of transport and strengthening of a system of protected areas, including the Natura 2000 network. But these are measures for which a very limited scale of resources will be committed and which are not integrated into a coherent system. They are of a selective nature, and result only from lobbying conducted by particular interest groups. In consequence, according to government forecasts, in the period 2003–2013, energy intensity will be reduced by only 18.5 percent, although the Polish economy is two to three times more energy intensive that EU15, and $CO_2$-equivalent emissions are projected to grow by almost one-third over current levels, although remaining 11 percent below 1988levels.[6] This contradicts Poland's 2003 Climate Policy, with its target of 40 percent $CO_2$ emission reduction in the period from 1988 to 2020. In order to achieve the target level provided for by the 2003 Policy, emissions in the period from 2013 to 2020 would have to be reduced by one-third (that is, by 138 million tons of $CO_2$ equivalent, equal to about 43 percent of present $CO_2$ emissions).

## ASSESSMENT OF SUSTAINABLE DEVELOPMENT IMPLEMENTATION IN POLAND

### Politics and Governance: Positive Processes

The period of 17 years since the memorable year 1989 was a time of fundamental change in the legal system for environmental protection. The Environmental Protection Law was adopted as a basis for environmental legislation. Many measures were introduced in Parliament concerning: nature conservation, waster management, forest management, geology, minerals abstraction, waste management, and a large number of other environmental and resource issues. At the same time, several dozen EU legal provisions on environment were adopted into Polish law. However, due to the pace and extent of these changes, resulting from the political decision for Poland to enter the EU in 2004, this law was highly imperfect, as evidenced by the multitude of amendments made over a short period of time after its adoption, as well as gaps, contradictions and overlapping legislative measures. This was aggravated by the slowness and weakness of the preparation of enabling acts. Despite these drawbacks, the whole process of fundamental change in the legal system should be regarded as positive.

The basis for change in the environmental protection system and related areas was the adoption of the First National Environmental Policy in 1991. As mentioned earlier, this was based on the philosophy of sustainable development. Later, in 2000, the Second National Environmental Policy was adopted (Council of Ministry, 2000), followed by successive strategic documents concerning the broad area of environmental protection. These policies included many principles consistent with the implementation of sustainable development, but their implementation was poor. Despite this, a foundation was built for modern thinking about environmental protection.

In 1990, local government was restored in Poland. As a result of the decentralization process, many decisions on the local environment are now taken locally rather than at regional or national levels.

A system of environmental funds was established at four levels: national, regional, county and local.[7] The revenues of these funds were derived from fees for the use of the environment and the release of pollutants into it as well as fines for failure to meet environmental requirements. At present, product charges also go to these funds. Another interesting solution was a debt-for-nature swap, in which Poland's creditors (states) agreed to a partial reduction in debt in return for the use of resources for environmental purposes (including climate protection, the prevention of acid rain, the protection of the Baltic Sea, the conservation of biodiversity and waste management). The EcoFund[8] was established for these purposes. A complement to this system is the Bank for Environmental Protection,[9] which grants preferential credits, in co-operation with the environmental funds.

## Politics and Governance: Negative Processes

After the Roundtable talks, when environmental issues took on political significance, they were never again high on the list of political priorities. An exception to this was the period of the negotiations with EU, where, in addition to agriculture, environmental protection was an important area of negotiations. The efforts taken by environmental non-governmental organizations to overcome this political barrier to sustainable development ended in failure. In the 1997 elections, a group of environmental leaders tried to support the Freedom Union Party. This attempt did not bring any benefits to the environmental movement, as none of its leaders was elected to Parliament and this group had no effect on the choice of the Minister of the Environment, despite promises made to them before the elections.

In 2004, the integration of some environmental groups with feminist groups and those supporting sexual minorities led to the establishment of the political party called the Greens 2004.[10] However, the Greens have negligible significance on the political scene. At present, none of the significant political parties supports sustainable development, meaning that there is no political backing for this idea.

In parallel to progress in economic development and access to EU resources, anti-environmental lobbies have an increasingly strong presence. These include the fuels and energy lobby, the motorway construction lobby, and the lobby for the construction of large hydro-engineering sites. For the most part, they are interested in the implementation of huge investment projects without any detailed analysis of the social viability, economic efficiency, or environmental efficiency of these measures. They are strongly connected with the political establishment which generally supports measures of this type. Decisions on such projects are repeatedly taken without wide public discussion, although they affect the public directly.

The essence of sustainable development is the integration of environmental policy into sector policies. In Poland's case, in the period in question, such integration was practically absent in the case of important strategic documents including the national development strategy, the energy policy, and the water management strategy. There were some attempts to achieve such integration in the case of the development of agriculture and rural areas. But even the adoption of the Government guidelines on integration of environmental policy into sector policies had no essential influence.

As mentioned above, the period 1989–2006 was characterized by basic and broad changes in environmental law. However, the system for implementation and enforcement lagged behind these changes. There are quite frequent cases of failure to issue enabling acts on a timely basis, and the State Inspectorate for Environmental Protection lacks sufficient means to carry out inspections which would allow for a broad assessment of the extent of compliance with the law.

Due to the wide reconstruction of local government, along with an insufficient number of persons qualified in the scope of environmental protection or, more broadly, sustainable development, administration at this level is weak. Only 43 percent of persons engaged in environmental protection at the local level had higher education and only one-third of them had graduated from a faculty related to environmental protection. In many of the almost 2,500 local governments, the persons responsible for environmental protection had many other duties of greater importance from the viewpoint of the development of the local community, so that they did not really have much time for environmental protection.

According to a 2001 study (Kalbarczyk, 2001), 40 percent of local environmental staff had insufficient knowledge as to how financial and investment applications should be prepared, 35 percent of them were unable to organize environmental education for adults, 34 percent did not fully understand the environmental law, 33 percent had no experience in organizing public participation, 32 percent had no knowledge of relevant technologies for environmental protection, and 28 percent had no knowledge which would allow them to perform economic analyses.

## Economy: Positive Processes

Starting from a base of extremely inefficient use of natural resources under Communism, the introduction of a market economy with a recession in its initial phase, combined with the introduction of modern technologies, led to economic development in Poland without increased use of resources during the period 1990–2005. In particular, this was the case with energy resources and water. The consumption of primary energy fell by more than seven percent from 1990 to 2005, while water abstraction for production purposes dropped by 19 percent. After 1992 the national product grew at a pace varying between 1 and 7 percent a year; in the period from 1991 to 2003 it doubled on a per capita basis (Main Statistical Office, 2006), even as resource use declined. This contributed to a substantial reduction in pollution released into the environment.

Despite the lack of determined support from the Government, green jobs increased, particularly through the growing number of organic farms, agrotourist sites and renewable energy sources. From 2003 to 2005, the number of organic farms grew by a factor of more than 3 (from 2,286 to 7,183 farms), with a 40-fold increase in the surface area of crops, reaching as much as 167,700 ha, with the number of organic processing plants growing by a factor of 4.5, to almost 100. There are now about 1,000 agrotourist sites.[11] During the period from 1999 to 2005, the share of renewable energy in total energy consumption grew from 4.0 percent to 4.7 percent (Żmijewski and Kassenberg, 2006). In recent years, the government's support for 'green' job creation has slowly improved.

The influx of foreign capital and the establishment of many foreign companies in Poland, particularly those with world-renowned brands, contributed to widespread improvement in the environmental image of companies in Poland. This is demonstrated primarily by their acquisition of ISO 14000 certificates and their policies of environmental and social corporate responsibility.

## Economy: Negative Processes

The process of economic transformation contributed to many fundamental changes. Still, the essence of this process is economic growth and the achievement of a high level of gross domestic product per capita. Accordingly, development in Poland has followed a similar path to that in highly developed countries, although it has done so under different technological and market conditions. Efforts to shape sustainable patterns of production and consumption have been less than sufficient. The basic investment policy entails the construction of new production or service capacity for its own sake rather than with a view to satisfying social needs in a manner that would be most efficient in economic, social and environmental terms. Eco-innovation is not part of this approach.

Despite the improved efficiency in use of natural resources, their productivity is two to three times lower (Kassenberg, 1999) than in highly developed countries, where there are also substantial opportunities for making resource use more efficient. There is no determined policy encouraging the use of these opportunities to gain a competitive edge on the market.

Despite the introduction of a system of environmental fees and fines in Poland, market-based instruments are still clearly underused to promote sustainable development. Specifically:

1. The category of external costs is not taken into account in the course of decision-making, nor is it compensated for in the tax system. For example, a study performed for OECD estimates that the external costs of transport in Poland represent 10 percent of the annual domestic product (OECD and CEI, 2002). These costs do not include congestion, which is calculated to represent 0.5 percent of the domestic product in EU15; unless there is improvement in this respect, its cost will reach one percent by 2010 (European Commission, 2001). Other studies estimated the share of the external costs of transport in 2001 in Poland at 6.33 percent of GDP, and forecast that the share would be 6.75 percent in 2006. In 2001, road transport represented 91 percent of these costs, and this share is expected to grow to almost 96 percent in 2006 (Ministry of Infrastructure, 2004).
2. When subsidies are introduced their adverse impact on the environment is not taken into account. For example, in 2003, which was the last year before the accession and the last year when the level of State aid was not controlled by the European Commission, subsidies reached a level of as much as 3.5 percent of GDP. Hard coal mining received the largest support, PLN 17.5 billion (about two percent of GDP),[12] 80 percent of which consisted of forgiven payments for: land usufruct charges, royalties payable to the National Fund for Environmental Protection and Water Management, as well as fees and fines for the economic use of the environment (Świerkula, 2005).
3. The possibility of trading in allowances to emit air pollution was introduced in Poland with a large delay, 13 years after the first attempts had been made, and only because it was adopted by the EU. This instrument is not used as part of the implementation of environmental policy regarding climate protection, but as support for the Polish industry and energy sectors. The 2nd National Allocation Plan for $CO_2$ Emission Allowances proposed an annual allocation of 279.6 million tons $CO_2$ for the period from 2008 to 2012, an increase of 16.9 percent over the period from 2005 to 2007 (Ministry of

Environment, 2006). This was done without an in-depth analysis from the viewpoint of the strategic dilemmas of climate policy and without fundamental validation of the production growth forecasts as presented by individual sectors and industries. According to the Climate Coalition of environmental organizations in Poland, the total allocation of $CO_2$ emission allowances should be 221 million tons $CO_2$, consistent with the government's own Climate Policy (Climate Coalition, 2002).
4. Despite some interest in environmental tax reform, as demonstrated for several years by the Ministry of the Environment and the establishment of a Polish–German intergovernmental group on environmental tax reform, the discussion on this policy has never gone beyond the initial phase.

The last 16 years have seen basic changes in the transport system in Poland, clearly leading towards unsustainable transport. Specifically ('Transport Policy', 2004):

- The conditions for competition between different modes of transport have become more and more unequal.
- Use of railways has declined by 16 percent and utilization of roads has increased by about 10 percent.
- The role fulfilled by public transport has diminished – the division between passenger cars and public transport used to be 10/90 (1989), now it is estimated at 30/70, and the official government projection for 2020 is 72/28.
- The amount of goods transported has fallen; however, at the same time, goods are more often transported by truck than by railway (80 percent share); the transport of goods by railway has declined by 50 percent.
- The number of cars purchased has increased, stimulated by advertising campaigns (with a peak in 1999 when the Poles bought 640,000 new cars) – the motorization rate is almost 300 cars per 1,000 inhabitants, and in some places (e.g. Warsaw) it is as high as 400 cars per 1,000 inhabitants.
- For more than two years Poland imported about 2 million used cars (50 percent of them are 11 or more years old).
- In the 1990s rail passenger transport was reduced by 72 percent, and the car traffic volume on national roads is twice as high as it was prior to 1989.
- Traffic congestion has become more and more burdensome.
- The number of accidents has grown from 50 thousand to 57 thousand yearly.

In addition to large companies of significance in the economy, hundreds of thousands of small and medium-sized enterprises (SMEs) have emerged, which have little interest in environmental protection and care of their environmental image. Based on the survey conducted by the Polish Confederation of Private Employers 'Leviathan', only 0.3 percent of such companies are interested in environmental protection. At the same time, the State Inspectorate for Environmental Protection lacks both the ability and the motivation to check whether SMEs comply with the provisions of environmental law.

The energy sector is another area of key significance for the implementation of sustainable development in Poland. Despite substantial progress, the process of restructuring this sector is very slow, as indicated in Table 12.1.

*Table 12.1 Selected energy statistics*

| | POLAND | EU 15 |
|---|---|---|
| Efficiency of electricity production by power stations | 36.5% | 46.5% |
| Energy-intensity of the economy (toe/million € GDP) | 462 | 170 |
| Energy intensive sectors (added value) | 36.8% | 27.6% |
| Thermo – insulation of apartments (kWh/$m^2$/year) | 150 - 350 | 40 - 90 |
| Energy costs of households ( as % expenditures) | 10.4% | 3.0% |

*Source:* Żmijewski and Kassenberg (2006).

At the same time, according to experts' assessment, the technical capacity for the use of renewable energy in Poland is 1,750 PJ, equal to 47 percent of the current consumption of primary energy (Żmijewski and Kassenberg, 2006). However, no revolution is expected to come in 2005–2015 in the scope of improvement in efficiency, since the efficiency of the economy is envisaged to improve by only one-fourth. It is interesting to note that the Government plans to double the capacity of power plants by 2025, while the branch organizations of the energy sector project that in the period from 2005 to 2010 electricity production will grow by 50 percent; this is not physically possible, but it clearly indicates their line of thinking.

The critical example of lack of integration between sectoral policies, especially energy and transport, and environmental priorities is in the area of climate change. Poland, with $CO_2$ emissions of 317 million tons per year, is one of the significant contributors, especially when it comes to emissions per capita – 8.4 tons of $CO_2$. At the same time, climate change has already led to significant damages in Poland, and this will continue in the future. The total cost of the protection of the Polish coast, given a 1 meter rise in sea level, is estimated to amount to USD 6 billion, whilst the cost of losses suffered by the Polish economy if no action is undertaken will exceed USD 30 billion (Sadowski, 2006). Therefore, if Poland wants to demand effective climate protection from other countries, it has to initiate decisive actions in this respect itself.

As was mentioned earlier, the Polish government adopted in 2003 a climate Policy with a target of a 40 percent reduction by 2020 as compared to the base year of 1988. The goal is still possible to achieve because as of 2005 emissions of $CO_2$ had already declined almost one-third relative to the base year. Poland has a huge potential for of GHG reduction – the carbon-intensity of the economy was 75 tons $CO_2$/1000 euro GDP in 2005 but potentially could be reduced to 22 tons $CO_2$/1000 euro GDP. Unfortunately the Government has not followed its own announced policies, and many new strategic policies involve significant increases in GHG emissions. These include: Energy policy up to 2025, Transport policy up to 2025, 2nd National Allocation Plan for $CO_2$ Emission Trading 2008–2012 and Strategy for Development of Poland up to 2015. A similar situation exists in almost all the new members of EU (NMS) for Central and Eastern Europe, excluding the Czech Republic and Estonia.

## Society: Positive Processes

The basic benefit brought by the changes initiated by the Roundtable Talks was that they started the building of a democratic system and civic society. It is difficult to imagine sustainable development without the related fundamental principles, including a democratic election of authorities, self-government, access to information and wide public participation or equal opportunities for using the justice system. Despite many shortcomings and implementation difficulties, such a political system has become a foundation for Poland's development.

In the 1980s, an independent environmental movement, led by the Polish Ecological Club, started to organize itself in Poland. Reform of the political system caused a radical increase in the number of organizations, both formally registered and informal ones. It is estimated that the number of such organizations reached 700. With the passage of time, some organizations became professional and stronger, establishing their offices and employing staff (Gliński, 2006). The organizations started to form coalitions, such as those for: sustainable transport, organic farming, wetland conservation or monitoring the spending of EU funds. Networks of domestic organizations were also established, such as those of the Polish Green Network, or those of international organizations, such as Bankwatch. International organizations, such as WWF, IUCN or Greenpeace, also opened their offices. In addition to the environmental movement, consumer organizations also were created to take care of consumers' interests. There is some co-operation between the environmental movement and consumer organizations, but it is limited.

From 1992 to 2004, a number of nationwide sociological surveys were conducted concerning the Poles' environmental awareness. These surveys identified an 'environment-friendly' group, which is estimated to represent 20 percent of the entire population. It consists of well-educated persons, with a high economic status, primarily of the younger generation, and living in big cities. Another major survey finding was that Polish society recognized a strong connection between health and the quality of the environment. The opinions as to why it is important to take care of the environment were as follows (it was possible to choose more than two reasons) (Burger, 2002):

64.9 % – our own and our children's health
24.6 % – quality of the environment
19.7 % – care of next generations
12.5 % – for the sake of nature itself
11.2 % – other reasons

Due to individual legislative initiatives, the need to implement EU legislation and the requirement to implement the provisions of the Aarhus Convention after its ratification, a formal system was created in Poland to provide adequate access to information and public participation in matters related to the environment.

Along with the development of the environmental movement, self-government and, primarily, civic activity, many initiatives began to be undertaken in the scope of environmental education, particularly at the primary school level.

**Society: Negative Processes**

Despite the education activities undertaken and the improved access to information, the level of public environmental awareness is low. The environment-friendly group is diminishing. At the beginning of the 1990s, it represented about one-third of the public and now it is only one-fifth of the public. A study conducted by the Public Opinion Poll Centre shows that young people aged about 15 from 21 sub-culture groups identify to the greatest extent (about 30 percent) with environmental organizations. However, when they become adult and can actively affect the direction of the development of the country through elections, only 3 percent of the public is ready to do it through a radical environmentally friendly political program.

A very disquieting factor is the low awareness of the need for nature conservation, including biodiversity conservation. There is a wide acceptance of the view that human needs come first and the protection of 'little flowers and birds' must be subordinate to these needs. In other words, despite the slogans of sustainable development implying that solutions which would reconcile its three pillars – social, economic and environmental – should be sought, natural aspects are not treated as equal. This is evidenced e.g. by the statement of the Polish Prime Minister that it was necessary to limit Natura 2000 sites, given the need to make investment projects in Poland. It should be noted that the sites of the Natura 2000 network constitute part of a pan-European system; they are designated by the Polish Government and largely coincide with the already existing system for the protection of Polish nature.

So far the problem of excessive, unsustainable consumption in Poland is limited to a small group of citizens. However, there are clear signs, including the increasing amounts of waste and the transport problems in big cities, that consumerism may soon become dangerous in social and environmental terms. The unlimited growth of consumption, proposed by many politicians as the main goal for all Polish citizens, is highly controversial. In the EU15 states, there is a distinctly higher level of environmental awareness, including an awareness of the risks posed by excessive consumption. In Poland, even the poorest social strata have become rapidly motorized, which is unprecedented on a world scale. Given the financial potential of Poland's citizens, determined by the size of its domestic product, the motorization indices should be three times lower (Institute for Sustainable Development, 1999). There is no full awareness of the adverse effects of the motorization of the public and no critical reflection on its environmental, energy and spatial to a reduction of the environmental burdens generated by transport.

In contrast to the clear development of children's and youth education, adult environmental education is distinctly insufficient and ineffective. This is particularly the case with future businessmen. Surveys conducted in the late 1990s by the Institute for Sustainable Development showed an extreme weakness of environmental education in this social group. In an assessment of 80 business colleges, education concerning the environment was conducted in less than one-fifth, and only in a few of them was it of satisfactory quality (Czarnecka, 1997).

As mentioned above, as a result of political transformation, legal grounds were created for access to information on the environment and for public participation in decision-making process in matters related to the environment. However, the practice in this area is far from satisfactory. The table below shows the results of the assessment of the implementation of Principle 10 of the Rio Declaration in Poland, which is concerned with the issues in question. The study used indicators for access to information, participation in decision-making processes, and the strengthening of the capacity of the administration and civic society. Table 12.2 shows the results of this assessment.

*Table 12.2 Synthesised statistical assessment of the implementation of Principle 10 of the Rio Declaration in Poland*

| Categories of assessment | Assessment score as a percentage (100 maximum) |
|---|---|
| Public participation in decision-making | 58 |
| Access to information | 57 |
| Development of the capacity of the administration and the public | 47 |
| Total result | 58 |

*Source:* Institute for Sustainable Development (2006).

Despite the existence of a substantial environmental movement in Poland, partly associated with the Greens 2004 Party, many enterprises operating in the environmental protection market, producers of 'green' projects and goods, and a large number of design and consulting companies in the broadly understood area of environmental protection, no environmentally friendly political force has emerged in Poland with significant influence on political and administrative decisions.

## Environment: Positive Processes

As noted above ('positive processes in the economy'), efficiency of resource management increased in the period from 1990 to 2005. During this period, Poland clearly achieved the decoupling effect sought by many countries. Water consumption fell by 23 percent. Moreover, with the falling consumption of primary energy, consumption of hard coal and lignite fell, respectively, by 34 percent and 9 percent. The consumption of crude oil and natural gas, however, increased respectively, by 41 percent and 35 percent (Main Statistical Office, 2006).

Along with the more efficient use of raw materials and application of improved technologies, as well as a result of changes in the structure of the economy, the amounts of pollutants released into the environment were reduced, as illustrated by Table 12.3.

*Table 12.3 Change in the amounts of pollutants released into the environment in Poland from 1990 to 2005*

| Pollution | | 1990 | 2005 | Change in % |
|---|---|---|---|---|
| Air pollution – $SO_2$ (million tons – 2004) | | 3.21 | 1.24 | –64.1 |
| Air pollution –$CO_2$ (million tons – 2004) | | 381.48 | 316.70 | –17.0 |
| Air pollution – $NO_2$ (million tons – 2004) | | 1.28 | 0.80 | –37.5 |
| Air pollution – VOCs (anthropogenic) (million tons – 2004) | | 0.83 | 0.60 | –28.8 |
| Air pollution – Particulates (million tons) | 1990-1999 | 1.95 | 0.82 | –57.9 |
| | 2000-2004 | 0.46 | 0.44 | –4.3 |
| Industrial sewage | | 1,800.8 | 841.5 | –53.3 |
| Municipal sewage | | 2,313.9 | 1,273.6 | –45.0 |
| Generated industrial waste (million tons/year) | | 143.9 | 124.6 | –13.4 |

*Source:* Main Statistical Office (2006).

In addition to improved efficiency of the use of resources, there was a distinct increase in the provision of environmental protection infrastructure. In the period from 1995 to 2005, commissioned sites included wastewater treatment plants with the total capacity of 3,240,000 m3/day, equipment for capturing particulate air pollution with the capacity of 1,501,000 tons/year and those for capturing gaseous pollutants with the capacity of 833,000 tons/year, as well as equipment for disposal and economic use of waste with the capacity of more than 22 million tons/year. These efforts allowed for significant pollution reduction.

In the years from 1990 to 2005, there was an increase in amounts of wastewater treated chemically or biologically from 41 percent to 64 percent of wastewater requiring treatment, and an increase in the degree of the reduction of particulate and gaseous air pollutants, respectively, from 95 percent to 99 percent and from 16 percent to 50 percent. As a result, the quality of the environment improved slowly. Both water quality in rivers and lakes and air quality improved over this period (Main Statistical Office, 2006).

Poland is a country with a long tradition of nature conservation. In the period in question, there was a substantial increase in the surface area of protected areas from 19.4 percent to 32.5 percent of the total territory of the country. Table 12.4 shows the increase in these areas by major categories.

*Table 12.4 Change in protected areas in Poland from 1990 to 2005 (in thousand ha)*

| Protected areas | 1990 | 2005 | Change in % |
|---|---|---|---|
| National parks | 165.9 | 317.2 | +91.2 |
| Nature reserves | 117.0 | 165.2 | +41.2 |
| Landscape parks | 1,215.4 | 2,516.9 | +107.1 |
| Areas of protected landscape | 4,574.8 | 7,044.5 | +54.0 |
| Total | 6,073.1 | 10,175.9 | +67.6 |

*Source:* Main Statistical Office, 2006.

## Environment: Negative Processes

Despite clear successes in traditional environmental protection, the period of transition, the related fast economic growth, and the emergence of consumer society brought new dangers. These include primarily (Main Statistical Office, 2006):

- mass motorization, creating increased vehicle-related pollution. In the period 1990–2005, the number of vehicles almost doubled (as demonstrated in Figure 12.1), while in the period 2000–2004, $CO_2$ emissions from road transport grew by 6.7 percent, representing nearly 11 percent of the total emissions of this gas. The number of persons exposed to excessive vehicle noise represents about 40 percent of the population.
- emissions and landscape fragmentation as a result of the construction of new roads;
- the increased mass of post-consumer waste, including packaging;

- the slow intensification of agriculture, along with increasing farm size, contributing to loss of biodiversity;
- the beginning of the urban sprawl process. In the period 1990–2005, the share of land other than farmland and forestland in the total territory of the country grew from 12.7 percent to 19.8 percent.

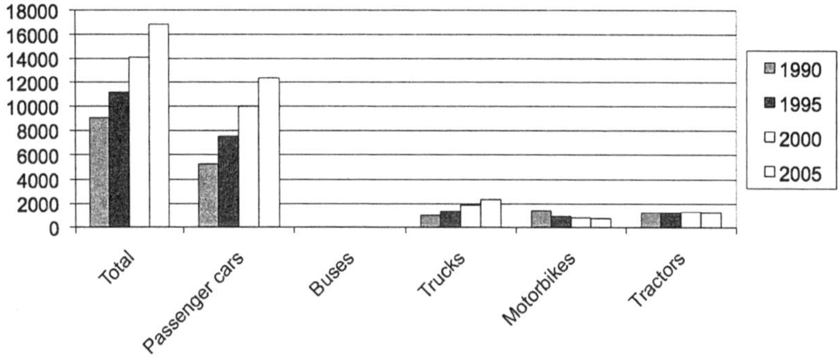


*Figure 12.1 Number of vehicles in Poland between 1990 and 2005 (in thousands)*

Loss of biodiversity has increased, with the faster loss in Western Poland. In addition to the impacts of transport and agriculture, biodiversity loss is aggravated by small and medium-sized enterprises locating in sensitive natural areas. Large investment projects are likely to lead to farther loss of biodiversity in the future. Examples of such proposed projects include: the program of motorway network construction, the dams planned on the Lower Vistula River, and the Olympic Games planned in Zakopane.

Despite substantial progress, water quality is still far from satisfactory; the same is true of soils and forests. Out of 1,360 water quality monitoring points on rivers, more than half have indicated Quality Class V or IV, the worst levels. At the same time, 30 percent of the monitored intakes of water for human consumption do not meet standards. In 2005, at more than 36 percent of measuring points, poor or unsatisfactory quality of groundwater was identified (Main Statistical Office, 2006).

In the period 1990–2005, there was a drop in emissions of basic pollutants, but the pace of this decrease clearly fell after the early gains from improved efficiency were realized, as shown in Figure 12.2.

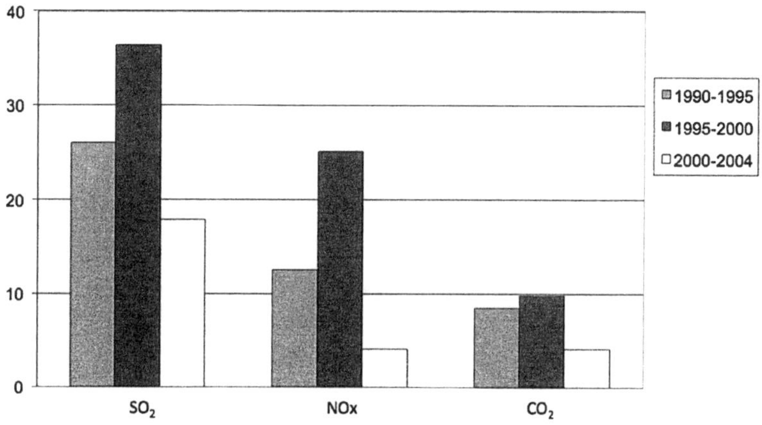


*Figure 12.2 Change in the rate of reduction in air pollutant emissions from 1990 to 2004 (each bar represents the percent decrease for that period)*

In subsequent years, as a result of strong support with resources from the EU budget for energy development, it is expected that pollutant emissions will grow in the period 2005–2020, as illustrated by Figure 12.3 for $CO_2$ and other greenhouse gases. This means that Poland will exceed the level of ten tons of $CO_2$ equivalent per person/year by 2020. To alter this unacceptable trend would require an effective integration of climate policy with strategy development plans. This would include:

- energy efficiency promotion including market-based instruments;
- much stronger support for renewable energy development including energy mix on the local level;
- continue support for combined heat and power plants;
- restructuring of coal industry and decline the role of fossil fuel in energy sector;
- promotion of design, technology and management in industry and services to decrease the use of energy per unit of product or service;
- changing people's behavior in more sustainable and environmentally friendly directions (for example increasing the role of public transport and railways).

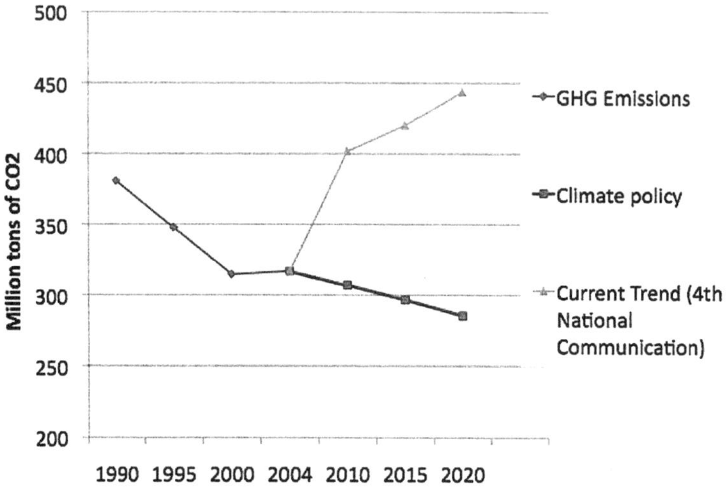


*Figure 12.3 Emissions of GHG in Poland 1990-2005 with projections for 2005-2020: current trend based on national development policy ($4^{th}$ National Communication) contrasted with Climate Policy (40 per cent reduction by 2020)*

# CONCLUSION

The period starting in 1989, when the process of fundamental transition began in Poland, was a time of both significant economic achievements and the building of civic society, as well as a time of significant hardships and high unemployment. From the viewpoint of sustainable development, with focus on its environmental aspects, three basic themes can be distinguished:

1. Substantial efforts were taken to build the appropriate infrastructure of environmental protection in order to satisfy basic civilization needs. These efforts were greatly stimulated by Poland's accession to the European Union. This included the construction of wastewater treatment plants, along with wastewater collection systems, air protection facilities, and improvement in waste management. The effects of these projects can already be seen, but there still remains much to be done, particularly in waste management and the construction of wastewater treatment plants. It should be expected that in another ten years Poland will meet the EU standards in this respect.

2. Given the huge waste of natural resources in the period preceding the transformation, Poland's economic development has unfolded with a general stabilization of resource consumption, including the use of energy or water resources. However, the opportunities for easily-obtained efficiency increases have become exhausted and, at the same time, there is a very strong tendency for further economic growth to increase resource use. The basic measure of economic performance still continues to be the domestic growth per capita. As a result, Poland is copying the bad patterns of highly developed countries in terms of excessive resource use. Although this copying takes place under different conditions, it will have similar environmental impacts if this trend continues. These effects will include higher greenhouse gas emissions and loss of biodiversity, along with increased landscape fragmentation and waste generation.

3. The position of the EU is ambiguous as, on the one hand, it promotes its Sustainable Development Strategy (the so-called Goeteborg Strategy), as updated in June 2006, and, on the other hand, it clearly supports, with its Structural Funds and the Cohesion Fund, a different type of development which leads to unsustainable economies and the promotion of over-consuming societies in the new EU Member States. A classic example of this is the very low development of rail infrastructure and the dynamic growth of road transport, with a resulting decline in rail transport. Proposals for different strategic solutions, involving eco-innovation, limitation of environmental impacts, and promotion of sustainable consumption, are not understood or accepted either by political elites or by common citizens. This is particularly unfortunate as the new EU members from Central and Eastern Europe (CEE) have great potential for reorienting development towards sustainability, which would contribute to progress in EU27 as a whole, including helping to achieve targets for carbon emissions reduction.

4. In Poland, both before and after the transformation, attempts have been made to build public pressure on the political elites so that they would incorporate sustainable development into national development strategies. So far it has proved impossible to create an effective lobby for sustainable development. The environmental movement, groups of independent experts or scientists, the Greens 2004 Party, and groups of environmentally aware entrepreneurs or common citizens represent a distinct minority and act in isolation rather than as a unified force with a significant political impact. Neither leftist, nor rightist, nor post-Communist, nor post-Solidarity parties are interested in promoting sustainable development.

An overall assessment of sustainable development in Poland thus indicates both positive and negative developments. Significant improvements have been made in environmental law and infrastructure, and resource efficiency has improved. Air pollution and waste emission levels have fallen, carbon emissions have declined, and protected areas have increased in size. But on the negative side, Poland now faces the danger that it will copy many of the environmentally unfavorable features of highly developed countries, including:

- Expansion of resource consumption and release of pollutants accompanying economic growth;
- Unwillingness of political and economic elites to adopt significant measures for protection of the environment, instead trying to 'buy time' by overexploiting environmental resources;
- Short-term decision-making, failure to internalize external costs, and environmentally harmful subsidies;
- An inadequate definition of sustainability, seeking only a compromise between economic development and the environment, rather than following the precautionary principle embodied in the Rio Declaration for the protection of planetary life support systems and cultural heritage.

In particular, policies aimed at promoting the expansion of energy production rather than improvements in energy efficiency threaten a significant growth in $CO_2$ emissions, contrary to Poland's stated Climate Policy of reducing emissions by 40 percent by 2020.

To alter these negative trends, a redirection of economic and political priorities in the direction of true sustainability is needed. Currently, however, a political consensus in favor of such a shift is lacking in Poland. Environmental awareness is strongest among the younger generation, which might offer hope, but few are currently willing to place the requirements of sustainability above the desire for economic and consumption growth.

## NOTES

1. Andrzej Kassenberg is President of the Institute for Sustainable Development in Warsaw, Poland, http://www.ine-isd.org.pl/.
2. Constitution of Poland from 2 April 1997.
3. Environmental Protection Law from 27 April 2001.
4. An effect of this is, among other things, the current need to expend EUR 35–40 billion to meet EU requirements in the field of environmental protection.
5. The Resolution on Environmental Policy of 10 May 1991 of the Parliament of the Republic of Poland.

6. As a transitional economy, Poland has chosen the base year of 1988 for purposes of the Climate Convention and Kyoto Protocol, so that a one-third increase in emissions over current levels will still amount to an 11 percent reduction below 1988 levels.
7. Available at: http://www.nfosigw.gov.pl/site/index_en.php.
8. Available at: http://www.ekofundusz.org.pl/us/index.htm.
9. Available at: http://www.bosbank.pl/i.php.
10. Available at: http://www.zieloni2004.pl/portal/index.php?s1=aktualnosci.
11. Rural Development Plan for years 2007–2013.
12. The Polish Zloty (PLN) was worth approximately $0.34 as of early 2007.

# REFERENCES

Burger, T. (2002), 'Rio Declaration in the Eye of the Society', in report no. 2/2002, Warsaw: Institute for Sustainable Development.

Climate Coalition (2002), *Position Paper of Climate Coalition on draft II National Allocation Plan for $CO_2$ Emission Trading for Second Period 2008–2012*, Warsaw: Climate Coalition.

Council of Ministry (2000), *Second National Environmental Policy*, Warsaw: Council of Ministry.

Czarnecka, A. (1997), *Business Schools in Sustainable Development*, Warsaw: Institute for Sustainable Development (in Polish).

European Commission (2001), *European Transport Policy for 2010: Time to Decide*, White Paper, Brussels: European Commission.

Gliński, P. (1996), *Polish Greens: Civic Moment during the Transformation*, Warsaw: Institute of Philosophy and Sociology, Polish Academy of Sciences (in Polish).

Institute for Sustainable Development (1999), *Alternative Transport Policy in Poland in Accordance to Sustainable Development Principles*, in report no. 4/99, Warsaw: Institute for Sustainable Development (in Polish).

Institute for Sustainable Development (2000), *The Roundtable. The Environmental Sub-Table after 15 Years*, Warsaw: Institute for Sustainable Development (in Polish).

Institute for Sustainable Development (2006), 'Assessment of Implementation Principle No. 10 from Rio Declaration' (Report TAI – The Access Initiative). Available at http://www.ine-isd.org.pl/.

Kalbarczyk, R. (2001), *Environmental Protection Problem of Local Communities in the Beginning of the XXI Century*, Warsaw: The Polish Ecological Club (in Polish).

Kassenberg, A. (1999), 'Sustainable Development and Dematerialization of Production and Consumption', synthesis of report done for Ministry of Economy, Warsaw: Institute for Sustainable Development. (in Polish)

Main Statistical Office (2006), *Environmental Protection 2006*, Warsaw: Main Statistical Office.

Ministry of Economy (2003), *National Development Plan 2004–2006*, Warsaw: Ministry of Economy.

Ministry of Environment (2006), *Draft II National Allocation Plan 2008–2012*, Warsaw: Ministry of Environment.

Ministry of Infrastructure (2004), *Sector Operational Program for Transport 2004–2006*, Warsaw: Ministry of Infrastructure.

Ministry of Regional Development (2006), *National Development Strategy 2007–2013*, Warsaw: Ministry of Regional Development.

OECD and CEI Subgroup on Environment and Transport (2002), *External Costs of Transport in Eastern Europe*, Vienna/Zurich: CEI Subgroup on Environment and Transport, OECD.
Sadowski, M. (2006) *Ocena potencjalnych skutków społeczno-gospodarczych zmian klimatu w Polsce [Estimate of potential socio-economic results of climate change in Poland]*, WWF, http://wwf.pl/informacje/publikacje_klimat.php.
Świerkula, E. (2005), *An Attempt to Identify Environmentally Harmful Subsidies in the Polish Economy*, Warsaw: Institute for Sustainable Development and Green Budget Germany.
'Transport Policy in the Context of UE Sustainable Development Strategy' (2004), paper presented at the conference 'Conditions and Mechanism of Sustainable Development', Białystok-Supraśl 1–3 July.
Żmijewski, K. and A. Kassenberg (2006), *Energy Policy of Poland. Declaration and Reality*, Warsaw: Institute for Sustainable Development.

# 13. Climate Change from the Investor's Perspective

**Adam Seitchik**[1]

While public policy initiatives on climate change are just now kicking into gear, investor interest is already substantial and accelerating rapidly. The Investor Network on Climate Risk (INCR), founded in 2003, has grown into an alliance of more than 60 institutional investors responsible for over $5 trillion in assets. The third Institutional Investor Summit on Climate Risk, held at the United Nations in February 2008, attracted more than 450 institutional investors, fund managers and financial professionals from around the world. INCR members have been active in encouraging the companies they invest in to address the business risks and opportunities associated with climate change and the global shift toward a less carbon-intensive economy. In conjunction with the Summit, nearly 50 leading US and European institutional investors pledged to invest $10 billion in prudent emerging business opportunities in clean technologies over the next two years.

Research on climate-related investment risk and opportunity has grown from next-to-nothing five years ago to the continuous publication of substantive reports on a variety of themes and industries. One important spur to research has been the UK-based Enhanced Analytics Initiative (EAI), an institutional investment consortium backed by over $2 trillion in assets. The EAI provides financial incentives for better and more detailed analysis of issues such as climate change within mainstream investment research. Leading global investment houses including Citigroup, UBS, Lehman Brothers, and Goldman Sachs are responding to this demand and publishing substantial reports on climate-related investment challenges and opportunities. Furthermore, a number of brokerage institutions now have dedicated research groups assessing the impact of environmental, social and governance (ESG) issues on investment portfolios.

Beyond research and analysis, early stage investors are making a major commitment to climate solutions. Venture capital has been pouring into this space under the banner of 'clean technology', or 'Cleantech'. Again, the motivation is primarily financial, as investors emphasize doing well financially while doing good. Cleantech technologies add economic value by optimizing the use of natural resources to reduce environmental impact, lower costs, and boost profits. The potential opportunity inherent in these strategies could rival or even eclipse earlier investments in information technology and biotech. The Cleantech Venture Network estimates that Cleantech is now the 3rd largest venture investment category, with 13 percent market share in North America and 18 percent in Europe (Parker, 2007). Global investment in clean energy has grown from an estimated $27 billion in 2004 to $71 billion in 2006, almost tripling in the space of 24 months (Liebreich, 2007).

The exploding capital market interest in climate solutions has little to do with social investing. Instead, it has everything to do with the disruptive power of climate to create both financial risk and opportunity. There are three essential reasons why investors are taking a strong interest in climate change: portfolio strategy, security selection, and capital allocation.

## 1. Portfolio Strategy

Most institutional investors, as well as many individuals, are broadly diversified: by country, sector and asset class. As long-term asset holders with exposure to both private assets like venture capital and real estate, and public securities such as stocks and bonds, these highly diversified 'universal owners' essentially own shares in the global economy. As a result 'their returns and consequently their ability to meet their fiduciary obligations depend to a critically large extent on the performance of the economy as a whole' (Hawley and Williams, 2006). Therefore, investors have a strong vested interest in public policy and private activity that lowers the global risk of climate-related economic disruption.

## 2. Security Selection

Regardless of how climate change plays out, better research will result in improved investment decisions. Until very recently, investors interested in how climate change might impact the fair value of any individual asset holding or industry were working in a virtual information vacuum. Few corporations estimated climate-related risks and opportunities as part of strategic planning, little research was published on the subject, and securities analysts essentially ignored climate change when developing pricing models. This is all changing fundamentally.

### 3. Capital Allocation

While most investing still occurs in publicly traded securities, the allocation of capital to less-liquid private investments has grown substantially since the stock market crash of 2000–2002. Green real estate, green hedge funds, and Cleantech venture capital are emerging as attractive choices for investment allocation. Also, institutional investors are pressing the fund management industry to develop targeted 'green' funds that trade in public securities. For the most part, these newly emerging investments are driven by the long-term economic and financial opportunities defined by a carbon-constrained world.

## THE IMPORTANCE OF CLIMATE CHANGE TO PORTFOLIO STRATEGY

In the long run, investors are paid for taking risk. Much of the risk in a diversified portfolio comes from participation in the markets themselves. As popularized in books such as *Winning the Loser's Game* in the 1980s and *Stocks for the Long Run* in the 1990s, the most important choices investors make are not in active stock picking, but broad asset allocation: their relative exposures to classes of investments such as real estate, stocks, bonds and cash. Similarly, climate will have its greatest portfolio impact through overall asset class returns, not the performance of any individual securities holdings.

Most of the advice around asset allocation focuses on the long-term, wealth-generating potential of investing in the stock market. This bullish view of long-term investing is a product of the post-War experience in market economies in Western Europe, Japan and North America. During the second half of the 20th century, stock returns in these markets were exceptional. However, recent research on global financial returns in the last century indicates that investing in the markets as a passive exercise does not always lead to positive outcomes. Market returns do not occur in a vacuum, but are the product of political, social, technological and economic trends that investors themselves help influence.

For example, a passive, risk-averse investor in German bonds would have lost 100 percent of their value during the hyperinflation of 1923, and a German equity investor would have lost 87 percent of value in 1948.[2] During the first half of the 20th century, Japanese equity investors essentially made nothing for 50 years, after accounting for inflation. So, long-term investing through broad market exposure is not an effective strategy at all times and in all places. Markets in the first half of the 20th century endured two World Wars, multiple financial panics, the Great Depression, the rise of communism and fascism, widespread labor discrimination, and the detonation of atomic bombs that killed several hundred thousand human beings. The result was US and global investment returns less than half as good as those post-war.[3]

Our perception of long-term market outcomes is colored by the positive developments that emerged in the five decades following World War II: no global wars, a regulated and insured banking system, limited nuclear proliferation, the Marshall Plan, expansion of the middle class, improved social justice via the civil rights movement and related legislation, national environmental policies, the end of the Cold War, healthy, less-volatile economic growth, and Federal Reserve interest rate management. The result was 50 years of phenomenal returns in a variety of markets, with global stocks rising nine percent annually in excess of inflation.

While efficient, broad market investment through vehicles such as index funds has gained widespread popularity, it has also led to a risky passivity among owners of capital. In fact, simple exposure to a market index (such as the S&P 500) has become known as 'passive' investing. However, as climate change and energy constraints loom, market returns will not necessarily be attractive in the long run.

No doubt, clear linkages exist between the performance of portfolios and the health of the overall economic system. Recently, this understanding has crystallized into a more formal analysis of the position of the Universal Owner (UO). The UO hypothesis 'states that a portfolio investor benefiting from a company externalizing costs might experience a reduction in overall returns due to these externalities adversely affecting other investments in the portfolio, and hence overall market return' (Thamotheram and Wildsmith, 2006).

Put simply, negative externalities are costs from economic activities that are borne by those 'external' to the transaction. Carbon emissions are a classic example of a negative externality, to the extent that the full cost of the pollution is not factored into the price of a barrel of oil but borne by society at large. The key insight from UO analysis is that for a diversified investor, there is no place to hide from these costs: they come back into the portfolio as taxes, insurance premiums, inflated input prices and the physical cost of disasters.

Being a passive investor abdicates fiduciary responsibility for the world that underpins economic and financial prosperity. The corporations that investors own exert tremendous global power relative to government and labor. Investors can and should demand that companies desist from externalizing environmental costs onto society that in the long run will harm portfolio-level returns.

From the perspective of a single company, it may be a profitable strategy, even in the long term, to avoid paying the costs of $CO_2$ emissions. Yet, from a portfolio perspective, this could lead to lower overall returns. For example, consider the profits that derive from the traditional energy sector. Investments in this sector account for about 10 percent of US stock market value. In 2006, fossil fuel companies occupied three of the top six spots in the Fortune 500 list of the largest US companies, and generated record profits of over $60 billion (Fortune Magazine, 2006).[4] These profits drove up the stock prices of the companies and thus appeared to benefit diversified investors in the short run. Over time, however, the disruptive portfolio influence of climate change, such as rising ocean levels and the damage from more intense storms, could easily overwhelm the short-term benefit of these corporate profits narrowly concentrated in the energy sector.

## Climate Risk and Fiduciary Responsibility

It is in investors' financial self-interest to take a leadership role in analyzing critical long-term risks and opportunities such as $CO_2$ emissions. Arguably, for trustees such as pension fund and foundation boards it is a key element of fiduciary duty. In recent years, the legal case for taking environmental, social and governance (ESG) issues into account when making fiduciary decisions has been strengthened. In 2005, the United Nations Environment Program's Finance Initiative commissioned a comprehensive global report by leading international law firm Freshfields Bruckhaus Deringer entitled: 'A Legal Framework for the Integration of Environmental, Social and Governance Issues into Institutional Investment'. The Freshfields' analysis concluded that 'integrating ESG [environmental, social, governance] considerations into an investment analysis so as to more reliably predict financial performance is clearly permissible and is arguably required in all jurisdictions.'

Paul Watchman, Partner at Freshfields Bruckhaus Deringer and senior author of the study, notes that 'Institutional investors have more freedom to integrate ESG issues into their decision-making than they think. Whilst normally we find ourselves encouraging our clients to be more cautious, in this case we can instead say "be more imaginative".'[5] An improved investor understanding of the importance of these risks has led to the development of the Principles for Responsible Investment, now backed globally by over $2.5 trillion in investor assets. The preamble to the Principles states that:

> As institutional investors, we have a duty to act in the best long-term interests of our beneficiaries. In this fiduciary role, we believe that environmental, social, and corporate governance (ESG) issues can affect the performance of investment portfolios (to varying degrees across companies, sectors, regions, asset classes and

through time). We also recognize that applying these Principles may better align investors with broader objectives of society.[6]

Securing attractive market returns in this century will likely require the aggressive management of climate change. It is all too easy to put seemingly environmental issues like this into the box of 'politics', disconnected from investment policy-making. But, while investors can debate the appropriate course of action, there should be little disagreement that dire outcomes are possible and imminently material. When shareholder activism can reduce market risk and enhance long-term returns, passivity is not the winning investment strategy.

The Investor Network on Climate Risk (INCR) has led in the development of institutional investment strategies to effectively manage risks and capture opportunities around climate change. In 2004, INCR published an *Investor Guide to Climate Risk*, identifying 10 key steps for investor action. They are shown in Table 13.1 on the following page and include assessment, disclosure, and solution-based activities.

At the INCR summit in February 2008, nearly 50 major institutional investors with assets of over $1.75 trillion endorsed an action plan intended to accelerate the pace of innovation around climate risk and opportunity. Signers of the plan included seven state treasurers, three state and city comptrollers, four public pension funds, seven labor pension funds, two foundations, and two religious institutional investors.

The action plan included a number of specific initiatives covering many of the above strategies. Commitments included:

- Deploying $10 billion of capital in clean technologies over the next two years;
- Improving the energy performance of real estate portfolios and investments;
- Urging comprehensive corporate responses to climate risks;
- Expanding climate risk scrutiny and collaboration by investors;
- Encouraging companies and investors to support government action on climate policy;
- Supporting policies to maximize energy efficiency;
- Encouraging the Securities and Exchange Commission (SEC) to require that companies disclose the risk associated with climate change as part of their securities filings.

A growing number of investors have emphasized the need for mandatory climate disclosure, in addition to voluntary disclosure through the Global Reporting Initiative and other means.

*Table 13.1 Ten key steps for investor action on climate risk*[7]

**ASSESSMENT**

*Expert Advice*

Find experts to raise awareness, assess climate risks, and convey fiduciary duties to plan beneficiaries, investment consultants, fund managers and portfolio companies.

*Risk Assessment*

Assess physical and policy risks of climate change in evaluations of companies, industry sectors, investment portfolios and property holdings.

*Networking with Others*

Join INCR and engage with others to promote climate risk assessments, greenhouse gas emissions disclosure and responsible public policy.

**DISCLOSURE**

*Public Statement*

Declare that climate change poses fiduciary and financial risks to be addressed through research, corporate engagement and long-term investment strategies.

*Public Disclosure*

State methods to assess and address climate risk in plan documents and require companies to identify material risks of climate change in securities filings.

*Emissions Accounting*

Ask companies to disclose emissions based on the Greenhouse Gas Protocol, and to account for GHG emissions from products and property holdings.

*Stakeholder Dialogue*

Adopt proxy voting guidelines to urge corporate action on climate change, and maintain and active dialogue with beneficiaries, fund managers and companies.

**SOLUTIONS**

*Investment Strategy*

Match long-term objectives with reduced climate risk exposure to optimize investment returns, and engage fund managers and companies to adopt best practices.

*Clean Energy*

Direct investment capital into emerging clean energy technologies and promote energy efficient products and building practices.

*Government Action*

Support government actions to promote investor certainty, including mandatory policies to achieve absolute reductions in greenhouse gas emissions.

Members of the Investor Network on Climate Risk (INCR) have written to the SEC Chairman (in 2004, 2006, and 2007) to request the enforcement of disclosure requirements on material risks such as climate change, the strengthening of disclosure requirements related to these risks, and the inclusion of proposals related to climate change in shareholder proxy statements.[8] In September 2007 a broad coalition of investors, state officials with regulatory and fiscal management responsibilities, and environmental groups formally asked the SEC's Division of Corporation Finance to immediately begin closely scrutinizing the adequacy of company climate disclosures under existing law.

Both companies and members of Congress are responding to these requests. In key industries affected by climate change, disclosure rates in SEC filings rose from 26 percent of companies in 2000 to 49 percent in 2005. Two of the six climate change bills before the Senate in April 2007 would require corporate disclosure of climate risk in SEC filings. Both the Sanders-Boxer and the Kerry-Snowe bills require an interim SEC statement acknowledging trends in global warming. The bills also require new regulations, issued within a two-year period, directing companies to disclose their financial exposure due to their emissions, and the potential economic impacts of climate change on the company.

Investor action is now moving to the public sphere, as the linkages between long-term investment returns and effective public policy on climate become clear. In March 2007, dozens of institutional investors responsible for $4 trillion in assets called on US lawmakers to enact strong federal legislation to curb the pollution causing global climate change. Joined by some leading US companies, the investor group outlined the business and economic rationale for climate action. They also called for a national policy to reduce greenhouse gas emissions consistent with the scientific targets needed to avoid dangerous global warming impacts. The 65 signatories included institutional investors and asset managers such as Merrill Lynch, Allianz, and the California Public Employees Retirement System (CalPERS), as well as leading corporations such as BP America, PG&E, DuPont, Alcoa, Sun Microsystems and National Grid.

## CLIMATE CHANGE AND SECURITY SELECTION

The fair value of any security is a function of its future profit stream, and the certainty (or lack thereof) of those expected cash flows. Climate change has the ability to influence virtually every investment on every important dimension that determines its price: projected costs, revenues, and the level of uncertainty about the future.

Good data are central to the investment management of carbon risk and opportunity. Cross-sectional information is needed to make judgments between companies, along with longitudinal data to monitor trends over time.

The Carbon Disclosure Project (CDP) has spearheaded efforts to improve corporate transparency on climate for investors. Launched in 2000, the CDP began by requesting information from the 500 largest global companies (the FT 500). The fourth annual survey, in 2006, was sent to an expanded list of 2000 companies globally, of which 900 responded. This questionnaire (CDP4) had significant investor weight behind it, including 225 institutional investor and asset management signatories.

Given the high level of material climate change risk, investors would benefit from required reporting in this area under a consistent set of disclosure guidelines. Despite the lack of a mandated framework in most countries, it is striking how much the data have improved in just the last few years – particularly from corporations in Europe. In the US disclosure is improving, but is uneven among large corporations and minimal for smaller firms.

Ceres, a non-profit organization that works with companies and investors to address environmental issues including global climate change, recently teamed up with the investment group Calvert to analyze responses to CDP4. While 72 percent of the 500 largest global companies (the FT 500) responded to the survey, only 47 percent of the primarily US-based S&P 500 companies filled out the questionnaire. In addition, one-third of S&P 500 responders only allowed their data to be available to the signatories of the CDP, limiting the investment analysis impact for research firms and asset managers. Furthermore, only one quarter of S&P 500 respondents disclosed measurable emissions targets. While many companies acknowledged physical risks from weather, few tied weather-related risk to climate change.

The analysis of S&P 500 CDP4 responses indicates that companies with the largest direct carbon emissions, such as those in the electric power and oil sectors, have the highest-quality disclosure. Most companies in sectors where carbon emission risks are indirect but very real, such as health care, retailing and banking, have not begun to analyze their strategic exposure to climate change.

When companies lag in their response to climate change, concerned investors increasingly are responding by filing shareholder resolutions. Shareholders have raised the issue of climate change with companies for years: Exxon received the first climate-related shareholder proposal in 1990. However, shareholder advocacy related to climate change has increased exponentially in recent years and shows no signs of peaking yet. Shareholders filed 150 climate-related proposals in the last five years. The number of climate proposals in the 2007 proxy-voting season broke all previous records, with a broad set of public pension funds, religious institutional investors and other asset holders filing a total of 45 climate resolutions at companies in diverse sectors including oil, gas, and coal companies; utilities; automakers; home builders; retailers; and insurers and other financial institutions.[9]

Not only has the number of climate proposals climbed, so have levels of support for these shareholder votes. The high-water mark for climate-related resolutions is 37 percent, very significant in a voting system favoring corporate management. While the proposals vary in how they ask corporations to address climate change, most request improved data disclosure and the development of a coherent climate strategy, including: (1) public reporting of greenhouse gas emissions, along with an assessment of risks and opportunities from climate change; (2) establishing goals and targets to reduce emissions of greenhouse gases; and/or (3) support for public policies that restrict greenhouse gas emissions.

As a result of their activism as corporate owners, shareholders have negotiated significant agreements with companies over the past several years. For example, shareholders helped convince major utility companies to call for new federal legislation to limit greenhouse gas emissions and give them greater certainty about future regulations, and to boost investments in integrated gasification combined cycle plants that could allow carbon capture and storage. Proponents have also convinced a number of oil companies to measure and disclose their greenhouse gas emissions, set reduction targets, and boost investment in renewable energy alternatives. A number of retailers and homebuilders agreed to implement new energy efficiency measures. Other companies, from automakers to banks and insurers, boosted their disclosures and in some cases adopted new policies to address climate-related impacts.

In order to improve the quality and consistency of corporate data in this area, a group of institutional investors released the Global Framework for Climate Risk Disclosure in October 2006. The Framework consists of four elements of disclosure:

- Total historical, current, and projected greenhouse gas emissions
- Strategic analysis of climate risk and emissions management
- Assessment of physical risks of climate change
- Analysis of risk related to the regulation of greenhouse gas emissions

There are a number of existing reporting mechanisms through which the Framework's disclosure can be accomplished. These include mandatory financial reports such as those required by the Securities and Exchange Commission (SEC), where material risks must be disclosed; the Carbon Disclosure Project itself (CDP); the Global Reporting Initiative (GRI), which is a set of guidelines for the comprehensive reporting on the economic, environmental and social dimensions of corporate activity; and forward-looking statements made in analyst briefings and other corporate reports.

Engaged shareholders understand that there is a strong business case for pro-active corporate approaches to climate change. As discussed in recent business strategy research, corporations have a clear self-interest in using environmental strategies to 'innovate, create value and build competitive advantage' (Esty and Winston, 2006). Analysts are identifying key linkages between climate change and business profitability. For example, in a recent *Harvard Business Review* article, Lash and Wellington (2007) offer prototype questions that companies (and the investment analysts that follow them) should be asking about potential climate-related revenue and cost drivers (Table 13.2).

*Table 13.2 Examples of cost and revenue drivers from climate change that influence fair value*

| Potential Cost Drivers | Potential Revenue Drivers |
|---|---|
| • How will regulatory policy affect costs? | • How will changes in customer demand patterns affect pricing? |
| • Will emissions be taxed? | • What percentage of climate-related costs can be passed through to customers? |
| • What capital expenditures will be required for emission reduction? | • What revenue streams can come from new low-carbon products? |
| • How much will raw materials prices escalate for the company and its suppliers? | • What new forms of income (for example, carbon credits) will become available? |
| • How much will energy costs rise? | • What threats are faced from low-carbon substitute products? |
| • How will the company's risk profile affect its insurance premiums? | • What will be the impact of weather patterns on revenue? |

Ceres worked with the Investor Responsibility Research Center (IRRC) to develop a comprehensive analysis of how 100 global companies in the ten most carbon-intensive industries in the US are managing climate risk and opportunity (Cougan, 2006). As part of their analysis, the authors developed a Climate Change Governance Checklist, a 100 point system covering five key areas: Board Oversight, Management Execution, Public Disclosure, Emissions Accounting, and Strategic Planning. The study covered 76 US and 24 non-US companies.

The Ceres/IRRC analysis revealed large differences in the estimated climate risk governance performance within the various sectors studied. Climate risk leadership was evident in companies like DuPont, AEP, Toyota and Alcan, with scores upwards of 60 (100 would represent comprehensive management of climate risk). Laggards scored in the 20s. In general, companies in the Chemicals, Electric Power and Auto sectors are paying more attention to climate than the Oil & Gas, Coal, Food and Airlines industries. Investors should take note of companies that, despite obvious exposure to climate risk, are slow-footed in the strategic management of climate change. The average industry scores are shown in Figure 13.1

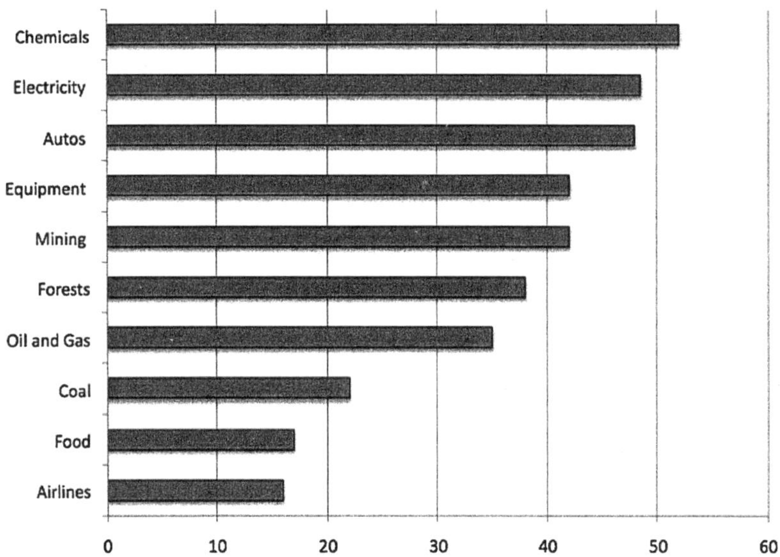


*Source:* Cougan (2006).

*Note:* 100-point scale includes Board Oversight, Management Execution, Public Disclosure, Emissions Accounting, Emissions Management, and Strategic Opportunities.

*Figure 13.1 Climate change corporate governance checklist*

## Developing Climate Risk Management Strategies

The Ceres report identified some common themes among leadership companies with best-in-class climate risk strategies. First, the Board and senior executives are working collaboratively to address climate issues. Second, the CEOs have identified climate as a near-term priority. Third, management is taking action, and establishing practical policies for dealing with climate risk and opportunity.

For the most part, investment analysis of carbon risk is a long-term proposition, as risks may be latent for many years and then emerge suddenly through, for example, weather-related events or new regulations. However, a higher 'risk premium' for a company should lead to lower current levels of fair value, and as investors sort through the data on carbon risk it could trigger a re-evaluation of corporate worth.

The research firm Innovest Strategic Value Advisors has developed industry and company-specific carbon risk metrics for over 1500 global companies. Innovest identifies three industry-level risk measures:

- Climate Change Direct Intensity; that is, the industry's emissions of carbon from its own operations
- Climate Change Indirect Intensity, which estimates the industry's demand for electricity and other carbon-intensive inputs
- Climate Change Demand Sensitivity, with high sensitivity sectors either producing goods that create significant greenhouse emissions, or having other kinds of exposure (such as through investing or insurance provision)

In order to evaluate the influence of carbon risk on stock prices, Innovest used its carbon risk framework to identify the 21 best-in-class responses from the first year of the Carbon Disclosure Project in 2002. These firms came from 12 carbon-sensitive sectors. When benchmarked against their sector peers, a portfolio of these carbon leaders outperformed by 2.3 percent annually over the subsequent three years (Kiernan, 2007). Effective management of carbon may in itself create improved stock price valuations, and also could be a proxy for a company's broader risk-reducing approach to complex strategic issues.

Conservation and efficiency measures go straight to the bottom line and can directly boost investment returns. Investors play an important role in improving economic efficiency by allocating capital to those corporations with the most effective resource and risk management systems. Given uncertainty about future risk, it is difficult to place a price on the management of climate change. That said, new research is emerging to quantify the potential investor benefit of sound resource deployment. One careful peer-reviewed study evaluated the investment returns of companies based on their 'eco-efficiency', defined as the ratio of the value a company adds with their products and services to the waste they generate. While industries with heavy environmental impact such as oil, gas, chemicals and utilities scored badly in general, the authors identified the best-of-sector performers in each part of the economy. The 'eco-efficient' portfolio created substantially better investment returns than the companies with less eco-efficiency (Derwall et al., 2005, pp. 61–63).

## CAPITAL ALLOCATION TO CLIMATE SOLUTIONS

Beyond developing climate-related portfolio strategies and security selection techniques, investors are making substantial capital commitments to early-stage climate solutions. The Cleantech Venture Network differentiates between the current market environment and prior efforts to finance environmental solutions in the 1970s through early 1990s. While earlier efforts were driven by regulatory changes and focused on 'end-of-pipe' technology (such as scrubbers on smoke stacks), today's Cleantech sector is profit-driven and responding to what appear to be enduring market trends (Parker, 2007). Specifically, the Network views the move from 'Enviro to Green to Clean' as creating a new emphasis on:

- First-mover activity driven by market forces, not regulatory change
- Productivity-based purchasing, not compliance-driven activity
- 'Front-of-pipe' technology, such as zero emission plants
- Biological and materials science, transitioning away from a reliance purely on chemical science
- Systems design and engineering;
- Rapid growth markets, moving from areas like waste management into solar, wind and energy efficiency
- An entrepreneurial mentality, replacing a save-the-world idealism
- Intensive use of information technology

There is no question that capital allocation to Cleantech is growing by leaps and bounds. The research firm New Energy Finance estimates that in 2006 at least $7 billion was deployed globally in clean energy venture capital and private equity. Public market fundraising accounted for an additional $10 billion, up from $4 billion in 2005. The sum total of all global investment, mergers, acquisitions and refinancing in clean energy during 2006 is estimated at $100 billion (Liebreich, 2007).

Green hedge funds are not as pervasive as Cleantech venture capital, but investor interest is likely to surface once additional attractive products are brought to market. While the unregulated nature of hedge funds means that the strategies employed are virtually limitless, a popular approach is 'long–short', limiting overall market exposure by going 'long' attractive securities and 'short' those that are judged to have lower financial return prospects.[10] Hedge fund providers such as Green Cay and Civic Capital Group already incorporate environmental risk and opportunity into their strategies. Access to an expanding body of research assessing carbon risk at the company and industry level allows investment managers to identify best practices and worst-in-class firms. Emerging hedge fund strategies will likely incorporate these data into their evaluation of risk on both the long and the short side of the market.

Another area very likely to benefit from increased capital allocations is 'green' real estate, such as buildings and other properties that incorporate sustainable design and construction elements, ranging from the selection of renewable or recycled building materials to energy efficiency, green roofs, and alternative power sources. In 2005, McGraw-Hill estimated that the market for environmentally friendly real estate could grow to $20 billion by 2010. However, even those projections may be too modest. A more recent survey by McGraw-Hill Construction and the National Association of Homebuilders estimated that by 2010 green builders may account for 10 percent of new home construction, or $38 billion (McGee, 2007).

While investment demand for green commercial real estate currently outstrips supply, the market is evolving rapidly as cities implement green building legislation. Boston and Washington, DC are now requiring all new large-scale projects to meet designated green building standards. Real Estate Investment Trusts are forming with 'green' mandates, and some banks and institutional investors have committed capital to building projects that meet specific environmental standards.

Risk in alternative energy investing and conservation technologies is driven in large part by the uncertain price of fossil fuels. This was clearly evident in the mid-1980s, when the collapse of oil prices decimated the fledgling solar power industry. From 1986 to 1998 the price of a barrel of oil was relatively stable between $15 and $25, even as general consumer prices rose steadily.

Despite continuing subsidies for oil and gas exploration and production, since 2003 supply and demand conditions have led to a breakout in fossil fuel prices out of their historic trading range. This has no doubt been a primary driver of booming Cleantech activity. The average price of a barrel of West Texas crude was $41 in 2004, $56 in 2005, and $66 in 2006. Prices rose to over $100 per barrel in the first half of 2008, and a surprise decline in fossil fuel prices that could undercut alternative energy and conservation technologies now seems unlikely.

The dynamism of the Cleantech and green real estate sectors is particularly striking given the absence of a coherent national public policy around climate change. The more investors are convinced that high fossil fuel prices are here to stay, the more capital we will see committed to Cleantech, conservation, and other environmental strategies.

The March 2007 investor Call to Action for the US Congress to address climate change, backed by $4 trillion in assets, noted that government policy 'would remove unnecessary risk in asset management and corporate governance and help to harmonize an increasingly complex regulatory landscape. With greater certainty, American businesses and investors could make capital investments and seize global leadership on clean technologies. American businesses could do what they do best – innovate'. The business and investment leaders emphasized that they 'are willing to play their part in bringing about a low-carbon future. But in the absence of strong federal leadership, there is a risk that US businesses may get left behind, losing ground against competitors in the rapidly growing global market for low-carbon solutions'.

Given the large economic threat from climate change, it is in the interest of investors to advocate for public policies that constrain carbon emissions and thus provide a stable planning environment. Fossil fuel price subsidies and cost-free carbon emissions are not in the interests of long-term investors, when fully incorporating the portfolio risks that accrue from business-as-usual emissions patterns. Thus it is not surprising that climate change is one of the very few areas where both corporations and investors are calling for more government regulation, not less.

## SUMMARY AND CONCLUSIONS

Most institutions and individuals have a long-term financial horizon that is placing climate change firmly on the investment agenda. Investors have been intensely active around climate in the last five years, with leadership coming from both the institutional investor and venture capital communities. The Investor Network on Climate Risk (INCR), an alliance backed by over $3 trillion in assets, has used the power of shareholder ownership to push for substantial changes in the approach to climate by the financial services industry and the corporations that it invests in. This has led to improved strategic planning and data disclosure by companies about climate risks and opportunities, as well as more and better investment research.

Investment managers and research providers are active in developing programs for assessing which companies are best-in-class in managing climate change, and where business-as-usual behavior is leading to investment risk. Recent research has identified a financial return premium for those companies that are leaders in the efficient management of environmental resources in general and of carbon emissions in particular.

Investors increasingly understand that short-term benefits created by carbon emissions in one portion of their portfolios will show up as costs elsewhere, particularly in the long run. Diversified investors are exposed to the health of the overall global economy, and thus the effective systemic management of climate change has become a central investment issue. This explains why the INCR and other large institutional investors are active not just in pushing for improved financial research and disclosure on climate, but also in calling for better public policy to ensure a rational financial planning environment for a carbon-constrained future.

American dynamism in venture capital investing has now turned to the clean energy sector, or 'Cleantech'. This is now estimated to be the third-largest venture area, eclipsing telecom. With venture capital deployments of at least $7 billion in 2006 and overall global capital allocation to clean energy of around $100 billion, investors are responding to high fossil fuel prices by reallocating capital to technologies in areas such as conservation, alternative energy, water purification, and materials-efficient production. Green investing is also moving into alternative asset classes such as hedge funds, and the greening of commercial and residential real estate is the mega-trend in property development. The number of green real estate investment trusts and mortgage pools is expanding at a rapid pace, and recent estimates suggest that green homebuilding could represent 10 percent of the market by 2010, creating $38 billion in investment activity.

Diversified investors accept that future market returns are perhaps the most important determinant of their long-term financial health. Furthermore, attractive long-term financial returns are contingent on the vibrancy of our economic and ecological systems. Short-termism is not only inconsistent with most investors' planning horizon, but is also in conflict with the kind of investment activity that will underwrite better risk-adjusted returns in the long run.

The investor push for better corporate management of climate risk and more effective public policy is consistent with fiduciary duty and in the long-term interest of all Americans. With an intermediated financial system as complex as ours, it is vital to remember that the citizenry are the underlying beneficiaries of mutual funds and retirement plans. This makes the effective management of climate an investment issue for virtually everyone. Asset owners both large and small must ensure that their interest in climate change risk reduction is firmly reflected in the behavior of their fiduciary boards, of investment managers who work on their behalf, and of the corporations that they own.

## NOTES

1. Executive Vice President and Chief Investment Officer, Trillium Asset Management Corporation. The author would like to thank his colleague at Trillium Asset Management

Corporation, Natasha Lamb, Steve Lippman at Microsoft, and Rob Berridge and Jim Coburn at Ceres, for their helpful comments and contributions to this chapter.

2. All market return data from Dimson et al. (2002).
3. The author first developed these ideas in 'Taking responsibility for market returns', Investing for a Better World, Trillium Asset Management Corporation, Fall 2006.
4. Exxon Mobil (#1), $36.1 billion; Chevron (#4), $14.1 billion; ConocoPhillips (#6), $13.5 billion. Source: Fortune Magazine (2006).
5. See Trillium Asset Management Corporation (2007).
6. UNEP Finance Initiative, http://www.unpri.org/principles/.
7. Excerpted from INCR (2004). Available online at www.incr.com.
8. See http://www.ceres.org/pub/docs/Ceres_INCR_SEC_letter_061406.pdf.
9. Data on climate-related shareholder resolutions provided by Ceres and from Doug Cougan (2007).
10. Going 'long' is investing in securities in the traditional manner, making a profit as prices rise. An investor who sells stock 'short' borrows shares from a brokerage house and sells them to another buyer. Short sellers are betting that they will be able to buy the stock back at a lower amount than the price at which they sold short. As the stock falls in value they are making a profit, as it rises they are incurring a loss.
11. See http://www.ceres.org/Call_to_Action/index.php.

## REFERENCES

Cougan, Douglas G. (2006), 'Corporate Governance and Climate Change: Making the Connection', Ceres, March 2006.

Cougan, Doug G. (2007), 'Environment: Global Climate Change', 2007 Background Report – J2, Institutional Shareholder Services, Washington, DC, February 28, 2007.

Derwall, Jeroen et al. (2005), 'The Eco-Efficiency Premium Puzzle', *Financial Analysts Journal*, **61** (2), 51–63.

Dimson, Elroy, Paul Marsh and Mike Staunton (2002), *Triumph of the Optimists: 101 Years of Global Investment Returns*, Princeton, NJ: Princeton University Press.

Esty, Daniel C. and Andrew S. Winston (2006), *Green to Gold*, New Haven, CT: Yale University Press.

Fortune Magazine (2006), 'Fortune 500 2006: Our annual ranking of America's largest corporations', 17 April 2006, http://money.cnn.com/magazines/fortune/fortune500/full_list/.

Hawley, Jim and Andy Williams (2006), 'Universal Owners: Challenges and Opportunities', introductory remarks at the Universal Ownership Conference, Saint Mary's College, Moraga, CA, April 2006.

INCR (2004), 'Investor Guide to Climate Risk: Action Plan and Resource for Plan Sponsors, Fund Managers, and Corporations', http://www.incr.com.

Kiernan, Matthew J. (2007), 'Climate Change and Global Investment Strategy', background paper for a presentation at the Institutional Investor Socially Responsible Investment Forum, New York, January 2007.

Lash, Jonathan and Fred Wellington (2007), 'Competitive Advantage on a Warming Planet', *Harvard Business Review*, March 2007.

Liebreich, Michael (2007), Presentation to the INCR Clean Energy Working Group, New Energy Finance, January 2007.

McGee, Suzanne (2007), 'Green Real Estate', http://www.financial-planning.com, March 2007.

Parker, Nicholas (2007), Presentation to the INCR Clean Energy Working Group, Cleantech Venture Network LLC, January 2007.

Thamotheram, Raj and Helen Wildsmith (2006), 'Putting the Universal Owner Hypothesis into Action', paper presented at the Universal Ownership Conference, Saint Mary's College, Moraga, CA, April 2006.

Trillium Asset Management Corporation (2007), *Mission-Related Investing for Foundations and Non-Profit Organizations.*

# Index